T0329044

CAMBRIDGE LIBRARY COLLECTION

Books of enduring scholarly value

Polar Exploration

This series includes accounts, by eye-witnesses and contemporaries, of early expeditions to the Arctic and the Antarctic. Huge resources were invested in such endeavours, particularly the search for the North-West Passage, which, if successful, promised enormous strategic and commercial rewards. Cartographers and scientists travelled with many of the expeditions, and their work made important contributions to earth sciences, climatology, botany and zoology. They also brought back anthropological information about the indigenous peoples of the Arctic region and the southern fringes of the American continent. The series further includes dramatic and poignant accounts of the harsh realities of working in extreme conditions and utter isolation in bygone centuries.

Report of Board of Officers to Consider an Expedition for the Relief of Lieut. Greely and Party

In 1881, Adolphus Greely led a U.S. Arctic expedition to gather meteorological, astronomical and magnetic data. It was poorly supported by the U.S. Army, neither Greely nor his men had experience of Arctic conditions, and their ship, the *Proteus*, sailed home once they had landed in Greenland. An inadequately planned relief mission failed to reach them in 1882, and a second expedition in 1883, including the *Proteus* (which was crushed by ice), also failed to locate the men or to land sufficient supplies. This official report was published in 1884, and proposes a further rescue mission, much more carefully planned and equipped. It includes, as an appendix, detailed information about Arctic conditions and means of survival from the British naval explorers George Nares and Albert H. Markham. When eventually found, only seven of Greely's original team of twenty-five were still alive. Other accounts of the expeditions are also reissued in this series.

Cambridge University Press has long been a pioneer in the reissuing of out-of-print titles from its own backlist, producing digital reprints of books that are still sought after by scholars and students but could not be reprinted economically using traditional technology. The Cambridge Library Collection extends this activity to a wider range of books which are still of importance to researchers and professionals, either for the source material they contain, or as landmarks in the history of their academic discipline.

Drawing from the world-renowned collections in the Cambridge University Library and other partner libraries, and guided by the advice of experts in each subject area, Cambridge University Press is using state-of-the-art scanning machines in its own Printing House to capture the content of each book selected for inclusion. The files are processed to give a consistently clear, crisp image, and the books finished to the high quality standard for which the Press is recognised around the world. The latest print-on-demand technology ensures that the books will remain available indefinitely, and that orders for single or multiple copies can quickly be supplied.

The Cambridge Library Collection brings back to life books of enduring scholarly value (including out-of-copyright works originally issued by other publishers) across a wide range of disciplines in the humanities and social sciences and in science and technology.

Report of Board of Officers to Consider an Expedition for the Relief of Lieut. Greely and Party

UNITED STATES BOARD OF OFFICERS

CAMBRIDGE
UNIVERSITY PRESS

CAMBRIDGE
UNIVERSITY PRESS

University Printing House, Cambridge, CB2 8BS, United Kingdom

Cambridge University Press is part of the University of Cambridge.

It furthers the University's mission by disseminating knowledge in the pursuit of
education, learning and research at the highest international levels of excellence.

www.cambridge.org
Information on this title: www.cambridge.org/9781108075008

This edition first published 1884
This digitally printed version 2014

ISBN 978-1-108-07500-8 Paperback

REPORT

OF

BOARD OF OFFICERS

TO CONSIDER AN

EXPEDITION FOR THE RELIEF OF LIEUT. GREELY AND PARTY.

BY AUTHORITY OF THE SECRETARY OF THE NAVY.

WASHINGTON:
GOVERNMENT PRINTING OFFICE.
1884

ROOM, BOARD OF OFFICERS, CONSIDERING
RELIEF EXPEDITION TO LIEUT. GREELY
AND PARTY AT LADY FRANKLIN BAY,
Washington, D. C., January 22, 1884.

GENTLEMEN: I have the honor to inclose herewith the report of the Board of Officers, created by Executive Order, dated December 17th, 1883, for the purpose of considering a relief expedition to be sent to Lieutenant Greely and party at Lady Franklin Bay.

The Board has been informed that in accordance with its invitation, communicated through the Department of State, Captain Sir George S. Nares, and other officers of the British Navy, have kindly signified their willingness to submit their views upon the proposed expedition.

The Board is also in daily expectation of receiving information, in response to its inquiries, in regard to the possibility of obtaining skin clothing for use on the proposed expedition. So soon as responses from Captain Nares and in regard to clothing shall have been received, I shall have the honor to transmit the formal minutes of proceedings of the Board, the exhibits referred to therein, and any other communications that may be received in the mean time.

I have the honor to be, very respectfully, your obedient servant,

W. B. HAZEN,
Brig. and Bvt. Maj. Gen'l,
Chief Signal Officer, U. S. A., President of the Board.

The Hons. SECRETARY OF WAR and
SECRETARY OF THE NAVY.

REPORT

OF

Board of Officers considering the Relief Expedition to Lieutenant Greely and his party at Lady Franklin Bay.

WASHINGTON, D. C., *January 22, 1884.*

To the Honorables,
The Secretary of War and
The Secretary of the Navy:

GENTLEMEN: The Board of Officers, convened by Executive order dated December 17, 1883, for the purpose of considering an expedition to be sent to the relief of Lieutenant Greely and party at Lady Franklin Bay, has the honor to submit the following report:

PRELIMINARY.

Before giving an expression of opinion upon the subject under consideration, the Board considers it necessary to state briefly, its general views as to the character and magnitude of the undertaking.

It appears from the records of the War Department that have been submitted to the Board, and which will be found in the Appendix (Exhibit M), that on the 13th and 14th days of August, 1881, Lieut. A. W. Greely, 5th U. S. Cavalry, in command of a force of two officers and twenty-two soldiers, citizens, and Esquimaux, landed from the steamer "Proteus" at Discovery Harbor, Lady Franklin Bay; this force constituting what is known as the Lady Franklin Bay Expedition.

This expedition was authorized by act of Congress approved May 1st, 1880, and legislation relating to its maintenance is to be found in the appropriations for Sundry Civil Expenses of the Government, approved March 3, 1881.

SUBSISTENCE.

It also appears from the records referred to, that this expeditionary force was furnished with articles of subsistence stores—the components of the Army ration or their equivalents—for three years. Of beans, coffee, sugar, and salt, a supply for about four and a half years was issued. Besides the articles composing the ordinary Army ration, there was supplied a very extensive assortment of canned fruits, vegetables, pickles, sauces, condiments, anti-scorbutics, and butter, which would probably be equal to another year's supply of food for this party.

On the 15th of August, 1881, Lieutenant Greely reported to the Chief Signal Officer that his " general cargo was discharged", including about one hundred and forty tons of coal.

On the 18th of August Lieutenant Greely mentions that he had already succeeded in collecting "three full months' rations of musk cattle".

EQUIPMENT.

For the purpose of carrying on exploration and effecting retreat, this expedition was furnished with a Navy steam-launch and three other boats adapted to the navigation of Smith Sound. Lieutenant Greely also knew that at Thank God Harbor, Polaris Bay, on the coast of Greenland, twenty-eight miles distant, was a serviceable ice-boat left there by the English expedition, and near Cape Sumner, at the mouth of Newman Bay, some thirty-eight miles distant, was a whale-boat, left there by the U. S. Steamer "Polaris" in 1872.

About seven miles from the Signal station exists a deposit of free-burning coal, in unlimited quantities, for the procurement of which implements were supplied.

Lieutenant Greely's detachment is quartered in comfortable wooden dwellings, affording ample accommodations for his party, and on the 25th of August he reports the construction of the buildings as very nearly completed.

ORDERS AND CORRESPONDENCE.

The vessel transporting Lieutenant Greely to Lady Franklin Bay sailed thence on the 25th of August, 1881, and since that date no news has been received from the expedition.

In the orders and instructions to Lieutenant Greely from the Chief Signal Officer of the Army, dated June 17, 1881, is found the following :

It is contemplated that the *permanent* station shall be visited in 1882 and in 1883 by a steam sealer, or other vessel, by which supplies for, and such additions to, the present party as are deemed needful will be sent. In case such vessel is unable to reach Lady Franklin Bay in 1882, she will cache * a portion of her supplies and all of her letters and dispatches at the most northerly point she attains on the *east side of Grinnell Land* and establish a small depot of supplies at Littleton Island.

Notices of the locality of such depots will be left at one or all of the following places, viz: Cape Hawks, Cape Sabine and Cape Isabella. In case no vessel reaches the *permanent* station in 1882, the vessel sent in 1883 will remain in Smith Sound until there is danger of its closing by ice, and, on leaving, will land all her supplies and a party at Littleton Island, which party will be prepared for a winter's stay and will be instructed to send sledge parties up the *east side of Grinnell Land* to meet this party. If not visited in 1882, Lieutenant Greely will abandon his station not later than September 1, 1883, and will retreat southward by boat, following closely the *east side of Grinnell Land*, until the relieving vessel is met or Littleton Island is reached.

Lieutenant Greely in his report to the Chief Signal Officer dated August 15, 1881, and previously referred to, states as follows: " In my opinion a retreat from here southward to Cape Sabine, in case no vessel reaches us in 1882 or in 1883, will be safe and practicable, although all but the most important records will necessarily have to be abandoned".

DEPOSITS OF PROVISIONS.

It appears that Lieutenant Greely, before leaving the United States, was aware of the existence of certain deposits of provisions left by

* The stores which composed this cache were such, in quantity and variety, as were suggested by Lieutenant Greely in letter to the Chief Signal Officer, dated August 17, 1881, (Exhibit M.)

previous expeditions to Smith Sound, the most important having been made by Sir George S. Nares, commanding the English expedition of 1875–6.

A deposit consisting of two hundred and fifty rations was left in 1875 at Cape Collinson, at an estimated distance from Lieutenant Greely's station of one hundred and thirty-seven miles. The same expedition left a depot at Cape Hawks, fifty miles further to the southward, consisting of bread, pickles, and preserved potatoes; this cache was examined by Greely while en-route to his destination. A deposit of two hundred and forty rations was also made by Nares near Cape Sabine, another at Cape Morton, and about one hundred and fifty pounds of meat at Cape Isabella, but these stores were not examined by Greely, neither did he see those at Cape Collinson. While en-route to his station, Greely made a deposit of two hundred and twenty-five bread and meat rations at Carl Ritter Bay, seventy-five miles south of Lady Franklin Bay. He also deposited six and one-half tons of coal at Littleton Island, and knew that at the Cary Islands were 1,800 rations left by Nares in 1875. At Lincoln Bay Nares also left a large depot; but these stores would be available only for exploring parties operating to the northward of Discovery Harbor.

It is well known that the supply expedition sent out by the War Department in 1882, found the entrance to Smith Sound blocked by ice, and the vessel was unable to communicate with the Signal station. A deposit of two hundred and fifty rations, a small quantity of fuel, together with a boat, was, however, made near Cape Sabine. A boat was also left at Cape Isabella, some twenty-five miles to the southward of Sabine. By the same expedition two hundred and fifty rations were cached at Littleton Island. It is understood that all these supplies were fairly well protected.

The relief expedition of 1883, commanded by Lieutenant Garlington, was unable to accomplish its mission, the steamer "Proteus" having been crushed by the ice near the entrance to Smith Sound. A considerable quantity of supplies, approximating five hundred rations, and a large quantity of clothing, was, however, landed near Cape Sabine, and are available for the use of Lieutenant Greely's party, should he retreat to that point.

NAVIGATION OF SMITH SOUND.

It is well known that the navigation of Smith Sound is, at almost all times, difficult and dangerous. The season of 1881 appears to have been exceptionally favorable and open, as evidenced by the fact that the "Proteus" was able to reach her destination in a period of eight days from the date of leaving Littleton Island. The expedition of Sir George S. Nares, in 1875, consisting of two powerful steamships, was twenty-eight days in passing over the same route, and twenty-five days in returning to Littleton Island in 1876.

It will be seen from the instructions previously quoted, that Lieutenant Greely had considerable discretion as to the date when he should vacate his station. He was required to abandon it "not later than September 1, 1883".

The experience of all explorers of Smith Sound shows that the most favorable season for navigating those waters by boat is in the month of August. If Lieutenant Greely left his station early in that month— which his instructions warranted him in doing—there is a reasonable probability that he succeeded in reaching the entrance to Smith Sound, but it may be regarded as extremely doubtful, did he delay his departure until September 1st, that the conditions would permit him to effect a retreat. He had already spent two winters at Discovery Harbor, and although there is no reason to believe the health of his detachment had been greatly impaired by his long residence in that rigorous climate, yet the Board considers it necessary to assume that either through impaired health or possible loss of boats and other means of transportation, he was unable to abandon his station as was contemplated. The Board, therefore, is of opinion that the relief expedition to be organized, and which is now under consideration, should have such an equipment that in any event it will be able to reach Lady Franklin Bay.

If Lieutenant Greely has successfully effected his retreat to Cape Sabine, or to the coast of Greenland adjacent to the entrance of Smith Sound, the work of relief will be vastly simplified.

Did he arrive at Littleton Island by the 15th of August, he would probably retreat to Upernavik, the northernmost Danish settlement in Greenland, and it is within the bounds of possibility that the Lady Franklin Bay party is now there in safety. But to assume such a probability is entirely unwarranted, for all the conditions must have been even more than extraordinarily favorable to have permitted such a result.

If the organization and dispatch of a relief expedition were to be deferred until the season is so far advanced as to permit communication with the Greenland settlements, it would be impossible in the present year to visit Lady Franklin Bay, or even Littleton Island, and the chance of ever effecting the rescue of the party would be very greatly impaired.

The conditions and difficulties which are to be met in effecting the rescue are, fortunately, entirely dissimilar to those which had to be encountered when the Franklin search began. The "Erebus" and "Terror," when last heard from in 1845, were about to sail into a region almost unknown to civilized men, and of immense extent. That the search for these lost ships and their crews should have occupied so many years and required so many ships and land expeditions is not surprising when we consider the vast area covered by the search, but the work now under consideration is surrounded with no doubts or uncertainties as to the locality of Lieutenant Greely.

The Franklin search, extending from 1848 to 1859, and employing some forty ships at various times, cost the English government many million pounds sterling. But under the most unfavorable conditions that can be named, the Board believes two properly equipped vessels will certainly be able to achieve success, and rescue the Lady Franklin Bay party.

RECOMMENDATIONS.

The Board, by the terms of the Executive order creating it, is required to make recommendations under the following heads, viz:
1. Transportation and Equipment.
2. Control and Conduct.
3. Organization of Personnel.

TRANSPORTATION AND EQUIPMENT.

Although a single vessel might be able to reach Discovery Harbor and return in a single season, as did the "Proteus" in 1881, yet all familiar with the navigation of Smith Sound agree that the seasons favoring such free navigation come at long intervals, and it is quite certain that in some seasons the strongest vessel ever built would be able to proceed but a short distance into Smith Sound. But four steam vessels have ever reached Kennedy Channel. One of them, the "Polaris", as is well known, was drifted out in an ice-pack and lost near Littleton Island, and another, the "Proteus", which in 1881 succeeded in reaching Lady Franklin Bay, in 1883 was crushed by the ice near Cape Sabine. On several occasions the vessels under the command of Sir George S. Nares were in imminent danger of being destroyed. In 1876, the "Pandora", under the command of Captain Allen Young, an experienced Arctic navigator, struggled from the 3d to the 28th of August in vain endeavors to effect an entrance to Smith Sound, but was unable to reach Cape Sabine, or any position above latitude 78° 45' N., twenty-five miles north of Littleton Island. In 1882, the "Neptune" was engaged in similar fruitless efforts from the 28th of July to the 5th of September, but never advanced beyond 79° 20' N., or about seventy-five miles above Littleton Island.

In view of all the facts in the case, the Board is of the opinion that the relieving expedition should consist of two vessels, each supplied for a cruise of two years, not only for its own crew but for the crew of the other ship, and those composing Lieutenant Greely's party at Lady Franklin Bay. Should one of these vessels be lost, even at the outset, the other would be able to continue her efforts for the rescue, and at the same time render succor to the crew of the less fortunate ship. As it may occur that these vessels, if successful in reaching Discovery Harbor the first season, will be unable to extricate themselves and return to the United States, they should be provisioned and prepared for wintering in the ice.

In the opinion of the Board, the best ships obtainable for the work in hand are the Scotch "whalers" or the Newfoundland "sealers". The "Proteus" and "Neptune" were of this latter class. The Dundee whaling fleet, consisting of some twelve vessels, are built with special reference to Arctic navigation; their cruising grounds are in Melville and Baffin Bays and adjacent waters, where extensive ice-floes are always encountered.

When organizing the Nares' expedition in 1875 (the most completely equipped and appointed Arctic expedition that ever sailed from any port, costing, it has been stated, a million dollars), the English Government purchased one of these whalers, known subsequently as the "Discovery", and she was regarded by Captain Nares as a better ship than the "Alert", an English naval vessel, specially strengthened and fitted for that voyage.

So far as the Board has been able to ascertain, there are on the Atlantic coast of the United States at the present time no American ships suitable for the purpose, and it is believed impracticable for any American ship-builder to build and equip vessels adapted to the work in hand by the time they should start.

In reaching this conclusion, the Board has given due weight to the opinions expressed to it by ship-builders, that thoroughly constructed vessels can be built in the United States and ready to proceed on their voyage by the 1st of May. But in an emergency where human life is at stake, it is thought to be unwise to place reliance upon the ability of a ship-builder, no matter how well equipped or reliable, to complete his contract for two vessels by a date which should find this relief expedition on its way.

The Board, therefore, recommends the immediate purchase of two full-powered steam whalers or sealers of from five-hundred to six-hundred tons, and that they be brought to a navy-yard of the United States, and properly fitted for the service intended. These alterations will consist principally of modifications in the accommodations for officers and crew, and in the addition of materials to give greater strength.

ADVANCE VESSEL.

Considering the contingency of delay from some unforeseen cause in the sailing of the expedition, it may be deemed advisable to procure and have fitted an advance ship, to be dispatched in time to reach the Danish settlements previous to the date which the Board has named as that on which the relief vessels should assemble at Upernavik. In the contingency of the delay of the other ships, this advance vessel passing through Davis Strait, Baffin and Melville Bays at the earliest possible moment—taking more risks than should the relief ships—may be able to rescue the party should they have effected a retreat to the entrance of Smith Sound or to the Danish settlements.

In this connection, the Board would invite attention to the communications addressed to the Secretary of the Treasury, dated November 4 and December 29, 1883, and that to Senator Miller, of California, dated January 4, 1884, signed by Captain Hooper of the U. S. Revenue Marine (Exhibit O), in which will be found suggestions that a U. S. Revenue cutter be fitted for service in the Arctic Ocean and dispatched in search of Lieutenant Greely.

It appears to the Board from these communications, that possibly a valuable auxiliary to the relief expedition could thus be secured at a small cost, by the employment of one of the vessels of the Revenue Marine, provided such vessel was properly fitted for the necessities of the service.

SUGGESTIONS.

The following suggestions are made, and it is recommended that all supplies be prepared under the personal supervision of the officers attached to the expedition, who should also supervise the modifications to the ships, construction of boats, sleds, &c.:

BOATS.

In case the vessels should be stopped by ice or meet disaster, it will become necessary to resort to combined boat and sledge journeys over ice and water. A thorough equipment of boats and sleds will, therefore, be required. Each of these vessels should be supplied with the following boats:

One steam whale-boat.

Two ordinary whale-boats about twenty-eight feet long.

Two ordinary whale-boats about twenty-four feet long.

One dingy (for two pairs of sculls).

One balsa.

One *oomiak* (if obtainable in Greenland).

In addition to the above, the Board would recommend that the expedition should be supplied with one of "White's" steam life cutters. The "Herreschoff" steam whale-boat, such as is used by the American whalers in the Pacific Ocean, the Board believes might be of very great use, even when the vessels are unable to proceed, for it sometimes happens that an ice-barrier but a few miles in width prevents the further progress of a ship; under such circumstances a "Herreschoff" steam whale-boat could be hauled across and launched in open water beyond, where the navigation was free. The other whale-boats should be built after the New Bedford pattern, as light as is consistent with strength and the rough usage they are to receive. The balsa, built with special adaptation to the work in hand, the Board believes may be of very great utility. The *oomiak*, or skin-boat, is used very effectively by the natives in navigating the water leads in Arctic regions; it is very light and will transport a very large number of persons.

SLEDS.

Two sixteen feet sleds, and
Two eight feet sleds, similar to those supplied the "Proteus" last year.

SHELTER ON SHORE.

On board of each vessel there should be material for the construction of a house ready to be put up on shore.

DOGS.

The supply of dogs in Greenland is, at best, uncertain. It is in evidence that of those (forty-two in number) taken by Lieutenant Greely, at the date of his last report, all but eleven had died of some epidemic disease. It is therefore recommended that at least sixty dogs, obtainable either in the region of Pembina and Mackinaw, or in Labrador, should compose a part of the equipment of the vessels.

It is also recommended that a naval vessel or tender be provided and proceed as far as Littleton Island or Cape Sabine for the purpose of contributing supplies for the use of the relief vessels, and to aid in any way the efforts to rescue Lieutenant Greely. It is not proposed that this vessel shall winter in the ice—her crew should be reduced to a minimum and supplied with provisions for eight months. All available space in the ship to be filled with coals.

In case the relief vessels are obliged to winter in Smith Sound, the naval tender, or auxiliary ship, will bring to the United States intelligence of their progress.

PROVISIONS.

It is recommended that the expedition be provisioned in accordance with the schedule as to variety and quantity which governed in outfitting the relief vessel "Rodgers", which sailed from San Francisco on June 16, 1881, and those which governed in the provisioning of Lieutenant Greely's party, and that stationed for two years at Point Barrow under the command of Lieutenant Ray, U. S. Army. It has been stated that the provisions supplied to the expeditions named were the best that could possibly be procured for any Arctic expedition. (Exhibit Q.)

MEDICAL OUTFIT.

It is recommended that the medical equipment of the expedition be made up in accordance with the schedules of similar supplies furnished

to the relief ship "Rodgers", to the U. S. Signal station at Point Barrow, Alaska, and to the Lady Franklin Bay Expedition, all outfitted in
1881.   (Exhibit R.)

Attention is respectfully invited to the able and interesting paper
(Exhibit K.) prepared at the instance of the Board by Surgeon-General Philip S. Wales, U. S. Navy, and it is advised that the commanding officer of the expedition observe, as far as practicable, the suggestions contained in this paper, not only in outfitting the vessels, but in
the steps to be taken to insure the health and comfort of the men under
his command.

CLOTHING.

Head-gear.—Woolen caps and fur caps to cover the ears, neck, and
chin; the latter with side extensions to cover the face, if necessary.

Hand-gear.—Woolen mitts; leather mitts, for use on deck; fur mitts,
having transverse slit at the wrist, and with cuffs.

Foot-gear.—Cotton woolen-lined stockings reaching above the knees,
re-enforced at the heel with chamois leather; blanket wrappers; moccasins with leggings; spare half soles of non-conducting material for
use with moccasins and for boots; tanned leather fishermen's boots for
use on deck; water-proof preparation for same; fur stockings; fur
boots; slippers of thick material, and rubber sandals having rough
soles.

Body-covering.—Best thick merino or red flannel underwear; closely
knit jumpers, extending just below the hip; thick cloth trousers; light
canvas working suits, with blanket lining, if necessary, for summer
work; fur jumpers with hoods; fur trousers.

All fur clothing to be made from reindeer skins, if possible; otherwise, from young calf-skins.

SLEEPING-BAGS.

Of reindeer skin, if obtainable; failing to secure that, of calf-skin.

BERTHING.

If practicable, a berth to be fitted for each man on board.

HEATING.

By steam, the pipes to be laid as near the decks as possible.

WATER.

A small distiller to be fitted in each ship, and distilled water to be
used for cooking and drinking purposes.

AUXILIARY BOILER.

A small auxiliary boiler to be put up on the berth or spar deck; the
bed for same should have an air space between it and the deck, to
insure against fire.

DECK HOUSE.

Material for deck house to be prepared for use in case the ships should winter north, to be put up in the fall. This house to be made double, with air-space on top and sides, to cover two or more hatches, and fitted with double doors, and to be lined with non-conducting material.

STEAM WINCH.

A steam winch to be placed on the spar deck for hoisting, warping, &c.

EXPLOSIVES.

Five-pound charges of gunpowder and gun-cotton, to be prepared for use in blasting.

FIRE-ARMS.

A supply of Springfield rifles for the expedition, and a proportion of breech-loading fowling pieces and the requisite ammunition.

COAL.

Each ship to be supplied with coal for thirty-five days' full steaming; and with fifty tons of Anthracite coal for depots. For steaming purposes, the best quality of soft coal.

METAL SURFACES.

Metal surfaces in the living quarters to be covered with a non-conductor.

TENTS.

To be of blue "Denim", in size and arrangements similar to those prepared for the "Proteus" in 1883.

PACKAGES.

Each package to have stencilled on it the list of its contents.

ESQUIMAUX, DOGS, AND CLOTHING.

The advance vessel or expedition to carry a letter from the Danish Government directing the authorities in Greenland to aid the expedition in obtaining hunters, clothing, boats, and dogs, should these animals be required. Timely request to the Government of Denmark should therefore be made.

SUN SPECTACLES.

Glass, wire, and hair goggles should be supplied.

STIMULANTS.

Wines and liquors, to be used for medicinal purposes only. Ordinarily, it is believed that tea is preferable to coffee or cocoa.

ICE TOOLS.

Ice anchors, chisels, small picks, and drills.

GOODS FOR TRADING.

A small supply likely to be useful to the Esquimaux, consisting of knives, carpenter's tools, matches, thread, needles, earthenware, &c.

CONTROL AND CONDUCT.

As the means employed to reach Discovery Harbor must necessarily be of a nautical character, it is recommended that the control of the expedition be committed to the Navy Department.

Should Lieutenant Greely have succeeded last autumn in effecting his retreat to Cape Sabine or Littleton Island, and supposing he has found a moderate supply of game in that region, he will necessarily, at the beginning of next summer, be very short of supplies. It therefore seems indispensable that the expedition should be on the ground at the earliest possible date.

Experience has shown that the navigation of Baffin and Melville Bays may be practicable at a date as early as the 1st of June. There is no record of a vessel having passed Cape York, north point of Melville Bay, earlier than the date given. The relief ships should therefore arrive at Upernavik, the northernmost Danish settlement in Greenland, not later than the 15th of May, and no opportunity lost to communicate with the natives at Cape York at the earliest moment, so as to obtain intelligence of Lieutenant Greely if possible.

The vessels should therefore be fitted and in complete readiness so that they may arrive at Upernavik on the date named.

GENERAL PROGRAMME.

The following general programme for the movement of the vessels is suggested as the one which will be most likely to result successfully, but it should be remarked that a wide discretion should be given the officer in command, for, as he will be held responsible, wide latitude should be allowed. The problem of reaching Lady Franklin Sound in a steamer from Cape Sabine can only be solved by the exercise of skillful seamanship combined with good judgment, unless Smith Sound should be found to be comparatively free from ice.

1. The two relief vessels, designated Nos. 1 and 2, to proceed in company to Saint John's, Newfoundland, fill up with coal and fresh provisions; thence to Disco, and, if necessary, to Upernavik; thence to Littleton Island, communicating with the natives at, and north of, Cape York.

2. The first depot to be established on Littleton Island (before proceeding north of that locality), or in the immediate vicinity, as may seem best to the commander of the expedition—to consist of one of the houses, fifty tons of coal, the steam life cutter, one whale-boat, and provisions and clothing for the entire party for one year. The house, coal, provisions, whale-boat, and clothing for this depot to be taken from No. 1; an officer or a petty officer and two men, to be left in charge of the depot.

After leaving Littleton Island and reaching the ice-barrier, the design of the expedition would be for No. 1 to take the first favorable opportunity to push to the northward, leaving No. 2 to serve as a base to fall back upon in case of disaster, or for a second attempt to reach Lady Franklin Sound.

3. No. 2 not to enter the ice-pack, but to manœuvre constantly to the southward of it, or to anchor in the immediate vicinity; to be ready to land a second main depot of provisions to consist of the same amount of material proposed for the first, but to include two whale-boats, in case No. 2 be required to proceed north in the event of disaster to No. 1.

4. Should Smith Sound be comparatively open, No. 1 should advance to the northward forming small depots at Washington Irving Island, and the vicinity of Cape Collinson and Carl Ritter Bay. No. 2, after forming a small depot of supplies at Cape Sabine, to proceed as far north as Dobbin Bay, beyond which point she should not advance unless the prolonged absence of No. 1 should give rise to the apprehension of her loss.

5. Should No. 1 be crushed or disabled, No. 2, before attempting to advance north, should land her house, two boats, and supplies for the whole party for one year, in the vicinity of Dobbin Bay.

6. Should neither vessel be crushed, and should neither succeed in communicating with Lady Franklin Sound, one should winter in Franklin Pierce Bay, and the other in the vicinity of Littleton Island.

7. On the way north the coast to be examined from Cape York to Cape Ohlsen on the east side and from Cape Isabella to Cape Sabine on the west. Cairns should be erected containing notices of the movements and intentions of the relief expedition at Conical Rock, Wolstenholme Island, Cary Islands, Hakluyt Island, Cape Isabella, and Cape Sabine.

8. The whalers from Dundee and the sealers from Newfoundland to be requested to keep a lookout on the ice-floes for Lieutenant Greely's party.

9. The naval vessel, or tender, to go as far as Littleton Island or Cape Sabine.

PERSONNEL.

As the relieving vessels may be detained for one or more winters in the ice, the complement of each ship should be reduced to a minimum, in order to give each man abundant air space. The crew should consist only of useful men, fitted for the rigorous service before them, between the ages of twenty-four and thirty-seven years. Preference should be given to seamen of American birth, and all subjected to a rigorous medical examination. The crew of each vessel should be made up in accordance with the following list:

COMPLEMENT OF EACH SHIP.

1 commanding officer;
3 line officers;
1 medical officer;
1 engineer officer;
1 ice master;
4 petty officers;
10 seamen;
1 machinist;
1 boiler-maker;
1 blacksmith;
1 carpenter's mate;
3 firemen;
1 captain of hold and yeoman;

1 ship's cook;
1 officer's cook;
1 officer's steward;
2 Esquimaux, or men to drive dogs and hunt; aggregating in all thirty-four persons.

ICE MASTERS

Should be men familiar with the navigation of Melville Bay and Baffin Bay.

DOG DRIVERS.

If dogs are procured from the northwestern portion of the United States or from Manitoba, a sufficient number of men accustomed to driving these dogs should be taken. If they are gotten in Greenland the same rule should be observed.

COST OF EXPEDITION.

Although not specially directed to make any estimation of the cost of the relief expedition, yet the Board would respectfully submit the following

ESTIMATE:

Two steam sealers or whalers, if purchased after sealing trip		$227,480
Alterations and additions to the outfit of same, including boats, sledges, and dogs		35,000
Provisions, independent of the Navy ration		50,000
Medical outfit		2,000
Clothing		20,000
Coal		6,000
Amount		$340,480
If vessels be purchased before sealing trip, add		30,000
		$370,480
If advance ship be sent, add—		
Cost of vessel	$38,920	
Outfit for same	15,000	
		53,920
Total cost		$424,400
If a smaller ship be purchased instead of one of the above provided for, deduct		8,712
		$415,688

CONCLUSIONS.

The best plan and the most complete expedition that can be organized may, from unforeseen cause, be delayed in its movements.

The track by which the Dundee whaling fleet reaches its cruising grounds is fortunately favorable to Lieutenant Greely. These vessels always pass in sight of Cape York and the Cary Islands before crossing the "north water" to Jones and Lancaster Sounds. The Cary Islands are about one hundred miles from Littleton Island, and it seems to the Board extremely advisable that the Government of the United States should give notice to the masters of these whalers that, if they should succeed in rescuing Lieutenant Greely's party, or in rendering him material assistance, a large bounty would be paid, provided Greely be found at, or north of, Cape York, and that no United States vessel is in sight at the date of rescue. For the offering of a bounty by Government for the purpose stated, the history of Arctic expeditions furnishes many precedents.

The minutes of the different meetings of the Board will be transmitted at an early date, as will also the various exhibits to which reference is made.

During the progress of the investigation the Board has heard the expression of opinion of a considerable number of gentlemen, experienced to a greater of less degree in Arctic life and exploration. Others who could not appear in person, forwarded papers containing an expression of views upon the subject under consideration. All such communications will appear in the Appendix, and will, it is believed, be found to contain valuable suggestions.

A large number of communications relating to the subject under consideration have been received by the Board, either direct from the writers, or by reference from the Secretary of War or the Secretary of the Navy. These communications will be forwarded with the minutes of the Board meetings. An abstract of them will also appear in the Appendix.

Upon the suggestion of the Board, the Secretary of War, through the Department of State, requested an expression of opinion upon the best means of effecting the relief of Lieutenant Greely from Captains Sir George S. Nares, H. F. Stephenson, and A. R. Markham, all of the British Navy. It is understood that the gentlemen referred to have kindly responded to the request. When these communications shall have come to hand the Board will forward them and ask that they be filed.

A chart of Smith Sound and adjacent waters is inclosed. (Exhibit U.) It was prepared by the Hydrographer of the Navy Department, and shows the tracks of the following-named expeditions, viz:

"Polaris", 1871–2...Hall.
"Alert" and "Discovery", 1875–6...........................Nares.
"Pandora", 1876 ....Young.
"Proteus", 1881 ....Greely.
"Neptune", 1882 ....Beebe.
"Proteus", 1883 ....Garlington

The caches of supplies which have been deposited on the shores of Smith Sound and Kennedy Channel are also indicated. Accompanying the chart is a description of the various depots, compiled from official reports and other publications.

We have the honor to be, very respectfully, your obedient servants,
W. B. HAZEN,
Chief Signal Officer.
JAS. A. GREER,
Captain, U. S. Navy.
B. H. McCALLA,
Lieutenant-Commander, U. S. Navy.
GEO. W. DAVIS,
Captain, 14th Infantry, U. S. Army.

———

The undersigned members of the Board, while heartily concurring in all the foregoing recommendations and suggestions, have the honor to further recommend:

That the complement of officers and crew of each relief ship be increased to forty persons, the increase in the *personnel* to consist of one officer and five enlisted men of the Army. The officer selected should be one who has had practical experience in the northwestern portion of the United States or in the Arctic, and the men selected with special reference to their fitness for the work in hand. The officer should also be trained in the use of the meteorological instruments which should be sent for comparison with those in use by the Lady Franklin Bay Expedition.

Should the relief ships be compelled to winter in Smith Sound, these Army detachments to be quartered on shore at the highest favorable point reached, as the commander of the expedition might determine, and from thence, as directed by the commander, to advance over the ice or along the coast with dogs, sleds, and boats to Lady Franklin Bay. Such a force, made up of men inured to the cold of Dakota and Montana, where every winter mercury freezes, equipped with the best dog-teams from the northwest would, it is thought, if added to the nautical equipment of the expedition, greatly improve the chance of final success—should the vessels fail to reach Lieutenant Greely's station, and operations over land and ice be the last resort.

The reasons for the employment of such auxiliary force detailed from the same branch of the public service which established the Signal station at Discovery Harbor—each and every man loyally co-operating with his naval associates in the humane work before them, and actuated by the same honorable motives, each striving to excel the other in efforts that may reach the limit of human endurance—are, in the opinion of the undersigned, so numerous and cogent, that to set them forth in detail, seems as unnecessary as does an argument in support of the recommendation to employ such a force.

W. B. HAZEN,
Chief Signal Officer.
GEO. W. DAVIS,
Captain, 14th Infantry, U. S. Army.

————

The undersigned members of the Board, in dissenting from the proposition to send two officers and ten enlisted men of the Army as additional to the projected complement of the expedition, have the honor to submit the following statement of their opinion in reference thereto:

1st. It is desirable that the expedition should be as homogeneous as possible, and to this end it should consist of but one branch of service, under one form of discipline, unless there are strong reasons to the contrary.

2d. It is universally admitted that the number of persons composing the expedition should be as small as possible, consistent with the successful performance of the work to be done; and they should, as far as practicable, be persons available for all kinds of service which will devolve upon the expedition.

3d. The service required will, up to a certain point, be on shipboard; after that point it may be, according to circumstances, either on the water by means of the relief ships, or by means of boats; or on ice and water, partly by means of sledges and partly by means of boats; or wholly on land by sledges. The last supposition is considered by the best authorities as the least probable.

4th. The question of the expediency of adding a contingent of officers and enlisted men of the Army to the Naval expedition, must be considered with reference to the three possible kinds of service above mentioned. If the first or the second supposition should turn out to be correct, no reason can be adduced for their employment, as in either case the service is purely nautical. There remains the third and least probable hypothesis that, after navigation and ice and boat journeys are found impracticable, it may be necessary and feasible to make a sledge journey on land. It is for the purpose of this journey, and for this alone, that an argument can be advanced for the employment of a detail from the Army.

In this connection, it may be well to quote from the late Lieutenant Payer, an Officer of the Austrian Army who, together with two jägers or mountaineers, accompanied Lieutenant Weyprecht in the Austrian Polar Expedition Ship "Tegetthoff," for the purpose of taking charge of sledge journeys.

Lieutenant Payer attained his highest point, accompanied by a Midshipman and a seaman from the "Tegetthoff," his mountaineers having broken down during the journey, and in writing to the *New York Herald*, after his Arctic experience, upon the subject of the Polar Colonization Scheme, a plan which involved primarily land service and land sledging, he says, "Seamen are better capable of maintaining discipline under such circumstances than members of any other profession, and therefore the colony should mostly consist of them."

Lieutenant Payer also says, in speaking of the selection of a crew for the Colonization Scheme, "It is often assumed that the ability to endure cold must be a crucial test of fitness. This is an error. A sense of duty, endurance, and determination are the most essential qualities. Habit soon overcomes cold."

5th. In determining the number of officers and men for the two vessels, the probability of land sledging, and of journeys over ice and water, was considered by the undersigned; and if the force is to be further increased, it would be, in our opinion, preferable to take more seamen.

6th. It is submitted that unity and efficiency will be better secured by confining expeditions of this character to a single branch of the two services; that it has been decided that the character of the expedition shall be naval, and that it shall be under the control of the Navy Department, and therefore it should be composed of persons in the naval service; that as few persons should be taken as possible, and they should be such as would be useful for all the work of the expedition; that undoubtedly the greater part of this work will be nautical, and probably all of it; that as far as land service may be required, no evidence can be adduced to show a general presumption of superior fitness in enlisted men of the Army over seamen, under the peculiar conditions to be met, but that, on the contrary, the efficiency of seamen for this service has been recognized by high authority; while, in reference to the officers, it must be remembered that the experience of the Navy in Arctic sledging, has been far greater than that of the Army.

7th. It has also been suggested that the two Army officers which it is proposed to send, should be trained in the use of the meteorological instruments which would be taken for comparison with those in use by the Lady Franklin Bay expedition. In reference to this, it is submitted that as officers of the Navy are required by their daily occupations to make the closest and most accurate observations with the instruments in question, both for scientific and professional purposes, it may be presumed that they are fully competent to perform any service of this character that may be required of them.

8th. The undersigned are of the opinion that the suggestion as to the specific conditions under which the proposed Army detachment is to be employed would, if adopted, have a mischievous result. It has been proposed that the detachment should proceed in the ships, presumably as passengers, for they could go in no other capacity, until the expedition should be compelled to winter in Smith Sound; that they should then be quartered on shore, at a point selected by the commander of the expedition; and that they should thence, as directed by the commander, advance over the ice or along the coast, with dogs, sledges, and boats.

The undersigned, having in view solely the success of the expedition, regard the proposed plan as prejudicial to that success, for the following reasons:

It comtemplates the increase of the complement, already large enough to meet the demands of all possible service, by the addition of twelve supernumeraries, who would be without occupation until the progress of the ship was finally checked. It requires of the commander of the expedition that he shall quarter the detachment on shore apart from the rest of his command, although the ships would furnish the most suitable place of abode, and that he shall entrust to this detachment specifically, the execution of any sledging operations that may be undertaken on the ice, or along the coast, leaving to his discretion only the selection of the place where they shall be quartered, and the general direction of the advance with the sledges.

Such an arrangement, would, it is submitted, result inevitably in that division of responsibility and command which is above all things to be avoided; it would necessitate the issue of particular and special instructions to those who were thus sent for a particular and special purpose; it would hamper the commander of the expedition, upon whom the ultimate responsibility of success or failure must rest, with conditions by which no commander would willingly be bound; and, finally, that it would create a command within a command, which, as in previous instances where such a plan has been adopted, would certainly be prejudicial to success.

JAS. A. GREER,
Captain, U. S. Navy.
B. H. McCALLA,
Lieutenant-Commander, U. S. Navy.

PROCEEDINGS.

SIGNAL OFFICE, WAR DEPARTMENT,
Washington, D. C., December 20, 1883.
The Board met pursuant to the following order of the President of the United States:

EXECUTIVE MANSION, *December 17,* 1883.
The following-named officers of the Army and Navy will constitute a board to consider an expedition to be sent for the relief of Lieutenant Greely and his party, comprising what is known as the Lady Franklin Bay Expedition, and to recommend to the Secretaries of War and the Navy, jointly, the steps the board may consider necessary to be taken for the equipment and transportation of the relief expedition, and to suggest such plan for its control and conduct, and for the organization of its *personnel*, as may seem to them best adapted to accomplish its purpose: Brigadier-General WILLIAM B. HAZEN, Chief Signal Officer, U. S. Army; Captain JAMES A. GREER, U. S. Navy; Lieutenant-Commander B. H. McCALLA, U. S. Navy; Captain GEORGE W. DAVIS, 14th Infantry, U. S. Army.
The board will meet in Washington, D. C., on the 20th instant.

CHESTER A. ARTHUR.

All the members were present.

An informal discussion then ensued as to the duties of the Board and the steps that should be taken in order to best fulfill the requirements of the order creating it.

It was agreed that at the next meeting, each member should submit a memorandum embodying his general ideas as to the character, organization, and equipment of the proposed relief expedition.

It was then decided that such persons as are known to have had experience in Arctic service, and are now in Washington, should be invited to appear and give their general ideas upon the subject under consideration; also, to invite persons remote from Washington, who have had like experience, to submit in writing their ideas upon the same subject.

The Recorder (Captain Davis) was instructed to request the Secretary of War to direct, by telegraph, Lieut. Frederick Schwatka, 3d U. S. Cavalry, to submit in writing whatever he might propose for the organization and conduct of a relief expedition to Lady Franklin Bay.

The Board then adjourned to meet on Saturday, the 22d instant, at 11 o'clock a. m., in room 88, Navy Department Building.

ROOM 88, NAVY DEPARTMENT BUILDING,
Washington, D. C., December 22, 1883.
The Board met pursuant to adjournment; all the members present.

A letter, dated December 21, 1883, from the Secretary of the Navy, (Abstract, Miscellaneous Correspondence, No. 1,) transmitting a letter, dated U. S. Training-Ship "Saratoga," New York Navy-Yard, December 19, 1883, from Commander Henry C. Taylor, U. S. Navy, (Abs., Mis. Cor., No. 2), was received and read.

The Recorder was directed to acknowledge receipt of letter from Commander Taylor, and to request him to invite Lieutenant Usher to submit a written statement of his ideas concerning the organization and conduct of a relief expedition.

A telegram from Lieut. G. T. T. Patterson, U. S. Army, was received and read. (Abs., Mis. Cor., No. 3.)

Lieutenant-Commander McCalla, U. S. Navy, read a memorandum entitled "General design for an expedition for the relief of Lieutenant Greely and party." (Exhibit A.)

General Hazen read a paper, which he stated had been prepared in his office, suggesting a plan of relief. (This paper will be found entire in the testimony of Lieut. Ernest A. Garlington, 7th U. S. Cavalry.—RECORDER.)

Captain Greer stated that he had prepared a memorandum, but as Lieutenant-Commander McCalla had covered the whole ground, expressing exactly his own ideas, he would not read the notes he had prepared.

Captain Davis stated he had not yet been able, owing to the press of other duties, to put into the form of a memorandum the ideas he entertained as to the proper steps to be taken to afford succor to Lieutenant Greely and his party.

An informal discussion then ensued, and the opinion was expressed by each member that the first step to be taken was to recommend to the Secretaries of War and Navy the immediate procurement of two vessels suitable for Arctic service, in order that timely preparations might be made to adapt them for the proposed work, and the Board accordingly directed that the following letter be addressed to the Secretaries of War and Navy, respectively:

WASHINGTON, D. C., *December 22,* 1883.

SIR: As preliminary to its general report, the Board of Officers appointed by the President to consider the relief of the Lady Franklin Bay Expedition, begs to recommend that the Secretaries of War and the Navy take immediate steps to procure, by purchase, two full-powered steam whalers or sealers, and to prepare them for service in the Arctic regions.

Although it is hoped, and even expected, that Lieutenant Greely's party will be succored during the coming summer, yet the contingency must not be overlooked of the inability of the expedition to extricate itself from the ice and return the same season, and an enforced detention of the vessels in Smith Sound during the winter of 1884–5 may occur.

Therefore, the Board would further recommend that a naval vessel be prepared to act as a tender to the expedition, for the purpose of going as far as Littleton Island or Cape Sabine, to bring back the latest news of the expedition, or, in the event of the loss of one or both of the steam whalers or sealers, to bring home the officers and men not necessary for the sledge journeys during the winter; to contribute supplies for the use of the expedition, if necessary, and to aid in any way the efforts to reach and rescue Lieutenant Greely and his party.

Very respectfully, your obedient servant,
W. B. HAZEN,
Brig. & Bv't Maj. Gen'l,
Chief Signal Officer of the Army, President of the Board.

The Board also directed that the Secretaries of War and Navy be informed that, in the opinion of the Board, the services of a stenographer would be indispensable to an efficient and speedy transaction of the duties imposed on it.

The Board then adjourned to meet at 11 o'clock a. m., December 26, 1883.

ROOM 88, NAVY DEPARTMENT BUILDING,
Washington, D. C., December 26, 1883.

The Board met pursuant to adjournment; all the members present.

The Recorder stated that the person detailed by the Secretary of War to act as clerk and stenographer was unable to perform the duties of both positions, and that the services of a reporter would be necessary.

The Recorder was then directed to make arrangements for the immediate employment of an experienced stenographer. Upon invitation, the Board then repaired to the office of the Secretary of War for a conference with that officer and with the Secretary of the Navy, and a discussion of the best means of giving effect to the recommendations of the Board, contained in its preliminary report, then ensued.

Upon returning to the Board room, Captain Davis read a memorandum embodying his views as to the organization and conduct of a relief expedition. (Exhibit B.)

The Board then adjourned to meet on Wednesday, January 2, 1884, at 11 o'clock a. m.

ROOM 88, NAVY DEPARTMENT BUILDING,
Washington, D. C., January 2, 1884.

The Board met pursuant to adjournment; all the members present.

By approval of the Secretary of War, Mr. James L. Andem, of Washington, D. C., was employed as stenographer to the Board, and C. H. Emerson, of the Record Division, War Department, was assigned to duty as clerk.

General Hazen then submitted a large number of papers and communications received from various parties, offering their services, suggesting plans, &c., for the relief of the Greely party. (Abs., Mis. Cor., Nos. 4 to 26, inclusive.)

Capt. GEORGE E. TYSON, of Washington, D. C., having been invited to appear before the Board, was interrogated as follows:

By Captain DAVIS:

Question. The Board would thank you to make a brief statement of the experience you have had in the Arctic regions, giving dates of such service, how, and where, employed.—Answer. I first sailed for the Arctic regions in the year 1850, and I was employed continually there, in the whaling service, until 1870, when I entered on board the "Polaris" as assistant navigator. We left New York on the 1st day of July, if I remember correctly, and sailed from New London on the 4th day of July, arriving at Polaris Bay, in Smith Sound, or above Smith Sound, on the 27th day of August, and were frozen in there on the 5th day of September, 1871, in Polaris Bay. We remained there until the next July, when, Captain Hall being dead, the sailing master concluded to return home. On coming down Smith Sound, I suppose you all remember, I got adrift on a floe of ice and drifted for one hundred and ninety-six days.

By General HAZEN:

Q What date did you get on that drift?—A. On the 5th day of October.

Q. At what point was it?—A. I got separated from the vessel close to Littleton Island, and was rescued by the steamer "Tigress" on the last day of April, 1873, just north of the Straits of Belle Isle.

By Captain DAVIS:

Q. You say that from 1850 to 1870 you were in the whaling service?—A. Yes, sir.

Q. In the Arctic regions?—A. Through Melville Bay, down the coast of America, Hudson Strait, Cumberland Gulf, and Repulse Bay.

Q. In sailing or steam vessels?—A. Sailing vessels.

Q. Have you had any experience in the Arctic regions since your rescue from the floe?—A. Yes, sir; I returned with Captain Greer in the "Tigress."

Q. On a search expedition?—A. Yes, sir; a search expedition. and in 1877 I sailed in the "Florence" on a preliminary expedition for a proposed government expedition which was to be made.

Q. Where did you go?—A. To the head of Cumberland Gulf, to collect material, and we carried Esquimaux over to Disco Island, expecting to meet the government expedition there, but did not meet them and we had to return home. Since then (1877) I have not been in Arctic service.

Q. Have you given the subject of the relief of the Lady Franklin Bay expedition thought and consideration, and have you any project for the accomplishing of Lieutenant Greely's relief that you would suggest?—A. Yes, sir; I think a steamer of three hundred tons, sailing from here in June or the 1st of July, would be time enough, touching at Cape York, and not finding Lieutenant Greely or his party there, hunting the coast along as far as water would permit, and not finding them there, I would go to the west coast, and finding no trace of them there, I should have two whale-boats prepared, well fitted and manned, to take the land or water, and those boats will go up to Lady Franklin Bay. But I would not put my steamer in the ice; it would likely enough lead to another catastrophe.

Q. And you think there is a reasonable probability of reaching Lady Franklin Bay with those boats?—A. I think so; you can always find a little land water where you can get a boat along. But I think it would be impossible to get your ship through, and in going up to Lady Franklin Bay, a vessel getting there late in the season and coming down, runs great danger late in the fall. In fact, I consider it almost impossible, unless it is a very open season indeed.

Q. And reaching Lady Franklin Bay, you would expect Lieutenant Greely to avail himself of his own boats to return?—A. Yes, sir; of course, the two boats would require to take back double the number of men they would require to go there. In fact they would bring the whole party down if it was necessary, that is the fact.

Q. I suppose you are aware of the number of persons in Lieutenant Greely's party?—A. Yes, sir; I believe there are twenty-five.

Q. You spoke of obtaining a steam whaler of about three hundred tons. Can you liken that vessel to any which you have seen in service; do you remember any one of a similar character, such as you would propose?—A. No, sir; I never have seen any as small as that. The "Tigress" is about three hundred and fifty tons.

Q. Do you think such a vessel, suitable for the purpose, is obtainable; and if so, where?—A. I think perhaps a suitable vessel could be obtained at Saint John's, Newfoundland.

Q. And how about the *personnel;* how many should compose the crew of such a vessel?—A. About twenty-five or thirty men.

Q. What reliance, if any, would you place upon sledges and dogs?—A. None whatever.

Q. Would you make no use of the Esquimaux as guides or as hunters?—A. No, sir; I think not.

Q. About what point in Smith Sound do you think you could safely expect to reach with a vessel?—A. I think it could possibly reach Littleton Island, and then above Cape Isabella.

Q. You would expect to be able to reach that point in any event?—A. Yes, sir.

Q. Do you take into consideration the fact that your vessel might be frozen in there, and that you might fail to reach Lieutenant Greely with your boats?—A. Well, I do not anticipate any failure in reaching Lieutenant Greely or Lady Franklin Bay with the boats.

Q. What length of time would you expect to consume in the boat journey from Cape Sabine or Cape Isabella to Lady Franklin Bay and return?—A. I would be gone about fifteen days.

Q. At what date would you wish to be at Cape Isabella?—A. I should like to be there on the 25th of July; the vessel should be there the 25th of July.

Q. And, therefore, by the 10th of August you would expect to have returned to the ship?—A. I should hope to return to the ship by the 10th or 15th of August.

Q. Do you remember anything of the attempt that Hayes made to reach a high point with boats and sledges, and the difficulties that he encountered?—A. Yes, sir; but that was at a different time of year; that was in April or May that he attempted to reach Lady Franklin Bay, or some high northern point, with his sledges.

Q. He also endeavored to take with him a boat, you remember?—A. Yes, sir; but he gave the boat up.

Q. Would you expect to make your voyage in boats on the west shore of Smith Sound or the east?—A. On the west shore.

Q. Would you place any reliance on present depots of provisions located along the coast, or expect to carry all of your own provisions?—A. I do not know exactly; I understand there are caches of provisions along the coast, but I should carry fifteen or twenty days' provisions in each boat.

Q. What would be the weight of the boat with its complement of stores?—A. I could not tell you. I know they are handled easily. I should use a whale-boat twenty-seven or thirty feet in length, such as we use in the whaling service, but, perhaps, build the garboard stakes stronger with oak and put a three-inch keel on her, and shoe with good oak, so that when you jump your boat out on a piece of ice you can run it across.

Q. And you would expect your crew to be able to pull the boat out very hastily?—A. O, yes, sir; I have pulled hundreds out with a crew of six men to each boat.

Q. If you think it would be so easy to reach Lady Franklin Bay, then you would naturally expect Lieutenant Greely easily to reach the same point without assistance?—A. Certainly. If Lieutenant Greely was alive, and not in trouble, he would have been down last July or August. It may be that he made an attempt to reach there last spring.

General HAZEN. His orders require him not to leave much before the 1st of September.

The WITNESS. Then it would be impossible for him to come down.

Q. You are familiar with Lieutenant Greely's orders?—A. Yes, sir.

Q. You expect, in any event, he will have made the attempt next spring to go south?—A. Yes, sir; if living and well I think you will find him at Littleton Island, or near by there.

Q. What do you think of his chances of maintaining himself, supposing he reached Littleton Island last fall?—A. Well, they have suffered some, no doubt. Are there no provisions at Littleton Island?

Captain DAVIS. Yes, a small quantity.

The WITNESS. Well, there are caches near by there, are there not?

Captain DAVIS. Yes, on the west side of the Sound.

The WITNESS. If he reached Littleton Island last fall they have suffered some, no doubt. But nineteen persons floating on the ice for six months and a half, with scarcely anything at all, shows what can be done, and at Littleton Island there is an abundance of game through the winter season, and walrus which they can secure.

Q. All through the winter?—A. Yes, sir.

Q. And in the dark?—A. Yes, in the twilight; they can catch them in the twilight, the natives capture them.

By General HAZEN:

Q. What is the method of taking walrus during that period?—A. The natives take them with a spear and line.

Q. To prevent their sinking?—A. Yes, sir. They get their spear in and hold them. They are very expert in catching them.

Q. You did not see much of the Esquimaux when you were on that expedition—on the "Polaris"?—A. O, yes, sir; I have lived with them years and years.

Q. Then your opinion is that if Lieutenant Greely succeeded in getting safely to Littleton Island with some supplies, he could get through the winter pretty fairly?—A. Yes, sir.

By Captain GREER:

Q. How about the question of fuel there?—A. They would have to make their fires from the blubber, the oil.

By General HAZEN:

Q. I take it, it would depend more on the heat of the body and their being well protected with good clothing?—A. Yes, sir; and if they can find plenty of animal food, they can survive whether they have a fire or not.

By Captain DAVIS:

Q. Did you see any indications at Polaris Bay that the Esquimaux had ever lived and hunted in that region?—A. I saw indication of where they had had their huts, and the skeletons of cattle.

Q. In recent years?—A. The stains of the blood were distinguishable on the bones of the cattle that were lying there. I found indications of where they had fires, and a number of huts, and dug their spear-heads up. But I saw no other traces; no living trace.

Q. You would not think the services of an auxiliary vessel or tender would be required?—A. No, sir; I do not think that would be necessary.

By General HAZEN:

Q. Have you ever used dog sleds?—A. Yes, sir; I have used them for twenty years.

Q. I understand you to say that you would not propose to use them in this expedition?—A. No, sir; not in that season of the year.

Q. Then that might be done at other seasons if the boats failed?—
A. Yes, sir; that would be done in the spring of the year; but we could not use them in the fall.

By Captain DAVIS:

Q. I notice a paper among those sent to the Board in which you tender your services for a relief expedition?—A. Yes, sir.

By Captain GREER:

Q. How many dogs would you provide for each sled, supposing you were going on such an expedition, allowing for loss by death; the number required to haul an ordinary load?—A. Nine to twelve dogs make a very fine team, and they will carry a heavy load.

Q. I will put my question in this way. How many dogs would you provide for each load, if you were going to use them?—A. I should provide eighteen or twenty dogs for each sled.

By General HAZEN:

Q. Then there are some driven along; they are not all in the harness at once?—A. No, sir. Twelve dogs make an excellent team on good ice, and carry a heavy load, but not on rough ice.

By Captain DAVIS:

Q. Nearly all the sledge expeditions that have been successful have been conducted in the spring of the year, have they not?—A. Yes, sir.

By General HAZEN:

Q. For how long a period, beginning and ending when, in Smith Sound?—A. Well, it would not be safe to have your sleighs out later than the 1st of July, beginning at any time in April.

Q. About three months, then?—A. Yes, sir; you could work three months there with sledges.

By Captain DAVIS:

Q. Are the dogs found in Cumberland Gulf and Hudson Strait the same as those on the Greenland side?—A. No, sir; those on the Greenland side are a little mixed; they are not so good as the Esquimaux dogs on the west coast.

Q. Supposing it was intended to take dog-sledges with the expedition there, what would you regard as the best locality in which to procure dogs?—A. Sailing at that time of the year, it would be hardly possible to get dogs from the west coast; you would have to find them on the east.

Q. How early in the season could you expect to get into Hudson Strait or Cumberland Gulf, where there is a supply of dogs?—A. In the middle of July, and that would occupy too much time. Cumberland Gulf is not always accessible at that time of the year.

Q. Have you ever been at Ponds Bay?—A. No, sir; but I have been opposite. I sailed for Ponds Bay once, but we were driven back by the ice.

Q. At what date in the spring would you think it safe for Lieutenant Greely to start to come down in boats?—A. He would have to use his own judgment about that. I think he could start the middle of July and make his way down.

Q. If he has dogs in good condition, at what date could he get down with them, starting in the spring?—A. He could get down there in a very few days.

Q. Starting in April ?—A. Yes, sir; in April, May, or June.

Q. Would you think there certainly would be no difficulty in his crossing Smith Sound with sledges in the spring?—A. In the spring, there would be no difficulty.

By Lieutenant-Commander McCalla:

Q. That depends, of course, upon the character of the ice.—A. Of course the character of the ice has something to do with it. What I mean is he would meet with no obstructions from water at that time.

By General Hazen:

Q. The ice would be strong?—A. Yes, sir.

Q. He might meet with considerable obstruction from the ice being rough and piled up ?—A. Yes, sir.

By Captain Davis:

Q. Was not Smith Sound and Kennedy Channel open a good part of the winter when you were there in the "Polaris"?—A. Polaris Bay was open during the greater part of the winter, but Smith Sound was never known to be open during the winter. It chokes there, and freezes and stays.

By Lieutenant-Commander McCalla:

Q. Have you been above Littleton Island many times in your life ?—A. Only twice; once in the "Tigress" and once in the "Polaris."

Q. Did you go above Littleton Island in the "Tigress"?—A. Yes, sir.

Q. How far ?—A. Just about there.

Q. Did you go as far as Life-Boat Cove ?—A. We were right opposite that, I think.

Q. Can you give me an idea on this chart of the track of the "Polaris" up and down between Littleton Island and Lady Franklin Sound, or in that vicinity? Please trace it with a lead pencil on that map.

(The witness drew, with a lead pencil, the line referred to, on the map of Smith Sound and Kennedy and Robeson Channels.)

By General Hazen:

Q: Do you know anything about the "Polaris" having left any stores opposite Lady Franklin Bay on the east coast?—A.. Yes, sir; there were stores left there, but I believe that Sir George Nares consumed most of them, if not all.

Q. Have you any information that he did do it?—A. No, sir.

General Hazen. We can not find any such information.

Captain Greer. Not in his book.

By Lieutenant-Commander McCalla:

Q. Did you land in the "Polaris" between Cape Sabine and the vicinity of Lady Franklin Sound?—A. Yes, we landed at Cape Frazer.

Q. Then the line you made should have gone in there. Is that the only place?—A. Yes, sir; that is the only place.

Q. How near the coast did you go on your way up?—A. We were sometimes within one hundred yards of it.

Q. Then this line you made does not represent your track, for this is about ten miles out?—A. We followed the sinuosities of the coast usually.

Q. Then this lead pencil line does not represent your track?—A. No, sir; it is a little too far off shore.

Q. That is the only part of the coast that you know, in the vicinity of Cape Frazer?—A. Yes, sir.

By General HAZEN:

Q. About what was the amount of the stores that the "Polaris" left?—A. That I can not tell.

Q. A large quantity?—A. No, sir; I do not think it was.

Q. Were they covered or shielded in any way?—A. They were put in the observatory.

Q. What reason have you to suppose that Sir George Nares did consume them?—A. I saw it published somewhere that he had asserted that the American stores left there were superior to his own.

General HAZEN. He does not mention having used them all in any of his reports, and he really had no occasion for them for he had an abundance of stores for his own use, and he made an extensive number of caches.

The WITNESS. Those caches are still there?

General HAZEN. Yes; Lieutenant Greely was under the impression that those stores were still at Polaris Bay.

By Captain DAVIS:

Q. If the Esquimaux should visit that point they would appropriate the stores, would they not?—A. I think that is doubtful, because the Esquimaux in that section do not know anything about such stores, and they would not eat them.

By General HAZEN:

Q. They would prefer their own food?—A. Yes, sir; they are not accustomed to any such thing.

Q. And you do not think there have been any Esquimaux there for many years?—A. They very seldom visit there.

By Lieutenant-Commander McCALLA:

Q. In speaking of two whale-boats with six men each, and provisions for fifteen days, where would you expect the whale-boats to start from, the vicinity of what point?—A. That is owing to circumstances. You might be fortunate enough to reach Cape Frazer with your vessel.

Q. You might go all the way up?—A. Yes, sir.

Q. Then you had no particular point in view that you would expect to start from?—A. No, sir; start when we met the ice.

Q. How many people are there in Lieutenant Greely's party?—A. Twenty-five, I believe.

Q. Then you would have thirty-seven men in the two whale-boats coming down?—A. I suppose Lieutenant Greely has a boat there.

Q. You said that you would be prepared to take them all in the two whale-boats?—A. Has not Lieutenant Greely a whale-boat there?

Q. He may have. But if you go up to relieve him, you would not take that into consideration?—A. Yes, sir; but they have been gone three years next July, and I suppose their number has decreased some.

Q. But you could not count on that in sending up a relief?—A. No, sir; we could not. But the two whale-boats, if absolutely necessary, could bring all those men down. I carried nineteen men in a whale-boat in an open sea.

Q. I understood you to say that you had had twenty years' experience in sledging with dogs?—Yes, sir.

Q. Where was that, do you remember ?—A. In Cumberland Gulf, and Hudson Strait.

Q. What use did you make of the dogs; for what purpose were you using them?—A. We used them sometimes during the winter for pleasure, to make trips from one station to another, and in the spring of the year we used them for the purpose of sleighing in bone and oil.

Q. Were you up there twenty years in that vicinity ?—A. I was there from 1850 to 1870.

Captain DAVIS. You mean, off and on ?

The WITNESS. Yes, every other year.

Q. You spent the winter there every other year?—A. Yes, sir; and sometimes two winters at a time.

Q. How many winters did you pass, do you suppose, in that vicinity ?—A. I believe I passed fourteen winters there.

Q. In what business were you engaged ?—A. In the whaling business.

Q. What clothing did you have when you were on the ice-floe coming down, after your separation from the "Polaris"?—A. I had on a pair of satinet pants, a satinet vest, a flannel undershirt, and a light jacket.

Q. Had you any skin clothing ?—A. No, sir; I had no skin clothing. I found an old pair of moccasins on the ice.

Q. Moccasins are very useful there, are they not?—A. Yes, sir.

Q. You had a coat or overcoat?—A. No, sir; no coat.

Q. Did you suffer any from cold ?—A. Yes, sir; a great deal.

Q. You had on the "Polaris" certain Arctic clothing, hadn't you ?—A. Yes, sir; we procured some on the coast of Greenland that was very indifferent.

Q. What did you get there ?—A. Dog-skin clothing.

Q. How many pieces ?—A. The jackets, coats, and pants were made of dog-skin.

Q. The coats buttoned ?—A. Yes, sir.

Q. What did you have for the feet ?—A. We had very indifferent foot-gear on board the "Polaris."

Q. I mean, what did you obtain in Greenland as coverings for the feet?—A. We obtained some deer-skin and dog-skin stockings.

Q. How high did they come ?—A. They came nearly up to the knees.

Q. You did not wear any of these?—A. I did not have any on when I separated from the vessel.

By Captain DAVIS:

Q. What temperatures did you have ?—A. On the ice; that I could not tell you. I had a thermometer that froze in February, but I could not tell after that.

By Lieutenant-Commander MCCALLA:

Q. You say the clothing you obtained in Greenland was indifferent; what was the matter ?—A. It is different from the clothing obtained on the west coast, which was very fine; clothing made of reindeer skin, very light and warm.

Q. Do the Esquimaux generally wear coats there?—A. I have never wintered on the Greenland side; I never have been there in winter. I have always been on the west coast in winter. They wear dog-skin clothing. I suppose they are compelled to in the winter season, but it is not so cold on the Greenland coast.

Q. You did not stop on the coast of Greenland, between Upernavik and Cape Farewell, going up in the "Polaris"?—A. We stopped at several places after leaving Cape Farewell. ·We stopped at Tessuissak.

Q. You got clothing there?—A. Some of it. We stopped at Fiskernais, Holsteinborg, Disco Island, and at Upernavik.

Q. Where did you get your clothing?—A. We got a little at each locality.

Q. None of your party had any of it?—A. No, sir.

Q. There were some Esquimaux in your party; what were they clothed with?—A. They had skin clothing, when they got adrift.

Q. Do you know how many pieces or garments they had on?—A. No, sir. They had their usual double jacket and a pair of deer-skin pants and their moccasins.

Q. You found them of great service for hunting?—A. I found one of them of great service in hunting, one named Joe.

Q. How many did you have in all?—A. I only had two men.

Q. But the other one was not of so much use in hunting?—A. No, sir; he was not.

Q. Was he of any service at all?—A. No, sir; I think he was more a source of annoyance.

Q. One of them did a great deal of hunting, I think?—A. Yes, sir; that was Joe.

Q. He saved the party several times from the pangs of hunger, didn't he?—A. I can not say that. I think if we had been without the Esquimaux, we would have suffered less from hunger, because we had to support nine Esquimaux there.

General HAZEN. You think they ate up more than they gained for you?

·The WITNESS. I think they ate up more than they caught.

By Captain DAVIS:

Q. How long were you in crossing Melville Bay in going up?—A. A very short time; I could not say how long.

Q. You met with no ice of any consequence?—A. No, sir. After leaving Tessuissak we were a very short time. We had a beautiful passage across.

Q. How early in the season do you think it probable that a vessel could reach Cape York in ordinary seasons?—A. I should think by the 20th of June.

By Captain GREER:

Q. Would not that oblige the vessel to take some very great risks, ordinarily?—A. O, yes, sir; but the whale-men have to take very great risks. because they must be on their whaling grounds the fore part of July, or as early as possible.

By Captain DAVIS:

Q. Did you ever see the "Proteus"?—A. No, sir; I think not. I have seen most of those English steamers, but my recollection of them is not good.

By Captain GREER:

Q. Had they any sheepskin clothing on board the "Polaris"?—A. No, sir.

Q. Have you ever seen it used?—A. No, sir; I never have.

Q. You have had no actual experience to enable you to determine upon its merits?—A. No, sir; I have not. I have always been travelling in a country where we found plenty of deer-skin, and had the very best of deer-skin clothing and deer-skin sleeping bags, covered with tanned seal-skin to keep the moisture away.

By General HAZEN:

Q. What do you consider the very best clothing for Arctic use?—A. Clothing made of reindeer skin.

Q. Is it in one thickness or more?—A. We made a double jacket, one with the fur inside and the other with the fur out.

Q. Have you any idea where any quantity of that reindeer-skin could be procured?—A. Yes, sir; you could procure an abundance of it in Hudson Strait.

Q. At what point?—A. I do not know that you can procure any at York Factory, but north of that, anywhere along the coast, I have seen deer as thick as cattle are anywhere. The skins you could procure at the factory.

Q. But would that be available for the expedition next year?—A. No, sir.

By Captain DAVIS:

Q. Do the Hudson's Bay Company trade in that clothing and send it to England?—A. I think so.

Q. Could it be found in London?—A. I do not know whether the reindeer-skin could be found there or not.

Q. But the Hudson's Bay people do trade in that clothing?—A. Yes, sir.

By General HAZEN:

Q. Have you any opinion as to sheepskin—its quality for that service?—A. I think it would be very serviceable, if you were not able to procure deer-skin.

Q. Failing to get deer-skin, you think that would be very serviceable?—A. Yes, sir.

By Captain DAVIS:

Q. Did you have any scurvy on the "Polaris" expedition?—A. No, sir.

Q. Did you make use of lime juice as an anti-scorbutic?—A. No, sir.

By General HAZEN:

Q. What anti-scorbutic did you make use of?—A. Fresh meat and potatoes.

By Captain DAVIS:

Q. Did you ever use lime juice in any of your winterings?—A. No, sir; I would not have it.

Q. You place no reliance upon it?—A. No, sir.

Q. What kind of provisions would you take in your boats, if you were starting up there on that trip, or for an occasion where you might be obliged to winter in your vessel?—A. I would take the provisions that all vessels going to the Arctic regions are equipped with, that is, with canned fruits and meats and pemmican; pemmican is very serviceable up there.

Q. The pemmican made and obtained where?—A. I think in Philadelphia.

Q. With the ordinary ship's provisions and with fresh meat, would you expect to maintain yourself and winter there without scurvy?—A. Yes, sir; with ordinary ship's provisions.

Q. How do you explain the breaking out of scurvy in other expeditions then, where they had an abundance of good provisions, including pemmican?—A. I attribute the great cause of scurvy to their having very inferior salt meat, very old, and where the nutriment had all gone from it. I would have good fresh pork, newly killed, and fresh beef, and plenty of canned meats, and vegetables, and fruits.

Q. But you can not expect to have fresh pork and .beef during the winter there?—A. But you can have it freshly killed here. There is no occasion to put so much salt in it when it is going to a cold climate.

Lieut. H. J. HUNT, U. S. Navy, having been invited to appear before the Board, was interrogated as follows:

By Captain DAVIS:

Question. The Board would thank you to make a brief statement of the experience you have had in the Arctic regions, giving dates of such service, how, and where, employed.—Answer. I was attached to the Arctic relief ship "Rodgers," and sailed in June, 1881, from San Francisco in search of the "Jeannette." The ship made a cruise during the summer in the Arctic regions north of Behring Strait, went into winter quarters in October at Saint Lawrence Bay, and was lost by fire the night of November 30th, 1881. From Saint Lawrence Bay, I came with the commanding officer overland through Siberia and Europe to the United States. The remainder of the crew returned by vessel from Saint Lawrence Bay.

Q. By what method did you cross Siberia?—A. To the first Russian town we travelled by dog sledge, a distance of about eight hundred miles. From that town we searched the coast to the westward, I mean with dogs, for a distance of four hundred miles. From there we travelled by reindeer sledges to Verkhojansk, an inland town, and then to Yakoutsk on horse back. That was in the summer. I was then detached by Captain Berry and ordered to join Lieutenants Harber and Schuetze, who were sent out during the summer to search for one of the missing boats of the "Jeannette."

Q. Have you given the subject of the relief of the Lady Franklin Bay expedition thought and consideration, and have you any project for the accomplishment of Lieutenant Greely's relief?—A. My views on that point I have put in writing in a communication addressed to the Board, which contains all I care to say on that subject.

The paper referred to was read, and is as follows:

WASHINGTON, D. C., *December 26, 1883.*

To Board for relief of Lady Franklin Bay Expedition.

GENTLEMEN: In accordance with the request of the Board to furnish it with any impressions I may have formed, concerning the organization and conduct of a relief expedition for Lieutenant Greely and party, I respectfully submit the following:

Organization.

The organization of the proposed expedition belongs properly to the Navy Department.

The officer to command it should be a naval officer of Arctic experience, selected by the department, and ordered without regard to volunteering. *Reason:* All officers are opposed to the practice of volunteering, and there are many efficient officers, well calculated, both by inclination and requirements, who would refrain from volunteering, even though it were made positively necessary to their eligibility: whereas the selection to command, by the Department, is such an honor that it would indeed be most unfortunate were it to hit upon a man who failed to appreciate the fact.

The officers of the expedition should be selected by the commander of the expedition, from all available officers of the navy, junior to himself. *Reason:* Officers of the navy are preferred, because each should be capable of navigating a boat, and of performing all the duties incident to the ship, besides having been educated to military discipline.

The crew should consist entirely of able seamen, selected by the commander of the expedition, from men who have served in the navy. *Reason:* The selection should be made by the commanding officer, in order that he may justly be held responsible for their efficiency and conduct. They should have served in the navy, that they may be thoroughly familiar with the discipline of that service. The necessity of discipline upon such an expedition is admitted by all, but its vital importance is impressed upon those who have taken part in Arctic work, when every man, not strictly under its influence, feels that he has a right to express and defend his opinion upon a subject not too well understood by any.

The ship should be either the property of the United States Government, or she should be an American ship chartered by the Government, without officers or crew. She should be selected by the officer who is to command her, from all available steam vessels, and be purchased, if a foreign ship. *Reason:* The ship should sail under the American flag, and no other.

The boats should be of the type known as the "New Bedford whale-boat," they being specially adapted, both by their model and construction, for navigating through ice, and being at the same time probably the best open sea boats in use. One or two lighter built boats should be furnished for use in quick sledge journeys over the ice, should such journeys be required. In these lighter boats particular attention should be paid to the fastenings, as with good fastenings almost any injury may be repaired. *Note:* Lieutenant Berry devised a skin balsa to take the place of light boats in quick journeys by sledge. I think the plan a good one, but it was not tried, through lack of necessity.

The ship should be provided, to take care of herself and the party she is to succor, for a term of two years. I believe no better guide can be followed than that adopted by the "Jeannette" Relief Board, of which the late Admiral John Rodgers was president.

Conduct.

The relief ship should sail in time to reach Upernavik at the earliest possible moment.

If the Greely party is not found at that place, and there is no information there to warrant another course, the ship should proceed with the utmost dispatch to Littleton Island, from which point the entire conduct of the expedition should be left to the commanding officer. *Reason:* The commanding officer, having been selected for his coolness, judgment, and other requisite qualities, and having full knowledge of all facts now possessed, will (when actually upon the ground, and with additional information) be the most capable person of judging of the proper course to be pursued.

Respectfully submitted,

H. J. HUNT,
Lieutenant, U. S. Navy.

By General HAZEN:

Q. Will you please state your opinion in regard to the different kinds of skin clothing?—A. In the latitude we reached there was no skin clothing required in summer. We had excellent clothing in winter, consisting entirely of reindeer-skin.

Q. Do you consider that better than sheepskin, or better than any other kind?—A. I think it is better than any skin. It has more warmth for its weight. It is much lighter.

Q. That is usually adopted by all Arctic people who can get it?—A. I think so.

Q. Have you any idea where it can be procured?—A. Not on this coast.

Q. Do you know where the clothing for the "Rodgers" was secured?—A. At Petropaulovski principally, and part of it at Saint Michaels.

Q. Ready-made, or did you buy the skins and make it up?—A. Both; we had some ready-made, and others we made up. After we landed, we had the native Chukches clothing, for which we traded.

By Captain DAVIS:

Q. Are the garments made of double thickness?—A. Yes, sir

Q. With the hair inside and out?—A. Yes, sir; the inner lining has the hair inside, and the outer the hair outside.

Q. What do they wear on their feet?—A. Reindeer-skin boots, coming up to the knee.

Q. With soles of thicker leather?—A. No, sir; the best soles were of the heavy seal-skin, with the hair inside, and some of them were fitted with bear-skin soles, with large hair outside.

Q. In what season of the year were these sledge journeys made?—A. We started from Saint Lawrence Bay a month before leaving the station. The delay was caused by the loss of Mr. Putnam. From that point we started on the 8th of February.

Q. And what average distance per day could you make with dogs during that journey, taking into account both the stormy and fair weather?—A. The distance is about eight hundred miles, and we actually made it, including all rests and stoppages, from the 8th of February to the 25th of March.

Q. That is, in about forty-five days?—A. Yes, sir.

Q. Did you travel on the land or on the ice principally?—A. Both; but principally along the coast on the land.

Q. How many dogs made up a team?—A. Our team consisted, at different times, of from fourteen to eighteen dogs.

Q. And what weight had they to pull?—A. The average weight, I think, must have been about twelve hundred pounds.

Q. Less than one hundred pounds to a dog?—A. Yes, sir.

Q. What is regarded as a proper load for a dog in Siberia?—A. For quick travelling, a dog is supposed to haul about half his weight, averaging from thirty-five to forty pounds, that is, for very rapid travelling. But they very often load as heavy as seventy-five or eighty pounds to a dog.

Q. Are the Siberian dogs heavier than those of Greenland?—A. I do not know the Greenland dogs. These dogs would average about sixty or sixty-five pounds.

Q. In the equipment of an expedition for that region, although you say that you would leave all discretion to the commanding officer, still he must have an equipment that will enable him to remain through a winter, if need be?—A. Yes, sir.

Q. Could you specify what supplies should be taken in the way of dogs, sledges, and boats, for operations away from the ships?—A. I think that two teams of fourteen dogs each would be sufficient. That is, I think thirty dogs would be sufficient. I think it would be well to have four whale-boats, in addition to the ice-boats, for light travelling. A New Bedford whale-boat is rather a heavy boat. It is very strong, and a most excellent sea boat.

Q. Would you expect to make use of boats and sledges in any single journey, combining the two?—A. I could not tell you that; I do not know the nature of the ice on this side at all.

Q. Do the natives in Siberia ever suffer from scurvy?—A. I never knew of a case.

By General HAZEN:

Q. You had no scurvy in your party?—A. I believe there were a few cases, light attacks of scurvy, after we separated from the party; but we had none in our party.

3

By Captain DAVIS:

Q. Was lime-juice issued, or was it included in the preparation of pemmican?—A. We had both lime-juice pemmican and plain pemmican.

Q. Were the men inclined to eat it; did they like it?—A. I think they were all very fond of it after the loss of the ship. Before that we did not eat pemmican at all. I was very fond of pemmican after we started.

By General HAZEN:

Q. Do you know where the pemmican was secured?—A. I think it was made by a firm in Baltimore, but I am not certain.

By Captain DAVIS:

Q. What number of persons would you think should compose the complement of a vessel to go up there on this errand?—A. I think that the ship should be a small one, but it would depend on the ship that is to go. They might find a ship of larger size that was stronger and better adapted to the purpose; but I should think that a ship which would be fully and well manned by a crew of twenty men would be best.

Q. And would be sufficient for your boating and sledging parties detached from the vessel, you think?—A. I think so.

By Captain GREER:

Q. Do you mean a total *personnel* of twenty?—A. No, sir; I mean twenty, not including the officers.

Q. That would be a total *personnel* of about thirty or thirty-five?—A. Yes, sir; about thirty, perhaps more, depending on the size of the ship. My opinion is that a smaller ship, provided you can get a proper one, would be better.

By Captain DAVIS:

Q. You feel a perfect confidence that such an expedition would be able to rescue the party?—A. Yes, sir.

Q. You would not think a tender or auxiliary vessel necessary?—A. I do not think it absolutely necessary, but I think it would be an additional precaution to send a tender. But she should have for her sole object the landing of stores and boats at Littleton Island.

Q. In the event of the relief vessel failing to reach Lieutenant Greely, or to rescue him next season, you would, of course, expect to winter?—A. Yes, sir; I think it very likely, too, that the best way of reaching Lieutenant Greely at an early period would be the way suggested by Captain Tyson, using these whale-boats, each of which could be navigated by four men and carry provisions for two months.

After a short recess by the Board, the examination of witnesses was resumed.

Lieut. ERNEST A. GARLINGTON, U. S. Army, in response to the invitation of the Board, appeared, and was questioned as follows:

By Captain DAVIS:

Question. The Board would thank you to give a brief statement of the experience you have had in the Arctic regions, giving the dates of such service, how, and where, employed.—Answer. I left New York City, June 12, 1883, in command of the Greely Relief Expedition on board the U. S. Steamer "Yantic," arrived at Saint John's, Newfoundland, there put my party on board the "Proteus" and took charge of her, left that port June 29, 1883, bound to Disco, Greenland, arrived there on the 6th of July, sailed thence on the 16th for Little-ton Island, where we arrived on the 22d of July, then headed for Cape Prescott, but in the afternoon were stopped by the ice; went into Payer Harbor and remained several hours. I then tried to work my way around into Buchanan Strait and along Bache Island, but on the evening of the 23d the ship was caught in the ice, crushed and sunk. The next day, with the part of the stores saved, we landed on Cape Sabine, remained there one night and part of the day, then left in two whale-boats, with the "Proteus" crew in three boats, crossed Smith Sound to Life-Boat Cove, followed along the coast down to Cape York, arrived there on August 10th, and remained in that vicinity until the 16th, when I started across Melville Bay and arrived at Upernavik on the 23d of August, the party being the same as when I left Cape Sabine, with the exception of the boat commanded by Lieu-tenant Colwell which had been detached at Cape York and sent direct to Disco. His boat had arrived at Upernavik the day before I did and gone on in a larger boat which had been borrowed from the Gov-ernor of the island.

Q. Have you given the subject of the relief of the Lady Franklin Bay expedition thought and consideration, and have you any project for the accomplishing of Lieutenant Greely's relief?—A. I have given the subject thought, and have submitted a project, dated the 19th of Novem-ber, to the Chief Signal Officer of the Army, made in conjunction with Lieutenant Colwell, the officer who had been with me on this expedition.

The paper referred to was read, and is as follows:

WASHINGTON, D. C., 19th November, 1883.

To the Chief Signal Officer.

SIR: I have the honor, in conjunction with Lieutenant Colwell, U. S. Navy, to sub-mit the following project of a plan for the relief of Lieutenant Greely and his party during the coming season.

The expedition to be commanded by myself, and the relief ship by Lieutenant Col-well.

This expedition should leave New York not later than the 10th of May.

Two vessels should be fitted out; the relief ship proper of not more than 500, nor less than 300, tons measurement (gross), and a convoying ship of larger size.

For the relief ship, one of the smaller class of steam whalers should be purchased. This purchase to be made, if possible, with the condition that the owners of the ship would re-purchase from the Government, if she were brought back in good order and condition, at a stipulated price. This vessel should be secured at once and put in thorough repair at one of the navy-yards. The hulls of these whalers are as strongly built as possible, and need little repair, but the equipment should be carefully and thoroughly overhauled under the personal supervision of the officer who will command her. Special attention should be paid to the boats, steering gear, navigating instru-ments, spars and rigging, hawsers, steam winches, capstan, boilers and engines. There should be a supply of ice saws, and ample facilities for ice blasting. The ship should be commanded as I have indicated. There should also be three watch officers, one engineer, and one surgeon. The crew should be specially enlisted for the cruise, the greatest care given to their selection, and should consist of three machinists, one steward, four quartermasters, one ship's cook, six firemen, and eight seamen. There should be from the Army, two sergeants (observers) from the Signal Corps, and eight enlisted men from the line, selected by the commander of the expe-dition, these men to be used for sledging. The services of two or three Canadian *voyageurs* should be secured if possible.

Supplies for fifteen months should be carried, although the probabilities are that the expedition would return to the United States in the fall of 1884. A sufficient number of sledges, made after a pattern to be determined upon after consultation with the best authorities on Arctic sledging, should be provided. Everything in the way of cloth-ing, provisions, arms and amunition, signalling apparatus, fishing tackle, &c., must be most carefully attended to, and advantage taken of the advice and experience of those who have been in that region. Supplies for six months only should be carried by the relief ship, and all available space utilized for coal, of which not less than forty days' supply should be carried.

The convoying ship could be one of the third-rate vessels of the Navy. It would be necessary to strengthen her about the bows, put sheathing along her entire water-line; she should be fitted with a two-bladed screw, and be provided with a spare-screw and rudder. Her complement of officers and men should be reduced to a minimum, and all available space utilized for coal and provisions, including the additional nine months' supply of the latter for the relief ship.

The Danish government should be requested at once to send orders to the Inspector of North Greenland to furnish dogs, drivers, dog harness, and interpreter, if possible. I do not think it advisable to get skin clothing in Greenland, but think it should be made in the United States. Duplicates of these orders should be requested, and given to the commander of the expedition, to guard against the failure of the ship arriving from Copenhagen.

The two ships should sail in company, the convoy having positive orders to go as far north as Cape Sabine. So early in the season as the end of May, it would probably be impracticable for the convoy to cross Melville Bay, while the whaler could force its way through. If, therefore, the ice was found to be very close and heavy in Melville Bay, the convoy, in the discretion of the commanding officers, should be allowed to return to Upernavik, and remain until the middle of June before again attempting the passage—it would probably be found feasible by the 1st of July. The convoy should not abandon the attempt to reach Cape Sabine earlier than the 1st of October. The relief ship should be pushed, at the opening of the season, with the first of the Jones Sound whalers. All efforts should be directed to opening communication with the Cape York Eskimo.

The ship could probably get within fifteen miles of Cape York early in June, when two lightly equipped sledges should at once be sent to communicate with the natives. If the Greely party, or any part of it, had reached Littleton Island, or were at that time anywhere along the Greenland coast, these people would, in all probability, be aware of it, as they now know that a large party of white men are in the far north endeavoring to come south.

If, from the natives at Cape York, it were ascertained that the Greely party had reached the Greenland coast, during the preceding winter or spring, the condition of the party and their necessities would be learned. Sledge parties should be at once organized, as many as possible of the natives with their sledges secured, and the parties started immediately for the camp of Greely.

The natives are acquainted with the sledge route along the coast, have excellent dogs, (superior to those of the Danish settlements) and with light sledge loads could make very rapid time. This party should have orders to await the arrival of the ship at, or near, Pandora Harbor, or at the place they find the party—taking all precautions to advise the ship of their location on the way to the northward.

Life-Boat Cove is but five days by sledge from Cape York in the season for sledging.

If no tidings of Greely were received, it would be reasonably safe to conclude that they had not yet reached the Greenland coast, and the sledges should return to the ship. The ship should then proceed north as opportunities offered, visiting Cary Islands and communicating with the natives on Northumberland Island and Saunders Island for possible information. If no traces or news of the party is received at Littleton Island, the ship should at once proceed to Cape Sabine, establishing a large depot at the most advantageous point in that neighborhood, then make a thorough examination there, and if nothing is found, return to Pandora Harbor and wait for the ice in Smith Sound to break up and pan out. From Cape Sabine, in the absence of news of the party, a boat and sledge party should be sent to northward with all possible despatch.

If the convoy should not arrive at Pandora Harbor by the 10th of July, the relief ship should cross to Cape Sabine; and if the condition of the ice was not favorable for the northward progress of the ship, a boat expedition of two boats, crews of one officer and six men to each, loaded with as many supplies as they could carry, should proceed north with orders to communicate with Lieutenant Greely. When a junction is made, the united parties should come south as rapidly as possible to meet the ship. The ship in the mean time should take advantage of every favorable opportunity to proceed north, taking advantage of all necessary delays to send parties to examine all likely camping places for tidings of Greely. Such places as Alexandra Haven, south side of Bache Island, Washington Irving Island, Franklin Pierce Bay, Scoresby Bay, Rawlins Bay, and the depot at Cape Hawks, Cape Collinson, Carl Ritter Bay, &c.

In case of disaster to the ship, all articles saved should be conveyed to the nearest land and a camp established.   One light boat, with four men, should be sent to Cape Sabine to communicate with the convoy, and one to the northward to communicate with the relief boats, assist them, and hurry their movements south with the Greely party.   The convoying ship failing to cross Melville Bay in company with the relief ship, should be able to accomplish it about the 1st of July, and should reach Pandora Harbor, or that vicinity, about the 10th of July, where she would meet her consort and all final arrangements would be made.   If she should find the relief ship gone, she should proceed at once to Cape Sabine, collect all the provisions in that vicinity and make one well-secured cache of the serviceable stores.   She should look for, and prepare, a suitable place on the west side of Smith Sound for the winter station (preferably Alexandra Haven), erect the winter house, and get the stores for the relief ship in readiness to land rapidly.   If she receives news of disaster to relief ship, the stores should be at once landed.   All available boats should be sent away to the assistance of the northern parties, and every precaution taken to avoid the possibility of the ships being blockaded in Buchanan Strait or Payer Harbor, retreating, if necessary, to Pandora Harbor, leaving a small party at the station established, to direct the parties as they arrived from the north.   Signal communication should be established between Cape Sabine and Littleton Island, and at the first news from the northern parties the convoy should proceed to Cape Sabine and be ready to render any assistance.   If no news was received by September 1st, preparations should be made for going into winter quarters at Life-Boat Cove, Foulke Fiord, or Pandora Harbor.   After October 1st there would be no prospect of getting the party south that season, and the ship should be prepared for the winter.   As soon as possible a lightly equipped sledge party should start up the east side of Smith Sound, and following approximately the track of Doctor Hayes in 1861, cross to the west side of the sound about Cape Hawks, where some news would certainly be obtained of the party.   The crew of relief ship should also endeavor to communicate with Cape Sabine and the convoying ship as soon after disaster or delay in ice as possible.

The Greely party, their records and valuables, should be brought to the camp established on the west coast, and as early as practicable moved across the sound to the winter quarters of the convoy.

This is an outline of the general course to be followed.   The many possibilities of the case preclude definite instructions being given to cover all emergencies.   The commander of the relief expedition should not be hampered with detailed orders, but should be directed to act according to his best judgment.

It is imperative that the commanding officers should have the same orders as far as the co-operation of their respective commands is concerned, and a thorough understanding between them should be insisted on before sailing from the United States, and at every point where the possibility of a separation could occur.   These agreements should be reduced to writing, and each officer held to a strict performance of his part. The selection of officers and men for the relief ships and sledging party, should be left entirely to their commanding officers.   The selection, preparation and disposition of equipments and supplies, should be under the personal supervision of the commanding officers, and no interference with their plans, by theorists with no practical knowledge of the work in hand, should be allowed.

To properly equip an expedition, steps to procure a ship should be at once taken. There are but three steam whalers owned in the United States, and their whereabouts is unknown.   Their owner has been communicated with, but he is now in San Francisco and no answer has been received from him.

A suitable vessel can be built in this country in about five months, at a cost of about $60,000.

The steam sealers of Saint John's are all over ten years old, with one exception, built in 1874, and are out of repair.   The price of the best of them is placed at $100,000 by their owners.

At Dundee, Scotland, where a fleet of steam whalers and sealers is owned, two comparatively new vessels are available, one two years old and one four years old.   Price unknown.   Vessels of the class of the "Proteus," (six hundred and forty-seven tons measurement, gross) costing about $80,000 to build and equip, can be built in five or six months.   As difficulty and delay are always experienced in obtaining dogs in Greenland, a supply might be procured from the Northwest Territory, with drivers to handle them.

A rough estimate of the cost of an expedition based on the foregoing would be about $150,000 for the relief ship.   The repairs to the ship being made at a navy-yard and the pay of the enlisted crew being from regular appropriations.

Since writing the above, have heard of four American whalers in San Francisco—one reported an excellent ship.

Very respectfully, your obedient servant,

        (Signed.)   E. A. GARLINGTON,
                                 1st Lieutenant, 7th Cavalry, A. S. O.

                         WASHINGTON, D. C., 26th November, 1883.

To the Chief Signal Officer:

SIR: In reply to your letter, I have the honor to submit an approximate estimate of the cost of the expedition, based upon the accompanying plan, for the relief of Lieutenant Greely. Total cost, $169,200, distributed as follows:

Purchase of ship	$100,000
Pay of crew, fifteen months	35,000
Subsistence sixty-nine men, fifteen months	15,000
Medicines	1,000
House	1,200
Extra and Arctic clothing	7,000
Incidental: dogs, dog food, oil stove, sledges, &c., &c	10,000
Total	$169,200

Very respectfully, your obedient servant,

        (Signed.)   E. A. GARLINGTON.
                                 1st Lieutenant, 7th Cavalry, A. S. O.

By General HAZEN:

Q. Have you any statement to add in addition to that?—A. No, sir; that is the plan, in the main. There are details as to the equipment, clothing, provision and sledges, the kind of boats, &c., which are not not touched upon in that plan.

By Captain DAVIS:

Q. You say in your memorandum or project, that the relief ship should be one of the smaller class of steam whalers. What inquiries have you made as to the availability of those vessels and the points from whence they can be obtained?—A. I looked into the subject while at St. John's, and made inquiries as to the whaling fleet sailing from Dundee, and since I returned here I have made inquiries in regard to whalers owned in America.

Q. What have you been able to ascertain in regard to American whalers?—A. All the United States steam whalers are on the Pacific coast. I think there are but three registered here, or were at the time the examination was made. But I have since learned that there are four in addition to those three; four have been built recently on the Pacific coast, which are pronounced to be excellent ships, and which fulfill all the conditions that are requisite in steam whalers. The best ships I have heard of are the "Thetis" and the "Resolute," of Dundee, Scotland.

Q. How old are they?—A. Two and three years.

Q. And what size?—A. About the same size as the "Proteus"—about 467 registered tons.

Q. Did you make any inquiry as to the possibility of having vessels built by American ship-builders in time for such an expedition?—A. Yes, sir; I have had some correspondence, and Lieutenant Colwell wrote to some ship-builders—to the firm who had built these whalers that are now owned in Maine—and received a reply stating that a vessel could be built, fulfilling the conditions required, in six months from the time the order was given. It would require at least that, and 1 think, from talking to naval men, it would require a longer time.

Q. Is there any difference in type, as you understand, between the sealers of Saint John's and the whalers of Dundee ?—A. In the "Proteus" and the "Bear," the newest of the Saint John's sealers, their engines are placed differently; there is one whaler built the same way, with the engine amidships. All the other whalers have their engines astern or aft; all the steam-whalers, except the "Arctic," that I have been able to learn about.

Q. Are those vessels full-powered ?—A. Yes, sir; I suppose they can make about seven or eight knots, and under favorable conditions they would make nine or nine and a half knots under steam alone. .

Q. What was the speed of the "Proteus"?—A. She could make about nine and a half knots. Her average was about seven and a half to eight knots.

Q. At that rate of speed, what was her consumption of coal per diem ?—A. About twelve tons.

Q. You are confident that these newest Dundee whalers are built with their engines abaft the main-mast?—A. I was so informed by sailing captains at Saint John's.

Q. You did not see any of the vessels?—A. No, sir; they were not in Saint John's. The "Bear," owned by Walter Grieve & Company, of Saint John's, is a good ship. She has new boilers, and is a sister ship of the "Proteus," of about the same size and dimensions.

Q. How old is she?—A. The same age—ten or eleven years. The "Neptune" is also a good ship, and I was informed by some parties in Saint John's that there are two small ships there of less than 300 tons burthen, the "Iceland" and "Greenland," I think. They are small ships, both have propeller wells, &c., and it is claimed, well fitted for this work; they are about the proper size, I think.

Q. What would you regard as the chance of getting a vessel into Lady Franklin Bay next season—a relief vessel I mean—considering all the probabilities of the case?—A. From conversation with people in Greenland, and as near as they can find out from records which they keep and information they get from people who have been up there, they seem to think there is an open season once in seven years. But that of course is merely guess-work; I think the chances are against it—against getting up to Lady Franklin Bay, always.

Q. Would you regard it as probable that a boat expedition could have reached Lady Franklin Bay last summer, judging from what you saw?—A. A boat expedition, purely, could not have done anything at all while I was there; could not have made any progress north. A sledging and boat party could have gotten at least to Cape Hawks or Cape Prescott.

Q. How much ice would they have been obliged to cross to reach the open water around Cape Hawks?—A. Ten or fifteen miles would have brought them to open water. At one time while we were there, we could have gotten to open water within a few hundred yards.

Q. From your experience in returning from Littleton Island, passing through such ice as you saw getting down to Melville Bay and through it, how large a crew for a whale-boat would you consider necessary to haul it out on ice?—A. With a whale-boat of the size we had, a crew of six men could get it out, if the ice was not over six inches above the water; more than six inches above it they could not pull it out. We had seven men in one boat and eight in another, and we had to "double up" every time the boats were pulled out. I think that the boats should be smaller. One of the boats I refer to was twenty-eight and a half feet long and the other thirty feet over all.

Q. When you speak of six men not being able to pull them out of the water, you refer, of course, to the boats and their contents?—A. Yes, sir; they were loaded with thirty days' supplies.

Q. And it took a relay of men to get them out—a "doubling up" of the crew?—A. Yes, sir; and there are times when it is impossible to do that. Boats have to be pulled up very hurriedly, and the boat's own crew should be able to get it out of the water.

Q. Did you have a steam-launch aboard the "Proteus"?—A. No, sir.

Q. Would an ordinary steam-launch be useful and efficacious in navigatiug the waters of Smith Sound in the autumn?—A. No, sir; I think not. The only steam-launches that would be of any use at all are those which use oil for fuel and have their screws under the boat in some way. I forget the name of the launch.

Q. You have not seen any such?—A. No, sir; but I have had them described to me; they use them on the Pacific coast. On account of the weight, there would be an objection to a steam-launch—getting it on the ice, pulling it out.

Q. Who has any knowledge of the boats you speak of?—A. Lieutenant Ray spoke to me of a boat of that kind, and I also talked with Lieutenant Colwell about them—he knows of a boat. I do not think he has ever seen one, but he knows about it from reading or otherwise. I think a boat twenty feet long, with bilge keels, would be better for that work.

Q. One that could be put on runners?—A. Keels serve the purpose, to a certain extent, of runners. The boats can be pulled on the ice without subjecting them to so much strain. When the ordinary boats are pulled out on the ice-floes, the whole strain comes on the keel and it is apt to break it.

Q. Where have keel boats, such as you describe, been recently used?— A. I do not know of their having been used except by one expedition, Parry's, long ago. But he made a more successful sledge-boat expedition than has ever been made since, with other appliances.

Q. What kind of clothing were you furnished with on your last Arctic expedition?—A. I carried from here buffalo overcoats, german socks, mitts made of the same material as the socks, some oil-tanned moccasins and arctic overshoes. I took some buffalo shoes also and sheepskin sleeping-bags, and in Saint John's I got a lot of seal-skin clothing, made in Greenland, for the expedition of 1882. This clothing was made up about Disco.

Q. You did not have occasion to make much use of your Arctic clothing?—A. We used it on the boat, coming back, to some extent.

Q. But you did not have any very low temperatures?—A. No, sir. I used it enough to form the opinion that clothing obtained in Greenland would prove inefficient in extremely cold weather.

Q. You say that was seal-skin clothing?—A. Yes, sir.

Q. Did you have any dog-skin clothing?—A. No, sir. You cannot get dog-skin clothing in Greenland; they monopolize that themselves and can't get enough for their own use.

Q. Were the buffalo overcoats of service to you?—A. They were good for sleeping in, but they are of no account when you have to engage in hard work, for they are made in a clumsy way, and the buffalo-skin is heavy.

Q. What were the sleeping-bags made of?—A. Of sheepskin.

Q. Have you seen clothing made of reindeer skin?—A. I have not, but every man who has been to the Arctic regions and has had any experience there sledging, &c., recommends it as the best clothing, beyond all question. I think sheepskin clothing for an inner garment would be as good, or very nearly so, as reindeer.

Q. Do you know anything of the possibility of obtaining deer-skin clothing in time for an expedition next summer?—A. There is no place where it can be obtained, except it be in Norway or Sweden. I think in some parts of Norway they have immense herds of reindeer.

Q. You think an inquiry there might show that it was obtainable?—A. I think so.

Q. Do you know whether the Hudson's Bay Company trade in it and have it as an article of merchandise?—A. I do not; but I think it extremely unlikely, because the English expeditions were not fitted with it at all; and none of the expeditions, so far as I have been able to find out, were fitted with reindeer clothing; they had to get it for themselves.

Q. You had no occasion to make use of your dogs in any sledging journey?—A. No, sir; I used them a little on the ice-floe after the ship was lost.

Q. Where were your sledges made?—A. They were made here.

Q. What was their capacity?—A. I think the larger ones would carry a ton.

Q. How many did you have?—A. Two large ones, and a small one which would carry about half that amount.

By Lieutenant-Commander McCALLA:

Q. I believe you said that the seal-skin clothing was not good or was not serviceable. Please state on what you base that opinion, if you did not use it much?—A. I did not use it myself, but some of the men did. Men in my party used it all the way from Cape Sabine to Upernavik.

Q. What was the difficulty in regard to it?—A. Seal skin is cold to begin with; it has no warmth, particularly the hair-seal, and if it gets wet it is just like a dish-rag; it absorbs water.

Q. It is not water-proof?—A. Not at all.

Q. Where did you get it?—A. In Saint John's.

Q. What clothing did you have for each man?—A. A double jumper and a pair of trousers; that was the suit.

Q. Any seal-skin covering for the feet?—A. No, sir; but I got a few seal-skin boots in Saint John's.

Q. Is that the only arrangement you made for the winter in the way of covering for the feet; I mean in regard to seal-skin clothing. I thought you might have bought some in Greenland?—A. No, sir; it has been stated repeatedly that the request from this government to the Danish authorities met with no response, so far as Greenland was concerned. Almost every man, though, got himself a pair of those Esquimaux moccasins or boots.

Q. How high did they come?—A. About half way up to the knee.

Q. The clothing that did not prove good, did it come from New-foundland?—A. No, sir; it came from Greenland. It was provided for the expedition of 1882, and was not used by them.

Q. Then it was clothing bought in 1882 in Greenland which remained last winter in Newfoundland?—A. Yes, sir.

Q. Was the hair taken off?—A. No, sir.

Q. The trousers were not double thickness?—A. No, sir.

Q. Anything for the head in the way of seal-skin?—A. No, sir; they never use seal-skin. We had fur caps.

Q. The jumpers had no hoods?—A. Yes, sir; they had hoods and they pulled them over the cap or whatever they wore under the hoods.

Q. Do you remember what rations were left at Cape Sabine?—A. I estimated the number of rations put by Lieutenant Colwell on that first boat, as five hundred rations; he thinks there were six hundred and fifty rations.

Q. That is simply an estimate?—Yes, sir.

Q. How far was it from the eastern extremity of Cape Sabine?—A. About three miles and a half to the west.

By Captain DAVIS:

Q. Did you see those stores after they were landed?—A. No, sir; I did not. They were landed by Lieutenant Colwell.

By Lieutenant-Commander McCALLA:

Q. You spoke of boilers being placed amidships. I suppose you mean well forward, where the vessel has the greatest beam?—A. Yes, sir. I do not know whether I stated it correctly, technically. I know nothing about naval architecture.

Q Then that is a non-professional opinion merely?—A. It is what I have learned from those sailing people, that when the engines or boilers are put amidships, it is impossible to brace the ship; they cannot get those cross-beams in there.

Q. Who told you this?—A. I talked with the chief engineer of the "Proteus" about it, and with Mr. Norman, the first officer of two of those expeditions, and also with Captain Pike, and with the officers of the "Proteus," going up.

Q. I think you said that the "Proteus" consumed about twelve tons of coal. Might not that have been about seven or eight tons, or as low as that?—A. I do not think so.

Q. Do you remember how you got the information about it?—A. From what Captain Pike told me. I do not state it positively but think that was about it.

Q. In your estimate of the whale-boat's dimensions, I think you said they were twenty-eight feet long?—A. One twenty-eight and a half feet and one thirty.

Q. How many did you have in the ship, furnished for the relief expedition proper?—A. I had two whale-boats and one dingy.

By Captain DAVIS:

Q. Where were the boilers and engines of the "Proteus"?—A. They were amidships.

Q. In the region of the boilers and engine of the "Proteus" was there a cross bracing?—A. There was only one beam or one brace about the engine room, a timber one. The "Proteus" had been caught in the ice at one time and kept in the ice all of one season and subjected to more or less strain, and after they got her out they put some diagonal braces in her, on the sides.

Q. They were not in the ship when built?—A. No, sir.

By Lieutenant-Commander McCALLA:

Q. Have you seen any of these Dundee whalers?—A. No, sir; but I have seen several of the Saint John's sealers that are built on the same plan. The "Thetis" and the "Resolute" are considered by everybody up there as the best ships afloat of that character, because they are new, and in building them they had the experience of years. I talked with several Newfoundland people about it.

Q. These whalers do not go to Saint John's, do they?—A. Not as a general rule, but some of them make a trip sealing before they go whaling. But a great many of these people are Scotchmen; go back and forth, and are acquainted with all these whaling captains.

By Captain DAVIS:

Q. Do you think there would be any difficulty next season in getting dogs for sledging in Greenland?—A. That depends upon whether they have any dog disease there this year or not. I could have gotten them the year I was up.

Q. You did get all the dogs you needed?—A. Yes, sir; but those dogs had been bought the year before, and had been left with the Governor of Disco. I left a request for thirty dogs to be furnished the expedition of this year, and also a request for as many dog-skin sleeping bags as could be got; but that number would be very few, because the dog-skins are very scarce, and, as I stated before, they keep them all for their own use.

By Lieutenant-Commander McCALLA:

Q. Did you leave that request with the Governor?—A. I left it with Governor Elborg at Upernavik to be sent down to the Inspector at Disco, by the mail this winter, as Commander Wildes declined to stop at Disco on the way back.

Q. When was the mail to go down?—A. They make one trip every year from Upernavik to Disco as soon as the season is favorable.

By Captain DAVIS:

Q. That communication is probably at Disco before this time?—A. No, sir; I think they make the trip in February, or about then.

By Lieutenant-Commander McCALLA:

Q. Then the request would not get there before February?—A. Not until spring, probably not until March, and then there is no certainty of his acting on it in the absence of instructions from his home government. They will not do much, if anything, unless they have orders, and whatever supplies are to be gotten from Greenland on this next expedition, duplicate orders should be carried by the vessel which goes up there.

Q. How is that mail taken down in February?—A. By sledges.

Q. Did you hear whether they ever failed to communicate by mail during any winter?—A. I did not; I was informed they made the trip once every winter. Doctor Pavy made the trip the year before he went up with Lieutenant Greely.

By Captain DAVIS:

Q. Of the provisions that you saw in caches, what portion of them could be relied on for use during the coming season?—A. I think everything was intact and in perfect condition in the caches left by Mr. Beebe. Of those I saw, left by the English expedition, I estimated that sixty per cent., at least, were in good condition.

Q. That is at the Cary Islands?—A. Yes, sir; and the probabilities are that seventy-five per cent., at least, would be eatable.

Q. Were there Esquimaux around Cape Ohlsen this season?—A. I saw no recent traces of Esquimaux until we got to Saunders Island; they had evidently been there within a month. There were also Esquimaux on Northumberland Island.

Q. Did not Mr. Beebe leave some supplies at Littleton Island?—A. He did.

Q. Did you examine that cache ?—A. I did not.

Q. I know there was some apprehension expressed by him in his report that the Esquimaux might get at those supplies and appropriate them, and it would be interesting to know whether they were intact ?—A. I do not think they have interfered with them, because he secreted the provisions, and left a record in the coal, describing the locality where they could be found.

By Lieutenant-Commander McCALLA :

Q. At how many points did you land on the west coast of Greenland south of Littleton Island, coming down ?—A. I landed at Pandora Harbor, Sontag Bay, Cape Chalon, Cape Saumarez, Cape Parry, and also near Cape Radcliffe, Cape Athol, and between Cape Athol and Potowik Glacier, and landed two or three times between that point and Cape York.

By Captain DAVIS:

Q. Where did you see your first Esquimaux in coming down ?—A. At Cape York.

Q. Did you mention having seen them at Saunders Island?—A. From the signs, I should judge they had been there about a month before. I saw an Esquimaux dog there.

The most important article of Arctic clothing is the foot-gear. That will all have to be made before leaving the United States. That has caused the most trouble to all expeditions.

Q. Could proper equipment for the feet be obtained around Assinaboine, Pembina, or in Montana ?—A. I think not.

By Captain GREER :

Q. From your reading and experience, of what should you say the foot-gear ought to consist ?—A. I think a soled canvas boot with blanket foot-wraps, blanket inner-soles, and soft pliable straw inside, is the best thing.

By Captain DAVIS:

Q. Have you seen such in use ?—A. I never saw them used. These northern people use something similar to that. The great difficulty about foot-gear is caused by perspiration. All these fur coverings cause the feet to perspire, and as soon as you stop, it is the same as if your feet were wet, then follow frost bites and inflammation of the feet. In this journey we had in the boats, I suffered a good deal with my feet on that account, and Doctor Harrison has not yet recovered from the effects of the same thing. I think that these german socks they use on the frontier and in the extreme northwest, and what they call shoe-packs, would be worth a trial any way. I think a variety of these things should be provided so that by trial you could get the best. You do not want anything to confine the foot or cramp it.

Q. Lieutenant Schwatka in his journey to King William Land, speaks of suffering very greatly from his feet being cut by rocks and stones when he was using moccasins ?—A. That is the reason I think a sole would be better. It is all rock up there on the coast, and there is no soil to walk on. As soon as you leave the ice you get on these sharp stones and it is very hard on the feet, as it is also in walking on hummocky ice, broken ice.

Q. Is the mainland down to the water covered with moss about Cape York, and above?—A. No, sir. Where it is not perpendicular rock it is either shelving sandstone rock, gneiss, or granite, and where there is anything approximating to a beach you only see little patches of moss among the boulders; but there is a good deal near old glaciers where there is much moisture. I think that the ship that goes there next year should be up to the ice by the 30th of May; otherwise I think the Dundee whalers will rescue the party if they come down.

By Lieutenant-Commander McCALLA:

Q. What time do the whalers leave Dundee and Peterhead?—A. I do not remember, but their aim is to get to the ice about the 1st of June.

Q. Do you mean to Melville Bay?—A. Yes, sir.

Q. Melville Bay, or further south?—A. No, up to what they call the northern passage.

By Captain DAVIS:

Q. Don't they first go to the mouth of Cumberland Gulf and cross from there?—A. No, sir; not to my knowledge. They go direct to Melville Bay and cross over. They have to be on the other side by July 1st.

Q. What do you mean by "the other side"?—A. Across Melville Bay in Jones Sound, and unless they do get across they generally abandon it, go down and take a southern passage.

Q. How early in the season have you heard of the whalers reaching Cape York?—A. June 12th is the earliest on record to 1873.

Q. On what date do they generally, or usually, get there?—A. Any time from that until the last of June; if they do not get across by the last of June they abandon it.

Q. Where do you think Lieutenant Greely will be found?—A. I think on the coast of Greenland.

Q. Above Cape York?—A. Yes, sir; unless his party has been weakened and rendered unfit to travel.

Q. Do you think he failed to start last fall?—A. I think so; because in the first place it was impossible for him to come down by sledge in the fall of the year, and if he started in his boats he would have had to start in the latter part of July or very early in August. I do not think he started that early, because he labored under the impression that the station was to be kept up another year, and it was contemplated he would be there about the first of September. In addition to that, I do not think the condition of the ice, from what I saw, was such as to allow him to leave Lady Franklin Bay in boats.

By Lieutenant-Commander McCALLA:

Q. Of course you could not judge of the condition of the ice in Kennedy Channel by what it was at Cape Sabine?—A. You could form some idea. If the ice had not passed out of Smith Sound, the supposition was justifiable that he was up there. Kennedy Channel is comparatively short, but he could not get down unless he had open water.

Q. Do you know how long Kennedy Channel is?—A. About sixty miles, I think.

By General HAZEN:

Q. Taking into consideration the fact that he was under orders to leave, don't you think he would have gotten away last summer?—A. No, sir; I do not think he would, because we know from all the attempts that were made last year to get to the Arctic regions, it was a very bad season.

By Lieutenant-Commander MCCALLA :

Q. Don't you think if he had found open water in Kennedy Channel and had been ordered to come south, he would have taken the steam cutter and come south ?—A. I think he would.

Q. And a northeasterly wind which would block Smith Sound at the entrance, would be likely to clear Kennedy Channel of ice ?—A. It depends upon what body of ice had passed out of Smith Sound at the beginning of the season.

Q. I speak with reference to what you saw when you went up there; you found it blocked ?—A. Yes, sir. If the ice in the lower part of Smith Sound had moved out and they had a north wind, the ice would come down. But if it did not move down, it would not necessarily clear Kennedy Channel.

By Captain DAVIS :

Q. Do you think there is any probability that Lieutenant Greely attempted last spring to send down to find out as to the success or failure of the Beebe expedition ?—A. He did not evidently get down as far as Cape Sabine, if such an effort was made. I think it would have been natural for him to have tried it, however.

Q. Supposing he starts next spring from Lady Franklin Bay, do you think he will have great difficulty in getting to Sabine by means of sledges ?—A. He would have to drag his sledges all the way and it would be a hard trip, of course.

Q. He had some dogs hadn't he ?—A. Very few; I do not think he had over three or four dogs. I gather from Captain Pike and those people who were with him there, that nearly all had died at the time the ship left.

Q. Do you think he would have any difficulty in getting across Smith Sound to Littleton Island ?—A. I think he would have difficulty in getting across with sledges. If he followed the track of Doctor Hayes I think very likely he would get across.

By Lieutenant-Commander MCCALLA :

Q. Of course it would depend entirely on the character of the ice, no matter whose track it was?—A. Of course I know it depends on the character of the ice, but I am speaking now of the probable presence of water between Sabine and Littleton.

By General HAZEN :

Q. Is there not a current setting through the sound?—A. Yes, sir; there is a strong current out of Buchanan Strait, a strong current in Smith Sound and a strong tide current. Doctor Kane's experience, and Hayes', and that of the "Polaris" people show there is always more or less water in the entrance to Smith Sound.

Q. The wind and currents keep it open?—A. Yes, sir; which makes it impossible for a sledge party to cross, and extremely difficult for a boat. But up above, striking over from Cape Inglefield they might find comparatively good travelling.

Lieut. P. H. RAY, U. S. Army, having been requested to appear before the Board, made the following statement in answer to interrogatories :

By Captain DAVIS :

Question. Will you please state to the Board what experience you have had in the Arctic regions, giving the dates of such service, how, and

where employed?—Answer. My experience in the Arctic regions com
menced in 1881 when I left the United States on board the steamer "Gol
den Fleece" for a voyage to Point Barrow. I passed into Behring Strait
in August of that year, reaching my destination on the 8th of September. I there established a station, maintained it, and carried on
the observations required of me by the Chief Signal Officer, from that
time until the 29th of August, 1883, when I broke up the station and
came back to the United States through Akotan Pass and by way of
San Francisco.

Q. You were at Point Barrow how long?—A. Two years, lacking
nine days. During that time I made three different expeditions from
the Point to the interior, with dogs. In 1881 I made a trip of a little
over one hundred miles into the interior for the purpose of procuring fresh meat. In the spring of 1882 I made an expedition
and travelled in all one hundred and fifty miles south, in a direct line.
In the spring of 1883 I also went eastward along the coast forty-five
miles to the mouth of a river I .had discovered. The sledging altogether, for hunting and exploration, footed up between seven hundred
and eight hundred miles, the most of which I did alone or with the
natives; I was the only white man.

Q. In what season of the year were these journeys made?—A. In
March and April.

Q. Did you have an equipment of dogs?—A. I used dogs; there is
no other transportation on that coast.

Q. Have you given the subject of the relief of the Lady Franklin Bay
expedition thought and consideration, and have you any project for the
accomplishment of Lieutenant Greely's relief?—A. I have given it considerable thought, and so far as my experience on the western side
would guide me, I think there is but one course to pursue, and that is
to have at least one strong vessel, probably with a tender, sent out; to
have that vessel strongly built and fitted for the ice, and to start so
that it will come up with the ice the latter part of May or the first of
June and follow it right up. If she should not reach him anywhere about the 1st of September, I should then land a small
party, well equipped, with a house, fuel, and everything prepared
to winter, and allow the ship to come south, with the understanding that the party left on land should push on to the point where
Lieutenant Greely was left, and, if possible, when the sun came back
in the spring so that sledges could be used, have him and his party
brought back down the coast to a point agreed upon before the vessel
left. All those details could be arranged by a person who knows more
about the region than I do. The party left there should have sledges
and dogs and be furnished with skin-boats for crossing water-leads,
and the sledges should be made so that the people could travel the
same as the Esquimaux do along the northern coast of North America
and Siberia. There they make long journeys of two hundred or three
hundred miles in March, April, May and June by having skin-boats,
which they put on their sledges and take along with them, and which
are easily put into the water and hauled out. These boats are of light
weight, say, one hundred pounds, and carry ten or twelve people.

Q. Of what is the frame-work of those boats made?—A. It is made
of spruce and other drift-wood that they pick up on the coast, lashed
together with whalebone lashings. These boats are from thirty to
thirty-four feet long, about seven feet beam, and flat on the bottom.
It takes three or four walrus hides to cover one boat.

By General HAZEN:

Q. Where are such boats to be obtained?—A. The nearest place I know is Saint Michaels.

By Captain DAVIS:

Q. They put to sea in them?—A. Yes, sir; I have seen them fifteen miles out at sea.

Q. They weigh how much?—A. Seventy-five to one hundred pounds, and some one hundred and fifty pounds, including frame-work and everything. I have had two men take them up and walk off with them, and I have seen twenty persons in one of those boats. A ton to a ton and one-half of freight is an ordinary load. The three timbers in the bottom make up the greater part of the weight. When the skin is wet the boat will weigh more. I give the dry weight. Four men at any time can pick up such a boat and walk off with it.

Q. Is it propelled by paddles?—A. Yes, sir; by paddles and sail. They run square before the wind, free, and in travelling alongshore, whenever the beach is open, they put dogs on a line and tow them like a canal boat, and make ten or fifteen miles a day in that way. That type of boat would be an excellent one to have along in addition to the ordinary whale-boats. In crossing the ice I know of no boat equal to them, and a number of whale-ships are adopting them; I saw several this year.

Q. Do they use them as whale-boats?—A. No; but they keep them in case of necessity and use them for light work paddling around. They are much handier than a dingy.

Q. Have you seen anything of the whalers of the Pacific—steam-whalers?—A. I have been on board of every steam-whaler in the Pacific, and on twenty-seven other whale-ships. I think I have been on all American whale-ships except three.

Q. How many of these steamers are there?—A. Four from San Francisco and three from New Bedford.

Q. Where were those vessels built?—A. Four in San Francisco, and the other three in New Bedford, I think.

Q. What is the size of the most improved type of the steam-whalers in the Pacific?—A. I cannot give displacement. The best type of the improved vessel is one called the "Narwhal." Her registered tonnage, new measurement, taking out engines, boilers, and cabin room, was $389\frac{67}{100}$ tons; registered horse power, 245, and draught, twelve feet; consumption of coal for twenty-four hours about four and a half tons.

Q. You are confident about the consumption of the coal?—A. Yes, sir; that was told me, and I took it down.

Q. What would probably be the displacement of that vessel?—A. I do not know. It is generally from thirty to forty per cent., in excess of the registered tonnage.

Q. What was the length and beam of that vessel?—A. I do not remember, and I could not get that information here.

Q. What speed could she maintain in a smooth sea?—A. I was on board the "Bowhead," a vessel of 395 tons, 280 indicated horse power, and drawing eighteen feet, when she was making eight knots in still water. But I have seen her make thirteen and a half knots under sail and steam.

Q. Has the "Narwhal" as great speed as the "Bowhead"?—A. Yes, sir. I have never seen that decided in any test, but the captain told me he could make better speed than the "Bowhead." The latter was built in 1882, and the other in 1883. The "Bowhead" was an experiment, and after trying her they built the other three.

Q. What was the rig of the "Narwhal"?—A. She was bark-rigged, full. The "Bowhead" is light rigged; her spars were lighter, but the others were all full-rigged barks.

Q. Where and how was the machinery of the "Narwhal" located? —A. Her boilers and everything were abaft the main-mast. Her smoke-stack was, I judged, fifteen or twenty feet forward of the mizzen-mast. Her shaft was not over forty feet long from the coupling, back to the screw. The engines were way aft.

Q. Where were the cabin of the officers and the quarters of the crew? —A. On deck above. The floor of the cabin is flush with the spardeck. They are deck cabins.

Q. And the waist of the ship was occupied by the coal, oil, and casks?—A. There are no casks on these ships. The lower hold is built in sections, of half-inch iron tanks, built to fit the ship exactly, and in between decks is the blubber room, in the waist of the ship.

Q. You have never seen any of the Dundee whalers?—A. I know nothing of them except from hearsay. These vessels for about eight or nine feet forward from the stem are solid timber. They are very heavy and strong. Their side timbers are only about four inches apart, are sawed out to fit accurately, and the outer sheathing is of oak. From two feet above the water-line down to the keel they are sheathed with six inches of white oak, and back from the cut-water forty feet and down to the keel they are sheathed with boiler-iron; the stem is very raking so that in running her into the ice, they do not hesitate where they wish to break through, to run right on, riding right up on the pack, and if that does not give way beneath, they slip back into the water.

Q. The sledging you did in Alaska was on land?—A. Yes, sir; principally. I did a little on one stretch along the sea where I travelled about twenty miles on foot. The tide is practically nothing up there, so that there is no ice-foot, and it is very fair travelling on the ice along the shore.

Q. What kind of Arctic clothing were you supplied with for your stay in Alaska?—A. the clothing I wore entirely during the winter was made of deer-skins by the natives and procured there. I bought the skins from them. Part of the men's clothing was made of skins purchased in Siberia by Captain Hooper and turned over to me in Plover Bay. Reindeer is the only clothing an Indian will use. You cannot get him to use seal-skin. There is no warmth to it; it is very cold and they will not use it even for boots.

Q. Is there any trader in San Francisco who would have this clothing on hand?—A. Not unless the Alaska Commercial Company have some. They make it an item of trade with the Indians at the mouth of the Yukon, and they may possibly have some skins on hand. When I was there in 1881 they had some skins I would rather have than deer-skins, these pup fur-seal.

Q. Are they expensive?—A. No, sir; they are valueless in the market. The natives on the island were allowed to kill 10,000 of them a year for food; these skins fall into the hands of the company and they use them for clothing and other purposes; they had a number when I went up there. They would make fine *artegas*. The ordinary dog-skin will make the best *artega* that I know of—that is the native name for jumper.

4

By General HAZEN :

Q. Do you think the native dog-skins here would be suitable ?—A. Yes, sir. Skins of dogs like the setter and the finer kinds of Newfoundland dog would make fine jumpers. The trouble with all that clothing which is made in that country is, that the Esquimaux do not know anything about tanning, except the Chukches. The Esquimaux simply dry and scrape the skin and it becomes offensive in a short time especially when wet.

By Captain DAVIS :

Q. What kind of foot-gear did you use?—A. The native foot-gear. The leg of the winter boot, up to the knee, is made from the skin taken from the leg of a reindeer that has short smooth hair, the snow will not adhere to it at all—the sole is of seal-skin, crimped to fit the upper.

By Lieutenant-Commander McCALLA :

Q. Are they water-proof?—A. No, sir; not water-proof. But that is not necessary until the snow begins to soften. These seal-skin boots that the whaling people use are not winter boots, and cannot be worn in winter; they are too cold. I tried to wear them, and found from experience they needed a fur cover for the upper part of the foot, and under the foot we always wore the scrapings of whalebone; we made a pad of that and put it underneath the foot. It absorbs the moisture from the foot, and is the finest foot-gear I ever saw.

By Captain DAVIS :

Q. What socks did you use?—A. There I found the natives wearing deer-skin, but from San Francisco I had some fine sheepskins, the wool cut off pretty close, and I had the natives make socks of them, and they preferred them.

By General HAZEN :

Q. It was sheepskin with the wool inside?—A. Yes, sir. I could give you the pattern. They need to fit the foot nice and snug. The moment you make them loose, you ruin the gear. I wore them, with my whole party, and we found them excellent.

Q. You had no frost bites?—A. No trouble at all. The longest trip I made on foot was forty-eight miles in thirteen hours with that kind of gear, and my feet were in as good condition when I came home as when I started out.

Q. What temperature have you had when travelling ?—A. Ranging between —30° and —45°. I had no tents; never used them. I slept in snow. I made an *igloo* every night. And any party going out there should be furnished with a long broad knife, made strong, with a handle that a man could take hold of with two hands, the same as the Esquimaux use.

Q. A kind of spatula?—A. Yes, sir; and with snow shovel and a knife—that would make up the gear.

Q. How many dogs to a team do they use?—A. That depends on circumstances. You rarely ever see more than four, but I used eight to carry my provisions for twenty days.

By Captain DAVIS :

Q. What do you know about the time taken to build those whalers in San Francisco ?—A. It is all derived from hearsay and information from those people. The "Bowhead" took between sixty and seventy days from the day the work was commenced on her until she was launched.

The "Belinda" and "Narwhal" were built under contract in sixty days and were launched on time. The "Orca" I do not know so much about. She is four hundred and sixty tons, new measure. There had not been a blow struck on the three ships on the first of November, 1882, waiting for the "Bowhead" to return with her catch and report. She was successful, and in December a contract was made; these vessels were at sea in March to my knowledge, for I saw them all in the Arctic Ocean in August.

By General HAZEN:

Q. How long would it take one of those ships to go around to New York?—A. I could not say.

By Captain DAVIS:

Q. Where are those ships now, probably?—A. I was informed that the "Bowhead" would lay up to receive tanks this winter. The others are probably in the South Seas off the coast of Australia. Before these vessels were constructed, these people sent experts to Dundee, New Bedford, and other ports; they came back and reported, and these ships were built with all the improvements they could gather.

Q. What do the sailors generally think of the vessels?—A. There seems to be but one opinion, and that is they are the best they ever saw. They are men of thirty years' experience, New Bedford captains, and the best of them are leaving the New Bedford fleet and sailing in these San Francisco vessels, with a smaller "lay" than on the other ships.

By General HAZEN:

Q. What kind of a ship was the "North Star" that was crushed? —A. She was a New Bedford ship, sister ship to the "Rodgers."

By Captain DAVIS:

Q. You were aboard the "Rodgers"?—A. Yes, sir.

Q. What decided differences were there in her construction from that of the modern whaler?—A. They are the same, bark-rigged. The San Francisco steamers were heavier than the "Rodgers." They had an additional sheathing of iron and oak which the "Rodgers" had not, and the experts say that in every way they are stronger vessels. I know this year a vessel of the same construction as the "Rodgers," the "Belvidere," was up there and would not go into the ice where the San Francisco ships went and passed right along without any difficulty. The "Belvidere" remained out.

Q. What was her steam power as compared to the others?—A. It is lighter. I do not know what it is exactly.

For foot-gear I have often thought if I was going again, instead of using the skin of the leg of the reindeer, which is very delicate and tender and will not hold thread well, that young calf-skins tanned with the hair on, in our fashion, would be better than anything else. They should be worn with the hair out.

Q. You would have it of double thickness also?—A. No, sir; they never wear them of double thickness.

By General HAZEN:

Q. Is the german stocking used there?—A. No, sir; I only saw the native clothing.

By Captain DAVIS:

Q. When the whalers have to winter in the ice are their crews afflicted with scurvy?—A. No American whaling ship has wintered on the North American coast, so that that has not been decided. The furthest north a ship has ever wintered was in Saint Lawrence Bay, south of Behring Strait.

By General HAZEN:

Q. What was the diet of your party, and what was its health during the two years you were there?—A. I took from the United States a full supply of bacon, canned corned beef, sugar, flour, coffee, and the necessary groceries for an ordinary diet, with dried apples, cranberries, a few peaches, and syrup, and there was sent me from the east about forty gallons of lime-juice. We had fresh meat at least three times a week, after the first four months, of either seal, walrus, bear, or rein-deer.

Q. What was the size of your party?—A. The first party, from 1881 to 1882, consisted of nine men besides myself; the second year there were eleven besides myself.

Q. What was the health of the party?—A. I never had a man on the sick report from the time I landed until I sailed.

Q. What was the latitude?—A. 71° 16' north.

Q. What was the average temperature in winter?—A. The annual mean was plus seven; the mean for the winter months I could not give accurately from memory, but I should say minus twenty. We had as low as minus fifty-eight by the corrected thermometer.

Q. Did you use lime-juice at all?—A. I issued it, but more as a lux-ury than anything else, because we never had any indication of scurvy, or any disease in fact. Besides the regular duty which the men per-formed, which was six hours out of the twenty-four, I required them to be one hour in the open air, which was compulsory during the whole time I was there, unless it was blowing so hard that a man could not stand up. We were seventy-two days without sunlight.

Q. How dark does it get?—A. At Christmas noon it was so dark that stars of the third and fourth magnitude were visible.

By Captain DAVIS:

Q. Your fuel was coal?—A. Yes, sir.

Q. What quantity per diem did you find it necessary to use to main-tain a fair degree of comfort in your shelter?—A. Two hundred and fifty pounds for two fires.

Q. What temperature did you aim to keep up in your living rooms?—A. Seventy degrees. Ice never formed in my sleeping-room or living-room, during the whole time I was there, that is, in the pitcher.

Q. Was it a board building?—A. A redwood building, sealed up; the studding was two by four, and the space at the bottom between the outside and the sheathing was tamped up with clay to make it air-tight so that there would not be any circulation of air in this space. The floor was ordinary inch and a quarter pine and was close to the ground, as close as I could lay it and get a level. The earth there is perpetually frozen. I used stoves for heating and cooking. I banked up the building with earth for about eighteen inches, and as soon as the snow was hard enough to cut I got a wall of snow built up around the house to the eaves, connected the building, by snow channels, with the astronomical observatories, and the snow drifted over until it was flush with the roof.

Q. What illuminating material did you use?—A. Kerosene oil, 150 fire test.

Q. Did you use alcohol in your sledging journeys?—A. No, sir; I think kerosene is preferable. I did not use a gallon on either one of my trips, and the last time I was out eleven or twelve days.

Q. Kerosene does not stiffen like lard oil, in those temperatures?—A. No, sir; it was always liquid.

By General HAZEN:

Q. Did you use pemmican at all?—A. I used it in my journeys.

Q. Where was it procured?—A. It was procured by the Chief Signal Officer at New York and shipped to me. It was excellent, and the best food for travelling I ever saw.

By Captain DAVIS:

Q. Did the men like it?—A. Yes, sir; it made excellent soup, and could be used cold. Eight ounces is a good day's ration. I could not eat over that while I was hard at work.

Q. Is there enough warmth in the summer to grow cresses or lettuce? —A. The first summer I raised a few radishes and some lettuce, but the second summer there was a frost every day, the ice hung on the shore and we could not raise anything. In 1882 many flowers appeared, but I did not see so many in 1883.

By General HAZEN:

Q. How deep does the soil thaw in the summer?—A. From eight inches to a foot. Black spots, where exposed to the sun, would thaw down to eighteen inches.

By Captain DAVIS:

Q. Did you have any experience in sledging over ice hummocks?—A. No. I went with the natives out to a crack five or six miles only, and through an old ice pack.

Q. Do the natives make long journeys across the ice?—A. No, sir; that is absolutely impossible. It took forty men thirty days to work a sled and boat out to a lead about a mile and a half away so that they could get through with their provisions, boat, and outfit. They were working day after day right along and putting in all their spare time.

I would like to make this suggestion, that any one going up there, should engage some of the *voyageurs*, who can be found around the Red River of the North. These men are expert with dog teams, thoroughly accustomed to cold, and, travelling in all seasons of the year, very hardy, and patient under hardship; I have had them under me and know what they are.

By General HAZEN:

Q. Do you know anything of the facilities for getting dogs with those men in that section?—A. There used to be some of the finest bred dogs at Pembina and Fort Garry before the railroad was built. At that time everything was carried by dogs, the mails and all.

By Captain DAVIS:

Q. Is there a reasonable probability that those dogs would stand the life above the Arctic Circle, and on the food that they would have?—A. Yes, sir; I took with me a dog from the United States, a setter, and brought him back; he was never sick a day; he travelled through the interior with the team and lived on their food. I could not see but what he stood it just as well as the Esquimaux dog. I think you could get some dogs at Mackinaw if you needed them; I have seen them there.

In regard to those whalemen, they had a boat I never saw used anywhere else, that is a steam whale-boat. It is about thirty-two feet long and has a " Herreshoff " engine and screw in the centre, working on a universal joint. It is made on the exact pattern of the ordinary whale-boat they use up there, and can be worked under steam or sail. In regard to sledging, every sledge should be rigged with a light lug-sail. That answers two purposes. When the snow begins to soften in the spring you can build up side walls of it and cover over with the sail; when the wind is on or abaft the beam of the sledge, it counts for a good many dogs.

Q. Did you see one of those " Herreshoff " launches ?—A. Yes, sir; I have been in one of them.

Q. How was the screw, amidships ?—A. Yes, sir; to lower or raise the same as you do the centre-board of a boat. When you haul it up you have a sailing vessel. You can run them up in the shallow water. With the screw they draw about four and a half feet.

Q. What fuel did they use ?—A. Coal.

Q. Do you know how much coal the boat you saw could carry, or for how many days steaming ?—A. They loaned me one, and I was steaming three days with what coal was on board, and we had considerable left, then.

Q. Did you make four or five knots ?—A. Part of the time we made seven knots with steam alone for a long distance. It is the fastest steam whale-boat that is made.

Q. It would take a large crew to pull one of these boats out of the water, would it not ?—A. That would depend upon your tackle.

Q. How long do you say these boats are ?—A. The ordinary whale-boat they use in the fleet is thirty feet, but these were two feet longer than the ordinary whale-boat.

Upon the conclusion of Lieutenant Ray's testimony, General Hazen stated that in regard to the matter of dogs for the proposed relief expedition he desired to submit a letter received from Lieut. Thomas J. Clay, 10th U. S. Infantry, which was read. (Exhibit C.)

A letter from Lieut. Frederick Schwatka, 3d U. S. Cavalry, giving his ideas as to the organization and conduct of an expedition to be sent for the relief of Lieutenant Greely and party was then read. (Exhibit D.)

The Board, then adjourned to meet to-morrow morning at 11 o'clock.

ROOM 88, NAVY DEPARTMENT BUILDING,
Washington, D. C., January 3, 1884.

The Board met pursuant to adjournment; all the members present except General Hazen.

Capt. RICHARD PIKE, of Saint John's, Newfoundland, appeared, in response to the invitation of the Board, and was interrogated as follows:

By Captain DAVIS:

Question. The Board would thank you to give a brief statement of the experience you have had in the Arctic regions, the dates of such service, how, and where, employed.—Answer. The first experience I had in the Arctic regions was in 1881, when I took Lieutenant Greely and party to Lady Franklin Bay. I left Saint John's on the 7th of July, and went from there to Godhavn, that is Disco Island. We arrived there on the 16th, and from there we went to Upernavik to get some dogs, and then proceeded on north. We proceeded up as far as Cape Lieber, and I think it was on the 10th of August that we met the ice there. We did not meet any obstruction at all in going up Smith Sound.

Q. You got to Lady Franklin Bay when?—A. We got to Cape Lieber on the 10th of August on our way up, and there we met a block right across; it was one solid block in Robeson Channel. When the break up came we were driven back to Franklin Island, and then we got a gale of wind from the western shore and sailed up the harbor. I think we arrived in Discovery Harbor about the 20th of August, and left it again on the 26th, and returned to Newfoundland without any difficulty.

Q. Preceding this, what Arctic experience had you had?—A. Nothing in the Arctic Seas, but I have had years of sealing on the coast of Newfoundland and Labrador, and last summer I went up again in the "Proteus."

Q. Have you given the subject of this relief expedition thought and consideration, and have you any project for the accomplishment of Lieutenant Greely's relief?—A. Well, I would advise two ships, for the reason that then you can run more risk with one ship if you have something to fall back upon, in case there should be an accident. I believe it was possible this year for a sledge to go right on to Lady Franklin Bay on the ice.

Q. You think Smith Sound was closed all the way up to Robeson Channel?—A. Yes; I think so.

Q. You think there was no chance of getting a vessel up?—A. Late in the season there might have been. I believe later in the season a vessel could have gone a good way up there.

Q. What kind of vessels should these two ships be that you propose to use?—A. Steam whalers.

Q. What time would you expect to reach Littleton Island?—A. About the latter part of July is time enough. That would give some of the ice a chance to be coming down out of the sound.

Q. You would work those two ships all the way up, conjointly?—A. Yes, sir; only be sure and keep one behind the other in safety.

Q. Have you made much use of pemmican?—A. No, sir; I never used any.

Q. Have you ever had scurvy in your ships' crews?—A. No, sir; I have never wintered north.

Q. In regard to Arctic clothing, what kind do you recommend?—A. Seal-skin for outside clothing is the best.

Q. Is there any difficulty about its getting wet?—A. It will get wet, but of course the sun will dry it again.

Q. Please describe the garments?—A. A double jumper, with the hair inside and outside, with a hood to pull over the head and with a little cap inside of it. In regard to the feet, seal-skin boots are the best, with soles of seal-skin, coming up to about the knee.

Q. Have you worn those in severe weather?—A. Yes, sir; we always use them in the seal fishery, but we have ours soled with leather, which is not as good for Arctic travel as seal-skin.

Q. Where do you get that clothing, in Saint John's?—A. No, sir; but then there is some brought over from Hudson Bay.

Q. Have you seen reindeer-skin clothing used?—A. I have seen very little of it.

Q. In your sealing expeditions, do you have to sleep on the ice at times?—A. No, sir; very seldom. There may be a few men get away from the ship who will be gone all night, but it is only when they cannot possibly find the ship.

Q. In the equipment of vessels you would propose to send up there, what kind and number of boats would you use?—A. A whale-boat is the best, perhaps twenty-eight feet long.

Q. How many men would it require to pull out one of those boats in a hurry?—A. You could not do it with less than six men, depending, of course, how high the ice is out of the water.

Q. How high out of water was the ice that you saw in Smith Sound last summer?—A. Some two and some three feet.

Q. Could you get out a boat on that with six men?—A. O, yes, sir. The stem of the boat must be very rounding. We had to haul our boats up some few times, on the route coming south.

Q. Have you done any sledging?—A. No, sir.

Q. So that you know nothing about dogs and sledges, of your own knowledge?—A. No, sir.

Q. Have you ever used a steam-launch in any of your sealing expeditions?—A. No, sir.

Q. You are aware that sledging expeditions in the autumn are difficult, but you have no doubt there was a good chance of their getting up there last fall by sleds?—A. I think so.

Q. Did you expect to take a boat along with the sledges, if you had gone up this fall?—A. I would have had nothing to do with the sledging part of it. I think the sledges Lieutenant Garlington had are very suitable.

Q. When you went up in the "Proteus" in 1881, was there an ice-foot all along the land in Smith Sound?—A. Yes, sir.

Q. Was the land covered with snow, or bare?—A. Not much snow at all after we got up north; not as much snow after we passed Littleton Island as south of it. There was very little snow on the tops of the mountains.

Q. What boats did you leave with Lieutenant Greely at Lady Franklin Bay, or what boats did he have with him when you left him?—A. He had a steam-launch, a whale-boat, a boat that was left by Sir George Nares, and a dingy; he had three boats beside a launch.

Q. Do you think a launch would be of great utility in a retreat?—A. I do not think it would be of much use. They had no means to get the steam-launch on land in winter, and that would be the great trouble. If she was left in the water there is no doubt the ice would tear her all to pieces. Of course he would try to erect temporary ways to get her out, but he had not when I left.

Q. Was there much ice in Discovery Harbor when you left?—A. Yes, sir; it was full; the winter ice was in there and had hardly come out at all. The new ice was beginning to make pretty thick through there on the 26th of August.

Q. When you got into Discovery Harbor was there any ice in Robeson Channel then?—A. Yes, sir; but when we came out, we had to cross over, to take the water on the east side, and it was all blocked with ice on the west as far as I could see, from Cairn Hill, with the telescope. On the eastern side was water, and the western side was full. The wind was northeast then. My experience is that the water keeps open on the east side more than on the west.

Q. You didn't cross over to Thank God Harbor, Polaris Bay, to examine the provisions there?—A. We could have landed there easy enough, but we didn't try to.

By Lieutenant-Commander McCALLA:

Q. Please draw a line of the general track of the "Proteus," up and down, in 1881.

(The witness made a dotted line on the map, as requested.)

Q. Did you have any conversation with Lieutenant Greely in 1881 with reference to his possible retreat?—A. No, sir.

Q. You have stated that you thought a sledge might have gone from the vicinity of Cape Sabine last summer to the vicinity of Lady Franklin Sound; of course, you could not judge of the condition of the ice, except for a short distance?—A. No, sir; but I could see, I dare say, twenty or thirty miles away with a powerful telescope that we had. Of course, you would not be able to see the condition of the ice there.

By Captain GREER:

Q. What was the daily consumption of coal on the "Proteus"?—A. About twelve or thirteen tons.

Q. What would she make in ordinary weather with that consumption?—A. About eight or eight and one-half knots.

Q. How much coal did she carry?—A. We have had eight hundred tons in her, as a cargo, including bunkers and all; we had about four hundred tons on that summer. The bunkers would hold one hundred and ten tons.

By Captain DAVIS:

Q. Was the consumption of coal on the "Proteus" about the same as on the Dundee whalers?—A. Yes, sir; on some of them.

Q. Have you ever seen any of the more recent vessels built in Dundee for the whaling trade?—A. There is one that was built two years ago for the whaling trade, the "Resolute." She is the newest one; there are two of them, the "Resolute" and the "Thetis."

Q. Do they differ in construction from the "Proteus"?—A. No, sir; only their engines are aft, and those on the "Proteus" were amidships.

Q. Do you regard that as a better construction for a vessel in the ice?—A. Well, I approve of it.

Q. Are they full-powered vessels or auxiliary power?—A. Auxiliary power, about the same as the "Proteus." They steam about nine knots.

By Captain GREER:

Q. Bark-rigged or barkentine?—A. All the Dundee boats are bark-rigged.

Q. Are the Saint John's sealers barkentines?—A. No, sir; only two. The "Proteus" and the "Bear" were barkentines; all the rest are barks.

By Captain DAVIS:

Q. What time do these Saint John's vessels engage their crews for the sealing trade?—A. All the time during the winter, but generally about Christmas time.

Q. This list of vessels which you have given General Hazen comprises all those with which you are familiar?—A. Yes, sir; I know those very well. The "Vanguard" and the "Iceland" are nice vessels, and the "Greenland" is a nice vessel, but hard on her propellers.

Q. Those vessels are eight to twelve years old, I see ?—A. Yes, sir.

Q. There are no sealers in the Saint John's trade that have been built within three or four years ?—A. No, sir.

Q. About what is the length and beam of the "Vanguard" and "Iceland"?—A. The "Vanguard" has about thirty feet beam and is perhaps one hundred and seventy feet long. The "Iceland" would not have as much beam. One is a Dundee-built ship and the other was built in Aberdeen.

Q. They are very much smaller vessels than the "Proteus"?—A. Yes, sir.

Q. What is their consumption of coal ?—A. About ten tons, I think. The "Vanguard" would burn fully as much as the "Proteus," but she has more power; I think she has one hundred and twenty horse power.

Q. Are these vessels all in Saint John's now ?—A. Three are at Harbor Grace, Newfoundland.

Q. Are they owned there ?—A. Yes, sir. The "Bear" is a fine ship; she had a new steel boiler last year. She is exactly the same size as the "Proteus."

Q. Has she a lifting screw?—A. Yes, sir; they all have lifting screws except the "Falcon."

Q. What time do these vessels generally start out on their first sealing trip ?—A. On the 10th of March.

By Captain GREER:

Q. Can an abundance of ice tools be obtained at Saint John's?—A. Yes, sir.

By Lieutenant-Commander McCALLA:

Q. Do you know what the nominal horse power of the "Thetis" and "Resolute" is?—A. I think about one hundred and ten or one hundred and fifteen horse power.

By Captain DAVIS:

Q. Do you remember the size of the "Thetis" and "Resolute"?—A. I think they are about four hundred tons, or perhaps a little more.

Q. What was the registered tonnage of the "Proteus"?—A. Four hundred and sixty-seven tons.

Q. The "Bear" is just like the "Proteus" except that she has new boilers ?—A. Yes, sir; exactly the same, built side by side, the same year. She is one ton larger than the "Proteus" I believe.

After a short recess, the taking of testimony was resumed.

Mr J. W. NORMAN, of Saint John's, Newfoundland, having been invited to appear before the Board, was examined as follows:

By Captain DAVIS:

Question. Please state what Arctic experience you have had.— Answer. I was mate of the "Proteus" with Captain Pike when we carried Lieutenant Greely up there in 1881, and I was mate of the "Neptune" and ice-master of her when we went up with Mr. Beebe in 1882.

Q. What other service in northern waters have you seen ?—A. I have been all my lifetime, sealing, with the exception of four years, and have been down at North Labrador in the summer amongst the ice chiefly, every year; I have never been up around by Davis Strait but twice.

Q. Have you ever been in the whaling trade ?—A. Never.

Q. Have you been in Smith Sound ?—A. I was through it once, and in it another time as high as 79° 20'.

Q. What are the chances of a vessel being able to get above Cape Sabine in any season ?—A. I think she is safe to get above Cape Sabine in any season, from what I have seen. The season of 1881 was a very open one, but the season of 1882 was a close one.

Q. But not certain to make a port or harbor for wintering on that side; not able to go to Cape Hawks ?—A. No, sir; not to Cape Hawks; it was impossible in 1882, at any rate.

Q. What time did you arrive at, and what time did you leave, Smith Sound in 1882 ?—A. We arrived there on the 28th or 29th of July, and met the ice, and left on the 5th of September.

Q. Could you see open water beyond the ice during any part of the time you were waiting ?—A. Not north, not up towards Cape Hawks, but I think there is always water by the land as you pass Princess Marie Bay. I noticed there was water nearly all the time across that bay, and across in Buchanan Strait where the " Proteus " was crushed, and that water ebbs and flows with the tide.

Q. When you were there in the " Neptune " in 1882, do you think that boats could have made their way north ?—A. No, sir; not keel boats, unless you could take them in pieces and pack them on sledges. Not whale-boats or ice boats, or anything like that. On the 10th of August—we had no sledges—it was suggested trying a boat, as we were within eleven miles of Cape Hawks, and it was quite practicable for us then to get to Lady Franklin Bay, if a party of men could have gone, not with a boat, but with sledges, and gone up on the ice-foot. From what I noticed of the ice-foot in Smith Sound, it is the easiest way of travelling, and with one of these portable boats, you could pack it on your sledges, and take it across these fissures that the land slides make.

Q. Have you ever seen such boats as you describe, capable of being taken on sledges and packed ?—A. I have seen a boat that we have for carrying in the country for fishing purposes.

Q. Have you had experience in sledging ?—A. Not in the winter; I have in the summer when I have been down on North Labrador with the Esquimaux dogs.

Q. In your trip on the " Proteus " to Lady Franklin Bay, did you hug the west shore and the head-lands ?—A. Not until we turned Cape Louis Napoleon.

Q. Have you wintered in the Arctic regions ?—A. No, sir; never..

Q. Then you have not been obliged to have an outfit such as Arctic explorers require, in the way of clothing?—A. No, sir; but I have been with the people of North Labrador and know their habits in the winter, for I was trading with them for twelve years.

Q. What kind of boats do you find best adapted for working in the water among the ice ?—A. Our common sealing boats are the ones we are used to. If you get them crushed they are easily repaired.

Q. How are they, compared with the ordinary whale-boat ?—A. They are lighter than the whale-boat and rougher. The Dundee whalers that go whaling in the summer put ashore their whale-boats and take these sealing punts in preference, for sealing on the ice. They are more easily hauled up on the ice, and if they are stove they are more easily repaired.

Q. How long are they?—A. About twenty-five feet.

Q. What crew does it require to manage one?—A. Four men. That crew can pull those boats on the floe easily, and haul them over and put them in the water.

Q. And they stand that jumping on the rough ice without material injury?—A. Yes, sir.

Q. Are they made in Saint John's?—A. They are built in Newfoundland.

By Captain GREER:

Q. These sealing punts are not good sea boats, are they?—A. I think they are. I have seen them in pretty rough water. They are not as large as the whale-boats.

By Captain DAVIS:

Q. In case of emergency, how many persons, with fifteen days' supplies, could those boats transport through Smith Sound for example, taking the chances of the weather?—A. We will say ten men; that would be the outside of it in smooth water. I have known an instance of a ship's crew coming in over two hundred miles on these sealing boats; and frequently when they are one hundred miles away from land they have brought them in safe; and that in the month of March or April, the stormy season.

Q. A boat of that size would probably weigh a thousand pounds?—A. No, sir; I should say she would not be as heavy as that.

Q. Upon what do you base your opinion that a party would have been able to get up to Discovery Harbor in 1882 with sledges?—A. From the fact that the year previous I had been there and I had taken particular notice of the ice-foot. We landed several times on Cape Leiber, and I tried to find Doctor Hayes' record, supposed to be left there, and two or three times a day I would go ashore to look out and see if there was any opening in the ice, and from Cape Lieber I often used to look at this ice-foot all the way up. When we landed at Cape Hawks it was the same thing. Last year we could see the ice-foot along shore when this water used to come in across the bay. It was different, I noticed, to the floating ice I had seen in 1882; that was very hummocky; but still it was possible with light sledges to go along the shore. I think it would be the hardest job to get ashore, but if we once got ashore, getting to Lady Franklin Bay would be comparatively easy on the ice-foot.

Q. Do you think the ice-foot would have been continuous?—A. I think it is continuous except where the land-slides are, and that would break the way for a half mile, or a mile, sometimes, and we would have to take to the water.

Q. You would require a boat?—A. Yes, sir; some light, portable boat to cross these fissures or cracks, whether made by the cracking of the ice, or land-slides, or whatever it was.

Q. At how many points did you land on the west shore of Smith Sound and Kennedy Channel, going up in 1881?—A. At Carl Ritter Bay, several times at Cape Lieber, and between that and Cape Baird, which is the south point of Lady Franklin Bay.

Q. Did you visit the depot of provisions that Sir George Nares left near Cape Hawks?—A. Yes, sir; and took a boat from it, a keg of rum, and a few other things.

Q. Did you examine the remainder of the supplies?—A. Yes, sir; there were some frozen down in the ice, and we cut the ice and hauled them further up on a place clear of ice, on a rock, and secured them better. Lieutenant Greely was there; we did it under his orders.

Q. Were they apparently in good condition?—A. Yes, sir; the bread was a little old, but everything else was in excellent condition.

Q. At what would you estimate the quantity?—A. There were, I think, about nine puncheons, I cannot say positively, but I have a memorandum of what was there and how they were marked; they were about one hundred and twenty or one hundred and thirty gallon casks.

Q. Was the cooperage in fair condition?—A. Yes, sir; the rum was about one-third out, and we left another keg about half full.

Q. Is that shelter behind Washington Irving Island a good one in winter?—A. No, sir; but in Dobbin Bay I think you could get in there.

Q. There is a bold coast all the way up?—A. Yes, sir.

Q. Was the whole body of Smith Sound open when you went up in 1881?—A. Yes, sir; all open, just loose floes. We got within eight miles of our destination and there it was blocked solid across.

Q. Was there any water in sight above Lady Franklin Sound?—A. No, sir; we could not get to Water-Course Bay. We got in shore, and we were from the 19th to the 26th of August before we could get out again. There was water all the time over in Hall Basin. The ice would drift down to Cape Morton and back again. You could see up past the mouth of Newman Bay, and I don't know but what you could see up past the mouth of Saint Patrick Bay.

By Lieutenant-Commander McCALLA:

Q. How was that bread packed at Cape Hawks?—A. In oak casks. It tasted old, but was quite eatable. Any man who was hungry could eat it.

By Captain DAVIS:

Q. Did you see any game on the west shore of Smith Sound?—A. Very little. We saw some musk oxen and one flock of ducks, and shot some seals there. When you enter Kennedy Channel you go beyond all life, but below that there are plenty of seals and game on the east side.

Q. You saw no reindeer around Cape Hawks or Cape Louis Napoleon?—A. No, sir; none. At Cape Hawks we saw the print of the teeth of bears on the casks, but they had not opened any of them.

Q. How large is that steam-launch that Lieutenant Greely has?—A. It is about thirty-five feet long, I expect.

Q. What sledges did he have?—A. He had four, if not more. We carried up forty-two dogs from Greenland and they had increased some, but when we left he had but eleven. The dogs had epileptic fits and we threw over as many as five in one day before we got there.

Q. You have never seen any scurvy in your service?—A. No sir; only what I have seen at sea. We had one case of scurvy in a year that we went down there, but it was not new on that voyage; the man had had it for years. I have seen scurvy in North Labrador among the people there.

Q. Have you made use of lime-juice in trying to prevent scurvy?—A. Yes, always at sea.

Q. You have confidence in its effectiveness?—A. I believe it is a preventive against scurvy.

Q. Did you see any walrus in Smith Sound?—A. Yes, sir.

Q. Any in Kennedy Channel?—A. No, sir.

The Board then adjourned to meet to-morrow at 11 a. m.

ROOM 88, NAVY DEPARTMENT BUILDING,
Washington, D. C., January 4, 1884.

The Board met pursuant to adjournment; all the members present.

Captain Greer stated that he was informed Surgeon-General Wales, of the Navy, had made a special study of questions affecting the health and sanitation of men employed in Arctic service.

The President of the Board was directed to request Surgeon-General Wales to embody in a paper, and submit for the information of the Board, the result of his observations on the subject mentioned.

A letter from Cyrus Smith, dated December 28, 1883, was submitted by General Hazen and read. (Abs., Mis. Cor., No. 27.)

Dr. EMILE BESSELS, of Washington, D. C., appeared, in response to the invitation of the Board, and was questioned as follows:

By Captain DAVIS:

Question. Will you please give the Board a brief sketch of your experience in the Arctic regions?—Answer. My experience in Smith Sound extends over about two years while I was Chief of the Scientific Department on board the U.'S. Steamer "Polaris."

Q. Previous to that, had you seen any Arctic service?—A. Previous to that I spent a whole season between Spitzbergen and Nova Zembla, along the west coast of Spitzbergen, and the ice pack that extends from the coast of east Greenland to the eastward.

Q. Did you see something of Arctic navigation in Lancaster Sound and Barrow Strait?—A. Yes, sir; after the "Polaris" was lost I was taken on board the "Ravenscrag" and transferred to the "Arctic," and we steamed up Lancaster Sound, entered Prince Regent Inlet and went to the westward of that, entering the various bays, and after surveying a part of the coast to the south of Fury Beach and Creswell Bay, we returned. But at that time there was very little ice in the sound, and we found we might easily have gone a greater distance to the northward. The ice to be met with in Lancaster Sound is entirely different from that of the Smith Sound ice, and that again is different from that to the eastward of Greenland, and that between Spitzbergen and Nova Zembla.

Q. From your experience in the Arctic regions and your study of meteorological conditions, what do you regard as the probable chance of reaching Lady Franklin Bay in a steam vessel?—A. It is always a risky thing to send a vessel up Smith Sound, because it is narrower than any other sound we know of in the Arctic region of a similar extent. The ice being heavy, the probability is that a vessel will not be able to get through; but she may. If she does, it is a mere chance.

Q. It is understood that you have lately prepared a paper on the subject of the navigation of Smith Sound, and that it has been read before the Naval Institute. Does that paper embody your general ideas upon the subject of the navigation of that water?—A. It does. I have meanwhile read of a plan proposed by Mr. Tyson to send a vessel up there, and I have proposed something similar and written to an English naval officer who has seen a great deal of Arctic service, Major Fielden, and I have a letter here from him on the subject. He was one of the officers of the Nares expedition. He says in this letter to me: "The escape of a steamer from Payer Harbor, in 1885, is almost a certainty." Payer Harbor is easily accessible, but a vessel might meet with a great deal of difficulty in steaming north. In the first place, she would have to watch her chance and follow the lead, and besides, the sound would have to be navigated during a period of time when westerly winds—which actually open the water—would not blow; that is, you would not reasonably expect winds to blow. The prevailing direction of the wind is northeast, and in some instances, but very seldom, southwest, and during the time the vessel might find a chance to go north, it would either be calm or you might have slight headwinds. The probability of two or three whale-boats creeping along the coast, is far greater than that a vessel might pass; the chances are much better than would be the case with a large ship. While the "Polaris" was drifting down the sound, we saw a great extent of open water following the coast of Grinnell Land. You always find some open water between the ice-foot and the moving pack.

Q. Then, if I understand you correctly, you regard the general plan proposed by Captain Tyson a feasible one?—A. Yes, sir; I have the same idea he has, and I wrote it out for the first time a fortnight ago, but was ignorant at the time of his having proposed the same method.

Q. He, I think, would object to taking the ship into the sound?—A. He proposed to take the ship to Payer Harbor and send out two whale-boats; unless there is a lot of open water, you might fail.

Q. Your idea is not to go up with the ship unless the navigation is easy?—A. Yes, sir.

Q. Have you no doubt of the ability of a boat's crew to navigate Smith Sound under the conditions you state, pulling the boats out of the water on the ice, and so making their way north to Discovery Bay and return?—A. I have no doubt about it. It might not be a bad plan to take one of those boats in tow, the *oomiaks*. They could easily be procured in Greenland, and the Greenlanders carry them overland sometimes to go to the interior of the fiords; if a letter be written in time to the Governor at Disco, one or two *oomiaks* might be prepared to be taken on board the vessel that makes her way north.

Q. Will you please give us a general description of these boats?—A. It has a wooden frame, and is about twenty-five or thirty feet long, five feet beam, flat bottom; capacity, three tons; covered with walrus hide, or with the hide of the bearded seal. The only difficulty you might have to encounter in using the *oomiak* is, that after they have been in the water three or four days in succession, the water will penetrate, and they have to be greased, especially the seams; but as far as portability is concerned, they cannot be surpassed. When Graah made his exploration on the east coast of Greenland it was entirely in *oomiaks* rowed, by Esquimaux women, with paddles.

Q. What is their capacity of flotation; how many persons could they carry with fifteen days' supplies?—A. Fifteen persons easily, where a whale-boat can carry but eight.

Q. Do they go out in rough weather?—A. They would not meet any rough weather, because they would keep amongst the ice and there is scarcely any swell, and in case of heavy winds they can easily be pulled out. The vessel about to be dispatched should not be over five hundred tons in size.

Q. A vessel after the type of the Saint John's sealers or the whaling ships?—A. I would get a good sailing vessel with an auxiliary engine; she should be provisioned for at least two winters.

Q. What experience did you have in sledging?—A. Sledging in Smith Sound under ordinary circumstances is extremely discouraging, inasmuch as the sound scarcely ever freezes over entirely, for the ice is on the move and the current being swift, at least the tidal current, with high winds in winter, the ice is very hummocky, so that you cannot expect to sledge under favorable circumstances more than fifteen miles a day; I would call fifteen miles a very good average. You might, however, make seventy or eighty miles a day if you got to places that were frozen over smooth, but it never lasts long.

Q. Is there practically any ice-foot along Grinnell Land?—A. It is extremely uncertain and unsafe, and you do not find it everywhere, while in some places you find the ice piled up to a height of thirty or thirty-five feet, in others it is entirely missing. You cannot rely on it.

Q. In moving north, then, from the position the vessel might gain, would you, or would you not, expect to use sledges in connection with your boats for a movement towards Discovery Harbor?—A. It would certainly be wise to have sledges on board, that is, have the sledge runners lashed on to the outside of the boat, and have the cross pieces extra. The sledges could be put together in case they are needed, and a marlin spike and spun yarn is sufficient to secure them.

Q. Did you do any sledging from the "Polaris" with dogs?—A. Yes, sir. We made several sledge journeys on the ice; one following the coast to Petermann Fiord, which was explored, and where the only smooth ice which was found on that trip was situated; between Thank God Harbor and Cape Tyson, and on Hall Basin, and along the shore. The ice was broken up along the mouth of Petermann Fiord, and was extremely hummocky to the south of Cape Lucie Marie and Cape Morton; at the latter place it could scarcely be travelled over. We tried to get to Cape Constitution, but after having rounded Cape Bryan we had to abandon our sledge and go on foot, partly climbing over the cliffs, the same way Morton had done in reaching Cape Constitution from the south.

Q. What season of the year was that?—A. April. We finally struck the water. It would not have been possible to have carried a boat, as the pack in the channel was moving up and down with the tide. The ice to the north along Polaris Promontory was so hummocky that it was never possible to double what we call the Third Cape.

Q. You presume that the ice conditions on the Grinnell Land side would be the same, ordinarily, and that sledging would be extremely difficult?—A. Yes, sir. There is a strong "set" sometimes into Lady Franklin Bay. We were never able to approach Hall Basin when we went out of Polaris Bay, but from the top of the mountains in the vicinity we could see large ice-fields moving into Lady Franklin Bay without ever coming out, and we supposed from that that it was an open strait, until Archer explored it and found it was a long fiord which can readily harbor extensive ice-fields. In a letter written by Captain Nares to the *London Times,* he states that in sledging out, passing Cape Baird, Lieutenant Greely would experience great difficulty.

Q. Do you remember what the provisions left at Polaris Bay or Thank God Harbor consisted of?—A. Of bread, canned meats, lime-juice, molasses, pemmican, and canned or dessicated potatoes.

Q. Expressed in rations, about how many should you suppose there were there?—A. We should have to find out first how much was used by the English. There was a list of provisions left at the observatory at Polaris Bay sent to the British Admiralty, and a letter to the Secretary of State states what the English have taken. It is not given in Nares' report or Beaumont's journal, I think.

Q. But you have not the data in regard to the quantity remaining there?—A. No, sir; I have not.

Q. You think the Admiralty communicated with our State Department, and that the information is in the Department of State?—A. Yes, sir; you will find it there. But I would not rely too much upon those provisions which were left, for they might not be able to take them up in winter.

Q. What kind of Arctic clothing were the people on the "Polaris" supplied with?—A. They actually did not have anything except what we picked up on our way up the coast of Greenland. They succeeded in obtaining sixty or eighty dog-skins, and picked up a few ready-made garments and two sleeping-bags; that was all we had. Captain Hall had relied on getting plenty of deer-skins, but deer had been very scarce for a number of years and there were none to be obtained.

Q. Did you have enough of such clothing to enable you to form an opinion as to the comparative utility and serviceability of seal-skin clothing and reindeer clothing?—A. I would give the preference to reindeer clothing, by all means, and to reindeer calf, if that can be obtained, because it is lighter and warmer than any other skin you can obtain, and besides it does not get stiff after it has been wet.

Q. About what is the weight of a complete suit of deer-skin clothing?—A. It would not weigh over ten pounds complete, boots and everything.

Q. Ordinarily, is deer-skin clothing obtainable in Greenland, with a little previous notice?—A. I would write to the Hudson's Bay Company in London, and get all the skins from there, because they have a large ware-house, and you will be certain to obtain them. Or you might write to Montreal, to the Hudson's Bay Company's agent there. That would be the only certain way to get it, because you cannot rely on getting the skins in Greenland. I think they can be obtained and made up here, if necessary.

By General HAZEN:

Q. What garments do you recommend?—A. A jumper with a hood and short pantaloons, and deer-skin sleeping bag, covered with sail-cloth on the outside, so that the skin part can be removed and pulled out, because if deer-skin gets wet from day to day the hair is apt to come out, and it begins to rot. Then I would advise you to have sleeping-bags made in a different manner from those which have been made up to the present time, because they are always difficult to creep into. You should have a slit made coming down to the lower third, with a flap over it that can be buttoned, and then the difficulty of cleaning it from ice will not be great, and besides it is much easier to get into and out of the bag.

By Captain DAVIS:

Q. Have you ever seen them made in that manner, or used them?—A. I made one myself, and found it superior to anything I have seen before or since.

Q. It is not difficult to keep the slit closed and to exclude the cold?—A. No, sir.

By General HAZEN:

Q. How much did you use the one you made?—A great deal; for a whole season.

By Captain DAVIS:

Q. Did you have scurvy on the "Polaris"?—A. We had one slight attack of scurvy, and, strange to say, the steward was the one to be taken down first. That was early in the spring, but it didn't

5

amount to anything. He was taken to the observatory, where it was dry, and in about ten days he got entirely over it. He did not show any swelling of the lower limbs. After the return of our party from Newman Bay we had three cases, Chester, Myer, and I had an attack of it.

Q. To what did you attribute this outbreak of scurvy?—A. Merely to the dampness of our camp. We were unable to keep it dry, and we stayed there over four weeks.

Q. You do not think it was caused in any way by your diet?—A. No, sir. On board the vessel the steward had everything, and still he was the first one to be attacked.

Q. How do you explain the breaking out of scurvy in Nares' and other expeditions?—A. I certainly would not attribute it to the want of lime-juice, because it occurs just as often where lime-juice is used, as where it is not. But if any one should wish to carry lime-juice or any anti scorbutic on a sledge journey, it would be decidedly best to take citric acid which is crystallized, portable, and which can be used to make lemonade as well, and a pound of citric acid will go a long way.

Q. How frequent were your issues of fresh meat on the "Polaris"? —A. They were quite irregular. We only killed one musk ox when we reached Polaris Bay, which was towards the middle of October, and we had only a few seals, not over five, during the whole winter. But early in the spring we secured twenty-one additional musk oxen and then we had fresh meat almost every other day until the bird season began and then we had it more frequently.

By General HAZEN:

Q. When does the bird season begin?—A. Not before the middle of June. You will find probably some eider ducks, and some brent geese and a few other aquatic birds.

By Captain DAVIS:

Q. Did the scurvy make its appearance during the interval when you were without fresh meat, or when you had a supply?—A. It was when we had a good supply of fresh meat. We attributed it to the dampness of our camp.

Q. I notice that Sir George Nares makes frequent mention of the use of gunpowder to make way for his vessel. Do you think an explosive of some kind would be of utility in shattering ice barriers?—A. It would not be of great utility for navigation particularly, because if the Sound is blocked all the gunpowder in existence would not clear it.

By General HAZEN:

Q. Would it be of use in easing the ship?—A. It might be very useful in making a dock for the vessel or in blasting ice fields of smaller extent. I would give preference to gun-cotton or dynamite.

By Captain DAVIS:

Q. Smith Sound between Port Foulke and Cape Sabine may be said to be open and closed, alternately, during all the winter?—A. Yes, sir; when Hayes wintered at Port Foulke he had open water during the greater part of the time, and the temperature was so high that it rained, I think, about Christmas eve. There is a very swift tidal current running along the coast there. When Inglefield followed the coast he talked about a permanent current, and set it down at a velocity of five knots an hour.

Q. Supposing Lieutenant Greely to come south next spring, say in July, or even in April, with sledges; what do you regard as his chance of getting across Smith Sound, without boats?—A. His chance would be slim. He might make it across, but if he carries boats on his sledges it will impede his progress to a great extent, and if he does not carry any and finds the Sound open he will not be able to cross.

Q. Would he find it easier crossing Smith Sound, or what is com· monly called Kane Basin higher up, and making Rensselaer or one of those harbors?—A. No; it would be much more difficult, because it is wider. When Hayes was first sent out by Kane to cross and make the coast of Grinnell Land his orders were to hold to the westward. He made the attempt and failed and returned, and then, contrary to his orders, he made a northwardly line and reached the coast. Lieutenant Greely might do likewise. He would have to be guided entirely by circumstances.

Q. Do you know if there is game around Hayes Sound?—A. The Esquimaux informed us that Hayes Sound opened to the westward, and that musk oxen were there, that is, around Princess Alexandra Harbor, but I have never visited the spot.

By Lieutenant-Commander McCALLA :

Q. At what points did you land on the east side of Grinnell Land. between Cape Sabine and Cape Baird?—A. Only at one point near Cape Frazer, between five and six in the morning. I was not on shore myself.

Q. Then you do not know, from your personal observation, the condition of the land at the water's edge, or the ice-foot on the east side of Grinnell Land between those points?—A. I have seen the ice-foot in crossing the Sound and it was extremely rough.

Q. At what distance did you see it?—A. At a distance of about six miles, from an elevation of about sixty feet, so that I got a good view of it.

Q. In reference to a projected boat expedition up the east coast of Grinnell Land, which I understood you to say you favored, would you expect the party to advance over the ice-foot, or on shore?—A. I would not propose taking to the ice-foot in boats unless I was compelled to, or if I could not find a piece of ice of sufficient size to secure the boats.

Q. Then, in your calculations, you would not expect to land or go on the ice-foot in your boats?—A. I would not land unless I was compelled to go to one of the depots of provisions.

Q. But you would expect to advance entirely by water or over floating ice?—Yes, sir; entirely.

Q. How did you obtain water for drinking on the "Polaris"?—A. The water was obtained by melting berg ice.

Q. You did not use a distiller at all?—A. No, sir; there is no necessity for it. The best way is to have a barrel in your galley, fill it with ice, and pour boiling water on it whenever you can get it.

By Captain DAVIS :

Q. Did you find any trace of saline matter in water thus obtained?—A. No, sir; not in berg ice. At the time the boat party would probably go north they would find plenty of water running from the bergs and old hummocks; you would not meet with many bergs. The "Polaris" did not meet a single iceberg north of Polaris Bay.

Q. At what date ought a vessel to reach Payer Harbor?—A. She should not attempt to cross the bay before the mean date of opening, which is the middle of June; she would run unnecessary risks and would not find Smith Sound open at an earlier date. I think Melville Bay opens about the middle of June. However, it would depend entirely on her transit how long it would take her to get to the bay.

Q. She should be there by the 1st of July, then?—A. O, yes, sir. Captain Nares, in a private letter, says he thinks it would be better not to attempt to go north before the latter part of August or the beginning of September, and I think Major Feilden states something similar. His letter is at your service if you desire it. (Exhibit E.)

Q. There ought to be no considerable difficulty in Lieutenant Greely getting across to Polaris Bay and availing himself of the stores and any game he might find there?—A. We made several attempts to cross from Polaris to Lady Franklin Bay. In the first place we wanted to find the cairn which Hayes claims to have left, and we wanted to follow that coast and sledge along it. But the ice was always moving, and the lanes of water between the hummocks were so small and narrow that they were not navigable, and they were too wide to be crossed by sledges. It was entirely impracticable to cross; and something similar may have happened to Lieutenant Greely. On our return journey south we made an attempt to cross it somewhere near Hans Island and we failed. We made several attempts besides that.

Q. Beaumont, early in the season, seems to have gotten across without much difficulty?—A. Yes, he got across; but returning in August, with a boat, he found it very difficult.

Q. Would Lieutenant Greely be likely to make effective use of the steam-launch?—A. Yes, if he would take a boat in tow with coal. I do not see how else he could make use of her. He could not carry coal enough otherwise. It would offer advantages and drawbacks too.

By General HAZEN:

Q. If he should have open water why could he not tow the other boats?—A. But if the ice closes suddenly you might find yourself in difficulty before you are fairly aware of it. Sir George Nares mentioned in his first report to the Admiralty that he found a number of skin-boats on Littleton Island and that he carried one of them to Cape Sabine. Probably those skin-boats are really *oomiaks*, and if Lieutenant Greely knows about their having been deposited there it might be of great use to him.

Lieut. J. C. COLWELL, U. S. Navy, appeared, in response to the invitation of the Board, and was examined as follows:

By Captain DAVIS:

Question. Lieutenant Garlington submitted to the Board a paper which gives an outline of a plan, which he mentions as having been made in conjunction with yourself, for an Arctic expedition. I presume that embodies your views in regard to the general plan for a relief expedition?—Answer. Yes, sir.

Q. And in case your relief vessel should be unable to make her way to Discovery Harbor, you propose to make use of boats and sledges in the attempt to reach that point?—A. Yes, sir; to use boats at once when we get to the edge of the ice on the 1st of July; to start one light boat at once, and a week or two later, if the ice shows no signs of making out, to take the vessel into the Sound and start two boats.

Q. You mean boats of a construction which would be easy to launch and pull out of water?—A. Boats that their crews could haul up on the ice in the case of its closing in.

Q. Taking the ordinary New Bedford whale-boat, what is the least number of men, from your experience, that could pull her out of water and get her on an ice-floe floating eight inches high?—A. The New Bedford whale-boat is too heavy. Boats ought to be built lighter, but, after the style of the New Bedford whale-boats, pulling five oars, and they should be built to be hauled out with their load by a crew of six men.

Q. I think you left some provisions at Cape Sabine. At what altitude above high water were those provisions placed, as you remember?—A. About ten or fifteen feet, and behind a corner of rocks which would protect them from the ice banking up.

Q. You feel that they are perfectly secure from any danger from ice?—A. Yes, the only trouble would be from water running down the side of the cliff and getting under them, or a snow-slide might cover them up. When we left there was no snow nor any water coming into this hollow where I placed them.

Q. Were they in a position where they might be destroyed by a slide of snow from above, or pushed out on the ice?—A. The cliff was almost perpendicular where I placed them, in a little crevice, and the chances are that a slide of snow would not come down in that crevice, but would go over it or pass around to one side. They are about thirty feet distant from the edge of the water.

Q. What is the rise and fall of the tide there?—A. About eight feet. When I refer to high-water mark I, of course, refer to high tide.

Q. Did you land on the west side or on any other point on Grinnell Land?—A. Only at Cape Sabine and Payer Harbor.

Q. Did Payer Harbor appear to be well protected, in which a vessel could lie with safety?—A. She could lie there, but there would be a great deal of ice fouling her. It is a clear channel and ice is continually driven in there, but nothing to hurt her.

Q. How strong a current is there through this channel?—A. About two knots on the ebb tide and probably about half a knot on the flood.

Q. Did you find Arctic clothing necessary on your retreat?—A. No, sir.

Q. You made several landings on the Greenland coast coming down to Cape York, I believe?—A. Yes, sir.

Q. And saw evidences of game in considerable abundance at various points, especially up by Port Foulke?—A. About Pandora Harbor considerable game was seen, many birds, and some reindeer and hare; and about Cape Athol were seen some musk oxen. Some of the men followed a herd back of Cape Athol. But we saw reindeer horns at several points where we landed.

By Lieutenant-Commander McCalla:

Q. You covered those provisions west of Cape Sabine with rocks and stones?—A. With two tent flies, and weighted the whole thing down with stones.

By Captain Davis:

Q. Have you anything in addition to say in connection with the project for the relief of Lieutenant Greely except what is contained in this paper; anything bearing on the question which you think important?—A. I do not remember exactly what is in the paper, so that I

may repeat what is stated there; but I think it necessary that
the expedition should go up as soon as possible. If Lieutenant
Greely is going to need relief, he is going to need it next spring. If
he comes down in the spring from his place up the Sound to Littleton
Island he will find no supplies there, and he will need them as soon
as a vessel can get there. I think a vessel should go up as soon
as possible and communicate with Littleton Island from Cape York;
if a vessel is not up at Cape York soon you will find a Scotch whaler
getting to Littleton Island first and bringing the men down. They
know now that these people are there, and it is only a day's run
out of their track when they are bound for the whaling regions; it
would pay them to make that day's run to see if those people are there,
and if so to bring them back, as a business speculation.

Q. You say the relief ships should communicate with them from
Cape York as early as possible; do you mean by land?—A. By land
or ice. At that season of the year, I think by sledges.

Q. If you can get with a vessel to Cape York are you not reasonably
sure to get higher?—A. The whalers are sometimes blocked in off Cape
York three or four days in the ice, and during those times the natives
communicate with them off shore.

Q. How many days' travel by sledges is Cape York from Littleton
Island?—A. Five days.

Q. What date should you say that your vessel ought to be struggling
to get to Cape York?—A. She should be at Upernavik before the 30th
of May. The whalers usually pass Upernavik before that time. They
are usually at Disco in May. They leave Dundee the last of April.

Q. What is the earliest date that you have heard of a whaler, or any
vessel, getting to Cape York?—A. I cannot remember the earliest.
The best account of a whaling voyage I have read was written by
Captain Markham; he got off and above Cape York on the 9th of
June, and does not speak of it as an unusual passage. Before the use of
steam as a motive power sailing vessels averaged it by the first week
in July. If those whalers do not make it by the first of July they give
it up and try the "middle water".

I have heard since I have been here this morning, some discussion
about Arctic clothing, and I may offer a few suggestions on that point.
The principal work of this expedition will be during the summer.
During the past summer we saw no weather colder than the ordinary
winter weather we have in the Middle States. The best clothing to be
worn would be a good quality of woolen throughout, and a suit of
Cape Ann oil-skins over the whole, for rainy or snowy weather.
For the feet, I would recommend the best quality of water-proof leather
boots, those known as loggers' or lumbermen's boots, are the best of
that sort. They are water-proof, not particularly heavy, and are
easy on the feet.

Q. Your programme takes into account the possibility of being
detained there during the winter?—A. For that reason there should be
a supply of the very heaviest winter clothing. But in conversation
with the captain of the "Sofia," which carried Professor Nordenskjold's
expedition, (a man who had spent nearly all his life in the Arctic
regions) he showed me his clothing, which was only woolen clothing,
and over it he wore a suit of white duck, the jumper having a
hood attached to it, and over that, in the coldest weather, he
wore a woolen cap, such as is worn by the Russian troops in northern
Siberia, with long strings of the same material as the caps, which,

wrapped around the neck, made a muffler; he told me that in the coldest-weather he wore a silk handkerchief tied around his face over the nostrils and mouth.

Q. Was he with Nordenskjold in his trip north of Siberia in the "Vega"?—A. He was not on that trip. He commanded the vessel that went around the coast of Asia to relieve Nordenskjold, and was wrecked. He spent two winters on the north coast of Asia, was wrecked once, and made a journey of 1,500 miles during mid-winter in Siberia.

Q. Do you remember his name?—A. I have forgotten, but he told me he never used the skin clothing, and found this rig answered the purpose in every way.

Q. What did he wear on his feet?—A. I do not remember. He did not wear moccasins, and he said those would never do for that sort of work.

Q. You, or some of your party, wore seal-skin on your retreat?—A. Some of the men did, but it was only because they had not a sufficient supply of good clothing; suits of Cape Ann oil-skin would have been better for them. Seal-skin wets easily, and when dry and stiff breaks, and lasts but a very short time.

Q. And when saturated it is very spongy?—A. Yes, sir; and very uncomfortable.

Q. Did your vessel coal at Kudlisit Mines?—A. No, sir; but the "Yantic" did.

Mr. GEORGE KENNAN, of Washington, D. C., appeared, in response to the invitation of the Board, and was examined as follows:

By Captain DAVIS:

Question. Will you please give a brief statement of your experience in northern regions?—Answer. My entire experience in the north is comprised in a three years' stay in northeastern Siberia.

Q. You have made many sledge journeys and other trips of that character?—A. I travelled in the aggregate, I think, about 4,000 miles on sledges in northeastern Siberia, counting only the journeys that were made as explorations. I afterwards came home across Siberia to Saint Petersburg, but that journey was mostly made with horses, and on roads. The 4,000 miles of which I speak were made through an untravelled and comparatively unknown country.

Q. Were any of your journeys across hummocky ice, or ice-floes?—A. Very rarely, only at intervals along the coast where we crossed arms of the sea or where we were compelled, in order to avoid mountains, to go out on the sea.

Q. Do the natives of that region have occasion to make long journeys along the coast on the ice-foot or on ice-floes?—A. No, sir. They cross arms of the sea as I did, and are compelled sometimes to go out on the ice, but they never make any long journeys over open sea-ice.

Q. Describe briefly the outfit of a dog team as you used it there, the most efficient kind.—A. A dog team in Siberia consists of from seven to thirteen dogs harnessed two abreast, with a leader. The lead dog is especially trained to obey the voice. They are driven without a whip, and are harnessed in couples to a long trace running down between the two lines of dogs, with the leader ahead. The advantage of this system of harnessing is that it enables the driver to keep the team under control better than where every dog has a separate trace—particularly in going over hummocky ice or through timber. If dogs are harnessed in the Esquimaux fashion half of them are apt to run on one side of a tree, ice-cake, or other obstacle, and half on the other, thus bringing the sledge to a stop. If, however, they are harnessed in the Siberian manner they are unable to separate or jump over one anothers traces, and as they all follow the lead dog the driver can guide them through a dense forest as well as if he controlled them by means of reins.

Q. How about sleds ?—A. I do not know that I could describe Siberian sledges to you without a model. Perhaps the most noticeable thing about them is the width of the runner. The Siberian sledge runner is much wider than that generally used by Arctic expeditions; I should say from four to six inches.

Q. Rigid, solid 'timber, or bending ?—A. It is bending. It is not a solid plank set up on edge; it is a skeleton runner, consisting of a broad shoe made of a strip of birch bent up at the end and connected with the body or platform of the sledge by uprights. The sledge is lashed together, has no metallic fastenings, there is not a joint in it that will not give, and it is almost indestructible. I have seen sledges loaded with three hundred or four hundred pounds fall a considerable distance down a very steep slope and overturn on the ice without breaking. In the spring the natives shoe their sledge runners with whalebone, and in the winter, when the weather is very cold, every native carries about his neck a bottle filled with water, with which he ices the sledge runners at intervals of an hour or two. That adds very greatly to the smoothness of the runner and makes it slip more easily over the snow. Another feature of the Siberian sledge, which seems to me valuable, and which has never been adopted by Arctic expeditions, is the bow or arch which spans the sledge transversely amidships. It is made of a bent piece of wood, perhaps two and a half inches in diameter, with its ends lashed to the sides of the sledge a little forward of the middle. This arch, which stands upright, is used as a handle by which the sledge is managed. The Esquimaux sledge has what they call an "upstander" at the back end, but I do not think it is as convenient as this Siberian bow which enables the man to pull his sledge one side or the other, or lift it in any direction.

Q. The width and the length of the sledge is about what ?—A. It is about twelve feet in length and in width two to two and a half feet.

Q. Capable of carrying a load of how many pounds ?—A. The larger of these sledges would carry a load of eight hundred pounds. I think it would even be possible to put a thousand pounds on the largest sledges made there. But that would not be practicable or prudent if the journey was over a rough, broken country.

Q. What kind of clothing did you use during your winter experience?—A. The Siberian fur dress, which I think is the best in the world, is made entirely of reindeer-skin. The feet and legs are covered with reindeer-skin stockings, coming to the knee or thigh, as the case may be (depending upon whether they are worn with pantaloons or not), and boots made of the skin from the fore-leg of the reindeer. The stockings are worn, as a rule, with the hairy side in, and the bottom of the boot is filled with dried straw or grass to absorb, to some extent, the moisture of the foot. If the boots are short, pantaloons are generally worn; if long, they are not—that is, not heavy ones. The most important part of the costume is a sort of jumper which is put on over the head, and is made long enough to fall to about the calf of the leg. It is very large and loose and is girded about the waist with a sash. The object of making it so loose is, so that when it is tied about the waist with a sash, it will lie in folds over the body so as to increase the thickness. In addition to that, it seems to be the intention to confine within this jumper a quantity of air, which becomes warmed by the body and remains there, acting as an additional protection. Of course, without the sash that object could not be attained. A jumper worn loose, it seems to me, is not nearly so warm as one belted about the waist, for the reason that the warm air from the body rises under the loose garment and escapes at the throat, and the cold air and wind blow up under it. If you tie it tightly about the waist with a sash that circulation of air is broken, and two or three gallons of warm air are retained all the time about the body. The natives carry bottles of water tied around their necks for the purpose of icing their sledge runners, as I have stated, and these water bottles rarely freeze, even in very cold weather. The head is covered with a hood of fox or wolf-skin, made to come well forward over the face. I think the hoods used in Arctic expeditions have been defective, in that they leave the face too much exposed. With the Siberian hood you can turn sidewise to the wind and have your face at least partially protected. One hood is fringed about the face with a heavy border made of the skin of the wolverine, bear, or some shaggy fur of that sort, so that in a gale with drifting snow the sides can be brought together over the face, and the wearer can breathe through the interstices of the fur which affords protection and keeps out at the same time the flying snow. Another valuable feature of the Siberian dress is the boa worn about the neck for the protection of the nose and cheeks. I have tried everything that has been used for the protection of the cheek and nose, including silk handkerchiefs and squirrel-skin masks, but, with the exception of this boa, I never found anything that afforded protection to the face for more than half or three-quarters of an hour. Whatever I used would then become a solid mass of ice from the moisture of the breath. The Siberian natives use a boa made of squirrels' tails, which they wind about the neck (they are perhaps ten feet in length) until the coils come up over the nose, then they breathe through the loose hair, and as fast as one portion becomes frosty they turn it around. In that way a boa will last a man all day and furnish him constantly with a warm and dry safeguard against frost bites.

Q. What is the weight of a suit of that clothing?—A. It varies according to the purpose for which the clothing is desired. I carried two suits, one to travel in and one for sleeping. The ordinary travelling suit weighs, I should say, fifteen pounds. The suit for sleeping would be double that.

Q. Is that clothing obtainable anywhere out of Siberia?—A. I think not. It could be made anywhere, but it is not obtainable ready-made anywhere out of Siberia, so far as I know. In such a dress as I have described I have slept out of doors, on the snow, without shelter, in temperatures as low as thirty-five degrees below zero, in perfect comfort; and when I say perfect comfort, I mean to be taken literally. I had a sleeping-bag in addition, of course. Our sleeping-bags were about seven feet long and three feet wide, and were made of wolf-skin.

Q. What kind of a rig would that be for men to work in who had to pull boats or sledges?—A. Very bad. This dress is intended for men who ride on sledges. It seems to me that a great mistake has been made by many Arctic expeditions in dressing their men too warmly when they were compelled to drag sledges, or do heavy work. One of the greatest dangers to be guarded against by a sledging party is becoming over-heated, and especially should they guard against perspiration. I think there is more danger from perspiration than from any other one thing. Men put on heavy furs, and go out and drag a sledge until their under-clothing is saturated with moisture, and then when they come into camp and the body cools down, there is a chill from the moist fur-clothing, and an atmosphere of dampness in their tent or place of shelter, then their clothing saturated with the moisture from their bodies freezes, and their tents, sleeping-bags, and all their gear have to be fairly broken up with hand-spikes before they can get into them the next morning.

Q. During your residence in Siberia did you see cases of scurvy?— A. Never.

Q. Have you any positive, decided ideas about the relief of Lieutenant Greely that would be of use to the Board?—A. There are several suggestions I should like to make for the consideration of the Board—general suggestions. I have never visited Smith Sound myself, but I knew Doctor Hayes very well, and have often discussed this whole question with him. I am, therefore, reasonably familar with the country and with what can be done in it. It seems to me that if I were a member of a whaling firm and had a crew up there situated as Lieutenant Greely's party is, that one of the first things I should do would be to offer a reward to any private individual or private ship which should succeed in affording relief to the party. That has always been done by the British government. It was done throughout the Franklin searches. It was done more recently when Leigh Smith was lost, and more recently still when the Dutch polar expedition in the "Varna" was missing. The whaling fleet from Dundee and Saint John's comprises I believe, from twelve to twenty ships. There were fourteen whalers from Dundee and Saint John's in Lancaster Sound before the "Proteus" sailed from Saint John's last year, and all that fleet had gone up Baffin Bay and across Melville Bay to Cape York, and then crossed the upper part of Baffin Bay and come down into Lancaster Sound; they were all there before the time the "Proteus" left last spring. It seems to me, therefore, that it is worth a few thousand dollars to afford Lieutenant Greely's party that additional chance. It frequently happens that a few hours difference in the time of arrival of a ship at a given point, may make all the difference between getting through and not getting through for weeks. There are so many of these whaling vessels, and their captains are so skillful and experienced in ice navigation, that there is a strong probability they will be the first ships on the ground next season. It seems to me therefore, that it would be well to stimulate effort on their part by offering a reward, as has been done repeatedly before.

In the second place, I should say that it was extremely important that a leader for this expedition should be chosen at as early a day as possible, in order that he may have the advantage of being connected with the expedition from the beginning. Everything that is purchased should be purchased under his supervision and with his consent, and he should manage, practically, the whole expedition from the beginning. I think the man should be, in the first place, one of as extensive Arctic experience as possible; that should be the prime requisite, and in the second place the character and general attainments of the person selected should be considered. I think he should not be too much hampered with orders. I think that a man who is competent to take charge of an Arctic expedition at all, is competent to take charge of it entirely, and I would have his instructions of the most general character, and would furnish him everything in the way of suggestions that I could possibly get from any source.

I do not know whether the Board has already anticipated a suggestion I am about to make now, that the Chairman of the Board should write to Sir George Nares, Captain Stephenson, Commander Markham and Professor Nordenskjold, asking them all for suggestions with regard to this relief expedition. The three first-named are probably better acquainted with the navigation of the upper part of Baffin Bay and Smith Sound than any persons now living, Commander Markham, particularly, and I think that the advice to be obtained from those sources would be of the highest value. If I were going up there myself in command of the expedition, I should request this government to ask leave of that of Great Britain to have Commander Markham accompany the party as an advisory officer, if he would do so.

There are two or three other things with regard to equipment that I think it would be well to mention. In the first place, regarding snow-shoes. The Siberian snow-shoe is made of a thin strip of board, perhaps seven or eight inches in width, and about five feet in length, turned up at the end like a skate, and covered on the bottom with skin from the fore-leg of the reindeer; this skin, which is bristly, is put on so that the points of the bristles are backward; this gives a firm foothold, and a man with these snow-shoes on can walk up almost any acclivity short of a precipice. They slide forward like glass, but the instant the foot is thrown backward they hold with a grip that is stronger than that of an ordinary boot. It is possible with such shoes, to drag a heavy weight over deep, soft snow, and I do not know of any other snow-shoe that you can do that with. The foot is never lifted, but the shoe is slid forward up out of the snow all the time.

I would also suggest that a sledging party going north should try the Hudson Bay sledge for deep, soft snow. It never has been tried by an Arctic expedition, so far as I know, but it would have been a very great advantage I think, in many cases, to the Nares expedition. The Hudson Bay sledge is practically an exaggerated and enlarged pattern of this Siberian shoe, and will sink only a very short distance in the snow. It would be possible for men mounted on snow-shoes, such as I have described, to walk right over soft snow with a lightly loaded Hudson Bay sledge, at the rate of a mile an hour, where Nares' sledges made only a mile in four or five hours. Of course, this sledge would be of no use in rough ice work, but it could be lashed on the top of one of the other sledges, adding very little to the weight, and it might be so made that, upon coming to deep, soft snow, the ice sledge could be run up on the other and lashed, and the two be turned into one Hudson Bay sledge. The records of the Nares expedition show that deep, soft snow was one of the greatest difficulties they had to contend with.

I should like to say a few words about tents, cooking-apparatus, and fuel. I think the most important things in a sledging expedition are, first, food; second, fuel; and third, shelter. I wish to suggest a form of tent which I think might be useful. I have never tried it myself, but I have thought of it since I returned from Siberia, and it seems to me it would save sledging parties an immense deal of suffering. The greatest difficulty we had to contend with in trying to use tents was the heavy wind; we could not make any sort of tent stand in the gales that swept over those Siberian steppes. The tent which I suggest should be made conical in shape, with a frame-work of poles lashed together at the top, very much as the ribs of an umbrella are fastened, each pole to be shod with a spike, and a loose thong of seal-skin to run a foot or so from the ground, fastened permanently to the pole, would govern the distance to which the frame-work could be spread when open. The frame-work could be shut up like an umbrella in a single round package the length of the poles. I would set up this frame-work and then secure it by means of anchors made of a piece of wood, perhaps two and a half or three feet in length, and twelve inches wide, with spikes running through and projecting two and a half inches on the under side, with a ring on the side to fasten a line to. I would fasten this anchor on the snow, run a loaded sledge on, then carry a line to the frame; there would be two such anchors. Having secured the frame-work, the whole operation could be performed in two minutes. I would hang the tent up *inside* of the frame-work, instead of attempting to pull it over. I would have the tent made like a conical oil-can, with the bottom sewed continuously to the sides all around, with a small ventilating hole in the top, and would have this rigging fixed on the tent, so that a man could take it off the sledge in his arms in any gale of wind, hang it to the top of this frame-work of poles, and then hang or secure it with loop and toggle fastenings to the poles all around. I cannot imagine any wind which would prevent that being done, unless it was a wind so severe as to tear the canvas to pieces.

Q. Have you ever seen such a tent?—A. Never; it has never been used. I would warm and light the tent with a "Florence" kerosene stove. A kerosene stove can only be used there under shelter. It has a chimney and requires a draft, and the wind would put it out. But in a tent that had a bottom, so that no wind could get into it, a "Florence" oil-stove could be used, and I believe it would do all the cooking and dry the fur stockings of the men, which is of the first importance.

The food I have always used on sledge journeys is dried fish, hard bread and tea. I have known men to do extremely hard work for more than a month at a time on a sledge journey with nothing else. The Siberians live without vegetable food practically; they live largely on dried fish, and I never heard of a case of scurvy in eastern Siberia. I never saw a man broken out with any disorder resulting from food. I have lived on dried fish and hard bread for weeks at a time, and I should take that food on a sledging journey if it was obtainable.

Q. How much would such a ration weigh?—A. I should say two and one-half pounds. I would not use pemmican if I could get anything else, for it does not seem to agree with men who are hard worked. The men of the Nares expedition had a great prejudice against it, founded on something, and I presume in the Nares report there are twenty references to disorders of the stomach and bowels attributed to pemmican.

Q. Do the Siberians who live on that food perform much manual labor?—A. If they are going over a rough, broken country they do a great deal of labor, for their sledges are heavy and require hauling and pulling, this way and that, although they do not do any labor as severe as drawing heavy sledges over hummocky ice and loading and unloading twenty times a day.

By General HAZEN:

Q. What distance could you make daily in Siberian travel?—A. From five to eighty miles, depending on the condition of the snow. In the spring I went across on the snow almost constantly, making eighty miles daily. When the snow is soft and deep, you may not be able to make a mile in five days.

By Captain DAVIS:

Q. Do you think the average American seaman would be inclined to accept the food you have described when employed on sledging journeys of from thirty to sixty days?—A. Judging from my own tastes, I should say yes. There is nothing about the dried fish in any way distasteful. It is a food that I ate with perfect relish and all the men of our party, native and American, ate it with relish.

Q. You made no attempt to cook it?—A. We would sometimes throw a split dried fish on the fire and leave it until the fat broiled out, and I eat it in that way. It is generally salmon, and seems to contain everything that the human system needs under severe labor and when exposed to severe cold. We did not confine ourselves at all times to this; we took fresh meat whenever we could get it.

By Lieutenant-Commander McCALLA:

Q. Did you use stimulants?—A. Not at all, and I should advise against their use, except as medicine in certain cases.

After some time spent in discussion upon the subject of clothing, the Recorder was directed to prepare and send letters to the President of the Hudson's Bay Company at London, England, and its General Agent at Montreal, Canada, requesting information of that Company as to its ability to furnish reindeer-skins suitable for making such clothing as is worn by their employés and the Esquimaux in the northern portions of British America.

The Board then adjourned to meet to-morrow morning at 11 o'clock.

ROOM 88, NAVY DEPARTMENT BUILDING,
Washington, D. C., January 5, 1884.

The Board met pursuant to adjournment; all the members present.

Captain GREER presented and read a memorandum of a plan to relieve Lieutenant Greely, prepared by Commander Frank Wildes, U. S. Navy. (Exhibit F.)

Mr. J. W. NORMAN, of Saint John's, Newfoundland, being present at the session of the Board, stated that, in addition to his previous suggestions, he would recommend that notice should be given to the owners and masters of vessels engaged in the sealing trade to preserve and make note of any articles that might be found on their voyages which would indicate the location of any exploring parties in the Arctic regions. Also, that if the goverment desires to secure the services of any of the men employed in sealing expeditions, it should be done before the 5th of March, as most of the men secure their berths for the summer by that time.

Capt. RICHARD PIKE, of Saint John's, Newfoundland, being present, was further interrogated as follows:

By Captain DAVIS:

Question.. Supposing Lieutenant Greely started from Lady Franklin Bay about September 1st of last year, either with boats or sledges, or both, what do you think are his chances of getting to Littleton Island? —Answer. I think he would get down.

Q. About what time should you suppose he would reach there?—A. I think by the 15th or 20th of September.

Q. What was the condition of the ice above Lady Franklin Bay when you landed him there?—A. Very heavy.

Q. Do you think you could have gone any higher with your vessel? —A. We could not when we landed, but when we came out we could have gone further up on the east side.

Lieut. J. C. COLWELL, U. S. Navy, recalled:

By Captain DAVIS:

Question. Do you wish to make any additional statement?—Answer. In the plan submitted by Lieutenant Garlington, a naval vessel was recommended as a convoy, a ship properly strengthened. That was only indicated as a make-shift and to lessen expense; but to do it properly, there should be two regularly fitted whaling steamers sent.

Q. Suppose those vessels fail to get above Cape Sabine, or to a harbor above Cape Sabine, would you winter them there?—A. One I would push into the ice and take the chances of having her lost; the other I should not try to get above Cape Sabine.

By Lieutenant-Commander McCALLA:

Q. In the plan submitted by you and Lieutenant Garlington, you recommend, in substance, that the expedition shall be commanded by an officer from the Army, and the vessel by an officer from the Navy?— A. I was going to refer to that yesterday. I said that, generally, I approved of the plan submitted by Lieutenant Garlington; but as to the officer in command of the expedition, I think there should be one officer in command, and that he should be a naval officer. For sledging work on shore, I think soldiers would be better fitted than sailors. The class of men we had with Lieutenant Garlington this last year, enlisted men of the Army, were better fitted for the work we did than seamen would be, although it was confined almost entirely to boating.

Q. Then the recommendation that the expedition should be commanded by an Army officer and the vessel by a Naval officer, does not represent your views?—A. No, sir.

Q. Did you do any sledging last summer?—A. Not much. When the ship was lost we rigged up the sledges and I caught six dogs and we hauled several loads across the floes to the boats, of stores saved out of the ship.

Q. How long did that take you?—A. Five or six hours probably.

Q. And that is what you refer to when you say you think soldiers would be better adapted to sledging on land than seamen?—A. From what I saw of these men, they stood the hardships we suffered better than would the same number of seamen taken from a man-of-war.

Q. You had no man-of-war's-men with you to enable you to make the comparison?—A. There was one of them along but he was also a soldier, and had served only one enlistment in the Navy.

Q. Do you think the enlisted men of the Army that you saw would be better in boats than seamen?—A. Yes, sir; better for the work we did.

Q. In boats?—A. Yes, sir. They stood the work better and did better in every way than any seamen I have seen. I could not of course say how men-of-war's-men would do.

By General HAZEN:

Q. Then you think in the general work, including the probability of sledging, and the general rough work which such an expedition is almost certain to have on land, that enlisted men of the Army are better for that work than men of the Navy?—A. I think a combined force on board of a ship, of sailors and soldiers, would be best. I think the corps feeling generated between these men would be the means of getting better work out of them than if they were all of one branch of the service.

Q. How did those sledges answer the purpose?—A. They seemed to do very well. I had to work in a hurry, and had to overload them; but what little work I did they answered the purpose well.

By Lieutenant-Commander McCALLA:

Q. Do you know of any Arctic expedition in which officers or men of the Army were taken for sledging?—A. In the Austrian expedition, which did about the best work of any of the northern expeditions; it was a joint one of Army and Navy men under Lieutenants Payer and Weyprecht; the expedition was commanded by them jointly.

Q. Were the men who did the sledging on the Payer sledging trip enlisted men of the Austrian Army, or mountaineers?—A. I don't know whether they were enlisted men of the Army at that time, but they had been in the Austrian Army previously. They had served under the command of one of those officers.

By Captain DAVIS:

Q. Do you know to what branch of the service Lieutenant Schwatka belongs?—A. To the Army.

Dr. EMILE BESSELS, of Washington, D. C., recalled.

By General HAZEN:

Question. At what date should a vessel leave Littleton Island in order to secure a safe transit south?—Answer. About the middle of October.

General Hazen was instructed to inform the Secretaries of War and the Navy, respectively, that the Board would be gratified to receive an expression of opinion concerning the proposed relief expedition from Captains Sir Geo. S. Nares, H. F. Stephenson, and A. R. Markham, all of the British Navy. (The responses of these officers will be found in Exhibit V.—RECORDER.)

A discussion then ensued as to the necessity of the immediate detail of a commander for the proposed expedition. After an interchange of opinions, it was unanimously agreed that he should be chosen from the Navy, and that the assignment should be made as soon as possible.

In accordance therewith, the President of the Board was instructed to forward to the Secretaries of War and the Navy, respectively, letters of which the following is a copy:

ROOM, BOARD OF OFFICERS CONSIDERING RELIEF
EXPEDITION TO LIEUTENANT GREELY AND PARTY AT LADY FRANKLIN BAY.
Washington, D. C., January 5, 1884.

SIR: As preliminary to its general report the Board desires to state, that in its opinion the selection of an officer to command the proposed relief expedition to Lady Franklin Bay should be made without delay, in order that he may be enabled to make timely preparations for the work before him. The Board is unanimously of the opinion that the commander of the expedition should be a Naval officer.

Very respectfully, your obedient servant.

W. B. HAZEN,
Brig. & Bvt. Maj. Gen'l,
Chief Signal Officer, U. S. Army,
President of the Board.

The Board then adjourned to meet on Monday, January 7, 1884, at 11 a. m.

ROOM 88, NAVY DEPARTMENT BUILDING,
Washington, D. C. January 7, 1884.

The Board met pursuant to adjournment; all the members present.

A communication from F. B. J. Rust, dated New York, January 5, 1884, was received and read. (Abst. Mis. Cor., No. 28.) The Recorder was directed in acknowledging the same, to invite Mr. Rust to submit a memorandum embodying such suggestions as he might be pleased to make, touching the organization of the proposed expedition.

Lieut. J. C. COLWELL, U. S. Navy, appeared before the Board and made the following additional statement:

I think I can make my statement already given to the Board somewhat clearer, by adding a brief explanation. I did not mean to recommend the use of soldiers for boating in preference to seamen, but what I do recommend, is a detail of enlisted men from the Army to accompany the expedition, every party sent away from the ships to be composed of men of both branches of the service. The reason I recommend soldiers is, that on general principles, I consider them better adapted for land work than seamen. There are many things a soldier can do that a seaman knows nothing of, and many things a seaman can do that a soldier can not do. This opinion I have formed from what I saw of Lieutenant Garlington's party, whom I considered particularly well-fitted for the work which had to be done in that region. The work we did was nearly all boating, the sledging amounting to nothing; but even at boating, though foreign to their usual occupation, they proved themselves better men, more enduring, and adapted themselves more readily to the various circumstances as they arose than would the average man-of-war's-man. They were under better discipline, and were more trustworthy than the average man-of-war's-man .The boat's crew I had I would not have exchanged for the best boat's crew on board the "Yantic." I had so much confidence in these men I had with me, that I intended to take the same boat's crew back north for the rest of the party—in case I failed to meet the "Yantic," or the "Yantic" refused to return north—without the addition of one man; and the men all expressed their willingness and desire to go with me. It should be remembered, however, that Lieutenant Garlington's men were picked men, and in the remarks I have made I have compared the average man-of-war's-man to the men of Lieutenant Garlington's party. They were picked men, and Americans. There would be no difficulty in obtaining plenty of volunteers from the Navy, as I saw from the temper of the "Yantic's" crew; but the right kind of men might not offer themselves. In Saint John's, when we returned there last fall, it was rumored that the United States Government was to purchase a ship at once and send her north, and that I was to go in command of her. A boatswain's-mate of the "Yantic" came to me with a list of seventeen men whom he said wished to go with me, and he said there were many more on board that ship who would like to go back north if they were assured about their pay after their terms of enlistment expired; but those men were not the class of men I would select; they were mostly foreigners. If I had the command of a vessel fitting for Arctic service, I would wish to have the selection of my own crew, and, as a rule, I would not select men-of-war's-men. I think a crew specially selected, and a detail of enlisted men from the Army to steady them, would, with their combined knowledge and the discipline of the soldiers, form a force that could not be improved upon for Arctic work.

In answer to a question the other day as to whether any soldier had ever been used on Arctic work, I did not state that it had been done; but some years ago Captain Black, in his expedition in British North America, had with him four artillerymen, of whose services he speaks in the highest way. They were Royal Artillerymen, taken from the fortifications about Montreal. He speaks of their steadiness, and of the confidence which the presence of those men gave as serving to steady the rest of the men, among whom an insubordinate temper had commenced to show itself. Their endurance and knowledge of the work in hand he also speaks highly of.

By Lieutenant-Commander McCALLA:

Q. Did your men suffer any from sea-sickness in the boat?—A. Yes, during heavy weather. Crossing Melville Bay I was for twenty hours in a gale of wind in a whale-boat, with a very heavy sea running, and three of my men were very sea-sick. That was the only time.

By Captain DAVIS:

Q. Would you expect to find rough seas and conditions that would make sea-sickness probable in Smith Sound and Kennedy Channel in the narrow water-leads?—A. I would not expect to find any heavy sea there.

The Recorder then read a memorandum, prepared at the request of the Board, from Lieut. N. R. Usher, U. S. Navy, forwarded through the Navy Department, containing a project for the relief of Lieutenant Greely and party. (Exhibit G.)

The President of the Board was directed to request the Secretary of War to have the daily record of the Board printed.

The room was then cleared, and an informal discussion took place in regard to the detail of two officers from the Signal Service and a small corps of enlisted men from the United States Army, and in regard to a preliminary report as to the advisability of offering a national reward for the discovery and rescue of Lieutenant Greely and his party.

The Board then adjourned to meet to-morrow, the 8th instant, at 11 a. m.

———

ROOM 88, NAVY DEPARTMENT BUILDING,
Washington, D. C., January 8, 1884.

The Board met pursuant to adjournment; all the members present.

A letter from Dr. Irving C. Rosse, acknowledging receipt of a communication from the Board, dated the 5th instant, was read. (Abs. Mis. Cor., No. 29.)

A communication from Sergeant Christian Madsen, Troop A, 5th U S. Cavalry, was received and read. (Abs. Mis. Cor., No. 30.)

A price-list from William Macnaughtan's Sons, of New York, N. Y., dealers in furs and skins, was then submitted, and the Recorder was directed to make inquiry of said firm as to their ability to furnish tanned reindeer skins sufficient for making one hundred suits of ordinary Arctic clothing.

Lieut. ROBERT M. BERRY, U. S. Navy, in response to an invitation, appeared before the Board, and was interrogated as follows:

By Captain DAVIS:

Question. Please state with what expeditions north of the Arctic Circle you have served.—Answer. I was on the "Tigress" when sent for the relief of the "Polaris" party in 1873, and I commanded the "Rodgers" when sent for the relief of the "Jeannètte."

Q. You have, no doubt, formed some opinion about the best method of proceeding with the organization and conduct of an expedition to relieve Lieutenant Greely. If you have, will you please give us the benefit of your judgment in regard to this matter?—A. I believe the best method of relieving him would be to get the most suitable ship possible, and she would require quite a number of alterations to fit her for this special service, such as the alteration of quarters, special arrangements for heating and for obviating dampness, in order to preserve the health of the crew. I also think that any vessel which could be found would require additional and very material strengthening. I think a ship of about four hundred tons would be the best size. In regard to the rudder and propeller, there would also have to be some alteration to put them in proper shape, so that they could be readily unshipped or the propeller well protected, one or the other, and the pipes connected with the machinery should be protected in such a way as to prevent their freezing. In addition to this, the vessel ought to be thoroughly fitted with boats, the best of which I think would be of the New Bedford whale-boat pattern, that being the most serviceable open boat that I know of, and there should also be a full outfit of sleds.

With regard to provisions and clothing, I do not think any better can be provided than those furnished the "Jeannette" Relief Expedition, with the exception that, if possible, I should supply more reindeer clothing in the place of sheepskin; the number of trading articles for that expedition would be in excess of requirements, because there would be but limited opportunity for trading with the natives of Greenland; but some articles would be supplied.

I think the ship ought to be under some thorough military organization, and I would advise no division of authority in any way. It seems to me also, that the commander should be some one who has had experience in the north, and I think the best men who could be found for the service would be those who could be selected from the Navy, men of good character, active, and between the ages of twenty-five and thirty-five. I do not know that I should make that an absolute requirement, but men of about that age should have the preference.

I believe a second ship for the expedition would be of great service. It would not necessarily need the same amount of strengthening and fitting that the first or principal ship would, because it would not be required to remain in that region during the winter. But she could take an additional supply of clothing, fuel, and such other articles as might be needed; and she could also be used in establishing depots of supplies, so that in case the first vessel—which is intended to push on as far as her commander might think practicable—should be crushed or disabled in any way, her crew would have means of retreat. These depots thus established, should consist of supplies for expeditions proceeding northward for Lieutenant Greely's relief, in case the main part of the expedition—as I should call the first ship—failed to reach him.

In regard to the time of starting, I would vary it somewhat with the season. Some seasons there are more open than others. But the ship should reach Cape York as early as possible after the ice opens, because in case Lieutenant Greely retreats in the spring and should reach as far south as that he would probably need provisions, and it might also prevent his taking the hazardous trip in open boats across Melville Bay. The best time, however, for reaching the highest point possible would be very much later, and I presume that the latter part of August or the first of September would be the best time to make the attempt to get north with the ship. After the ship had gone into winter quarters, as she would have to do some time in September, (of which her commanding officer would be the best judge) then fit out the boat expeditions and in the autumn proceed as far north as you can, placing depots of stores along in the intervals, leaving them well protected from the bears, wolves or other animals that might prey upon them, and also marking them as prominently as possible with flags and cairns. These stores, of course, might be of great assistance to Lieutenant Greely in case he should reach them. Directly after going into winter quarters it might be of advantage to attempt an expedition with boats. They might, if they did nothing else, much more readily carry a large quantity of provisions and stores for depots than could be done with sleds. Of course, the spring is the best time for sledging north, and if there was nothing heard from Lieutenant Greely or his party in the fall, that would be the most favorable time for making an effort with sleds. With regard to sleds, I should have them provided both for hauling by men and by dogs. If you can get a road which is at all smooth you can travel much more rapidly with dogs than you can with men. On the other hand, if the ice should be particularly rough, then you would get along better with men. But both should be there for use. The best style of dog-sleds I believe to be such as the Chukches use; they make them from drift-wood, from birch principally, and they are held together entirely by lashings. They might also serve for hauling by men, but it would be well to have other sledges similar to the McClintock pattern.

I should recommend in addition to the boats that go with the ship, some species of balsa, to be determined upon after experiment. They would be very useful at any time in carrying large quantities of provisions, and would not be so liable to swamp or capsize as the boats, because they could be made water-tight and covered over.

I believe also in having some natives along, as they are far more expert dog drivers and hunters in those regions than white people, and have always been very efficient in taking game. They know the habits of game and will catch it when white men cannot.

Q. Where do you think the best vessel for this purpose could be obtained?—A. I have not considered that matter. The "Rodgers" was a vessel well adapted to Arctic work. She was built in Maine, and was of the modern style of whaling vessel. Her steam power was hardly sufficient, however. Her speed, under the most favorable circumstances, was about six and one-half knots, and in a head wind reduced very rapidly, because of her heavy spars. I do not know of any vessel in the east adapted to the purpose.

In regard to the balsa, the most I have seen appear to me to be too heavy. I think a lighter balsa could be made by using in its construction some other material than wood; light steel, or even tin might be used inside. I would have an open space in them which might be closed water-tight—a place to store provisions. I think the shell of the balsa less likely to be cut by thin ice than a boat.

Q. For the transportation of fifteen persons with fifteen day's supplies, what would be the weight of such a balsa?—A. I could not say.

Q. How does the clothing used in Greenland by the natives compare with that used in Siberia, as to warmth and suitability for a cold climate?—A. That which I saw in Siberia made by the Chukches was far superior, although the clothing we obtained at Saint Michaels was nearly on a par with that which you obtain in Greenland. They seem to select better skins in Siberia, fall skins, and they are tanned and made very pliable and durable. Skins taken later may be heavier, but are not as durable; the hair breaks. They use the fall skins for the *parki*, as they call it, and the trousers; and for boots and gloves they use the leg-skins of the reindeer. The soles of the boots are made of large seal-skin, *ookjook*, or else young walrus skin; they use other boots, especially in sleeping, the legs made in the same way, and the soles of bear-skin, with the hair left underneath. They give great warmth made in that way. The socks are made of fawn-skin.

Q. Of what garments did the Siberian suit consist?—A. Of a cap, sometimes, and generally a hood, which comes over the head, projecting somewhat, with straps passing around the shoulders, also a roundabout, or jacket, fitting closely around the neck and coming down to the middle of the thigh, with a belt around the waist. They are very large and loose so that the wearer can draw his arm inside and warm his hands. The trousers come to the middle of the waist and are drawn tight by cords there and at the ankles. They generally wear the shoes inside the trousers with the trousers tied around outside over the top of them, which excludes the snow completely. In some cases they let the trousers come down and the boots come up below the knee and are tied around the calf of the leg. But in either case the outer covering must be made snug and close; otherwise the fine snow works its way in. I think the trousers coming outside and tied around the top the better plan.

Q. Then the suit consisted of a pair of socks, boots, trousers, coat, and cap or hood?—A. Yes, sir; and then the under-coat, with the hair worn next the skin, drawers the same, and an outer coat with the hair outside. The outer coat is something like a jumper.

Q. If men are obliged to pull sledges, would they find that clothing adapted to the work?—A. More so than any other I know of, because nothing gives the same amount of warmth for its weight. The reindeer-skin has the advantage of having straight hair, and the natives carry with them a light bone stick made of a piece of horn flattened out, which they call a "beater," and, whenever the fur gets full of snow, they take the stick and hammer the snow off each other, or frequently pull off the outer coat and hammer it with the stick themselves, and the snow falls out. That is not the case with sheepskin, as we found the weight of our sleeping-bags increased rapidly because we could not beat the snow out. They also wear under the chin a deer-skin flap which projects and falls over, and around the head there is a light fur fringe of either dog or fox skin, which adds materially to the warmth of the face and protects it to a certain extent by retaining for a time the warm breath as it passes from the mouth. I know of no way in which you can protect the nose and cheeks except by having something of that kind projecting in that way. If you place anything over your nose and cheeks and breathe through it, the ice and frost form upon it and eventually the covering becomes a mass of ice throughout. Their gloves are also made of reindeer-skin, which I prefer to the buffalo gloves furnished the "Jeannette" expedition; they are more pliable and soft and collect less ice on the inside.

Q. Are they gloves or mitts?—A. They are mitts; finger-gloves would be impracticable. These mitts are made with a slit at the wrist inside, enabling the wearer to withdraw his hand, leaving the mitt still attached to the wrist, the hand bare and free.

Q. In the organization of such a corps, would you give preference to Americans?—A. To Americans, or any of the north country people living in our country, would be well suited for the purpose.

Q. I believe you had no experience with sleds on the Greenland coast?—A. No, sir.

Q. Did the "Rodgers" develop any defects of a character that could be guarded against in the fitting of vessels for similar service?— A. I think not, except with regard to her heating apparatus which might be improved, and her quarters. But her outfit of food, provisions, &c., seemed to me well adapted to the wants of the party.

Q. For a vessel of four hundred tons, what number of persons do you think should compose the crew—officers and men?—A. Not to exceed thirty-five.

Q. Had you any scurvy aboard the "Rodgers"?—A. Not while I was with her. After I left, in the crew while quartered at Saint Lawrence Bay, I believe there were some slight touches of scurvy, while they were living in villages.

Q. During your experience, have you had to travel over any very rough and hummocky ice?—Yes, in some places where we were forced from the beach by abrupt cliffs, for short distances.

Q. In rough, hummocky ice, dogs are not effective?—A. I think not. But I think from what I have read in Kane's account, and in other books of Arctic travel, the ice-foot could be travelled upon in Smith Sound, and in that region.

Q. But I understand that you would not expect to make any very effective use of sleds in the autumn, moving up from Smith Sound?— A. I should say, in a case of that kind, do all you can, but I should not expect them to gain a very great distance. The autumn is the season of gales and snow, the days are growing shorter, and other circumstances are against travelling; the drift is also very much greater. Sometimes in the autumn we would find the drifting snow so great for several days that we were unable to move at all; we could not see our way. In the spring there is much better weather, and the winds are not as severe.

Q. Do you think a steam-launch would be of very much use in addition to the equipment of your vessel?—A. I do not.

By Captain GREER:

Q. Would you advise the employment of an ice-master?—A. I would if the commanding officer is unacquainted with the ice; otherwise I would not, and I think, as a rule, he would not be of material service any way.

Q. How many reindeer-skins would be required for the clothing of an average-sized man?—A. Two skins will make it, independent of the foot-gear. Probably a large sized suit would require three.

Q. In ordinary ice travelling, how many men would be required to manage a sledge with ten dogs?—A. If it was a light sled I should think about six men. The sledges ought not to be made too heavy, especially for rough ice. I think it would be better to increase the number of sledges so as to avoid heavy loads. I do not think a sled should weigh over 1,200 or 1,500 pounds, loaded. With these light weights the sleds are less liable to be broken, because the men can guide them better.

By General HAZEN:

Q. Was the clothing for the "Rodgers" made from special patterns for that service, or was it adopted from patterns used before?—A. From patterns used before. We took up a full supply of sheepskin clothing made here, because we did not know whether we could get reindeer clothing; and for the reindeer clothing we took the same pattern that the natives used, which I do not think could be improved upon.

By Captain DAVIS:

Q. What would be the proper load, per dog, in Siberian sledge work?—A. In heavy work, where you did not travel too far, a dog would haul from fifty to seventy pounds, depending on the distance travelled. If you desired to make forty or fifty miles a day, which could be done over smooth ice, an average-sized dog should not haul over twenty-five pounds. A dog can haul sixty or seventy pounds over smooth ice, travelling slowly.

Q. How does the Siberian compare with the Greenland dog?—A. There are several varieties in Siberia, one variety fully equal to the Greenland dog. I think they will compare favorably with those you get in Greenland. While on the "Tigress," I saw some dogs at Littleton Island much finer than any of those we had gotten in Greenland. First-quality Siberian dogs are about the same as those we found up there; the others were inferior.

Q. In the reports of English officers who went on sledging expeditions in the Franklin search, they frequently speak of loads one hundred pounds per dog, and two hundred pounds per man?—A. Well, a dog might haul that, but he would go at a very slow pace. Those we had ranged from fifty to seventy-five pounds, and I should think one of them might very readily haul his weight and make a fair trip.

Q. In sledging in Greenland, would you harness your team after the Siberian or Esquimaux method?—A. I think I should adopt the Siberian method, and put them in pairs, with one leader.

After a short recess, the Board resumed its session.

Lieut. JOHN W. DANENHOWER, U. S. Navy, appeared in response to the invitation of the Board, and was examined as follows:

By Captain DAVIS:

Question. Please state in what Arctic expedition you have served?—Answer. With the "Jeannette" Arctic Expedition, as navigator. I joined the ship in the spring of 1878, and since that time have devoted myself to the subject of Arctic explorations.

Q. Have you formed an opinion as to the best method of relieving Lieutenant Greely and party?—A. I have given that matter considerable thought and attention. In my opinion such an expedition should be fitted out to reach Lady Franklin Bay as an objective point, but there is every probability that Lieutenant Greely will be found at Cape York or Littleton Island, or perhaps on the west side of the channel at Cape Sabine. ·I think two vessels should be procured as soon as possible, vessels of three hundred tons, and I think they could be procured at Baltimore or Boston. For example, the fruiters which go to the Mediterranean are about that size, and the West India traders and coffee traders. They should be taken to a navy-yard and strengthened. They should be ceiled with pine planking about four inches in thickness, and the transverse strength should be given by bulkheads. They should be engined and fitted with two-bladed screws, and shifting rudders. They should also have a wrought-iron casing to cover the stem and strips going up, and should be given a sheathing of American elm. In my opinion the best rig would be that of an hermaphrodite brig, and fitted with good sail power so as to be able to work under sail with the screw triced up. They should have a complement of twenty-eight, or not exceeding thirty men, the party under the command of two naval officers, and be provisioned for at least eighteen months.

In addition to the two vessels just mentioned, there should be a supply or store ship sent as high as Upernavik, not to go beyond there, to carry extra coal and provisions for this party. The relief vessels should not leave New York or Saint John's too heavily laden; they should be in good trim, and the supply ship should carry the extra stores necessary to complete the equipment of the others for eighteen months. After leaving the northernmost station, Upernavik for example, the general plan of operations should be to reach Cape York as soon as the season will permit, in the early part of June if possible, and then both ships should go to Littleton Island, the senior officer should cross over to Cape Sabine, and the second in command should remain at Littleton Island. The ships should be prepared to withstand heavy nips, but not to force the ice of Smith Sound by ramming, and I think that after the preparation already stated, they would be in a stronger condition than the "Alert" and "Discovery" were when the English expedition went up in 1875–6. As to forcing the ice in Smith Sound by ramming, it is an impossibility for any ship to do it.

The ship on the west side of the channel under the commander-in-chief, should be handled with skill and judgment and work her way north in a similar manner to the "Alert" and "Discovery." The ship on the east side should remain at Littleton Island and form a permanent base to fall back upon in case the first was crushed. But the second on reaching Littleton Island should send out a sledge party up the eastern side (it is a mooted question which would be the most open at this season, the eastern or the western side), consisting of a lieutenant, an assistant surgeon, and eight seamen. This party should have, in my opinion, two McClintock sledges with two thirteen feet dorys, one mounted on each sledge. They can carry all their provisions and stores in those two boats. From studying the subject I conclude that the difficulties in travelling there are very similar to those encountered by us in our journey over the ice, and I think the best organization for a sledge party would be what I have mentioned, and the sledges should be handled by man power; dogs are not as effective. In case they come to any open water, for example leads or any open bays, they can launch both boats and cross. This will also give them the advantage of boat capacity for Lieutenant Greely's party when found.

While this is being carried out, of course the west ship should be working up as the English expedition did, and if they are delayed and can not proceed they should throw out a sledge party on the west coast to work along the ice-foot, over the ice and through the water as we did. In preparing these sledge expeditions we have to consider the succor that is to be given Lieutenant Greely when we meet him, and also our ability to bring him back with us. These two thirteen feet dorys would be sufficient to transport a large party. They may have to make two fleets, but they are much better than a whale-boat. The lightest whale-boat obtainable is clinker-built, weighing about 1,500 pounds, including outfit. The two dorys will weigh not much more than half that. The dory is the best boat used on the American coast. It is used by fishermen who run out in heavy gales of wind, and has more capacity for its size and general dimension than any other form of boat, and is considered the safest.

That is the general scheme which I have in mind; the vessel on the west side taking every risk that the judgment of the commander thinks proper, to reach Lady Franklin Bay, in the mean time the coast on both sides will have been searched. This vessel should carry a signal gun. Night signals are not necessary, because it is daylight all the time there at that season.

Another thing to be considered is the weather. The principal part of the work will take place in July and August, when it is thawing. A thin coat of young ice might form during the night, but that is not very likely until after the middle of August. The men should be clad expressely for that summer work, and I think the best kind of clothing for the boat and sledge work is what is called the "Hard-times" suit used out west, a light canvas suit, lined with blanket stuff. Each man should be provided with a heavy suit of underclothing, red flannel, with a fur waistcoat. There is generally a great deal of rain and misty weather there, and fur is of no use outside. When wet, hair comes out at once, and it is soft and flabby. When I came over the ice I used a fur waistcoat, with a canvas coat over it, and I found I had the best rig of anybody in the party; it was so considered. Gloves at that season are not specially important; men can work bare-handed.

Special attention should be given to the outfit of the sledge party in the way of provisions, and as it is pretty wet work, the provisions should be carried in water-proof bags or carefully prepared tin canisters. The advantage of the method I have suggested is, that the provisions need not be shifted; they can he stowed in the boats, and five men could handle one boat if the difficulties are not great. If they come to a rough place, ten men would not be enough to move a whale-boat and provisions, but ten men could move a dory, mounted as I have stated, with ease.

There should be a regular system of signals between the parties in case they meet, and in every permanent camping place on the ice-foot or shore, there should be a memorandum left by the officers in charge. The two officers should be able-bodied and capable of working with the men. I think the men should be seamen, because it is principally boat-work, and seamen are handier at such work than anybody else. I know frequent expeditions have been made overland with western men who were very hardy and enduring, and I would not say anything which would disparage them; but still I think for that particular kind of work seamen are the best. If the party were commanded by a lieutenant in the Army, and all the men were seamen, good results could be expected.

In case the first ship is unable to reach Lady Franklin Bay, or unable to find Lieutenant Greely's party, they should come back to Littleton Island, and that ship should remain there another winter, and the second ship return and report. But there is every reason to suppose that the party will be found during that summer. The experience of Doctor Kane, Doctor Hayes, and the Polaris people shows that effective sledging and searching cannot be done in the autumn or spring; summer is the only time, and July and August the only two months.

The object of the supply ship is to wait until they get news, or until the party is found and rescued, when proper quarters can be afforded, nursing and care. On the little ships they would not be able to quarter them, because they would be crowded. The easternmost sledge party would, in all probability, be able to reach Lady Franklin Bay in July or August; but the easternmost ship should not be risked beyond Littleton Island; it should be put in quarters in a safe harbor, and if there is no safe place, she should go over where Doctor Kane wintered, on the adjoining eastern coast; she will find a safe harbor there.

I also believe in offering a very large reward to the Dundee whalemen, in case they are in the "north water," as it is called, for picking up the party, or bringing news of them. I would also suggest that these two small vessels, if they return safely, could be used effectively as naval vessels in the inland waters of Alaska and other places, and therefore the money spent would not be lost. But if we employ two sealers, or steam whalers from Dundee, that would be a loss, pecuniarily, to the Government.

The special articles needed by the sledging party, are Liebig's extract, tea, pemmican, and hard bread. A person can get along on that diet for sixty days without any trouble. And as they are going to do special work in a limited time, it might be well to give them stimulants, although for continued Artic work I do not believe in the use of alcoholic liquors. But where the most work is to be done in the least time, I believe in stimulants.

The dorys I speak of I have examined recently at Provincetown; that is the best place to obtain them.

I would have *picked* men for this work, selected from volunteers in the Navy, and, if they can be obtained, whalemen or Cape Cod fishermen. They are excellent men for the purpose. I believe they should be Americans. Their avoirdupois should not be specially considered, but I think vigorous men of medium size are better for the work than large men.

The officer in command of the expedition should be the man to do the work on the west side and take the risks. The second in command is simply to back him in case of accident. I believe also in taking natives from Upernavik in order to be able to talk with the Etah Indians and gain intelligence from them; that the fur clothing for the expedition for one winter should be made in New York, and that no dogs should be taken, because they will not prove effective in that work.

Q. What length of time do you think would be required to fit those vessels for Arctic service in the manner you describe?—A. I think if the vessels were selected and at the New York, or any other navy yard, by the first of March, they would be ready by the first of May.

Q. What speed are those vessels able to attain under ordinary conditions?—A. They make under sail 10 to 12 knots, and under good circumstances, should make under steam alone, in smooth water, about 9

7

knots. They should be fitted with the best of everything, engines and all, and should be able to make 9 knots, which is sufficient.

Q. Did not the ships of the English expedition do a great deal of ramming?—A. I think not; ships cannot stand it. I believe the capability of a ship to ram ice is exaggerated. I have seen the "Jeannette" try it, and her masts would shake like whip-stocks every time, and she accomplished nothing. If a ship puts her bows between two large fields of ice and goes ahead slowly, she can accomplish something, if there is no wind. But as to going headlong against the ice with a ship, I do not believe it can be done effectively.

Q. Is not the ice in Smith Sound in the summer in softer condition than the ice you saw north of Siberia?—A. That probably comes from the ramming and jamming together of the ice. That posh ice is the worst kind to work in. It banks up all around and you are hemmed in fast before you are hardly aware of it.

Q. Are not the Dundee vessels obliged to attack the ice and force their way in and out of the inlets and bays?—A. Yes, they attack ice of moderate thickness about 4 to 6 inches, but I do not believe they ever attempt to force such ice as is encountered in Smith Sound, sea ice, with an average winter growth of 6 to 10 feet. It thaws in the latter part of June and July to a thickness of 5 or 6 feet.

Q. Would any explosive, such as gun-cotton, be useful in relieving the ship from pressure, or making docks?—A. Docks have been effectively used by the whale ships in the ice-foot, or in young ice. If it is not too heavy they might be able to blow up part of it and dock the vessel temporarily.

Q. What progress could be made by five men, hauling their own provisions on a sledge and dory equipped as you have described, in the region over which you travelled?—A. With two boats fitted in that way, in the worst part of our travelling, we could have made at least 5 miles a day, although there was one occasion where we only made 1,000 yards after working 12 hours. But our boats and outfit were much heavier than those I propose.

Q. What time do you think it would take two sledges thus equipped, under similar conditions to those you encountered in retreating with the crew of the "Jeannette," to make the distance between Cape Sabine and Discovery Harbor?—A. The distance is, perhaps, 200 miles. I should say a sledge party in the month of July ought to average 15 miles a day, if not loaded down too much. The maximum weight given for a man to drag in the English service was 240 pounds; that was the limit. Two hundred pounds is much preferable. This party would not have much more than 200 pounds to haul with that outfit.

Q. You think the sledge party on the east side would be the one most likely to reach its destination?—A. I know the "Polaris" party had no difficulty in reaching a high latitude on that side. If the west side is closed the east is more apt to be open, and *vice versa*. The Polaris had no difficulty in reaching Thank God Harbor at that season.

Q. About what is the weight of this dory?—A. A 13-foot dory would weigh about 500 pounds.

Q. And carry how many persons?—A. It will carry more, for the general dimensions, than any other boat. Very heavy loads of fish are put in them. They ride out gales on the banks of Newfoundland. One great advantage is, that in a rough sea they can use a drag.

Q. Would you propose offering any rewards to the crew of the vessel for faithful service and success?—A. Yes, increased pay. I do not think $25 a month, which was the pay on our expedition, was adequate to the service performed.

Q. Do you think steam cutters could be made effective in such an expedition ?—A. I do not, because they cannot be hauled out on the ice by the number of men carried, and you cannot conveniently carry fuel. The fuel of a sledge party should be alcohol, and I would suggest methylated alcohol, or alcohol with some acid in it, rendering it unpalatable to those who wished to drink it. For camp stoves alcohol is the best fuel. A pint will do the cooking at each meal for a party of eight men. Each party of ten men should have a stove.

Q. Do you regard reindeer as better than seal-skin clothing ?—A. For the winter, yes; but it would not be needed until September.

Q. Would you carry material with which to build shelters on shore ?—A. Yes, and if it was decided to establish a depot of provisions on the east shore, I would provide a guard also of four men to protect them from wandering natives. An important thing respecting the boats is to have them painted black, and the tents and boat-sails should be a tan-color, so as to make them conspicuous objects, not only for the party you are seeking, but for your own men. To protect the eyes, snow goggles of glass should be worn, and the party should work during the p. m. hours when the sun is lowest. It is misty or cloudy generally at about midnight, and the men can get along without wearing goggles.

Q. Did you use wire-gauze goggles?—A. Yes; we covered the frames with red flannel or velvet.

Q. You think dogs would be no addition to an equipment ?—A. I am convinced they would not, but rather a disadvantage. Our dogs were of no use to us. If we had not taken the dogs and the food they consumed, it would have been better for us.

Chief Engineer GEORGE W. MELVILLE, of the United States Navy, appeared, in response to the invitation of the Board, and was interrogated as follows:

By Captain DAVIS:

Question. In what Arctic expeditions have you seen service ?—Answer. I was in the "Tigress" with Captain Greer and in the Jeannette expedition.

Q. You have formed doubtless some general ideas in regard to the relief of Lieutenant Greely at Lady Franklin Bay. We would like to hear what you have to say in regard to that.—A. When I received orders to appear before your Board I took the liberty of writing out some notes, as I thought I could probably remember my ideas better in that way. If the Board has no objection I will read these notes as they are, and discuss them as we go along.

My general plan is for two vessels; one steamer of 400 tons, properly fitted with six whale-boats and two years' supplies for forty officers and men; one schooner, to carry three officers and ten men, to go as far as Upernavik as store and supplementary ship, with two whale-boats and one dingy; the schooner to carry 300 tons of coal and six months' supplies for thirteen men. As Upernavik is easily accessible in the spring, the schooner is to be there as early as possible and await the arrival of the steamer; one of our Coast Survey schooners will answer the purpose. Upon the arrival of the steamer at Upernavik, to fill up with coal from the schooner, and take from her one whale-boat, officer and crew, with sixty days' rations of pemmican, bread, alcohol, and tea; the steamer to stop at Tessuissak to make inquiry for Greely and to leave twenty days' rations for the boat's crew. When the steamer arrives at Cape York, launch the first search-boat and crew, with forty days' provisions, and work back to Tessuissak, take a rest, pick up his twenty days' supplies, and on to Upernavik, join his vessel, and await the return of the steamer, the steamer to work her way as early as possible to Littleton Island, land two whale-boats and ninety days' provisions for the whole ship's company, land one officer and one boat's crew to guard the stores and await the return of the steamer, both whale-boats being fully equipped. The steamer then to continue cautiously north toward Lady Franklin Bay, having two expeditionary whale-boats and sledges, fully equipped with sixty days' supplies, in readiness to proceed to the northward from the ship and reach Fort Conger, at Lady Franklin Bay; the steamer to follow up carefully, taking advantage of open water as offered. In case accident now happens to the ship let the crew take to the two remaining whale-boats and retreat on Littleton Island, carrying with them what stores they can. The expeditionary boats and sledges are to go to Fort Conger and find definite information of Greely before returning, retreating on Littleton Island, where they know there is a depot of supplies, steamer or no steamer *en route*. The expeditionary boats and sledges to start north from the first ice-barrier that prevents the advance of the ship, provided it is not to the southward of Cape York. Upon the return of the expeditionary boats, if the steamer is safe, the whole party to embark with their stores. If Greely has gone south to Littleton Island continue the search from there south.

Cairns and records left by Greely should tell of their movements. Returned to Cape York, one of two courses lie open for Greely from Cape York, viz, to make the passage to Tessuissak or to the Danish settlements, or to look out for a whale-ship, as Buddington did in his retreat from the "Polaris." If no information of Greely has been found up to this point, detach two boats with crews to research Melville Bay to Tessuissak, the ship to skirt the eastern edge of the western pack as it drifts to the southward, and keep a lookout for the whalers. By this means a complete search can be made with perfect safety in one season. The details of ship, crew, boats, provisions, expeditionary provisions, sledges, clothing, equipment, arms, &c., will be discussed under appropriate heads.

Q. How many men would you have left in the ship after you had made all your detachments of boats' crews?—A. I propose to start with ten officers and thirty men, making forty people. The schooner at Upernavik to transfer one boat with officers and equipment of sixty days' provisions to the steamer, the latter to go north and touch at Tessuissak to make inquiries and land twenty of the sixty days' supplies at that point. Then transport our supplementary boat, which would work its way back to the schooner. We have thirty men and ten officers remaining on board the ship. If the ice-barrier at Cape York prevents the steamer from going north at this season, start the two expeditionary whale-boats and sledges. The probabilities are we will be able to work to the northward, with good sledging beyond Cape York. We will then carry our whole ship's company of ten officers and thirty men as far as Littleton Island. Land ninety days' supplies for all hands, the whole ship's company of forty men; detach one officer with a short boat's crew, say six men, and two boats fully equipped with tents, &c., to stay there. That officer to stay and amuse himself and gather provisions as well as he can during the absence of the steamer. The steamer proceeds then with nine officers and twenty four men, and goes as far north of Littleton Island, towards Fort Conger, as she can with safety, keeping the two expeditionary boats and sledges, with two officers and their crews, in readiness. That will detail two officers and seven men, at least, for each boat's crew. In the month of June it is doubtful if seven men can haul a whale-boat without going twice over the track, but that we can discuss afterwards. That will leave seven officers aboard the ship and ten men. Now, we have ten men with seven officers remaining in the ship, the medical officer, the engineer, and the paymaster to be in charge of all the stores and supplies.

Q. Would that be enough to work the ship?—A. I think so. They would have to come down to hard work. I think they would have less labor than the men who were sledging. The steamer to proceed with the expeditionary parties in readiness to launch out. If the steamer can go all the way to Fort Conger, of course no expeditionary sledges and boats are started. But when they come to the point where they can go no farther, start the boats and sledges, with sixty days' provisions, to go through to Fort Conger; that is their duty, it makes no difference to them what becomes of the steamer.

By Captain GREER:

Q. Would you leave any shelter for the party at Littleton Island?— A. Yes, sir; land tents with them. [Reading.] The ship to be of wood, cased with iron for forty feet abaft the stem. No keel to project below doubling, except false keel. The doubling to commence at the keel, 12 inches thick or depth of present keel, and to terminate at spar deck 6 inches thick. A light deck to cover the ship in, fore and aft, to be as light as possible and give sufficient strength to work ship from it, made in form of "turtle-back" frames, the deck beams of this structure to be of "T" iron. This will billet every man above deck and give large stowage for coal and stores below. The wood ends of the doublings should terminate well out to the end of the stem piece and should entirely encase the fore-foot, which in turn should be clamped with iron. The inside of the light deck or house should be lined with felt and covered with light tongued-and-grooved three-quarter inch pine. The fore-peak should be built in solid, and three water-tight bulk-heads should be fitted water-tight against the inner skin and frames. to prevent the water passing by the frames where the bulk-heads are, and the timbering spaces should be filled in with half-stuff from the floor to spar-deck. This can be done by pouring it in from above in wake of the bulk-heads. These were weak points in the "Polaris" and "Jeannette." The fore-foot of both carried away, and the keel was pushed right out of the "Jeannette." All water-tight bulk-heads leak by the frames in wooden ships. Rig, brigantine or schooner, compound engines, and boilers to be in thorough repair, and new boilers if necessary. A steam-pump in each compartment, with steam supplied from main boilers, an auxiliary boiler and hoisting engine on deck, rigged to hoist cargo, work main-deck pumps or hand-pumps, a pair being placed in each compartment, this being an economical arrangement for long and serious leaks and pumping. This boiler to heat apartments and radiators to condense the drinking water for ship's use. The propeller to be hoisting, if possible, and to be of Mahaffie-steel; have one spare propeller. The rudder to ship outside of the deadwood, like a Galliott, to be as small as possible to do its work, and to turn on a continuous bulb beam or gudgeon, so as to be readily raised or lowered and to be in action at any draught of water from a foot all the way down to its seat. Rudder and propeller to be raised by sheaves in main-boom. Cabin and ward room to contain ten apartments, occupying 35 feet of after part of ship, and a berth

for each man of the crew forward, with an air space 3 feet wide sur-
rounding the men's apartment, their berths opening on a common passage in the center. All officers to mess together to economize space;
all men require the same amount of healthful breathing space. There
should be steam pipes throughout the ship for extinguishing fire.

Q. Where could such a ship be obtained?—A. The "Tigress," a Newfoundland sealer, was a much better ship than the "Jeannette." Fitted
and stored as I describe, her draught would be about 12 feet if she is
of 400 tons burthen. She should go not less than 6 knots an hour.
I would not have a ship too fast for ice work, because if you are not
careful you will stave in her bows and knock her all to pieces. If the
boiler and engines were in a ship I would not alter them to suit this design. All this other work, excepting the moving of the engine, could
be done any time.

Q. How much battering and ramming would such a ship as that be
able to endure. I mean what effective work?—A. If you meet ice 8
inches thick and the floe extends half a mile, put that ship at full tilt,
say 7 miles an hour, and strike all standing; the blow would not hurt her.
Back her off and try two or three times, and you *might* split that floe,
and perhaps not, but the chances are you would split it, without endan-
gering the ship much. In regard to plating the ship's bows—the "Jeannette" was plated with flat-iron bars, 4 inches wide and three-quarters
of an inch thick. That was not good. They were placed apart probably two or three inches and the ice cut through so that the planking
was cut more than half way. The iron plates should come close together.

By Lieutenant-Commander McCALLA:

Q. What period elapsed from the time you entered the ice-pack in the
"Jeannette" until you were fairly beset?—A. About four days.

Q. Did you have any scurvy at all during that expedition?—A. There
was one case that most of us supposed was scurvy—Alexis, the Indian;
that is, he had all the symptoms of it and the doctor applied the remedies
he would in case of scurvy. Doctor Ambler said it was not scurvy, but
it seemed to be a well defined case.

Q. You used distilled water, I believe?—A. Yes, sir; altogether.

Q. Was there any daily distribution of stimulants?—A. No, sir. We
had lime-juice daily. [Resuming his statement.] Tents, if used, should
be of blue "dungaree," double at the bottom and for 18 inches up, with
a floor space of 6 by 10 feet to accommodate seven persons. The peak
of the tent and bags that receive the tent-poles to be well re-enforced.
The tent to be set with four poles, but to prevent racking by too great
a strain, guy ropes and a ridge-pole should be used. The sleeping-bags
should be made of deer-skin with the fur turned in. There should be an
old buck-skin for the bottom of the bag next the ice, and a light fawn-
skin for the top. Each man should be measured for his bag so that it
will fit. In form it should be two frustums of cones, joined at the
shoulders with elliptic ends at head and foot, about 8 by 12 inches
in diameter of axes. It should be slit across at the shoulder, with
a flap to cover the face, or slit from the face far enough down to get
in, and then fastened with toggles. A good bag should not exceed
in weight thirteen pounds. The cooking stove should be made of light
galvanized iron. Those designed for the Jeannette were of simple form
and efficient, but were too large and heavy. The kettle of light planished
copper, should hold about twelve pints, with upper dish or pan to hold
half that quantity. The drinking cups should be of light planished cop-

per, tinned inside, frustums of cones, so as to fit within each other without
beads or wires and to hold an exact pint, to be used as a measure.   The
bottom of the kettle should be concave so as to hold the heat.   An apron
within the body of the stove to make the heat hug the kettle.   A circular wick of asbestos with argand burner should be fitted, and proper
attention paid to ventilation of lamp, to insure perfect combustion.
Light copper pans, tinned inside, not to exceed a quart capacity, and to
set inside each other, to be used as mess-pans.

The cooking gear of the "Jeanuette" party was larger and heavier
than necessary.   Tea, sugar, and salt should be carried in small bags,
and all the cooking gear should stow inside of the fire pot and kettle,
the lid to fasten down with hooks, the whole carried by a bail.   There
should be one large spoon for each man in the mess.   No mess-box
is necessary.   Luxuries add to weight.   All the small bags should
be stowed inside of one large rubber bag 12 inches in diameter by
30 inches long, the top to lace in as near water-tight as possible to
keep the clothing dry.   One pair of deer-skin stockings should be
stowed in each sleeping-bag, to put on when turning in to keep the feet
warm.   A rubber blanket to cover the floor of the tent to keep the bags
dry should be supplied each boat, with eyelets around the edge, to pass
a lacing so as to keep the sleeping-bags dry while in the boat.   The
boat-box should be supplied with saw, hammer, nails, snow knives, &c.
Boats should have small dry-boat compasses, sextant, and tables, two
breakers for water and alcohol to each boat.   Pocket chronometer for
each boat and a couple of watches, and a number of small pieces of
cedar plank for patching the boat.   Each boat, in addition to painter
and drag rope, to have 25 fathoms of light strong flax line, an iron
ring, and canvas to make a parachute for a drag about 8 feet area
and have a buoy attached to float it.   A stone can be used for an anchor.
A mast coat to peak the boat-cover at the mast and bows of boat.

Clothing for travelling in summer time: Red flannel undershirt and
drawers; first class woolen socks, to come above the knees; heavy
cloth trousers, either fitting tight from knee down, or knee-breeches,
so that the moccasin leg will come over it; the breeches should not be
fly-fronts; they should button up squarely to keep out the cold, and
should be kept up by a waist-belt not too wide; sheath-knife; moccasins should be oiled-tanned without hair—what is known as water
boots; one canvas and six flannel or cloth inner soles, stitched down
the center for convenience in drying, are necessary to keep feet away
from the ice.   One pair blanket foot-nips; hay is sometimes used, but
not always obtainable.   A pair of rubber sandals with toe and heel
guards and strap across the instep will save the soles of moccasins in
summer travel.   The sandals should have a large diamond mesh or
rough surface much after the manner of rubber door mats.   A blue
flannel overshirt, with neck handkerchief.   A fur cap, with ear-laps and
large visor to protect face and eyes.   A short, close-fitting cloth and
lined *llammy*, coming to the hips, with two breast pockets and mittens,
complete the costume.   A fur jacket and knee trousers for camping at night are a good thing to prevent taking cold; a sleeping bag,
winter or summer; a tent in winter, but it may be dispensed with in
summer, using boat cover and sail for shelter.   In a small rubber bag
carry one pair of socks, one pair of foot-nips, one undershirt, one pair
of drawers, patches and sewing material.   One jacket and trousers are
to be carried in the boat for general service.

By Lieutenant Commander McCalla:

Q. On the retreat from the "Jeannette" could you have done without tents?—A. Yes, sir; but we could not have been comfortable without them. In the day-time they shaded our eyes from the sun. We had white tents and the glare on the eyes was painful. The men would turn in with no trouble about their eyes, but looking at the top of the tent their eyes would become inflamed.

Q. What kind of guard for the eyes did you find most useful?—A. Goggles made of horse-hair, plaited in about one-sixteenth inch meshes. [Resuming his statement.] As detached parties are contemplated, a greater number of officers and crew are required, say ten officers, i. e., commanding officer, five lieutenants, surgeon, paymaster, engineer, and ice pilot. Mechanics, such as carpenters, boat-builders, smiths, and machinists should be numerous among the crew.

Boats should be all American whale-boats, New London or New Bedford make, 26 feet long—the two expeditionary boats being lighter—all fitted with bevel side pieces, fastened to sides of keel so as to give bearing to the runner, 6 inches wide, and shod with one-eighth inch iron, two bilge keels or short runners fitted on the bilges to keep the boat upright in transporting it without the sledge, and to rest the boat on when set on the sledge for transportation. Smooth built, as they are easily repaired if stove in. Sockets and stanchions fitted to inside of rail, and cover fitted to make high weather cloths or half-decked boat. Lug-sail with boom, so as to be able to shore it out to prevent danger from jibing. In addition to usual equipment each boat should have two light ice-axes and picks combined, and two ice-chisels on light poles. The boats should be painted black and sails dyed black.

Provisions: In addition to the usual canned provisions, many of which are poisonous and unpleasant to the taste, there should be fresh roast meats and poultry of all kinds roasted in the usual manner and closely packed in half or quarter casks that had been previously charred within, and filled up with hot, sweet lard. This would keep the meat sweet and leave the lard for cooking purposes. Fresh potatoes, fried and put down in the same manner; potatoes boiled with the jackets on, under-done, and covered with fluid gelatine would keep; dessicated potatoes are worthless. They were not served in either Arctic ship in which I sailed. Bacon, although salt, should enter more largely into the dietary than I have seen heretofore. Fresh eggs boiled and scalded with hot lard, as in case of the roasts, will keep indefinitely. All the casks should be fitted with an air space, so as to insure their floating in case they should get overboard, and an iron ring should be in both heads of these casks to facilitate handling in case of emergency. No package to exceed one hundred pounds, and fifty pounds might be better.

Expeditionary provisions should consist of pemmican, hard bread, tea, sugar, and alcohol for fuel. One pound of pemmican and a half pound of bread (six hard biscuits), one-quarter ounce of tea, and one ounce of sugar per day being ample for a man. With a proper cooking-stove one-half pint of alcohol will produce ten pints of boiling water from summer snow. All pemmican should be put in tin cylinders and then in light wooden casks, so as to float them. The packages are heavier and bulkier for the weight of food, but then we lose none in transportation, either by spoiling, by being pierced, or in sinking when dumped overboard. Bread in India-rubber bags. Ship's bread, barreled.

By Captain DAVIS:

Q. Is dried fish a suitable food for use of sledging parties?—A. We had none except for dog food, but I think it would be very good. [Resuming his statement.] Arms should consist of rifles and shot-guns, all of each kind, of the same make and caliber. In the "Jeannette" all magazine-guns got out of order. The only gun that stood the test under all conditions was the Remington breech-loader, navy pattern, and for accuracy of fire was true enough. For shot-guns get the best quality hard-finished paper cartridges, with no shot heavier than duck-shot. Have a good assortment of small shot. Get good guns with strong stocks for rough usage. For killing walrus and bear, explosive bullets are the only certain means; unless struck in a very vital part a bear or walrus will get away with half a dozen rifle-balls. Have plenty of ammunition to encourage hunting among the crew, as it brings in some game and gives healthful exercise.

Dogs for long and continued labor, such as is before the present relief party, are not effective. They eat half as much as a man and do only one-eighth his work. Their feet give out in about ten days. In Siberia a dog was fed four pounds of fish daily and broke down under it. Their load was about forty pounds and they could carry but ten days' supply of food alone. A man can haul food for ninety days. For quick, light work, with numerous depots of supplies, dogs in the hands of skillful dog-drivers can do good work. White men haven't got the patience to drive dogs. When game is plentiful dogs can be worked to advantage, but a ship could not carry stores enough to keep a pack of forty dogs in working condition for any length of time. One good team of nine or eleven large dogs might be used experimentally, and if not efficient could be turned adrift or destroyed.

Sledges to be built both for boats and provisions, twelve and sixteen feet long, with double bow-runners, and bow-strung girder to receive the cross-pieces. The vertical posts extending from bow to bow without break. The deck or floor girders to rest on cleats riveted onto posts, the whole tied in by iron tie-rod, and the runners for boat sledges five inches wide and shod with iron, the edges of shoes are to be turned down three-sixteenths of an inch to cut in and prevent the side slide of the sledge, which is most destructive. The boat sledges to have a dip or reverse curve in the upper bow to accommodate the bilge of the boat. All lashings to be made of white flax small-stuff. The boats to be shored out where the holding-down lashings come.

By Captain DAVIS:

Q. In your judgment. how much time might be consumed by the boat expeditions in reaching Lady Franklin Bay and returning to the ship, provided a start was made from about Cape Sabine in the month of August?—A. I think it could be done in about forty days, travelling light. With water to manage the boat, less than forty. To sledge it without boats, in thirty.

Q. What progress, with properly equipped boats and sledges, do you think could have been made by Captain Markham, north from the position of the "Alert"?—A. They hauled their boats and sledges and made a mile and a half or two miles a day, and that was about our travelling. We had eight pieces of baggage and were travelling in the spring. When we started the snow was very heavy and soft. In the summer we could transfer all our baggage by going over the floe five times. We at first passed over the floe thirteen times; we travelled thirteen miles in making one; and we came down afterwards to as low as five trips.

Q. At what time do you think the expedition should leave the United States?—A. Not later than the first of May. The whalers get up off Cape York early in June.

Q. Do you believe in any system of rewards for the officers or crew of the expedition?—A. No, sir.

By Captain GREER:

Q. Do you think it advisable to employ an ice-master?—A. Yes, sir; I think the services of an ice-master would add essentially to the efficiency of the expedition. I have recommended an ice-master because I thought it was well to have him, and also a paymaster to have control of the stores and supplies.

[Resuming his statement.]

Clothing for winter travel: Entire suit of flannel clothing next to the skin. Light skin-trousers and shirt, with hair next to the undercloth-ing; deer-skin stockings, with hair next to the woolen-stockings; moc-casins of deer-skin to come to the hip; a pair of loose wide-legged knee-breeches of hair, made to put on while sledging, or not travelling on foot, and a long *cooly-tang* of deer-skin, with hood to cover the head; a tight skull-cap of fur covering the head, ears, neck, and chin, leaving a very small portion of the face from the eyes to the lower lip exposed; a small patch of fur, with elastic band, is sometimes used to cover the nose—this can readily be removed, and the ice knocked off—the nose is usually frosted, and a scab forms which protects it from further freezing; a breast-guard of fur, with a chin-piece, can be hauled up to cover the chin and keep the cold out of the necessary slits in the cloth-ing at the neck; fur mittens should be doubled so as to turn inside out, and thus permit the inside fur to dry; woolen underclothing next the skin is necessary to take up the moisture from the body. Skin-cloth-ing being impervious to air keeps the moisture of the body in, which soon wets the skin-clothing, and it in turn freezes. Canvas and woolen inner-soles or hay stuffing must be used in moccasins. For foot travel the *cooly-tang* and knee-breeches will have to be removed, as they impede travel. A man gets too warm, wets his clothing with perspira-tion, and his clothing freezes on his body.

The Board then adjourned to meet to-morrow at 11 a. m.

— —

ROOM 88, NAVY DEPARTMENT BUILDING,
Washington, D. C., January 9, 1884.

The Board met pursuant to adjournment; all the members present. A letter was read from Dr. F. E. Coulter, who offers to accompany the proposed expedition. (Abs. Mis. Cor., No. 31.)

After a long consideration of the various details of the expedition the Board adjourned to meet to-morrow at 11 a. m.

———

ROOM 88, NAVY DEPARTMENT BUILDING,
Washington, D. C., January 10, 1884.

The Board met pursuant to adjournment; all the members present. The Recorder laid before the Board a copy of a letter from Sir Edward Thornton, Minister Plenipotentiary from Great Britain, in relation to the deposit of stores at Polaris Bay. (Exhibit H.)

Additional statement of Lieut. ROBERT M. BERRY, United States Navy:

The pemmican on the "Rodgers" was put up in tins of twenty and forty pounds. We found great difficulty in serving this out in cold weather, owing to the fact that when we attempted to cut it up for rations it broke into fine pieces and some portions were lost. I would recommend that it be packed in cans in one-pound pieces in the same manner that laundry soap is packed.

Mr. G. C. GOSS, representing the firm of Goss, Sawyer & Packard, ship-builders, of Bath, Me., appeared before the Board and made the following statement:

We propose to build one or two vessels similar to those we build for the Arctic whale-fishery, which, under all circumstances, have proved themselves able and strong and have done their work well; to be bark-rigged, with steam power sufficient to propel them ten knots, and consuming seven tons of coal a day; with sail power they would go twelve knots. They work like pilot-boats under canvas. They should have a two-bladed propeller and an extra propeller to take along in case they break one. We propose to build them of extra strength, and brace the bilges so that it would be an impossibility to crush them. They would be of about five hundred tons, gross register, with freight capacity of six hundred tons, besides the accommodation for a crew of thirty-five men. We could have them built by the 1st of May if arrangements were completed so that we could commence work on the 1st of February, and would guarantee that, with bonds to the satisfaction of the Government.

By Captain DAVIS:

Q. Your plan does not contemplate a lifting propeller?—A. Not to hoist up; but a two-bladed propeller.

Q. Has not the advantage of a tricing propeller been fully demonstrated by the whalers?—A. They are very complicated, and, I think, impracticable in the ice. We built one in San Francisco, and found it did not work.

Q. Please state, approximately, the value of such a ship.—A. I should say, approximately, $100,000. We propose to put in heavier machinery.

Q. What are the resources of your firm for prompt and efficient work?—A. We have built one hundred and eighty vessels; we have the machinery and timber on hand constantly, and if any one wants dispatch he generally comes to us. We hold the same relation to wooden-ship building that John Roach does to iron-ship building.

The Board then adjourned to meet to-morrow at 11 a. m.

ROOM 88, NAVY DEPARTMENT BUILDING,
Washington, D. C., January 11, 1884.

The Board met pursuant to adjournment; all the members present.

A letter from S. K. Parson, general agent of the Hudson's Bay Company at Montreal, Canada, in response to a request of the Board, was received and read. (Abs. Mis. Cor., No. 32.)

The Recorder submitted a letter from William Macnaughtan's Sons, in reply to a communication from the Board of the 8th instant. (Abs. Mis. Cor., No. 33.)

The Recorder was directed to telegraph the above firm, asking estimates for dressed reindeer skins with hair on.

General Hazen submitted a letter, referred to the Board by the Navy Department from Frank Reynolds, dated Boston, January 8, 1884, in relation to the building of a vessel for the expedition. (Exhibit I.)

Upon the suggestion of the Recorder, the President of the Board was directed to request the Secretary of War to furnish copies of all instructions and orders to Lieutenant Greely regarding the establishment and maintenance of the United States signal station at Lady Franklin Bay; also copies of all reports or communications to the Chief Signal Officer of the Army from Lieutenant Greely which may relate to his future movements or which may contain suggestions as to his relief.

General Hazen submitted a communication from the Chief Clerk of the War Department, dated the 10th instant, relative to the request of the Board respecting the printing of its daily proceedings. (Abs. Mis. Cor., No. 34.)

In regard to the matter of having a chart or map prepared to accompany the proceedings, the President of the Board was directed to address the Secretary of the Navy a request that the Hydrographer of the Navy Department be instructed to lend his assistance in the preparation of a skeleton map, which it is designed shall accompany the report of the Board.

The Board at 12.30 p. m. took a recess until 2 o'clock.

Upon re-assembling, the room was cleared and a general discussion ensued upon the various subjects the Board have had under consideration, and at 3 o'clock p. m. the Board adjourned to meet at 11 a. m. to morrow.

———

ROOM 88, NAVY DEPARTMENT BUILDING,
Washington, D. C., January 12, 1884.

The Board met pursuant to adjournment; all the members present.

A letter from William Macnaughtan's Sons, in response to a telegram from the Board of the 11th instant, was received and read. (Abs. Mis. Cor., No. 35.)

The Board then took a recess until 1 o'clock.

Upon re-assembling, the room was cleared and an informal discussion took place relative to transportation, control, and conduct, and the *personnel* of the expedition.

At 3.30 p. m. the Board adjourned to meet on the 14th instant at 11 a. m.

———

ROOM 88, NAVY DEPARTMENT BUILDING,
Washington, D. C., January 14, 1884.

The Board met pursuant to adjournment; all the members present.

The Board, by invitation, met in consultation the Secretaries of War and the Navy in the conference room of the War Department, and discussed the preliminary recommendations heretofore made.

Upon re-assembling, General Hazen submitted a letter from Surgeon-General Wales, United States Navy, transmitting a paper entitled "Sanitary Suggestions for the Guidance of Arctic Expeditions." (Exhibit K.)

By reference from the War Department, the Recorder read a communication from G. C. Goss, of the firm of Goss, Sawyer & Packard, Bath, Me., offering to build a steamer for Arctic service. (Exhibit L.)

Lieut. P. H. RAY, United States Army, being present, was recalled and interrogated, as follows:

By Captain DAVIS:

Question. In this relief expedition to be sent to Lieutenant Greely and his party let us assume that sledging becomes necessary—what should be the composition of a party sent from Cape Sabine for Greely's relief?—Answer. Not to exceed five men besides the officer commanding. The length of time it would take to procure dogs at Pembina or Mackinaw I could not state positively, but not more than fifteen or twenty days. A skin or canvas boat, which would answer all purposes, should be carried along. It could be constructed in New York.

By General HAZEN:

Q. Do you think such a boat would be as good as those used and constructed by the natives?—A. Not as good, but good enough for the purpose. Any boat which can be handled easily would answer.

Q. How many days could you subsist on one of these light expeditions?—A. With two persons besides myself and with eight dogs and one sled I could carry provisions for thirty days, without depending upon the country.

Q. What do you think is the best outfit for such an expedition?—A. It would depend altogether upon the time of the year you started out. If in the early spring or winter you would need one flat-top sled for carrying the boat, and then two or three sleds for provisions and baggage.

By Captain DAVIS:

Q. What is your opinion of calf-skin as a substitute for deer-skin?—A. I would about as soon have it for ordinary wear. With our people at Point Barrow we never used any fur clothing, except when travelling, or when the observers had to be in the observatory continuously. We did not consider it necessary in the ordinary work around the station; we all wore heavy woolen clothing and native boots. In summer we wore no native clothing at all. Light calf-skins from animals one or two months old, tanned as we tanned them, would make excellent clothing.

Q. Suppose on the 15th of July you were ordered to proceed from a ship at or near Cape Sabine to Lady Franklin Bay, your party equipped with boats and sleds; what organization would you require in order to relieve and bring back Lieutenant Greely and party, supposing it to consist of twenty five persons, and the distance to be travelled 225 miles?—A. There are so many possibilities and contingencies covered by that question that it is impossible for me to answer it. There are so many questions that I cannot possibly answer now, and which cannot be answered by any man until he comes up to the ice. If, however, I was at Cape Sabine and found any open leads of water I would take a sufficient number of boats to bring his party back. I should take at least, four whale boats, built lighter than the ordinary whale boat, with a heavy hardwood garboard strake, with a little deeper keel than is usual, two heavy strips of hardwood about 18 inches from the keel on each side running fore and aft. Keel and bilge keels to be shod with steel. A boat of this character could be run over the large ice-floes with facility. I should allow four men to each of these boats. I believe that number of good, strong men could handle them. I do not think it advisable at that season of the year to incumber the boats with sleds, dogs, and the necessary dog food. If Lady Franklin Bay can be reached at all at that season, provided the ship cannot reach there, it will have to be reached by an outfit of that kind, and not by sledging. Four boats of the kind I describe would bring Lieutenant Greely and his party back. They could be manned on the trip up by four men each.

Q. Do you prefer these boats to the *oomiak*?—A. I would at that season of the year, but early in the spring I would not. But at the season that a ship could reach Cape Sabine, and supposing she was prevented from going further, I believe the boat expedition to be the most practicable. A party intending to winter there should be provided with skin-boats and the necessary sleds.

Q. Suppose the boat expedition fails, what method of procedure would you then recommend ?—A. That a party of one or two officers and five men be landed at or near Cape Sabine, or as far north as practicable, with one year's provisions for Lieutenant Greely's party, besides their own supplies. They would house themselves there for the winter. This party should be provided with four sleds and one canvas or skin boat. The sleds should have a carrying capacity of 1,500 pounds each. In the latter part of the winter I would send out a party and establish a cache about midway between the winter quarters and Lady Franklin Bay. I would place here twenty days' rations for thirty men and thirty-two dogs—say 1,800 pounds of carefully selected stores. Then as soon as the sun returned I would start north with the whole party, except one man left at the home station. I should take thirty days' supplies for thirty men and thirty-two dogs, and should push on with all possible speed until I reached Lieutenant Greely. After passing the cache previously established, I should make a cache of provisions along the trail wherever I could do so with safety—that is, on the land where most convenient. This would lighten the sled loads and leave a supply all along the home trail, and the sleds would be available for any disabled men there might be in the party. Only one light boat would be necessary, to be used in ferrying across cracks and leads, as I believe there is not much open water there at that season; the sled carrying it would also transport at least 800 pounds of supplies. Natives, say two or three, should be taken to kill seal, if nothing else. It would be better if the party winter in the vicinity of the natives. Walrus hide is excellent food for dogs, and I would prefer it to anything else.

A communication signed by Robert Laidlaw, E. Heimbacher, and E. S. Eveleigh, photographers, received by reference from the Navy Department, was read. (Abs. Mis. Cor., No. 36.)

The room was then cleared, and the Board resumed discussion of the matter under consideration, and directed the Recorder to submit at the next meeting a draft of a report for the consideration of the Board.

At 4 p. m. the Board adjourned to meet at the usual hour on the 16th instant.

————

ROOM 88, NAVY DEPARTMENT BUILDING,
Washington, D. C., January 16, 1884.

The Board met pursuant to adjournment; all the members present.

A letter from F. B. J. Rust, in response to request of the Board of the 7th instant, was submitted and read. (Abs. Mis. Cor., No. 37.)

A communication from L. Y. Coggins, for Otis Young, addressed to Hon. W. P. Frye, and by him referred to the Navy Department, was laid before the Board and read. (Abs. Mis. Cor., No. 38.)

In response to the request of the Board, of the 11th instant, to the Secretary of War, General Hazen submitted certified copies of all instructions and orders to Lieutenant Greely relative to the establishment and maintenance of a Signal Service station at Lady Franklin Bay, together with all reports and suggestions from Lieutenant Greely to the Chief Signal Officer in regard to future movements and plans for his relief. (Exhibit M.)

A letter from the Secretary of War, dated January 15, 1884, transmitting for the information of the Board, copies of letters dated the 11th and 12th instants from the State Department, inclosing copies of dis- patches from United States Minister to Great Britain, was received and read. (Abs. Mis. Cor., No. 39.)

A communication addressed to the Board by J. W. Norman was re- ceived and read. (Abs. Mis. Cor., No. 40.)

Capt. W. H. Clapp, United States Army, being present, was re- quested by the Board to furnish a memorandum relative to the construc- tion of sleds and such other information as might be useful to the pro- posed expedition.

The Board, at 12.45 p. m., took a recess till 2 o'clock.

Upon re-assembling, the Recorder submitted a rough draft of report prepared by him in regard to the transportation, equipment, control, conduct, and *personnel* of the proposed expedition, and, after some time spent in discussion, the Board adjourned to meet at 11 a. m. to-morrow.

ROOM 88, NAVY DEPARTMENT BUILDING,
Washington, D. C., January 17, 1884.

The Board met pursuant to adjournment; all the members present.

A communication from Capt. W. H. Clapp, United States Army, de- tailing the construction of sleds, tents, and sleeping-bags for Arctic serv- ice, was received and read. (Exhibit N.)

Captain Clapp being present was further requested to submit a plan or drawing of the sled furnished to Lieutenant Garlington for use on the Proteus expedition.

The room was then cleared, and, after discussion of certain recommen- dations that should be embraced in the final report, the Board adjourned to meet at 11 a. m., on the 19th instant.

ROOM 88, NAVY DEPARTMENT BUILDING,
Washington, D. C., January 19, 1884.

The Board met pursuant to adjournment; all the members present.

Copies of correspondence between the Treasury Department and Capt. C. L. Hooper, of the United States Revenue Marine, respecting the Greely expedition, was, upon reference to the Board by the Secretary of the Navy, submitted and read. (Exhibit O.)

General Hazen submitted a letter from E. M. Philibaum, which was read. (Abs. Mis. Cor., No. 41.)

General Hazen submitted copies of correspondence between the State Department and the United States consul at Saint John's, N. F., trans- mitted to the Board by letters of the 18th instant from the Secretary of War. (Abs. Mis. Cor., No. 42.)

The Recorder then submitted for consideration an amended draft of a report, which, after discussion and further amendment, was adopted and signed.

General Hazen submitted a draft of a recommendation to accompany the report of the Board, to be signed by himself and Captain Davis.

After a prolonged discussion it was arranged that at the next session of the Board, the naval members thereof should submit their views upon the proposition to include an Army detachment in the *personnel* of the relief-ships.

The Board then adjourned to meet to-morrow at 11 a. m.

ROOM 88, NAVY DEPARTMENT BUILDING,
Washington, D. C., January 21, 1884.

The Board met pursuant to adjournment; all the members present.
Captain Davis submitted the following proposition :

"That the recommendation which was made at the last meeting and
appended to the report of the Board, signed by General Hazen and
Captain Davis, be withdrawn, and that those who propose to recommend
the addition of an Army detachment to the complement of the relief-
ships file a paper setting forth their views upon the subject, and simul-
taneously, those who dissent from this proposition, to file a paper setting
forth their reasons for dissenting."

This was put to vote and lost

Lieutenant-Commander McCalla then submitted the following proposition, which was agreed to :

"It having been proposed in the Board that a detachment of one officer and five enlisted men from the Army shall be placed on board each
ship, additional to the complement herein recommended, the Board finds
itself unable to agree upon this point, its members being equally divided ;
and it has therefore been decided to append to the report separate state-
ments, embodying the views of the members respectively, supporting
and dissenting from this proposition."

The Board then adjourned to meet to-morrow at 11 a. m.

ROOM 88, NAVY DEPARTMENT BUILDING,
Washington, D. C., January 22, 1884.

The Board met pursuant to adjournment; all the members present.

The Recorder submitted a communication, received from Mr. George
Kennan, proposing to substitute for his remarks made to the Board on
the 4th instant, copy of a letter dated June 16, 1882, addressed by him to
Lieutenant Greely.

The Board, after deliberation, declined to make the substitution proposed, but directed that a copy of the letter referred to be appended to
the record. (Exhibit P.)

General Hazen submitted letter from the Navy Department calling
attention to communications heretofore referred to the Board by that
Department without reference indorsements. (Abs. Mis. Cor., No. 43.)

The Recorder submitted and read a letter from Mr. Hugh M. Suther-
land. (Abs. Mis. Cor., No. 44.) Also a communication from Mr. Frank
Reynolds, dated Washington, D. C., January 22, 1884, asserting his
ability to construct proper vessels within 90 days from date of receipt
of the order for same. (Exhibit I.)

General Hazen, on behalf of himself and Captain Davis, and Captain
Greer, for himself and Lieutenant-Commander McCalla, submitted in
writing their views, respectively, upon the employment of an Army detachment as a part of the complement of relief-ships.

The papers were ordered to be attached to the report of the Board.

There being no further business before the Board requiring present
attention, it adjourned to meet at the call of the President.

ROOM 88, NAVY DEPARTMENT BUILDING,
Washington, D. C., February 4, 1884.

The Board, pursuant to the call of the President, met at 12 o'clock m; all the members present.

The Recorder submitted and read the following communications, received since the last meeting of the Board, viz:

Letter from William Gibson, United States vice-consul at Glasgow, Scotland, dated January 11, 1884, with inclosures. (Abs. Mis. Cor. No. 45.) Also letter from the Secretary of War, dated January 22, 1884. (Abs. Mis. Cor., No. 46.) Also letter from Capt. W H. Clapp, United States Army, dated January 22, 1884. (Exhibit N.) Also letter from William Macnaughtan's Sons, dated January 23, 1884 (Abs. Mis. Cor., No. 47.) Also letter from H. Clay, dated January 25, 1884, referred by Hon. Albert S Willis, of Kentucky, to General Hazen, and by him to the Board. (Abs. Mis. Cor., No. 48.) Also letter from Dr. T. H. Carroll, dated January 26, 1884. (Abs. Mis. Cor., No. 49.) Also letter from J. W. Norman, dated January 28, 1884. (Exhibit S.) Also letter from William Macnaughtan's Sons, dated January 29, 1884, inclosing copies of correspondence had with the Hudson's Bay Company. (Exhibit T.) And letter from Navy Department, dated January 29, 1884, with inclosure. (Abs. Mis. Cor., No. 50.).

The Board, at 1 p. m., adjourned to meet subject to the call of the President.

ROOM 88, NAVY DEPARTMENT BUILDING,
Washington, D C., February 21, 1884.

The Board met at 2 p. m., pursuant to the call of the President; all the members present except Lieutenant-Commander McCalla.

General Hazen submitted to the Board a communication from the Navy Department transmitting copy of a letter from Capt. Sir George S. Nares, R. N., to our minister at London, together with a copy of a letter addressed to the President of the Greely Relief Board, signed by Captains Nares and Markham, R. N., and Major H. W. Feilden, H. B. M. A., containing suggestions from these officers regarding the conduct and equipment of the relief expedition. (Exhibit V.)

General Hazen also submitted two communications addressed to himself dated February 2, 1884, from Hon. Thomas N. Molloy, United States consul, Saint John's, Newfoundland, regarding the purchase of a steamer and the procurement of certain supplies for the proposed relief expedition. (Exhibit W.)

The Recorder submitted and read a letter from the Commissary General of Subsistence, transmitting list of subsistence stores furnished to Lieut. P. H. Ray, U. S. A., for use of the Point Barrow expedition, and also a list of similar supplies furnished Lieutenant Greely in charge of the expedition to Lady Franklin Bay. (Exhibit Q.)

The Recorder also submitted a letter from the secretary of the Hudson's Bay Company, dated London, England, January 29, 1884. (Abs. Mis. Cor., No. 51.)

General Hazen submitted a communication from the Secretary of War, transmitting copy of letter from Maj. H. W. Feilden, H. B. M. A., dated Royal Artillery Barracks, Woolwich, January 9, 1884, offering his services to accompany the proposed expedition. (Exhibit E.)

The President of the Board was requested to prepare and transmit to the persons addressed, the following communications.

[Room, Board of Officers considering Relief Expedition to Lieutenant Greely and party, at Lady Franklin Bay.]

WASHINGTON, D. C., *February* 21, 1884.

SIR: I have the honor to inclose herewith, a communication addressed to Captains Nares and Markham, H. M. Navy, and Major Feilden, H. M. Army, acknowledging the receipt, through the Navy Department, of their very interesting and instructive report embodying suggestions for the organization of the relief expedition for Lieutenant Greely's party, and to request that you will cause the same, with inclosures herewith, to be forwarded.

The Board begs to suggest the propriety in transmitting this communication to its destination, of conveying to the gentlemen who have so kindly given us the benefit of their extended experience in the waters of Smith Sound, the thanks of the Department for the interest they have taken in this subject.

I have the honor to be, very respectfully, your obedient servant,

W. B. HAZEN,
Chief Signal Officer, President of the Board.

The SECRETARY OF THE NAVY,
    Washington, D. C.

[Room, Board of Officers considering Relief Expedition to Lieutenant Greely and party at Lady Franklin Bay.|

WASHINGTON, D. C., *February* 21, 1884.

GENTLEMEN: I am requested by the Board of officers considering the relief of the Lady Franklin Bay Expedition to acknowledge the receipt on the 16th instant, through the Hon. J. R. Lowell, Minister of the United States in London, England, of your joint report embodying valued suggestions for the conduct of the expedition, made in conformity to the request of the Board in its communication dated January 5, 1884.

I am also directed by the Board to express its gratification that Captain Nares should have deemed it advisable to secure an expression upon this subject from Major Feilden, H. M. Army, in relation to the conduct of this expedition.

The communication referred to has been read, and will appear in the printed proceedings of the Board, and when published, copies will be sent you.

The Board observes with satisfaction that its own recommendations in regard to the organization, equipment, and conduct of the proposed relief expedition, coincide so nearly with the suggestions of officers possessing the extensive experience in Arctic navigation and exploration of Captains Nares and Markham and Major Feilden.

I beg to inclose herewith three copies (proofs) of the report of the Board dated January 22, 1884.

I have the honor to be, very respectfully, your obedient servant,

W. B. HAZEN,
Chief Signal Officer, President of the Board.

Capt. Sir G. S. NARES, *Royal Navy;* Capt. A. H. MARKHAM, *H. M. S. Vernon;* Maj. H. W. FEILDEN, *H. B. M. Army.*

[Room, Board of Officers considering Relief Expedition to Lieutenant Greely and party at Lady Franklin Bay.]

WASHINGTON, D. C., *February* 21, 1884.

SIR: I have the honor to inclose herewith for your information a copy of a letter addressed to the Honorable the Secretary of the Navy, inclosing to him a communication acknowledging the receipt, through the Navy Department, of a report signed by Captains Nares and Markham, H. M. Navy, and Major Feilden, H. M. Army, embodying their suggestions, made upon invitation of the Board, as to the organization and conduct of a relief expedition to Lieutenant Greely and party.

I have the honor to be, very respectfully, your obedient servant,

W. B. HAZEN,
Chief Signal Officer, President of the Board.

The SECRETARY OF WAR,
    Washington, D. C.

[Room, Board of Officers considering Relief Expedition to Lieutenant Greely and party at Lady Franklin Bay.]

WASHINGTON, D. C., *February* 21, 1884.

SIR: On the 22d of January last, I had the honor to submit a report embodying the recommendations which the Board was directed to make by Executive Order dated December 17, 1883, relative to the relief of Lieutenant Greely.

In the letter transmitting that report allusions were made to the expected receipt of communications from certain officers of the British Navy, embodying their suggestions in regard to the proposed expedition, and also to the receipt of replies to the Board's inquiries concerning the availability of reindeer-skin clothing.

The communications referred to have come to hand, and will be embraced in the proceedings of the Board, which are now being printed. So soon as this work can be accomplished the Recorder will deliver to the Secretaries of War and the Navy, respectively, copies of the printed proceedings of the Board, together with all exhibts referred to therein.

I have also the honor to state that the duties imposed upon it by Executive Order dated December 17, 1883, have been completed, and the Board has adjourned.

I have the honor to be, very respectfully, your obedient servant,

W. B. HAZEN,
Chief Signal Officer, President of the Board.

The SECRETARY OF WAR,
    Washington, D. C.

(Same to the Secretary of the Navy.)

There being no further business for consideration the Board adjourned.

APPENDIX.

APPENDIX

APPENDIX.

EXHIBIT A.

General design for an expedition for the relief of Lieutenant Greely and party.

1. As the proposed expedition is solely for the relief of Lieutenant Greely and his party in Lady Franklin Sound, and as the means employed to reach him must of necessity be of a nautical character, whether the vessel proceed direct to Lady Franklin Sound, or whether, in case she should be detained south of that point, it becomes necessary to resort to combined boat and sledge journeys over ice and open water, the officers and men of the expedition should be taken from the Naval Service.

2. The relief expedition to consist of two (2) full powered steam sealers or whalers, each with a complement of thirty-one officers and men (see list) and one Eskimo; and a naval vessel without guns, and with a reduced crew, as a tender.

As two of the steamers of the relief expedition may have to winter in the Arctic regions, the complement of each ship should be reduced to a minimum in order to give each man as much "air space" as possible, and at the same time to reduce the consumption of provisions; and should consist only of useful men, accustomed to ship life

3. The two sealers or whalers to be purchased at once and to be equipped and prepared for wintering in the Arctic region. Each of the two steamers to be supplied with clothing, provisions, and boats sufficient for two years for the entire relief expedition, and also for Lieutenant Greely's party; each steamer to be supplied with a house ready to be put up on shore, and with sledges and dogs.

4. The two relief vessels to proceed in company to Saint John's, N. F., fill up with coal and fresh provisions; to proceed to Disco, and, if necessary, to Upernavik; thence to Littleton Island and until they meet the ice pack in Smith Sound.

5. The first depot to be established on Littleton Island (before proceeding north of that island) or in the immediate vicinity, as may seem best to the commander of the expedition, to consist of one of the houses, 50 tons of coal, 4 boats, and provisions and clothing for the entire party for one year. The house, coal, provisions and clothing for this depot to be taken from steamer No. 1, *i. e.*, that of the commander of the expedition; an officer or a petty officer and two men to be left in charge of the depot.

After leaving Littleton Island and reaching the ice-barrier the design of the expedition would be for the commander of the expedition in steamer No. 1 to take the first favorable opportunity to push to the northward, leaving steamer No. 2 to serve as a base to fall back upon in case of disaster, or for a second attempt to reach Lady Franklin Sound.

6. Steamer No. 2 not to enter the ice pack, but to manœuver constantly to the southward of it, or to anchor in the immediate vicinity; to be ready to land a second main depot of provisions, to consist of the same amount of material proposed for the first, in case it should become necessary to proceed north in the event of disaster to steamer No. 1.

7. The problem of reaching Lady Franklin Sound in a steamer from Cape Sabine can only be solved by the exercise of skillful seamanship combined with good judgment; unless Smith Sound should be found to be comparatively free from ice.

8. Should the west side of Smith Sound be comparatively open, steamer No. 1 should advance to the northward, forming small depots at Washington Irving Island, and in the vicinity of Cape Collinson and of Carl Ritter Bay. Steamer No. 2, after forming a small depot of supplies and landing two (2) boats at Cape Sabine, to proceed as far north as Dobbin Bay; beyond which point she should not advance unless the prolonged absence of steamer No. 1 should give rise to the apprehension of her loss.

9. Should steamer No. 1 be crushed in the ice, steamer No. 2 before attempting to advance to the north should land her house, three (3) boats, and supplies for the whole party for one (1) year in the vicinity of Dobbin Bay.

10. Should neither vessel be crushed, and should neither succeed in communicating

111

with Lady Franklin Sound, one (1) should winter in Franklin Pierce Bay, and the other in the vicinity of Littleton Island.

11. On the way north, the coast to be examined from Cape York to Cape Ohlsen on the east side, and from Cape Isabella to Cape Sabine on the west. Cairns should be erected containing notices of the movements and intentions of the relief expedition at Conical Rock, at Wostenholme Island, Cary Islands, Hakluyt Island, Cape Isabella, and Cape Sabine.

12. The whalers from Dundee and the sealers from Newfoundland to be requested to keep a lookout on the ice-floes for Lieutenant Greely's party.

13. The Danish Government to be at once requested to instruct the authorities at Disco to prepare skin clothing and secure dogs for the expedition, and two (2) Eskimo hunters.

14. The naval vessel or tender to go as far as Littleton Island or Cape Sabine, for the purpose of bringing back the latest news from the expedition; or, in the event of the loss of one or both steamers, to bring home the officers and men not necessary for the sledge journeys during the winter; to contribute supplies for the use of the expedition, and to aid in any way the efforts to reach or rescue Lieutenant Greely and his party.

PROPOSED COMPLEMENT OF EACH WHALER OR SEALER.

1 commanding officer.
2 commissioned officers.
1 engineer.
1 surgeon.
1 ice master.
2 captains tops or B. mates.
2 quartermasters.
9 seamen.
1 machinist.
1 boiler maker.
1 blacksmith.
3 firemen.
1 officer's cook.
1 officer's steward.
1 ship's cook.
1 carpenter's mate.
1 yeoman.
1 captain hold.
1 Eskimo.
—
32 total.

EXHIBIT B.

Preliminary notes by Capt. Geo. W. Davis, U. S. A., upon the steps necessary to be taken to afford relief to Lieutenant Greely, at Lady Franklin Bay.

Purchase and have fitted for Arctic service by May 1st, 1884, a steam whaler of strongest build of about 500 or 600 tons displacement, full steam power, and provisions for 18 months for 70 persons. A naval vessel to be also prepared of about the size of the "Yantic;" for service as a tender, to be protected about the bows and water-line with outside sheathing, crew reduced to a minimum, provisioned for six months, and all available space filled with coal.

The tender to take on board lumber, and other building material sufficient for a structure capable of accommodating a detachment of 35 men. Additional provisions, &c., to be taken in the tender for 45 men for 18 months.

The officers and crew proper of each ship, assumed as 40 men for No. 1, and 60 men for No. 2, to be made up from the *personnel* of the Navy—the commander of the expedition to be also a Naval officer.

On board the relief vessel (No. 1) to be taken a detachment from the Army of 2 officers, a doctor, and 10 enlisted men, and on board No. 2 a similar detachment. The officers to be selected by the Secretary of War, and the men specially enlisted or selected for Arctic service.

Procure on the coast of Greenland four dog-teams, and three or four Esquimaux hunters if possible. Each of the vessels to be off the Greenland coast by May 10th, so as to secure the dogs and other equipments to be drawn from that region, filling up with coal from the Waigat mines if necessary, and be in a condition to reach Cape York (communicating with Upernavik), by June 10th (which is the earliest date that whalers have been able to reach that point), moving north as rapidly as possible, the ships remaining in company, examining all bays and promontories, leaving a record at Cape York if practicable, certainly at the Cary Islands, and at any other points likely to be visited by a party retreating south in boats.

The expedition should arrive at Cape Alexander or Littleton Island by July 15th to 20th, or possibly earlier. Make a careful examination of the east coast, islands and bays, to Refuge Harbor, of the west coast from Cape Isabella northward to Sabine, if possible. Should the pack prevent an early entrance to Smith Sound up to Sabine, say by August 15th, land the sledging party from No. 2 at Life-Boat Cove or Port Foulke, immediately put up the shelters and prepare for winter, and at once, with lightly equipped dog-teams, send out expeditions searching for traces of Lieutenant Greely to Rensselaer Bay.

No. 2 to lie at Littleton Island or Port Foulke, and No. 1 to watch for any available opportunity to get north, not desisting from the attempt until the season has so far advanced as to make further efforts injudicious.

If by September 15th No. 1 succeeds in getting to Dobbin Bay, and is unable to proceed further, put her into winter quarters, say, behind Washington Irving Island or in Franklin Pierce Bay. If detained by ice near Cape Prescott, land boat and sledging party and push forward, making use, if possible, of steam-launch.

Should Smith Sound be found more open in the east than the west, let the vessel go up into Kennedy Channel, and so communicate with Lieutenant Greely.

Reaching Lady Franklin Bay by either route, the detachment, with their records, instruments, &c., to be taken on board and the retreat begun.

Arriving at Littleton Island, pick up the detachment left there and return to the United States.

Should No. 1 be compelled to winter, let every effort be made during the autumn by boats and during the spring by sledges to communicate with Greely and afford all relief possible.

As soon as the sledging detachment is comfortably quartered at Life-Boat Cove, let systematic boating and sledging operations begin, depots advanced towards the the north and west, and the best efforts made to succor the men at Discovery Harbor, who, when reached—which should not be later than September 5th—will retreat towards the south, and if No. 1 be still above Sabine, Greely's detachment should be placed on board.

If No. 1 has not been able to reach Greely nor to get to Cape Prescott, let her, at the latest date consistent with safety, land at Alexandra Haven her Army detachment, materials for shelter, 50 tons of coal, provisions for 35 men for 18 months, boats, sleds, and dogs, and with her consort return to the United States.

If No. 1 should have been crushed and sunk, then her crew should return to the tender if possible, and if not lost, go into winter quarters at the most available port, communicating with the detachment at Life-Boat Cove.

. The tender to return home in any event, leaving Littleton Island by about September 15th, or as the condition of the ice may determine.

Each vessel should be supplied with all necessary boats of the most approved pattern, adapted for transportation over the ice, and, if obtainable, each should have a steam-launch, with enginery adapted to the burning of petroleum, the screw protected as best may be.

If launches depending upon the fuel named cannot be provided, then take those adapted to the burning of coal. If the ships should return to the United States in the autumn without affording relief, leave the launches with the detachments.

So long as the vessels remain north the conduct of the expedition to devolve upon the commander.

If sledging detachments are left as contemplated, the command to devolve on the senior Army officer present, who should be junior to Lieutenant Greely.

These are my general ideas upon the relief of Lieutenant Greely, subject to such modifications as may hereafter be found necessary.

If Lieutenant Greely be not rescued next summer, it will, of course, be necessary to send up a vessel in 1885.

EXHIBIT C.

FORT BRADY, MICH., *December* 16, 1883.

General WILLIAM B. HAZEN,
    Washington, D. C.

DEAR GENERAL: In view of the contemplated expedition for the relief of Lieutenant Greely and party next spring, I write to ask you if you do not think it would be a good idea and a wise precaution for the Government to engage three or four Indians, and about five dog-teams and *toboggans*, at this or some other northern point, to take along with the expedition, so as not to have to rely altogether on the Esquimaux for such transportation, for it may happen with this expedition as it has happened with others, that they will not be able to obtain either dogs or drivers from the Esquimaux. Dog-teams are used considerably in this country in the winter, for carrying mails, etc., through the woods. They usually drive three dogs, tandem, to a *toboggan*, which is capable of carrying all the way from two hundred and fifty (250) to four or five hundred (500) pounds, owing to the roughness of the country over which they have to travel. With two hundred and fifty (250) pounds they can go almost anywhere, and I think they would be better adapted for Arctic travel in the spring and summer than the runner sleds which they use in the Arctic regions, for they can go over soft snow very easily, and without cutting through, and I believe they can go over and around places that a runner sled could not. I also believe that snow-shoes, as are worn here, would be a good thing for a sled party to have along, as they could then walk over ravines, etc., which are filled with soft snow, without the danger of breaking through. A man on snow-shoes can walk over ice, that would not sustain his weight without them. The very best *toboggans* thoroughly fitted up, with three pieces or strips of sheet iron on the bottom to prevent their wearing, lashings for securing the load, and canvas cover, which laces on top of load, can be gotten made to order for about fifteen dollars ($15) each. And I don't think there would be much trouble in getting twenty (20) or thirty (30) well-trained dogs for five dollars ($5) each. Two Indians here, who have had great experience in dog-team travel (John Boucher and Antoin Piquet) could be hired for about fifty (50) or seventy-five (75) dollars a month each, and two younger Indians could be hired for two-thirds as much. John Boucher and Antoin Piquet, some years ago, while carrying mails between here and Saginaw, made three hundred and fifty (350) miles, on snow-shoes and with a dog-team in six days and five hours. When Lieutenant Danenhower of the Navy was here last summer, I showed him a *toboggan*, which he said he thought would answer admirably for Arctic travel.

I hope, General, you will pardon the liberty I take in thus addressing you, as I am prompted solely by the interest I take in the preparation for the relief of Lieutenant Greely and party.

Very respectfully, your obedient servant,

THOMAS J. CLAY,
2d Lieut. 10th U. S. Infantry.

EXHIBIT D.

HEADQUARTERS DEPARTMENT OF THE COLUMBIA,
Vancouver Barracks, Wash. T'y, December 21, 1883.

General WM. B. HAZEN, *U. S. Army,*
President of the Greely Relief Board, Washington, D. C.

GENERAL: In compliance with telegraphic instructions from the Adjutant-General of the Army, stating that the Secretary of War directs "that I shall prepare and send by mail, with least practicable delay, to you, whatever I am prepared to recommend as to organization and conduct of a party for relief of Lady Franklin Bay Expedition," I would recommend as follows:

The construction or purchase of the best steam vessel, especially adapted for Arctic work, compatible with the appropriation to be made by Congress, and, if made in time, the preference to be given to construction, and under the immediate supervision of the cc · mander of the expedition, the ice-masters, navigating officers, and such other inspection as proper authority may see fit to order.

The construction, purchase or charter (preferably one of the latter two) of a steam vessel (No. 2.) adapted for ice navigation with strengthened bows and oak sheathing so as to combat all ordinary ice impediments, as "ramming," collisions, etc.; or, in short, about the usual service required of steam whalers, Greenland traders, or sealers, the latter (No. 2) to act, in part, as transport or tender to the former (No. 1). I give preference to purchase or charter, so that only a naval inspection will be needed, and no supervision of construction of two vessels going on at the same time will be required.

Ice masters for the two ships should receive not less than $3,000 to $4,000 per year, with an increase of 25 to 50 per cent. based on the certificate of the commander of the expedition, if they have managed their ships safely through and accomplished the main object of the relief. It is simply impossible to overestimate their importance in this expedition. As masters of whalers, the best ice-masters often make the above in a single season, and the Government has no reason to expect the best service in this art for any less, while the increasing *percentage* is necessary not only as an incentive, but also, if administered as above, to keep the proper relations between the commander and these bold, bluff masters of their rude art, that are seldom used to being commanded. In fact it would be a good idea if the commander had some such power, to a limited degree, with all employés. Ice-mates could be given the usual compensation of from $600 to $900 per year, with the same limitations. All persons taken from existing branches of the Government should have their pay doubled after crossing the Arctic Circle (as done by other governments in such service), except the commander, should be so chosen. If all subordinates know that their commander is working *solely* for the reputation to be gained, they will understand at once that their percentage of pay is in the hands of one who will accept nothing but good service for good character. If ice-masters are placed on supervising boards of construction they might receive proportional "shore-duty" pay while so engaged. The cost of such vessels as recommended can be better estimated by those engaged in such manufacture and those nearer the markets where they would be built.

Vessel No. 1 is intended to follow as closely as possible upon all favorable opportunities to reach Greely's position and relieve him *by ship;* and its *personnel* and equipment should be accordingly. It should have the best ice-master and mates of the two; should have a powerful propeller, with easily adjusted blades in case of breakage, and adequate machinery to drive it; should be of strong construction, with heavy horizontal and transverse struts or beams, well strengthened bows, sharp lines, and as small and light as possible, so as to be easily lifted in ice-pressure; should have plenty of small boats (whale-boats) to rescue crew (and Greely's party if aboard) if crushed, and to load Greely's party and records rapidly when the position is reached, and its commander should carry orders for this officer to abandon everything except records and valuable instruments, as such vessel is presumed to be there under circumstances admitting of the very least possible delay. Its navigating officers and ice-master should be chosen more with reference to their success in daring matters than their success by cautious movements.

Vessel No. 2 is to accompany No. 1 as far as Hudson Strait, Cumberland Sound or the ports in Greenland where a sledging party can be outfitted with dogs, native drivers, and other essentials for a winter in Smith Sound, when No. 1 will proceed on her journey as indicated, first transferring to No. 2 everything not absolutely essential for a sharp, decisive encounter with the ice, carrying not over six weeks' provisions for her crew, but of the best; all this that she may float as high and be as light as possible in case of "nipping" by the ice. No. 2 will then visit Hudson Strait (and Bay, if necessary), Cumberland Sound, and Greenland ports, or as many of them as may be needed in order to perfect the best possible outfit for sledging and of not less than two, and, if it can be done, four sledges of a half a ton each. This done, the vessel should attempt to reach Greely's position by taking advantage of every fair opportunity, and zealously avoiding any severe encounter with the ice, following it up only as it offers reasonable opportunities for penetration. By this time the season will be (presumably) favorable for such cautious movements. From the highest port in Greenland, a *possible* route, on which No. 2 will proceed to and No. 1 return from Smith Sound, will be agreed upon by a council of proper officers, before the separation, the highest discretion being allowed for contingencies. No. 1, having been successful, will leave notification by cairns flying flags (at every available land point) in certain order of color, from top to bottom, to be interpreted by No. 2 in case pack-ice prevents their reaching them to read the records left in the cairns; and these signals will be arranged before separation. Information will also be left with all natives to be conveyed to No. 2. If No. 1 is unsuccessful, she will remain upon the ground as high in latitude as possible, and at all risks, until relieved by No. 2. When the two ships have joined, and it shall appear reasonably evident, by lateness of season or other cause, that Greely's position cannot be made, the sledging party and outfit and one year's provisions, will be left with No. 1, and she will winter in the best harbor, in the highest latitude, the ice will allow in Smith Sound, No. 2, returning to the United States to return to Smith Sound next year. It is thus seen that No. 2 is a transport, a relief vessel for No. 1, in case of disaster, and the conveyance for the sledging party, or last resort, in case of failure by the ice-masters.

No. 1 might take on a single sledge with outfit at some readily-reached Greenland port, in case of the failure of No. 2, which failure would not be very likely in the light of the comparative risks of the two. With this sledge and even only two or three white men and a couple of Esquimaux, Greely could be reached if this party had a winter's supply of provisions left with them.

The commander of the expedition should have unlimited discretion as to the ship he will use as his own of the two, except that he must remain with the one that winters in the sound, if that becomes necessary. No. 1 will be the most brilliant for him if successful, but as this success depends on her ice-master, No. 2 will be the most important in case of No. 1's failure. Unforeseen contingencies could change this importance, however.

Greely's party may be met escaping from the sound, having been compelled to abandon their records to save life, and such contingency should be anticipated at Washington, and orders given as to whether the present expedition should winter in order to recover them, if they have been safely deposited in some secure place unde such expectations.

All other recommendations of which I can think, as number of sledging party, white and native, the construction of the sledges and dog-harness, and number and kind of dogs, the quality and amount of ship's provisions for whites and natives, the material for wintering the ship properly, the kind and quantity of the arms and ammunition and other hunting and fishing supplies, and everything else necessary in equipment and *personnel* are of secondary importance, that is for recommendation, in that they can be safely left with an intelligent commander, or through him and under his supervision with his subordinates in their respective capacities.

Any other information that is in my power to give will be most gladly furnished, either by mail or telegraph, as the Board may request, but I think it proper in closing to warn them against too much reliance in the subject of experience, as applied to Arctic affairs. The whole history of continued Arctic expeditions under one commander will show a far larger list of retrogradations than advancement in success, noticeably the continued expeditions of Franklin, Parry, Barentz, Hudson, Hall, Kane, McClure, Back, and probably a score of others who had served previously as commanders or in subordinate capacities; and all this I can account for only on the ground of a too rigid application of their principles of experience.

An active mind, fertile with resources for a multitude of rapidly varying circumstances, is a higher quality, which, if tempered with experience, would be invaluable, and this is the more important the higher the position in the expedition.

I am, sir, your obedient servant,

FRED'K SCHWATKA,
Lieut. 3d Cav., Aide-de-camp to General Miles.

EXHIBIT E.

WEST HOUSE, WELLS, NORFOLK,
November 5, 1883.

MY DEAR SIR: It is not long since I returned from a tour of duty in South Africa, where I passed over two years in Natal, Transvaal, and Zululand.

My heart always reverts to Arctic enterprise, and I feel confident that you will forgive me intruding on your valuable time when I beg for a little information as to what is to be done next year towards the relief of Lieutenant Greely's party in Smith Sound.

I do not think that too much dependence ought to be placed on the report brought back by Dr. Nathorst from Cape York natives that Lieutenant Greely's party had reached Littleton Island.

I am very much afraid that the Eskimo of Cape York in conversation with Hans Hendrik assumed that Mr. Beebe's party from the "Neptune" in 1882, or the shipwrecked crew of the "Proteus," 1883, was identical with the Greely party.

From the log of the "Proteus" published in *New York Herald* Sept. 18th, 1883, it appears that the "Proteus" people were on Littleton Island on the 25th of July. Had Greely's party been there, surely some trace of it must have been found.

On the 10th of August, the "Proteus" people are in communication with the Eskimo of Cape York, who must have known as much of what was going on as the members of the tribe who were interviewed by Dr. Nathorst and Hans, and no mention appears to have been made of anything relating to Greely's party.

The "Proteus" people left Cape York on the 16th August. If Dr. Nathorst communicated with Cape York prior to that date, he may, I am afraid, assume that there is no foundation in the Eskimo report that Greely's party had reached Littleton Island, for if such had been the case the "Proteus" party must have found traces of them.

If Dr. Nathorst communicated with the natives of Cape York after the "Proteus' party passed along their coast line, then I am afraid the Eskimo reports refer to "Proteus" people, not Greely's party.

I am very much afraid that Greely's party, if alive, are still ice-bound in Discovery Bay. I have no doubt that the United States Government, with its usual energy and munificence, will organize relief next year on an efficient scale.

If I am correct in my surmise that Greely's party had not reached Littleton Island this summer, then the relief expedition should consist of two steamers next year.

Why did the "Yantic" not keep company with the "Proteus"? Had the two ships been in company the "Yantic" might have remained at Pandora Harbour or Payer Harbour.

The "Proteus" people would, in the case of disaster (as happened), have had the "Yantic" to fall back on. Great suffering would have been avoided, and in all probability the "Proteus" would not have been thrust into the ice to meet her fate on the 23d of July—a date, I think, too early to attempt to *force* a passage up Smith Sound, judging from our former experiences.

In my humble estimation, it appears to me that a great effort should be made to relieve or recover Greely's party next year.

The coast line from the Devil's Thumb to Cape York should be searched in case the Eskimo report be true that Greely's party reached Littleton Island and attempted to get south. The search should be carried along carefully from Cape York to Littleton Island. Supposing that one steamer did that, the other might go on to Pandora Harbour or Port Foulke.

Premising that both our ships are at Port Foulke in the beginning of August, I would suggest that they move across the sound to Payer Harbour, one to remain there, the other to be ready to take advantage of any clearance in the ice, so as to make a rush up to Discovery Bay. Supposing that this proves impossible, then I am afraid the fate of Greely's party would be sealed. The winter of 1884-'85 would be beyond hope. Still, it would be incumbent to recover the records and solve the fate of the Discovery Bay party. To this end (the necessity, I trust, may never come to pass) one ship should be left to winter in Payer Harbour, and from thence push sledge parties to Discovery Bay in the spring of 1885.

I do not think there would be any great or insurmountable obstacles in carrying out the sledge schemes. I feel confident it might be done.

The escape of a steamer from Payer Harbour in 1885 is almost a certainty.

With great regard, believe me to be, very sincerely,
H. W. FEILDEN,
Major, Army Pay Dep't,
H. B. M. A.

Dr. EMIL BESSELS,
Washington, D. C.,
United States America.

WAR DEPARTMENT,
Washington City, February 21, 1884.

GENERAL: I have the honor to transmit herewith a copy of the letter of Major H. W. Feilden, Army Pay Department, Royal Artillery Barracks, Woolwich, January 9th, 1884, relating to certain inquiries looking to the procuring of suitable vessels for the Greely Relief Expedition and offering his services to accompany the expedition. I also inclose a copy of the reply of the Chief Signal Officer, to whom the foregoing letter was addressed, and of his indorsement referring the correspondence to this office.

Very respectfully,
ROBERT T. LINCOLN,
Secretary of War.

General WM. B. HAZEN, *U. S. A.,*
President of the Greely Relief Board,
Washington, D. C.

[Inclosure 1.]

(Private.)

ROYAL ARTILLERY BARRACKS, WOOLWICH,
January 9, 1884.

GENERAL: The information imparted to me confidentially, yesterday, that Captain Chadwick, U. S. N., your attaché in London, had received telegraphic instructions to inquire about two vessels in England, suitable for ice navigation, has given me the most lively satisfaction. I trust that Captain Chadwick may be successful. I believe he left London for Dundee last night.

If my local acquaintance with the shores of Smith Sound, from Cape Isabella to Discovery Bay, might be of use to your forthcoming expedition, I would not hesitate to offer them, provided that my government granted me leave of absence, which I presume it would do.

Trusting that the deep interest I take in this matter, may be considered a sufficient excuse for my again addressing you,

I am, General, your obedient servant,
H. W. FEILDEN.

[Inclosure 2.]

SIGNAL OFFICE,
Washington City, January 21st, 1884.

Respectfully forwarded to the honorable the Secretary of War, with copy of note sent in reply. It will be remembered that Major Feilden was one of the officers of the Nares expedition.

W. B. HAZEN,
*Brig. and Bvt. Maj. Gen'l,
Chief Signal Officer, U. S. A.*

[Inclosure 3.]

OFFICE OF THE CHIEF SIGNAL OFFICER,
Washington, D. C., January 21, 1884.

MY DEAR SIR : I am in receipt of yours of the 9th January, to which I beg to reply that the selection of the *personnel* of the new expedition to Discovery Bay is in the hands of the Secretaries of the War and Navy Departments, to whom I will immediately refer your letter.

Very truly, yours,

W. B. HAZEN,
Brig. and Bvt. Maj. Gen'l, Chief Signal Officer.

Major H. W. FEILDEN,
*Army Pay Department,
Royal Artillery Barracks,
Woolwich, England.*

EXHIBIT F.

Memorandum of a plan to relieve Lieutenant Greely, by Commander Frank Wildes, U. S. N.

Two (2) ships of about 300 tons; of as light draught, as economical engines, as large coal capacity, and as great strength as can be found; to be still further overhauled and strengthened; provisioned, equipped, and supplied with clothing for two years; officered and manned by the United States Navy and under American colors; the commander to have had some Arctic experience if possible; 7 officers and 36 men (25 of whom to be able seamen) to each vessel; each ship to be fitted with patent reefing and furling topsails; to carry not less than 6 boats, spare-rudder, spare-screws, saws for cutting docks, electrical apparatus, powder in 5 and 10 lb. tin cans for blasting ice.

The senior officer to command expedition. To leave Upernavik about July 10th to 20th, and having reached the "north water," to separate; one vessel to search the coast so far as circumstances will permit, from Cape York to Three Sister Bees, including Wolstenholme Sound; the other the coast and island from Three Sister Bees to Cape Alexander, including Cary Islands; ships to rendezvous at Pandora Harbor.

Receiving no news of Greely, one vessel to remain in Pandora Harbor as base; the other (the senior officer) to cruise to Cape Sabine and search in that vicinity, and should the season appear favorable, push north as far as practicable, following the inshore leads; in no case to thrust the vessel blindly into the pack.

The great success of the English expedition was owing to the high qualities of its *personnel*, to a careful study of the movements of the ice as influenced by winds and tides, and to the increasing vigilance and watchfulness by which no opportunity to advance was lost.

Should the pack continue close and immovable and the season unfavorable, the vessel to endeavor to reach Alexandra Haven; thence dispatch two boats to Lady Franklin Bay; boats for the service to be fitted as Sir Edw. Parry's were in his attempt to reach the pole from Spitzbergen (1827?), viz, two deep bilge keels, to be used as sledge runners.

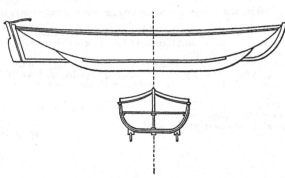

As late as Aug. 25th this vessel should be prepared to take advantage of open water to proceed north.

Physical conditions in Smith Sound vary from comparatively navigable ice and moderate weather found by "Polaris" and "Proteus" (1881), to closely-packed ice and constant storms experienced by the "Pandora" during the entire month of Aug., 1876. This vessel was 3 weeks in making a landing at Cape Isabella, and was finally driven out of the sound. It was even uncertain if she could have reached Payer Harbor. Therefore, the instructions to commander of the expedition must be largely discretionary.

Pandora Harbor is best anchorage on coast, but Foulk Fiord abounds in animal life, Dr. Hayes having killed 100 reindeer in Oct. and Nov., and continued to get them through the winter and spring. He states emphatically that one hunter can support 20 men with the products of chase.

Littleton Island and Life-Boat Cove can present no special advantages. Walrus. and birds abound on the former, but a vessel can remain but a short time at either place.

Should the ice move south, the vessel in Pandora Harbor is liable to be blocked in for the winter, but that may happen at any point. This vessel receiving no news from her consort by Sept. 1st, then to set up frame house on shore, land provisions, and prepare to winter.

It will be impossible next season to procure coal on the Greenland coast north of Ivigtut. A small amount might be obtained at the Kudlisit mines, with a good deal of labor, or at some of the other outcroppings, say at Hare Island, but it is very uncertain.

EXHIBIT G.

NAVY DEPARTMENT,
BUREAU OF NAVIGATION AND OFFICE OF DETAIL,
Washington, January 4, 1884.

Brevet Major-General WM. B. HAZEN, *U. S. A.*,
   President of Board considering steps for the relief of Lieut. Greely, U. S. A.:

SIR: By direction of the Secretary of the Navy, I have the honor to forward herewith a letter from Lieutenant N. R. Usher, U. S. N., containing a project for the relief of Lieutenant Greely and party.

I am, sir, very respectfully,

J. G. WALKER,
Chief of Bureau.

[Enclosure 1.]

U. S. S. "SARATOGA," 3D RATE,
Navy Yard, New York, 29 *December,* 1883.

To the Board for relief of Lady Franklin Bay Expedition:

GENTLEMEN: In accordance with permission received through Commander H. C. Taylor, U. S. N., commanding this vessel, I beg to submit to the Board the following project for utilizing what has not, in any previous expedition, been found available, viz, a steamer of high speed capable of maintaining her search during any reasonable period, and one at the same time of such strength and build as shall, to some extent, render safety from many of the dangers from young ice, or ice of recent formation. I would respectfully propose that the party consist of a small number of men selected from the enlisted men of the Navy, men and officers to be of American birth; this party to be organized at once, that they may learn to pull together while under the most favorable circumstances.

I would propose that the vessel have good speed, say at least (12) twelve knots per hour, and capable of maintaining this speed under all ordinary circumstances. The vessel could, I believe, be found among those used for clearing away the ice in the Delaware and Chesapeake Bays. These vessels, many of which are paddle, though some of them are fitted with screws, push their way through ice of considerable thickness, their peculiar build causing the forebody of the vessel to rise upon and crush by its weight the ice in front. Vessels of this character are strongly built, and where they have good speed can avoid any danger from being frozen in. A good speed would enable her to avoid to a great extent any danger while running through leads in the pack-ice, and would enable the officer in command to take advantage of every opportunity to push his way along the coast in his search. Such a vessel should be capable of keeping the sea in all weathers, and should one of the bay ice-tugs be selected, it could be easily made seaworthy by stout whale-backs, supported by iron frames forward and aft. What deck-houses are found on vessels of this kind could be converted into quarters for the ship's company and the members of the party sought for. That a vessel of the kind described may be used, it will be necessary to provide some means of supplying fuel in adequate quantity. To do this I would suggest the use of a fuel unknown in this country at the present time save in one or two instances of manufacturing firms, where it is used with stationary boilers. I refer to the fluid refuse from the petroleum oil refineries. At Hunter's Point, in this port, this may be had in any desired quantity at little or no cost. This fuel is now in use, and has been in use for years past in the merchant steamers and war steamers used by the Russians on the Caspian Sea, the substance being obtained from the oil wells near the military post of Baku, where it is to be had in great abundance. The vessels using this substance as fuel have boilers of the usual form, no alteration being found necessary beyond an arrangement for feeding the fuel to the furnace, using a steam jet to accelerate its flow from the tank holding it. The iron coal bunkers with which vessels are supplied would afford the space for stowage, either calking the bunkers and making them tight to hold fluid, or removing the bulk-heads and replacing them by the water-tanks, such as men-of-war are usually fitted out with. I am well aware of the objection to anything of an experimental nature to be used on an expedition of this kind, but must submit that where fuel of this kind has been used for a long time with success, as it has been in the Caspian steamers, and for such important service as transporting troops and war material to supply the Russian column when an advance was made on Golk Tepé, in Central Asia, and the cruising Russian men-of-war on the Caspian, it cannot be considered experimental. It is at present in use with appliances, the nature of which, and mode of use, can be easily had of those now using it, and within a short time, through the Intelligence Office of the Navy, and it offers such advantages in stowage and such power of heating effect, any given quantity of this refuse petroleum replacing effectively four times the same quantity of coal, that it would appear the very thing for a vessel where a supply to last a long time is of consideration. The climate of the Caspian has periods of intense cold, as well as great heat, and no trouble is found in handling or making use of this substance, and it would seem that taking the precautions now made use of in the Caspian steamers, no greater danger in carrying it would be found than they overcame, while the great advantage of quadrupling the supply of fuel available cannot be overestimated.

A vessel thus fitted out, strong in build, of good speed, capable of keeping the sea in any weather, and of pushing her way through new ice, if necessary, not hampered by the deck load with which the cruiser in the Arctic is usually hampered, could start from the most available northern port at the earliest available time, and, if necessary, continue her labors until the end of the season, with no need to renew her fuel supply. Upernavik affords a convenient station from which to start the search. There a supply of this proposed fuel could be left, and from thence the vessel commence her cruising, examining every accessible part of the land, and, where possible, throwing out search parties where a probability of their usefulness was seen.

To the end that the parties leaving the ship should be easily and effectively outfitted for journeying ashore on ice or afloat, I would suggest that whale-boats, such as have been supplied and made use of by the English naval authorities on the African coast for landing parties and use in the surf, be supplied in addition to the vessel's proper complement of boats. The boats which I suggest are built of stout frames hinged in the center, built of tubular metal or stout, tough wood, and covered with the stoutest canvas. They are built to fold in a small space. When complete, weight about 500 lbs., and are each capable of carrying 12 to 20 persons, and a landing outfit to last three (3) days. They are carried at sea abreast the vessel's boat davits that they may be easily put together and gotten overboard when needed. These boats, taken apart, could be converted into sledges for use ashore or on the ice, and parties, when making camp could make use of the boat as shelter. These boats are practical, have been used, are found good sea-boats and of good carrying capacity. Taken apart and used as sledges they practically make two sledges each, one being loaded with the boat canvas, oars, &c., and the other being available for transporting stores, &c. These boats can be put together in (20) twenty to (25) twenty-five minutes, and are then as stout and sea-worthy as the heavy wooden boats or metallic boats carried as life-boats, save only their vulnerability to sharp edges of ice. These boats, held in reserve till auxiliaries to the vessel's complement of boats are needed, would perhaps be of much use at a time when other means of transport would have to be extemporized. A vessel thus built and equipped would seem to possess the most desirable qualities for the proposed search, both at sea and along the coast, and be enabled to work effectively during an entire season, avoiding entering the ice. I would say that there was, some time since, a trial of this proposed fuel at this Navy-Yard, the report of it being, on the whole, unfavorable. But the trial was chiefly to determine a particular mode of using the fuel and to try one person's apparatus for that purpose, and the objection found was the tendency of the pipes to clog and impede a free flow of the fluid.

I venture, then, to recapitulate the points of the plan I would propose:

1. A limited number of officers and men to be drawn entirely from the Navy, or, if men are taken from civil life, American citizens. To be gotten together at the earliest possible moment and put aboard the selected vessel.

2. The use of a northern port, as Upernavik, as a base.

3. A vessel, rigged as a schooner if possible, built to crush ice—having a speed of at least (12) twelve knots and capable of maintaining that speed. If necessary the vessel to be fitted with "whale-backs" forward and aft.

4. At least four (4) boats in addition to the ordinary outfit of boats, these extra ones whale-boat shape, canvas over wooden or tubular metal frames, and capable of compact stowage and convertibility into sledges on the ice.

5. The vessel to be put in shape for cruising at once, and used to convey to the point selected as a base any extra supplies of fuel, &c., considered advisable, and to accustom the officers and men to their craft.

I am, gentlemen, very respectfully, your obedient servant,

N. R. USHER,
Lieutenant U. S. Navy.

EXHIBIT H.

WASHINGTON, *April* 26, 1877.

SIR: In a note, dated the 23d of January, 1875, which I had the honor to receive from Mr. Fish, he transmitted a copy of a letter from the Secretary of the Navy, of the 19th of that month, in which he forwarded a list of the stores and provisions deposited on the west coast of Greenland by the Polaris expedition, and was good enough to state that all or any of these stores were at the service of the Polar expedition to be dispatched in that year by Her Majesty's Government. He added that in the event of their use, the Navy Department would accept such inventory and appraisement as might be made by the order of the commander of the expedition.

It has been reported by Sir George Nares, the commander of the expedition, that in regard to the provisions deposited at Polaris Bay by the United States Polar Expedition, the whole of the provisions were used by the sledge parties from Her Majesty's ships "Alert" and "Discovery," and that the depot no longer exists.

In consideration that the depot was thus disturbed by the British Expedition, Her Majesty's Government would be glad to make payment for the whole of the original supply of provisions, and in compliance with Lord Derby's instructions I have therefore the honor to ask that the Navy Department of the United States will furnish me with a statement of the value of the provisions in question, in order that the wishes of Her Majesty's Government may be carried out with regard to their payment.

I have the honor to be, with the highest consideration, sir,

Your obedient servant,

EDW'D THORNTON.

The Hon. FREDERICK W. SEWARD, &c., &c., &c.

EXHIBIT I.

BOSTON, *Jan'y 8th*, 1884.

Hon. W. E. CHANDLER,
Secretary of the Navy:

DEAR SIR: As many are making suggestions about the relief of our friends in the Arctic, I think I have a right to a place among others.

I placed the first machinery in a vessel for Arctic use and made a voyage to see how it worked, and since have fitted five others and made four voyages—three north and one south, where I spent twenty months in the ice, and as I am a practical engineer, as well as knowing all about constructing a proper hull or vessel of any sort, and my long experience in the icy regions, I claim to know what is wanted and am ready to fit you a vessel ready for sea in every branch, and have all complete in time for the expedition.

My experience has taught me that people do not learn the requirements of these voyages in once trying, and the first thing is a suitable ship, and to my certain knowledge there is none now fit to make this hazardous voyage. I have been left in the ice myself, and am willing to give you my experience to help save our friends. Can refer you to the best men of New York and Pacific coast if you wish to hear more from me.

FRANK REYNOLDS.

WASHINGTON, *Jan'y 22nd*, 1884.

Honorable W. E. CHANDLER,
 Secretary U. S. Navy, and Advisory Board:

GENTLEMEN: I come here to represent New York and eastern ship and engine builders of reputation, and as there has been numerous suggestions concerning Lieut. Greely and party now in those desolate regions of ice, and knowing the necessity of immediate action on the part of the Government for their relief, I take the liberty of making a few remarks on the subject.

There seems to be but little doubt at the present time of finding experienced and suitable men for the carrying out of such voyage. There are always plenty of men ready to volunteer that know nothing of the requirements or dangers liable to occur, and especially to inexperienced men. Men who have voyaged in that country and are willing to go again, are brave enough to again attempt such voyage, deserve the respect of all nations and it seems to me a wrong thing to ask such men to risk such voyage until we have at first done all that human skill can advise to warrant them a successful voyage and safe return.

Now what is to be done? I would suggest that the Government contract immediately for one or more suitable vessels for this purpose. Said vessel or vessels can be constructed and got ready in ample time, if the order is given soon. To my certain knowledge there is no vessel now to be had in any way suitable for this voyage and my long experience in those regions warrants my making this broad assertion, and I am willing to give my experience, backed by the best builders in the country, to construct a vessel or vessels that will be a credit for the Government to own. There may be those that know what is required in the construction of vessels for this voyage, and I am here to say I do know what is wanted, and am ready to contract to build in ninety days said vessels, equipped ready for sea except boats and provisions. I would advise carrying four New Bedford whale-boats as life-boats, as there are no other boats to take their place in rough water, and with two light boats fitted with sleds, would be all that would be required for the voyage. These boats I can have built and fitted with all the necessary requirements if desired, as I am thoroughly conversant in all these matters.

Hoping you will give this prompt attention and consideration,
 I am, most respectfully,
FRANK REYNOLDS.

Address "Delamater Iron Works, West 13th street, New York."

EXHIBIT K.

NAVY DEPARTMENT, BUREAU OF MEDICINE AND SURGERY,
January 11th, 1884.

SIR: I have the honor to transmit, in accordance with your request of the 4th inst., the accompanying embodiment of my views in relation to the sanitary precautions for Arctic expeditions and hints as to the best methods of preserving health in high latitudes. I beg to state that the list of medical stores for the Rodgers seems to have proven satisfactory.

Very respectfully,
PHILIP S. WALES,
Surgeon-General, U. S. N.

Bvt. Major-General W. B. HAZEN, U. S. A.,
 Chief Signal Officer and President of Board, &c.

[Enclosure 1.]

Sanitary suggestions for the guidance of Arctic expeditions.

The exacting requirements of Arctic life display the cardinal importance of selecting persons of the most vigorous vital powers and of the highest moral qualities for expeditions, of whatever character, undertaken to penetrate the solitudes and to encounter the dangers of high latitudes. The physical and moral qualifications of the *personnel* should be scrutinized minutely, both as regards early history and present condition, with the view of determining these indispensable questions. The ages between which these qualities are found most highly developed are twenty-five and thirty-seven, or during the third and fourth decennaries of life. The average age of the twenty-three enlisted men of the "Jeannette's" crew was about 28 years, the oldest person being 48 and the youngest 18 on leaving San Francisco. The average age of the officers and civilian staff was 35, the eldest being 45 and the youngest 29. There should not be manifest any unusual tendency to corpulence or thinness, as both extremes suggest suspicions of defective health. The physiological proportion of the weight to the height may be stated generally as within the limits of two and two and a half pounds to the inch of stature. Persons of moderate height, between 5 feet 6 inches and 5 feet 10 inches, have usually more endurance than those of wider ranges. It will be advisable not to select any recruit who presents evidence of past constitutional disease, particularly scrofula, syphilis, and rheumatism, or tendency thereto, although he may be of apparently robust constitution.

The temperament best suited to Arctic service is that known as the sanguine; persons of this sort are endowed with a more vigorous power of assimilation, active circulation, florid skin, large firm muscles, and capacity for brisk movements and prolonged exertion. Another notable quality is a superior power of eliminating animal heat under low temperatures, so justly esteemed by Sir John Ross as of first importance to sojourners in high latitudes. The heat-producing power is possessed in varying degrees by persons of the same seemingly vigorous organization. A degree of extreme cold that would be simply invigorating to one might produce in another painful or even exhausting depression. The view of Ross was that the sensations of cold are not entirely dependent upon the physical effects of greater or less hygrometric saturation, the velocity of the wind, the actual temperature, the amount of exercise, or the quality and quantity of the food. These are, it is true, circumstances which affect the power of generating animal heat, but this power is, at the same time, as much a portion of the original constitution as are the muscular or mental energies, and deserves the first attention in the selection of a crew. This fact is seen in every-day experience, and is referred to by Arctic travelers. Unfortunately there is no ready test to determine this desirable quality, yet it may be asserted that it is possessed by northern peoples, Norwegians, Danes, Swedes, Canadians, and New Englanders, in greater degree than by those of the south, a circumstance due in part to inherited powers and in part to acquired adaptability, and by men of the largest appetites and most perfect digestion; feeble stomachs, whether dyspeptic or merely unable to receive much food, are found in men who suffer most from cold, and who never generate heat enough to resist external impressions. This doubtless explains, in a great measure, the resisting powers of the Esquimaux, whose consumption of food is sometimes enormous and often incredible.

It would be advisable, as far as practicable, to recruit Arctic ships from northern regions, and from persons of the type and character above described, particularly from those who have already had experience in Arctic traveling. It has been advised by certain writers on Arctic service, that they should be of one nationality which is calculated to secure closer ties of sympathy and interests. The sanguine temperament presents the most desirable moral qualities, as also power of resistance to the depressing influences of prolonged Arctic nights and daily hardships and dangers; and it is linked with a humorous, lively, good-natured, and hopeful disposition, so essential to the successful and harmonious prosecution of such enterprises. The reverse of this temperament is that including persons of portly habit, sluggish movement, dark complexioned, with feeble heart power, tardy circulation, and inclined to indulge in gloomy emotions—a class of individuals little fitted for such service. Professor R. L. Newcomb, of the "Jeannette," in a private communication, assures me that he can testify, from personal experience, to the value of the above suggestions in selecting men for Arctic service. Lieutenant Danenhower informs me that "the crew of this vessel was composed of 13 Americans, 4 Germans, 4 Swedes, 2 English, 2 Irish, 2 Danes, 2 Chinese, 2 Alaska Indians, 1 Hollander, and 1 Russian, making an entire complement of 33, of which 8 lived in the cabin and 25 forward. In the cabin seven were American and one Irish born, but a naturalized citizen. Probably a more cosmopolitan crew was never before detailed for Arctic service, and it may be interesting to study the national peculiarities of this mixed crew, and to judge to what extent they harmonized. Less than one-fourth of the men in the forecastle were Americans, though there was no other nationality in excess of that number. The men always seemed to get along well together, with little or no bickering or quarreling about their respective countries. Most of them had been following the sea for many years in such mixed company, and that may account for it. After the ship was crushed the officers and men had to live together, and we had good opportunities for judging of how the men got along with each other. They all labored so cheerfully and well that it is impossible to decide which nationality should be most praised. The two Chinamen were always treated fairly and well, but among the men there was an undercurrent of prejudice against them that occasionally came to the surface. The Orientals stood the extreme cold very well, and always did their share of the work most faithfully.

"Notwithstanding our satisfactory experience with a congenial cosmopolitan crew, I am of the opinion that the crew of an Arctic ship should be of one nationality, and that of an American ship should be native born, or at least citizens of the country. It is true that the Germans and Scandinavians are very tractable and easy to get along with, but it is also true that in times of danger and emergency the American and Irish-American elements are the leading men.

"About one-half of the crew was selected from a large number of candidates at New York, and the remainder from a lesser number at San Francisco. They were men of fine physique, averaging 5 feet 10 inches stature and 170 pounds weight. About one-third of the complement had light hair, florid complexions, and sanguine temperaments, while the others, particularly the Americans, had dark hair and quiet dispositions. There was not a really morbid or unhappy disposition in the party, though quite a number were subject to slight attacks of low spirits. The quality of pleasing others was not especially considered in making the selections, but we found quite a number had such qualities, and good nature and sociability prevailed in the forecastle.

"The two Indians, Alexie and Anequin, aged respectively about 30 and 20 years, got along very well with the officers and crew. They were generally quite happy, but at times were low spirited, and probably suffered from homesickness more than anybody else."

The same officer, in considering the selection of men in the different pursuits of life, remarks that "the question has often occurred to me : Is there any other class of men better adapted to Arctic sled-work than sailors?

"The average sailor seldom does a day's work like the continuous labor of the hod-carrier, for example, or the farmer during harvest. The sledding season is the harvest-time for Arctic explorations, and wrestling with sleds and boats over the Arctic pack is far worse than carrying bricks or following the plow.

"There is a class of men in the Pacific States who are 'packers' of goods to and from the mines. They are very hardy, carrying heavy loads day after day, and having wonderful endurance. Among our soldiers on the Western plains a very hardy element could be found.

"The Chouckches, the Tunguses, and the Cossacks of Siberia are all very hardy men. After considering these various classes of hard workers, I arrive at the conclusion that the seamen class is the best from which to select Arctic sledders.

"First. It comes more in their line of business.

"Second. Seamen can adapt themselves to circumstances probably better than any other class of men.

"Third. Although there is usually really not very much sailorizing in a sled trip, yet there is considerable, when working over ice-fields and through cracks and fissures.

"Fourth. The very fact that sailors have not generally been subjected to such hard work as hod-carriers, packers, or farm-hands, increases their chances of withstanding the severe work of sledding, for which they have not lowered their stamina by overwork."

The sanitary condition of the ship is of no less importance than the procurement of a healthy and vigorous crew; for without the former the latter will soon degenerate and become as inefficient as a crew originally defective in health. The obtainment of appropriate sanitation is somewhat more difficult in Arctic ships than under ordinary circumstances, on account of the extreme cold and the prolonged darkness, the ill effects of which are, in some manner, almost irremediable. It is unquestionable that ships intended for this service ought to be built with special reference to the peculiar and exceptional surroundings of Arctic voyages, but this has not hitherto been done, and the consummation of this desirable object rests with the future. Ameliorations in the structure of ships of ordinary character may, however, be attended with great success in attaining better conditions of sanitation.

The men ought to be provided with berths. They add greatly to their comfort and happiness. Every man, and especially a seaman, on board an Arctic ship likes to have a little place which he can call his own, and to which he may retire when he wishes. During the retreat, Newcomb says he often heard the men tell about the comfort they had in their berths, and how otherwise it would have been had they been required to sleep in hammocks. Aside from this there is a serious practical objection to hammocks. There must be a place to stow them, and that will doubtless be a very cold one. Therefore, when the hammock is lashed and stowed in the morning, with its more or less damp bedding, the dampness will be condensed and form frost. When the hammock is brought in at night it will be so cold that the moist air of the forecastle will be condensed on the bedding, making it very damp and unhealthful.

The principal points demanding attention are the heating, lighting, and ventilating contrivances. The most perfect method of heating the living-deck of an Arctic ship would be by steam coils fitted in appropriate adits, by means of which fresh air of the proper temperature could be delivered below. This has not yet been realized, and the old plan of warming the air after gaining admission to the apartments prevails exclusively. This is accomplished by steam coils in the most improved vessels, such as have been built as whalers, and of this type was the "Rodgers."

The usual or exclusive method of heating, up to the time of Nares' expedition, was by stoves scattered at convenient points around the deck and communicating with the external air by pipes, a plan which leads to the production of cold draughts, deleterious at once to health and comfort.

On board the "Investigator," in 1853, what is known as Sylvester's stove was used. This consisted of an ordinary heater placed in the hold from which pipes were led into the various apartments to be heated. This was reported as being a good apparatus, the consumption of coal being about 70 pounds per diem. On the "Alert" a number of stoves were distributed about the deck and were used as required, sometimes all together. A plan said to answer admirably was adopted on the "Discovery," of fitting a small stove with hot-water pipes, which gave out a large warming power. The maintenance of the heat below will be greatly assisted by building housings over the hatches, with double doors, and covering the upper deck with snow one or two feet deep, and, when possible in winter quarters, by banking it against the ship. The necessity for strict economy in fuel which may arise will often place embarrassing difficulties in the way of obtaining the requisite elevation of temperature for comfortable living. It may be here remarked that it is neither necessary nor desirable to raise the temperature very high. One not exceeding 55° Fah. is perfectly compatible with health and comfort, and avoi·s at the same time the inconvenient aqueous condensation at higher degrees. The temperature of the "Alert" was maintained between 40° and 50° Fah. during winter. There is not usually more than a degree or two difference between the temperature of the air of the upper deck and that of the outside, although this deck is protected by the usual housing. Professor Newcomb says that "the ward-room of the 'Jeannette,' where six of the eight officers slept, was not heated, and proved a comfortable placed to sleep, with less moisture than any other of the inhabited parts of the ship. Many a comfortable night's rest have I enjoyed there. By not having a fire the frost which penetrated was dry, and in the spring could be chipped off before it thawed much."

The proper illumination of Arctic ships is a difficult matter, but no effort should be spared to obtain its benign influence. As Martin has truthfully observed, "Light is the very life-blood of nature, without which everything material would fade and perish." The light gains access below through the skylights and bull's-eyes, which should be kept in good order. The ordinary oil lamps and candles, as is well known, consume the oxygen of the air and at the same time diminish its respirability by eliminating carbon dioxide, and the extent of this is readily appreciable when it is stated that one pound of oil demands for complete combustion 138 cubic feet of air and produces 21 feet of carbon dioxide, and a single sperm candle burning twenty-four hours produces 11.6 cubic feet of carbon dioxide. In breathing, a man adds 1 per cent. of carbonic acid to $53\frac{1}{2}$ cubic feet of air in an hour, which vitiates the air at the rate of 1 cubic foot per minute. The electric light will furnish a boon of inestimable benefit during the period of darkness, but has not as yet been utilized for this purpose.

Ventilation of the lower decks must be carefully attended to; but, as may readily be appreciated from the excessively low temperature of the external atmosphere, the very frequent renewal of air heated in the ordinary way after admission is an impossibility; so that the methods hitherto adopted are, so to speak, a sort of compromise between the cold and an impure air. When it is recollected that the volume necessary for health is 3,000 cubic feet every hour, and that the space allowed each person on a ship of 800 tons is only, at most, 150 cubic feet per man, it will be seen that, to insure the former quantity, the air would have to be changed twenty times, which would be impossible, both on account of the intense cold and the draughts that would be engendered.

In our temperate latitudes air cannot be renewed more than six times in this period without the production of damaging currents. The simplest plan, in the absence of an aspirating apparatus, is to have tubular ventilators communicating externally, and supplied with proper hoods and valves, by which the quantity of air may be regulated, as the great difference between the temperature of the outside and inside, always from 80° to 100°, will induce very strong currents.

The opening and closing of the doors of the hatch-housings in the ordinary routine of ship work will aid in introducing fresh air. One of the officers of the "Alert" adopted the ingenious plan of connecting his room with the external atmosphere by means of a rubber tube which enabled him to control the supply. Much assistance may be derived from a funnel-shaped hood inverted over the galley, which will increase the draught and conduct away the smell and moisture of the cooking. No apprehension need be felt from the bilges eliminating odorous or deleterious gases during the winter, as decomposition will be stayed by the low temperature; and in case of sickness, fæcal emanations should be avoided by the us of earth-closets.

A troublesome quality of the air of the living apartments of Arctic ships is dampness, proceeding from several causes: from the cutaneous exhalations of the men—

and the quantity of this may be appreciated when it is remembered that an ordinary sized person eliminates from 25 to 40 ounces of moisture a day, containing 240 grains of organic matter—and from the cooking operations, which being necessarily conducted below will supply no inconsiderable amount.

These are the constant sources; and then again dampness may be engendered by neglecting to dry the clothing of working parties, or by introducing the hammocks from the low temperature of the upper deck, for the moment they are brought into the warm air of the berth deck they speedily become wet, and hence the necessity of stowing them below whenever the thermometer falls under zero. Men returning from work should divest themselves of their clothing in the drying room set apart for the purpose before passing to the living-deck. All exposed metal surfaces should be covered with leather, or protected with a coating of cork composition, which will effectually prevent deposits upon them. The excess of moisture dripping from the beams should be removed with cloths promptly and regularly, which will greatly contribute to both comfort and health. It may be necessary, in order to avoid wetting of the bedclothes in the bunks, to protect them from the dripping by conducting the water away by a canvas overhang. Various special devices have been adopted by Arctic explorers to eliminate the evils of condensation. Lieutenant Berry, of the "Rodgers," informs me that, in his opinion, the officers' and men's quarters should be surrounded by air spaces, and overhead there should be at least two feet of non-conducting material, which, with the warm draughts recommended, will, he thinks, exclude all dampness. If possible, a house within a house, with the thick roof referred to, he is sure would attain the object desired. Sir John Ross caused apertures to be made in the upper deck above the galley, oven, and after passages, and over these iron tanks were inverted, into which the vapor passed, became condensed, and was removed in the shape of frozen masses amounting to as much as a bushel a day. To effect the same purpose, dry chloride of lime may be used; five pounds of this exposed on the deck will produce a very sensible effect on the humidity of a closed apartment in three hours. It has been suggested placing metallic plates in the hatchways to act as condensers. Another important mean in preventing the deposition freezing, as well as to maintain the heat, is to line the sides of the living-deck with a non-conducting imperishable cloth; in the Nares expedition the fabric known as "fearnaught" was employed.

In order to increase the air space of the living-deck, it has been proposed to build about the hatchways, including a space around them, snow walls with a roofing. The area thus inclosed being cut off from the outer air, free communication could be kept up with the lower deck by removing the hatch covering. On the "Jeannette" the men's quarters consisted of the forecastle and the deck-house. The forecastle was not roomy, but it contained twenty berths, arranged on each side and amidships. On either side of the old galley-room, which was situated immediately abaft the forecastle, there were two small rooms, each of which berthed two petty officers. The two Chinese lived in a portion of the cook-house, which was fitted with two berths. The deck-house was put up early in the fall, and it afforded a good place in which the men could work and smoke.

A hatchway was located just abaft the forecastle, and adjacent to the petty officers' rooms, and made them so cold that they acted as condensing apartments for the moist, warm air of the forecastle, thus rendering them very uncomfortable for their occupants, who had frequently to dry off the wet beams and bulkheads. These quarters were heated by one large cylindrical stove, the furnace of which was filled in with tiles so that the body of the fire was very small. Twenty-five pounds of coal per day were allowed. There was another such stove in the deck-house that was used for drying out when the forecastle became very damp.

The ventilation of the forecastle was effected by two doors in the after bulkhead and by a small circular skylight at the forward end. The skylight was fitted with a double tube about 3¼ inches in diameter, perforated and arranged so that it could be opened or shut.

Each day at 11 a. m. the forecastle doors were thrown open, the skylight removed, and the cover in the deck-house roof immediately above the skylight was taken off to give free egress to the heated air.

The place remained open and empty until 1 p. m., when the crew returned from exercise. When the thermometer was below minus 30° F., this mode of ventilation was only partially carried out. During the rest of the day the constant opening and shutting of the doors, the draught of the stove, and the small tube afforded sufficient ventilation.

At 10 p. m. each day the surgeon visited the forecastle to record thermometers (wet and dry bulbs), and he always looked out for ventilation. In very cold or in windy weather the small auger holes in the doors would be found plugged by the men.

The surgeon frequently tested the air of the forecastle. The amount of carbon dioxide was about the same as that found in the quarters of men-of-war.

The forecastle was lighted by a box lamp at the forward end and by candles and small hand-lamps on the tables. Olive oil was used.

The officers' quarters consisted of a cabin and ward-room. The former was a poop-deck cabin, which contained on the starboard side, counting from forward, first, the captain's room; second, the chart and work room, in which the chronometers, books, instruments, &c., were kept; and third, a water-closet and bath-room (the latter not useful after the ship entered the ice). On the port side was situated, first, the executive officer's room; second, the dispensary; third, the work-place of the naturalist and taxidermist; also a place for the meteorologist; fourth, the dark room for photographic work. Abaft of all was the tiller-room, which formed a very important condensing chamber. The midship portion of the cabin, which was about nine feet wide and thirty feet long, extending from the forward bulkhead to the propeller well, was used as a mess and living apartment by all the officers.

The cabin was heated by one large cylindrical stove, like the one in the forecastle, had furnace bricked up similarly, and the same allowance of coal (twenty-five pounds) was used. There were five small ports (six inches in diameter) on each side, three of which could be opened and shut, and two were covered with fixed glass plates. A small skylight abaft the mizzen-mast was fitted with a tube similar to the one already described. The cabin was lighted by an ordinary Walton lamp and by candles. The ward-room was situated directly below the cabin. It was small, and contained four small rooms and two berths, arranged as follows, counting from forward: Starboard side—navigator's room, with small store-room attached; naturalist's berth, surgeon's room. Port side—meteorologist's room, ice pilot's berth, chief engineer's room. Forward of the ward-room a large store-room was situated. The hatchway, a ventilating scuttle abaft the mizzen-mast, and a series of auger holes bored through the deck above each room and berth, afforded the means of ventilation. There was a large stove in the ward-room country, which was used every Saturday evening for melting snow and warming up the place so that the officers could bathe with more comfort. It made everything so damp by thawing the frost and snow that had collected during the previous week that its use was discontinued.

The following means were employed for ventilation: From 11 a. m. to 1 p. m. each day the cabin was open for ventilation, except when the temperature was below minus 30° F., when the rule was slightly modified. On one occasion a pocket anemometer was used, and it was found that the out-going warm current had a velocity of 122 feet per minute, and that the cross-section was about one-third of the doorway space. The incoming heavy cold current had a velocity of 78 feet, and a cross section equal to about two-thirds of the doorway space.

An interchange of warm and cold currents also took place in the skylight tube. On several occasions experiments were made with thermometers, and it was found that while the upper spaces of the cabin were at 50° F., the thermometer near the deck was at the freezing point. When the temperature showed 60° on the bulkhead, about five feet above the deck, the lower portion of the cabin atmosphere was very cold, and every one suffered with cold feet. There was very little vertical circulation below an imaginary plane passing through the bed of the fire, and it is suggested that in heating Arctic ships that the apparatus be placed as low as possible so that the rising columns of warm air will heat the spaces just above the floor. It would seem that steam pipes arranged near the floor as in the Pullman cars would be the best mode of heating.

The tiller-room was an important adjunct to the cabin, for it was a very efficient condenser. The cook-house should be apart from the quarters, as the amount of steam would make the latter very uncomfortable by liquifying on cold surfaces. The lighting should be with the best quality of oil in the market, such as Pratt's astral oil or mineral sperm oil. As these oils are derived from petroleum, and are explosive, some people might prefer a vegetable oil, such as rape seed, which gives a very brilliant light with a French moderator. Stearine candles were found very useful. The electric light cannot at present be employed unless there should happen to be a coal mine near by.

Cleanliness both of the ship and crew must be maintained as an important auxiliary to health. The deck should be cleansed with hot water and quickly dried by rubbing; and great advantage will accrue from shellacking or painting the decks thoroughly, which will prevent the absorption of moisture by the wood and at the same time render the cleansing more speedy and effectual. An apartment should be specially set apart for the ablutions of the crew, and this is best located on the lower deck, where hot water may be attainable. Bathing should be made compulsory at least once in two weeks. Professor Newcomb stated to me that "the officers of the 'Jeannette' bathed more frequently than he did. They also seemed to suffer, or at least to complain more of the cold. He bathed his feet, often took a dry rub, and kept clean underclothes. With the exception of being poisoned by eating canned tomatoes he was not sick a day, ate and slept well, and not only weighed more than ever before, but averaged it up to the loss of the ship." The clothing of the crew should be washed at stated intervals, once in ten days or two weeks, in the room appropriated for the purpose, and under no circumstances should this work be allowed on the living deck, to supply additional moisture. The bedding may be aired once a month. The men should be provided with a comfortable water-closet, which can be reached from the main deck when this is housed over, as is always done in winter quarters. It may be constructed of light materials, projecting from the side of the ship; and to exclude draughts and cold the snow may be built quite up to the platform, forming a sort of well. When cleansing becomes necessary the frozen mass of fæcal deposits may be removed with the snow, and a new snow wall raised as before. In this connection it may be mentioned that during sledging operations the warm snow hut or tent occupied the night previous for sleeping quarters will serve in the morning for latrine purposes before resuming the march. This convenience will be fully appreciated with a temperature, perhaps, of 50° or 70° below zero.

Regulated exercise is indispensable for the maintenance of health under all circumstances. Professor Newcomb says "it is a most important measure, and that hot tea to remove the cold lump often felt in the stomach after exercising is an excellent remedy." The intense cold and other incidents of Arctic residence, especially during the long, dark winter, dispose to inaction, and hence the necessity of inciting the crew to take a sufficient amount of body exercise to ward off disease. The ordinary routine of ship life will usually supply ample range for this purpose in the manifold labors demanded of mariners. In winter quarters, when ship-board work slackens, the men should be encouraged to employ their time in hunting or amusing themselves in pastimes that demand muscular energy. The cooks and servants particularly, who are not usually called upon for active labor, should be looked after and compelled to take open-air exercise. It may be stated, in general terms, that at least five or six hours daily should be occupied in this way, to maintain robust health under the conditions of Arctic life. This sort of training, so necessary to health, may be turned to practical advantage by making short journeys and establishing outlying depots of provisions and stores before the sledging season sets in, when the greatest drafts will be made upon the physical energies.

While moderate and regular exercise in labor or amusement, as indicated, conduces to health, and powerfully aids the system in warding off scurvy, it must be borne in mind that excess in this particular is equally capable of prostrating the vital powers and inviting scurvy, hence the need of great prudence and judgment not to overtax the men in long journeys, but to give them spells of rest to recruit their strength and energy; nor is it advisable in starting from a ship to press those unaccustomed to hard work in the early days of traveling, as continuous moderate labor is less wearing than sudden and severe strains. For a healthy man a journey of nine or ten hours is not too much; equivalent to about 350 foot-tons. By the adoption of this plan long distances have been accomplished by persons worn out by depressing influences of cold and disease. Whenever the exigencies of service demand extraordinary and long-sustained exertions, as frequently occur in Arctic experiences, as in breaking through the hummocks and in making roads, extra rations of tea or cocoa should be issued.

Great judgment should be exercised in graduating the weights of the sledge loads to the strength of the men and the nature of the ice to be traveled over. Under favorable circumstances 200 pounds on the short, and 240 pounds on the long sledges are proper, but no very great distance can be accomplished when the weight exceeds 220 pounds. Upon smooth roads the dogs can be depended on for material help in dragging, each animal being weighted to 100 pounds, or about one-half of a good average pull for a man. For rapid progress, as in exploration, or in the event of the necessity for quick communication between distant points, snow shoes of the Canadian pattern will furnish the least fatiguing means; for sledge dragging they are useless.

As regular clothing, stout woolen underwear is recommended as possessing more advantages than garments made of other fabrics, although persons of experience in Arctic service have used with satisfaction materials of chamois and silk. For coat and trowsers, a fine textured, thick and elastic material should be employed, and, when occasion demands, these should be supplemented by the warm and durable garments of fur, such as used by the Esquimaux.

Ross says that in the way of clothing every expedient should be adopted for resisting the impressions of the extreme temperature; nothing will, however, compensate for the want of the heat-generating energy, and external heat is but too often an imperfect expedient. "It is of little use to clothe him who will not in himself produce heat; it is like the attempt to warm a piece of ice by means of a blanket. The mistake is too common that the expedient which can only preserve heat is capable of producing it."

In sledging parties, the head can best be protected by a close-fitting woolen cap, shielding the ears, and over this the usual seal-skin covering. The feet should be enveloped by woolen stockings reaching above the knee, covered with flannel or blanket wrappers, and over these boots, or preferably skin moccasins of the Esquimaux, fitted with leggings. For the hands, woolen mittens with seal-skin outer covering will serve all the purposes of convenience and comfort. Much satisfaction will be derived from the use of a wide flannel roller encircling the belly. The Esquimau wears next his body a shirt made of bird-skins, neatly sewed together with the soft down inwards; over this a loose jumper of fox skin, which is tight around the neck when the hood is attached to it. The jumper is lined with bird-skins and trimmed with fox fur. The breeches are made of bear-skin, reaching down to the knees and upwards so far as just to be in contact with the jumper when the person stands erect. In stooping the body is exposed between the two garments. Bird-skin socks are worn with a padding of grass, and over the whole bear-skin boots.

Professor Newcomb, in regard to clothing, remarks in a private letter, "Your suggestions about clothing are good. I did not try chamois or silk, but found woolen underclothes to answer well; in fact, where working facilities are so poor I think undergarments made partly from cotton will answer better, shrink less, and are more durable. Cotton and woolen stockings are much more serviceable than all wool, and are warm. I have arrived at this conclusion after trying all kinds. Exterior fur clothing I consider indispensable. Reindeer is warmest. Seal-skin is strongest, and will stand more wetting. In extreme cold I used deer-skin and young hair-seal stockings or foot-nips inside my boots, but over my other stockings, which latter would have been better had they covered the knees. My head-gear was similar to that which you suggest. My mittens were made gauntlet fashion, with woolen linings, fur-seal backs, and buckskin palms. Condensation would occur, and until I lined the palms with mink-skin they would freeze in very cold weather, even on the hands, particularly if the position of the arm was such as to induce the flow of blood back from the fingers. The best cold-weather mitten is used by the Tunguses in Siberia. This mitten is made with an opening in the front below the palm. By this arrange-

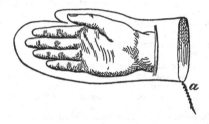

ARCTIC GLOVE.

Sketch showing the hand out, ready for use; "*a*" is lanyard to hang it up.

ment one can readily uncover the thumb and fingers without exposing the whole hand. I can indorse this mitten from experience."

Lieutenant Danenhower states that "the blanket-lined canvas suits used by the miners, stage-drivers, and prospectors on the Pacific slope were found to be very good and serviceable, especially for summer work, when the canvas turns the water. The underclothing should be of heavy flannel, doubled about the chest. The fur garments for winter use should be deer-skin frocks, seal or deer-skin trousers, with seal-skin boots."

The men should be protected by water-proof tenting that will not crack or become damaged when subject to wet and freezing. The experience of the Nares expedition showed engine-room sheet insertion to be well adapted to this purpose. Attention should be paid to the character and adaptability of the knapsack, which should be manufactured out of such material as will not crack with the low temperature nor permit dampness or water to gain access to the clothing and other articles contained therein. Professor Newcomb writes: "The knapsacks provided for our use would not stand water. I improvised one from a pair of oil-cloth pants of the ordinary kind in use among fishermen about Cape Ann. Sewing up the bottom strongly, I stowed my belongings in the same, and, tying it up securely with a rope-yarn, I rigged a rope to sling it across the shoulders. I used to grease it outside whenever a seal was shot. It worked admirably. Some improvements may be suggested, but for keeping things dry, and for this particular kind of work, there was nothing in camp that excelled it."

The Siberian dress consists of fur socks over the ordinary ones, fur stockings outside the socks, and fur boots inclosing all. Over the ordinary dress they wear a sheep-skin coat, with the wool outside, and fastening tight about the neck. Outside of this a deer-skin coat reaching to the ground, with a broad collar and long sleeves.

Not less notably in Arctic life is the character of the mental and moral impressions for good or for evil. Cheerfulness should be cultivated by all practical means, and intellectual tastes catered to by such diversions as are readily attainable by developing the various qualities possessed by the men composing the ship's company. Theatrical displays, orations, recitations, and musical entertainments are among the most advantageous methods that can be had recourse to for the purpose of counteracting the tendency to mental despondency so common during the season of Arctic darkness, and from which, according to Kane, the dogs themselves are not exempt. Professor Newcomb says, "Too much value cannot be attached to anything (within reason) which assists to keep up a healthy mental and moral influence. A contented mind is said to be a continual feast, and I think a properly filled stomach does much towards supplementing this influence."

The sanitary precautions above all others in importance to sojourners in high latitudes refer to food supplies. In consequence of the absence of wood and other fuel in the regions over which the Esquimaux roam, they have no means of creating artificial warmth other than that afforded by burning blubber in a stone lamp trimmed with a wick of moss. This heat, with that radiated from the bodies of the persons occupying the hut of snow or stones chinked with moss, sustains a temperature under which the ordinary household duties are performed without apparent inconvenience or discomfort. On the other hand, the families while traveling from point to point, and the men while out hunting on the ice, are exposed for many hours to a temperature often reaching minus 70°, and yet rarely succumb to this intense cold.

This endurance and resistance to cold is in great part due to the large amount of animal food, particularly of the hydro-carbonaceous sort, consumed. The quantity is almost incredible. Captain Cochrane says, in his "Journey through Siberia," that he has repeatedly seen a Yakute or a Tougousi devour forty pounds of meat in a day; that he has seen three of these gluttons consume a reindeer at one meal; nor are they nice as to the choice of parts, nothing being lost, not even the contents of the bowels, which, with the aid of fat and blood, are converted into black puddings. Dr. Hayes has often seen an Esquimau hunter, when preparing for the hunt, eat from six to twelve pounds of meat, about a third of which was fat, and he places the daily consumption of the man at from twelve to fifteen pounds. The food is mostly taken raw. Dr. Rae states that during his service in the Arctic regions the allowance for a man was eight pounds of fresh venison; four pounds for a woman; and two pounds for each child. When the water afforded supplies, three large whitefish were allowed a man, two to a woman, and one to a child; these fish ranged from three to four pounds each. Failure in the proper quantity and quality of these is sure to impair the strength of the men and invite disease, especially when conjoined with absence of sunlight, dampness, impure air, low temperature, defective cleanliness, want of exercise, and mental despondency. The diet should be varied as the circumstances of the situation will admit, and should consist of a due proportion of animal and vegetable food.

Lieutenant Berry reports to me the interesting fact that the Tchoutches use no salt in their food, and will detect its presence when a white man will not. Rations of fresh meats should be served out from the regular supplies as often as four times a week. This may be done oftener with advantage when such food can be procured by the chase; any opportunity presenting for such extrinsic supplies should be embraced with a view of economizing the ordinary provisions, and as affording materials preventive of scurvy. Such supplies are offered by the musk ox, polar bear, rabbits, ptarmigan, and the various species of water fowl and their eggs. There are persons to whom the flavor and smell of the flesh of the ox are extremely distasteful, especially that of the old bulls; the flesh of the cows is, in this respect, much less objectionable. The seal, walrus, porpoise, and whale may also be depended upon as valuable sources of fresh meat which usually need no particular means of preservation as long as the temperature remains below the freezing point. Dr. Kane noted the fact, however, that the flesh of a deer killed by his men became nearly uneatable from putrefaction, and the liver and intestines utterly so, in 24 hours, and remarks that the rapidity of such a change in a temperature as low as minus 35° seems curious; but the Greenlanders say that extreme cold is rather a promoter than otherwise of the putrefactive process. Esquimaux are in the habit, even in the severest weather, of withdrawing the viscera immediately after death and filling the cavity with stones.

The flesh of these animals has a peculiar flavor, a repugnance for which requires time, perseverance, and a good appetite to overcome in certain persons, while others care little about it and consume their rations with a zest. The food from these sources is believed by the whalemen to be superior to that obtained from the reindeer in warding off scurvy. Walrus meat and the skin of the narwhal enjoy a high reputation among the Esquimaux as anti-scorbutics, the natives of Disco using these in connection with scurvy-grass and the *Angelica officinalis*. Soups should never be substituted for meats, but may be appropriately used as adjuncts. Professor Newcomb writes, "I agree with you in saying 'soups should never be substituted for meat.' The sensation of being comfortably full is one which, after my experience on the 'Jeannette' party retreat, I most heartily indorse."

A common Russian article of diet called *pilmania*, much used in Siberian traveling, consists of meat made into balls and covered with an envelope of dough; it is carried dry in bags. A double handful dropped into a gallon of water is boiled for a few minutes and makes a substantial soup or stew.

For sledge journeying and traveling it is all important to reduce the weight of the food supplies to the least amount compatible with the work to be done, and hence the necessity for highly concentrated preparations. To supply this desideratum the natives of the northwest dry their venison by exposing thin slices to the heat of the sun on a stage under which a small fire is kept, more for the purpose of driving away the flies by the smoke than for promoting exsiccation, and then they pound it between two stones on a bison hide. In this process the pounded meat is contaminated by a greater or smaller admixture of hair and other impurities. The meat, in drying, loses more than three-fourths of its original weight.

The Hudson Bay Company prepare pemmican by drying venison or buffalo meat over a fire or in the sun, which, after pounding, is mixed with an equal weight of melted or boiled fat; the whole is then packed in the skin of the animal furnishing the meat. Occasionally a fruit, known as *saskatum*, or service-berry, is added.

Richardson, in setting out on his boat expedition through Rupert's Land in 1851, was supplied with a superior preparation of concentrated food. It was prepared in the following manner: A round of bullock or beef, of the best quality, having been cut into thin steaks from which the fat and membranous parts were pared away, was dried in a malt-kiln over an oak fire until its moisture was entirely dissipated and the fiber of the meat became friable. It was then ground in a malt-mill, the resultant powder was mixed with nearly an equal weight of melted suet or lard, and to render it more agreeable to the unaccustomed palate a proportion of the best Zante currants was added to a part of it, and part was sweetened with sugar. After the ingredients were incorporated by stirring they were transferred to tin canisters and rammed down, and the air was completely expelled and excluded by filling the canister to the brim with melted lard through a small hole left in the end, which was then covered with a piece of tin and soldered up. This process of preparing pemmican was adopted by Hall as entirely satisfactory; the article supplied the United States ship Rodgers was manufactured in a similar manner.

In the last English expedition two kinds of pemmican were furnished, the plain and the sweet; the plain made of beef cut into thin slices, the fat and coarse fiber having been removed, and dried slowly for twenty-four hours on oak sawdust spread on a floor heated from below. By this process 70 per cent. of water was gotten rid of, and the dried meat was then ground to a powder and mixed with clarified suet in the following proportions: Powdered meat, 4 pounds; suet, 4 pounds; cayenne pepper, one-eighth of an ounce. Sweet pemmican differs from this in containing one-half pound of sugar.

Of the physiological value of pemmican as a food, De Chaumont gives the following analysis as the mean of the two kinds: Nitrogen, 5.283 grains per cent.; carbon, 61.112 grains per cent.; nitrogen to carbon $=1:11.6$.

In a ration of one pound: Nitrogen, 370 grains; carbon, 4.278 grains. Potential energy of one pound, 3,338 foot tons.

Water	8.285
Albuminates	33.646
Fat	53.391
Carbo-hydrates	2.740
Salt	1.544
Total	99.606
Loss	0.394
Total	100.000

With the animal food regular rations of fresh or canned vegetables and fruits should be served. Among the best of these are potatoes, either fresh, desiccated, or preserved in molasses—the latter are the best; cabbage, particularly in the form of sauerkraut; turnips, carrots, soused pickles, and onions. Variety may be gained by adding beets, okra, asparagus, and rhubarb. Among the fruits rank oranges, lemons, limes, preserved apples, peaches, grapes, cranberries, currants, and gooseberries. These should be expressly canned immediately before the voyage. The best charcoal tin should be used, and not the ordinary ("B v") tin of commerce, which contains a large proportion of lead, and makes the danger of lead poisoning greater.

There should be a good allowance of cayenne pepper, condiments, and appetizing sauces to relieve the sameness of the Arctic diet, and to render it palatable. Codfish, bacon, pork, and beans make an agreeable change with the canned meats.

One of the most valuable antiscorbutic substitutes for fresh, succulent vegetables is lime-juice, which should be supplied the men daily in the quantity of one ounce mixed with an equal weight of sugar. It is recommended that the issue of lime-juice begin after leaving port, when the supplies of fresh vegetables have been exhausted, and that an officer should see that each man has taken the prescribed quantity. This last suggestion is important, since, if it is left to individual caprice or fancy, it may be neglected; acid wines and spruce beer (the latter may be prepared on shipboard) are valuable agents in preventing scurvy. It is of much importance to supply the men, if possible, with fresh bread made from new flour preserved in tin canisters hermetically sealed.

It may be well to note the fact, in the event of loss or expenditure of the ordinary supplies of succulent vegetable food and antiscorbutics, that, in the highest regions yet attained, there may be found plants possessing, in some degree, antiscorbutic power, such as scurvy grass, sorrel, reindeer moss, and others; but neither large nor regular supplies can be obtained.

The same remark also applies to the two most easily cultivable annuals, cress and mustard, as the dearth of room and the deteriorating influence of darkness impose restrictions upon their quantity and quality. They have to be put alongside of the stoves, and require from sixteen to eighteen days to grow, presenting a yellow instead of the usual green color of the healthy plants. During the summer, however, when it is reasonably warm—say, July—lettuce, onions, peas, and other plants may be successfully cultivated in the open air, and for this purpose light frames should be made use of.

It is very desirable that an abundance of various seeds should be furnished the Arctic ships for horticultural purposes.

The Esquimaux eat the contents of the stomach of the reindeer, which are composed in part of vegetable matter, and doubtless contributes to their exemption from scurvy. The Arctic whalemen attribute great virtue to the blood of freshly-slaughtered animals. Other reputed antiscorbutic remedies, as citric, tartaric, and malic acids, which form one-twelfth part by weight of lime-juice, and the alkaline salts of these acids should be furnished the ships with the view of determining their influence, should suitable opportunities offer. The indispensable necessity of lime-juice in the sledging parties, and the difficulties of carrying and preparing it for use, induced the suggestion of combining the juice and pemmican in the proportion of one ounce to a pound of the latter. A large quantity of this preparation was furnished for use in the sledging parties of the "Rodgers," but this vessel was lost before its value could be tested. The pemmican is greatly improved in taste and flavor, and will, it is believed, be more assimilable. This is an important advantage, as there are persons who cannot eat the ordinary article.

To avoid delay and labor under similar circumstances in serving out the food, it is recommended that single rations of articles, particularly tea, which should be compressed, shall be prepared before the sledges leave the ship. All food, when possible, should be taken hot.

An admirable article of lime-juice, prepared by evaporation in shallow earthenware pans, at a temperature not exceeding 140°, was furnished the "Rodgers" for traveling parties. It presents the consistence of a semi-solid, and when dissolved possesses the properties of the juice unimpaired. Each pound represents a gallon of the solution of the ordinary strength, so that this quantity contained in a sealed tin can will supply proper rations for eight men sixteen days. A single ration, when frozen, will not exceed a walnut in bulk, and may be then carried in a canvas bag or capsule, and when needed can be melted, if there be a scarcity of fuel, by the warmth of the body in the sleeping bag. The plain juice freezes at + 25° Fah.; that fortified with 10 per cent. of spirits at + 15°. Preserved potatoes may also be transported dry in bags. Edwards' prepared potato was used in the Nares expedition, and was generally liked by the men; after slight boiling it was ready for use.

The following tables show the sledge ration of the Nares expedition, and the proposed one:

British dietary.			Proposed dietary.		
	Lbs.	*Ozs.*		*Lbs.*	*Ozs.*
Per day, per man:			Per day, per man:		
Pemmican	1	0	Lime juice } combined	1	0
Biscuit		14	Pemmican }		
Bacon*		4	Biscuit		14
Potato		2	Cheese		2
Rum (fluid ounces)		2½	Dried potato		4
Chocolate		1	Dried onions		¼
Sugar for chocolate		¾	Tea		1
Tea†		⅓	Sugar		2
Sugar for tea		1½	Condensed milk		1
Stearine		3	‡Alcohol or petroleum (fluid ounces)		4
Spirits of wine		1	Tobacco		½
Tobacco		½	Salt		½
Salt		⅓	Pepper		1/10
Pepper		7/10	Curry powder		¼
Onion or curry powder		½			
Total weight	2	14.9	Total weight	2	13.5

* Increased in some cases to 6 ounces, at request, in lieu of pemmican.
† Double allowance of tea was carried in lieu of rum.
‡ Four fluid ounces alcohol of 75 per cent. will weigh about 3½ oz. avoirdupois. Average load hauled by each man on leaving ship, 234¼ pounds.

It will be observed that spirits have been altogether omitted from the proposed dietary, tea having been decided by an immense majority of Arctic travelers to be more advantageous as a comforting and strengthening beverage, and upon which more work can be done. The Siberian Russian drinks large quantities of hot tea while traveling, and many who are addicted to stimulating drinks while at home abstain altogether from them on the road, and drink nothing but tea. A convenient form of tea is known as "brick tea," which is compressed in bricks of two-pound weight, and which can be cut up as used.

In Kane's experience the men, after repeated trials, preferred coffee in the morning and tea in the evening, the former seeming to be more enduring in its effects and delaying hunger, while the latter was more soothing after hard work and disposing to sleep. There are important differences as to the action of the two agents according to Dr. Smith; while both are powerful respiratory excitants, increasing the elimination of the carbon dioxide, coffee causes specially an increase in the respiratory and circulatory rate, diminishes perspiration and thereby the loss of heat, and promotes the action of the bowels. Tea, on the other hand, lessens the force of circulation and perspiration and cools the skin, and does not congest the mucous membranes. Hence, in certain respects, coffee and tea are physiological antidotes of each other. It is suggested that the use of maté and cocoa in emergencies requiring excessive exertion may prove advantageous; the extract, made up into pills, may be carried in the pocket.

Rum was used in the Nares expedition, and a cheering influence attributed to it, taken after the day's labor when the men had gotten into their sleeping bags. It was universally pronounced a failure in increasing working power and endurance. Hayes says he has known most unpleasant consequences to result from the injudicious use of whisky for the purpose of temporary stimulation, and strong able-bodied men to become utterly incapable of resisting cold in consequence of the long-continued use of alcoholic drinks. Condensed milk and egg-powder are valuable additions to the sledge dietary. Eggs, hard boiled and preserved in vinegar, will keep for months. As regards tobacco, it has been observed that smoking tends to lessen the inclination or ability for work, but the fact of the difficulty of keeping the pipes going in open air will restrict this practice to the evening hours in camp. Chewing is regarded by some as antiscorbutic in a slight degree.

Supplies of potable water are most commonly obtained by melting snow; that from the old ice will be found the best. Two or three feet of the upper portion of floebergs are fresh-water ice, and below this it becomes saline; so that chemical tests should be constantly had recourse to in determining this point. Occasionally, on long journeys, which can only be made inland without boats, fresh pools are encountered, which will supply an abundance of sweet water. The use of snow is to be deprecated, as rather tending to increase than to assuage thirst; for one gets as thirsty in very cold as in tropical weather, and the temptation is strong to eat snow. The Esquimaux, when compelled to use it, squeeze the snow in the hand, and breathe through the mass thus compressed, the warmth of the hand and expired air together producing water, which may then be sucked out. Dr. James M. Ambler, of the "Jeannette," was very particular on this point, and recommended the use of distilled water, which was used during all the experience in the pack while aboard ship. There was no fresh-water ice in the vicinity. During the sled parties, and on the retreat, snow was used from the highest hummocks for cooking and drinking. The pool-water was too salty.

On sledding expeditions suitable sleeping bags should be furnished. They are best made of reindeer skin upon the under side, which is in contact with the ice, and of lighter materials upon the upper side. Their length may be the height of the persons using them and their shape somewhat that of the outline of the body, so as to avoid the extra weight of quadrangular bags.

It is believed that a close adhesion to the sanitary suggestions now made will remove any fear of the occurrence of scurvy during the service of the United States steamers in the Arctic regions.

In this connection it will be proper to call attention to the common diseases and injuries liable to occur, that they may be speedily recognized and treated by those in charge of the sledging parties when unaccompanied by a medical officer, as must necessarily often happen.

Scurvy is one of the most redoubtable enemies of the Arctic resident. It consists of a peculiar alteration in the properties of the blood, which becomes impoverished in nourishing materials by errors in diet, the most immeasurably frequent of which is the absence of succulent vegetable matter. The disease begins insidiously, the skin assuming a yellowish or earthy hue; is dry, rough, and unperspiring. Dark-red or brownish flecks of small size and round outline break out on various parts of the body, and later the discoloration presents large purple blotches; the gums are tender, swollen, and of a dark color, bleed readily, and separate from the teeth; pains in the joints of the legs, particularly in the hams, are generally complained of, and are often confounded with rheumatism. There are muscular weakness and feeling of lassitude, ordinary exertion producing exhaustion, palpitation of the heart, and breath-lessness. The mind partakes in the general debility of the body and there is more or less disposition to despondency. In the more confirmed stages of the disease, swell-ings occur in the hams and other parts from the bloody and fibrinous effusions, and the bones and internal organs suffer in various degrees.

These are the salient points in scurvy, and every precaution should be adopted to detect its presence at the earliest moment, especially by a periodical monthly exam-ination after the ships are settled in winter quarters. It should be remembered that paleness of the countenance is an inseparable circumstance in those who have spent a winter in the Arctic regions. There is nothing like acclimatizing a European, for experience has shown that in every expedition the crews have been more sickly the second than the first year. Middendorf asserts that the high north deteriorates the constitution of the blood, and that after three winters very few can stand the fourth. It is a familiar fact that continuous low temperature impairs the appetite and inter-feres with sleep. It was noticed by the officers of the Alert that during the winter when the moon was up, which lasted about a week each month, more food was con-sumed than during the dark part of the month. This was at least in part due to the greater amount of exercise during moonlight. These facts militate against the suc-cess of the colonizing plan in Arctic exploration. It cannot, however, be doubted that much can be done in delaying the advance of this constitutional impairment and in supporting and prolonging the ability for active exertion in the Arctic regions by a close and persistent adhesion to the sanitary points already fully dwelt upon, especially when the colonists are comfortably housed in well-lighted rooms. To what extent, if at all, the ordinary artificial or electrical lights can replace or substitute that from a solar origin in its action upon the process of nutrition, I am unable to say.

It is particularly important to examine the men selected for sledging parties, to see that they are free from scorbutic taint, inasmuch as the hard work incident to this service would inevitably disqualify a person with such tendencies in a brief period, and embarrass the party with an invalid. The proper means of preventing this dis-ease have been already fully indicated.

The most frequent trouble in the Arctic region is frost-bite. The men should be fre-quently asked if they perceive loss of sensation in any part of their bodies, as frost-bite may occur unawares, especially on a sudden rise of temperature. If on examin-ing the part it presents alteration in color to a dull waxy or purplish livid hue, with the formation of vesication or bladders, an effort should be made at once to restore the circulation slowly by frictions with the hands, or rubbing the part with melting snow, or plunging it into cold water for some time. Professor Newcomb found this about the best remedy.

Lieutenant Berry writes me that the Tchoutches are always very careful to have all hand and foot gear as soft and pliable as possible, which permits the joints to play freely and promotes thereby circulation, rendering them less susceptible to cold. Men unaccustomed to extreme cold are frequently frosted before they are aware of it. There is always a tingling sensation in the nose and cheeks just before freezing. The freezing can frequently be prevented by ungloving the hand and placing it over those parts for a short while. In severe weather the natives of Siberia will frequently be seen repeating this operation.

When the nose or cheek is frozen the best method of thawing it out is the one de-scribed. The plan of rubbing on snow is erroneous, for before the frozen part thaws a portion of the snow is melted, and the part being wet, if in the open air, at once freezes again. When the circulation is established, dress with glycerine and cotton batting, and cover the whole with a bandage. Great care should be taken not to use stimu-lating applications at first, otherwise acute inflammation, followed perhaps by mortifi-cation, will result. Should these efforts fail of success, the frost-bitten part should be dressed with carbolized cosmoline and cotton batting, and the patient made as com-fortable as possible, being placed, in case the legs and feet are affected, in a sledge. Lieut. F. Payer states that a mixture of iodine and collodion proved most efficacious against frost-bite during the Arctic voyage of the "Tegethoff" in 1872.

In very cold weather the face-cloth should be worn, and traveling by night adopted, as far as can be done, so as to enable the men to sleep during the day, when there is less likelihood, from the higher temperature, of frost-bite. It is advised, to prevent the effects of cold upon the exposed surfaces, to rub them with unctuous applications, as cosmoline. Professor Newcomb tried a mixture of glycerine and burnt cork on exposed parts of the face and nose to prevent frost-bite. The results were good, though it looked dirty. To avoid the action of the cold drinking-vessels upon the lips, the rims should be rubbed with the gloved hand.

The glare of the snow upon the eyes produces the condition known as snow-blind-ness, particularly in traveling during the spring and summer months. To prevent its occurrence, when the sun reappears the men should be provided with goggles of neutral-tinted glass; and on the march or in sledging parties a dark patch may be affixed to the backs of the men, upon which, when in line, the eyes may be directed instead of upon the snow. Professor Newcomb recommends that variously-colored garments be worn. The relief to the eyes thus obtained is very great. The leading man on the drag-ropes should be changed frequently to the rear, and the eyelids may be smeared with charcoal and grease. Professor Newcomb says he also rubbed some of the mixture of glycerine and burnt cork about the eyelids to relieve the glare of light, and with some success. The treatment of this disease is cold applications, astringent and sedative colyria, and the exclusion of light by bandaging the eyes. Professor Newcomb noticed an unusual brittleness of the finger-nails most of the time he was in the Arctic regions.

Sometimes sledge labor causes exhaustion and fainting, and when a case of this sort occurs the person should be immediately placed upon his back, with the head low, and the clothes about the neck loosened. He should be given a little warm tea, a teaspoonful of aromatic spirits of ammonia or brandy, and allowed to rest for awhile. The occurrence of perfect unconsciousness and of complete exhaustion requires the person to be at once removed to the tents, rubbed with hot flannels, and the above-mentioned stimulants given from time to time until he recovers. He should then be dressed warmly and allowed to rest in his sleeping bag for a few hours. To meet the emergencies of accidents and diseases of a slight character which may occur in the sledging journeys, the officers in command should be instructed by the surgeon of the vessel in the application of simple means and furnished with suitable supplies for these purposes.

EXHIBIT L.

WASHINGTON, D. C.

To the Honorable ROBERT T. LINCOLN,
Secretary of War :

DEAR SIR : We will build a steamer (bark-rigged), a duplicate of the steam whaler "Thrasher" (now in San Francisco, Cal.), and have her completed ready for service in three months from date of receiving the order. With the labor and material at our command, we could build this steamer in sixty days. We have a duplicate of the "Thrasher's" engines nearly completed. We have built five steamers for the Arctic whale-fishing, and the four that have been tried have proved able and efficient for the service.

Mr. Frank Reynolds, of New York, has made four voyages into the Arctic in these steamers, and many of the improvements in strengthening of the "Thrasher" were by him, and he superintended her construction. Mr. Reynolds could furnish you valuable information, no doubt, as to the requirements of vessels for this service.

The dimensions we propose to build are 144 feet measuring length; 33 feet beam; 16 feet deep; hold, 9 feet; between decks, 7 feet. The type of engines we have is same as we put in the "Thrasher," and the steamer "Jesse H. Freeman," which was examined by Commodore Jouett and one of the engineers of the Brooklyn Navy-Yard, and has their indorsement. They were built and designed by Messrs. C. H. Delamater & Co., of New York, and no pains or expense was spared to make them strong and efficient for Arctic service. They have two boilers of the Scotch type, with sufficient steam capacity to propel the boat ten knots on a consumption of seven tons coal per day.

While the "Thrasher" was admitted to be the strongest and best adapted to the Arctic service of any vessel we have built, we should make some improvements to strengthen her bilges by braces, which could not be done in a whaler, as they would interfere with her storing capacity. We should also sheathe her with boiler-plate iron, say six feet wide (where she would take the ice), to abaft her main rigging. This vessel would have some canvas, as a bark without steam, and would work and sail as well with two-bladed propeller, which would be protected by stern-post when in the ice and not used. Her speed under canvas alone would be from 10 to 12 knots. These vessels work admirably under canvas in a narrow sea-way.

As we have the plans and molds made and the timber in yard to commence on, we could lay the keel in five days from date of receiving the order. It would necessarily cost more to build this vessel in the limited time we should have, and our price would be $100,000—same price as the Government paid us for the "Rodgers." We beg to refer you to Mr. Dingley, of Maine, who represents the district (where we build) in Congress, and is acquainted with our facilities and ability to perform what we undertake.

Respectfully, yours,

G. C. GOSS,
Representing the Firm of Goss, Sawyer & Packard, of Bath, Maine.

E X H I B I T   M .

[Special Orders No. 97.]

WAR DEPARTMENT, OFFICE OF THE CHIEF SIGNAL OFFICER,
Washington, D. C., June 17, 1881.

I. By direction of the Secretary of War, the following-named officers and enlisted men are assigned to duty as the expeditionary force to Lady Franklin Bay:*
First Lieutenant A. W. Greely, 5th Cavalry, Acting Signal Officer and Assistant.
Second Lieutenant Frederick F. Kislingbury, 11th Infantry, Acting Signal Officer.
Second Lieutenant James B. Lockwood, 23rd Infantry, Acting Signal Officer
Sergeant Edward Israel, Signal Corps, U. S. Army.
Sergeant Winfield S. Jewell, Signal Corps, U. S. Army.
Sergeant George W. Rice, Signal Corps, U. S. Army.
Sergeant David C. Ralston, Signal Corps, U. S. Army.
Sergeant Hampden S. Gardiner, Signal Corps, U. S. Army.
Sergeant William H. Cross, General Service, U. S. Army.
Sergeant David L. Brainard, Co. L, 2nd Cavalry.
Sergeant David Linn, Co. C, 2nd Cavalry.
Corporal Daniel C. Starr, Co. F, 2nd Cavalry.
Corporal Paul Grimm, Co. H, 11th Infantry.
Corporal Nicholas Salor, Co. H, 2nd Cavalry.
Corporal Joseph Elison, Co. E, 10th Infantry.
Private Charles B. Henry, Co. E, 5th Cavalry.
Private Maurice Connell, Co. B, 3rd Cavalry.
Private Jacob Bender, Co. F, 9th Infantry.
Private Francis Long, Co. F, 9th Infantry.
Private William Whisler, Co. F, 9th Infantry.
Private Henry Bierderbick, Co. G, 17th Infantry.
Private Julius Fredericks, Co. L, 2nd Cavalry.
Private James Ryan, Co. H, 2nd Cavalry.
Private William A. Ellis, Co. C, 2nd Cavalry.
II. In accordance with special instructions from the Secretary of War, Lieutenant Greely will contract at Disco, Greenland, with Octave Pavy, M. D., who will thereafter remain on duty as Acting Assistant Surgeon, U. S. Army, with the expeditionary force.
III. First Lieutenant A. W. Greely, 5th Cavalry, Acting Signal Officer and Assistant to the Chief Signal Officer, is hereby assigned to the command of the expedition, and is charged with the execution of the orders and instructions given below. He will forward all reports and observations to the Chief Signal Officer, who is charged with the control and supervision of the expedition.

W. B. HAZEN,
Brig. & Bvt. Maj. Gen'l,
Chief Signal Officer, U. S. A.

Official copy from the records of the Signal Office.

W. B. HAZEN,
Chief Signal Officer.

1, 15, '84.

[Instructions No. 72.]

WAR DEPARTMENT,
OFFICE OF THE CHIEF SIGNAL OFFICER,
Washington, D. C., June 17, 1881.

The following general instructions will govern in the establishment and management of the expedition, organized under Special Orders No. 97, War Department, Office of the Chief Signal Officer, Washington, D. C., dated June 17, 1881.
The *permanent* station will be established at the most suitable point north of the eighty-first parallel and contiguous to the coal seam discovered near Lady Franklin Bay by the English expedition of 1875.
After leaving St. John's, Newfoundland, except to obtain Esquimaux hunters, dogs, clothing, &c., at Disco or Upernavik, only such stops will be made as the condition of the ice necessitates, or as are essential in order to determine the exact location and condition of the stores cached on the east coast of Grinnell Land by the English ex-

---

* Corporal Starr and Private Ryan relieved and returned in the "Proteus." Jans Edward (Eskimo), and Frederick Thorley Christiansen (half-breed), engaged at Proven, accompanied the expedition. See Greely to C. S. O., August 15, 1881, page 42.—RECORDER.

pedition of 1875. During any enforced delays along that coast it would be well to supplement the English depots by such small caches from the steamer's stores of provisions as would be valuable to a party retreating southward by boats from Robeson Channel. At each point where an old depot is examined or a new one established three brief notices will be left of the visit, one to be deposited in the cairn built or found standing, one to be placed on the north side of it, and one to be buried twenty feet north (magnetic) of the cairn. Notices discovered in cairns will be brought away, replacing them, however, by copies.

The steamer should, on arrival at the *permanent* station, discharge her cargo with the utmost dispatch, and be ordered to return to St. John's, N. F., after a careful examination of the seam of coal at that point has been made by the party to determine whether an ample supply is easily procurable. A report in writing on this subject will be sent by the returning vessel. In case of doubt, an ample supply must be retained from the steamer's stores.

By the returning steamer will be sent a brief report of proceedings, and as full a transcript as possible of all meteorological and other observations made during the voyage.

After the departure of the vessel the energies of the party should first be devoted to the erection of the dwelling-house and observatories, after which a sledge party will be sent, according to the proposal made to the Navy Department, to the high land near Cape Joseph Henry.

The sledging parties will generally work in the interests of exploration and discovery. The work to be done by them should be marked by all possible care and fidelity. The outlines of coasts entered on charts will be such only as have actually been seen by the party. Every favorable opportunity will be improved by the sledging parties to determine accurately the geographical positions of all their camps, and to obtain the bearing therefrom of all distant cliffs, mountains, islands, &c.

Careful attention will be given to the collection of specimens of the animal, mineral, and vegetable kingdoms. Such collections will be made as complete as possible; will be considered the property of the Government of the United States, and are to be at its disposal.

Special instructions regarding the meteorological, magnetic, tidal, pendulum, and other observations as recommended by the Hamburg International Polar Conference, are transmitted herewith.*

It is contemplated that the *permanent* station shall be visited in 1882 and in 1883 by a steam sealer or other vessel, by which supplies for, and such additions to, the present party as are deemed needful will be sent.

In case such vessel is unable to reach Lady Franklin Bay in 1882, she will cache a portion of her supplies and all of her letters and dispatches at the most northerly point she attains on the *east coast of Grinnell Land*, and establish a small depot of supplies at Littleton Island. Notices of the locality of such depots will be left at one or all of the following places, viz, Cape Hawks, Cape Sabine, and Cape Isabella.

In case no vessel reaches the *permanent* station in 1882, the vessel sent in 1883 will remain in Smith Sound until there is danger of its closing by ice; and, on leaving, will land all her supplies and a party at Littleton Island, which party will be prepared for a winter's stay, and will be instructed to send sledge parties up the *east side of Grinnell Land* to meet this party. If not visited in 1882, Lieutenant Greely will abandon his station not later than September 1, 1883, and will retreat southward by boat, following closely the *east coast of Grinnell Land* until the relieving vessel is met or Littleton Island is reached.

A special copy of all reports will be made each day, which will be sent home each year by the returning vessel.

The full narrative of the several branches will be prepared with accuracy, leaving the least possible amount of work afterwards to prepare them for publication.

The greatest caution will be taken at the station against fire, and daily inspections made of every spot where fire can communicate.

In case of any fatal accident or permanent disability happening to Lieutenant Greely the command will devolve on the officer next in seniority, who will be governed by these instructions.

W. B. HAZEN,
Brig. & Bvt. Maj. Gen'l, Chief Signal Officer, U. S. A.

Official copy from the records of the Signal Office.

W. B. HAZEN,
Chief Signal Officer.

1, 15, '84.

* Not printed.—RECORDER.

(Telegram 6 W. Received at —, July 1, 1881, 10.45 a. m., from St. John's, July 1.)

To SIGNALS, *Wash'n:*

Letters mailed noon to-day reach us; shall make formal start July fourth, dropping down to anchorage in bay, awaiting one hundred packages freight due on Hibernian Wednesday.

GREELY, *Lieut.*

Official copy from the records of the Signal Office.

W. B. HAZEN,
Chief Signal Officer.

Nov. 9, 1883.

ST. JOHN'S, N'F'D, *July 5, 1881.*

MY DEAR GENERAL: We leave St. John's to-morrow, and I am glad to be on my way. We have had much to contend with here in a people with whom it is hardly possible to deal except by written contract. I get away, however, leaving little, if any, more money than I expected. I have had to duplicate some things here, fearing that the Allen steamer will not bring them. I have tried to be as economical as I possibly could be, and hardly think that much can be charged to extravagant purchases. I would advise you by all means to seek proposals for next year's vessel immediately on the return of the "Proteus." I am quite certain they will attempt to run up the price on us next year to $25,000, or perhaps more, but by good management a vessel should not cost to exceed, say, $20,000 as a limit, and possibly down to $15,000. I will write fully as to the "Proteus" on her return. I hope to have papers in shape to send estimates in some detail from Disco. The men are all behaving well, but the naval engineer man keeps very full of beer. We sail to-morrow, if the Hibernian gets in. I do not understand how such delays occurred in the forwarding of ammunition, photographic material, &c., all of which should have been here ten days since.

A gloom has been cast over us by the terrible attempt on the President's life, but I am somewhat encouraged by your welcome telegram. Give my kindest compliments to Mrs. Hazen.

Faithfully and sincerely yours,

A. W. GREELY,
U. S. Army.

Official copy from the records of the Signal Office.

W. B. HAZEN,
Chief Signal Officer.

Nov. 9, 1883.

ST. JOHN'S, N'F'D, *July 6th, 1881.*

CHIEF SIGNAL OFFICER OF THE ARMY:

SIR: Referring to the items for repairs of steam-launch "Lady Greely," No. 66, in the bills of Mr. Gemmel and J. & W. Stewart, who paid the last bill to save extra sets of vouchers; I have to say that the machinery has proved thus far too slight and has broken three times without any extraordinary cause. She works very finely now, is an excellent sea-boat, and if the engine holds together will do well hereafter.

I am, resp'y, y'rs,

A. W. GREELY,
1st Lt. 5 Cav., A. S. O. and Ass't, Com'd'g L. F. B. Expedition.

Official copy from the records of the Signal Office.

W. B. HAZEN,
Chief Signal Officer.

Nov. 9, 1883.

ST. JOHN'S, N'F'D, *July 7, 1881.*

CHIEF SIGNAL OFFICER OF THE ARMY:

SIR: I enclose herewith description of the "Proteus." She has broken her way through *new ice* over two feet thick the whole length of the harbor. She has been pronounced by the officers of the U. S. S. "Alliance" as the best ship for ice work they have ever seen. Every shipmaster and every man with whom I have conversed agree that there is no better vessel on this coast for such work; one or two others are of the same build and probably as good. The captain is mentioned in the description. The mate, engineers, and crew are selected from the entire sealing crew of the firm. I might add that the firm has not been able to effect any insurance, and are certain in no event to cover more than the hull. This may complicate the hiring of a vessel at this price next year.

I am, resp'y, y'rs,

A. W. GREELY,
1st Lt., 5 C., Ass't, Com'd'g.

Official copy from the records of the Signal Office.

W. B. HAZEN,
Chief Signal Officer.

Nov. 9, 1883.

[Inclosure 1.]

The "Proteus" was built at Dundee, Scotland, in 1874; Alexander Stevens & Co. She is barkentine rigged, and has a gross tonnage of 619 tons and a registered tonnage of 467 tons. Her register is British; dimensions as follows:

	Feet.
Length over all	190
Breadth of beam	29
Depth of hold	18

One pair compound engines, 25 and 50 in. cylinders, with 30-in. stroke; one cylindrical boiler, 13 ft. diameter and 10 ft. long; three furnaces; horse-power, 110. The ship is built of oak, with a sheathing of "iron-wood" from above the water-line to below the turn of the bilge; the prow armed with iron; capacity 8¼ knots an hour. Capt. Pike has made six sealing and whaling trips *in this vessel on the Labrador and Newfoundland* coasts encountering and breaking through ice each trip. He says the vessel is capable of breaking her way, with occasional backing to free herself, through new ice to the thickness of eighteen inches. The vessel was built expressly for this kind of work, as she is provided with a spare-rudder and two spare-screws and shafts.

Official copy from the records of the Signal Office.

W. B. HAZEN,
Chief Signal Officer.

Nov. 9, 1883.

(Telegram received at 9,26, 1881, 9.54 a. m., from Disco, Greenland, July 18th, '81.)

To Gen. HAZEN, *Wash'n, D. C.:*

Arrived Disco July sixteenth, nine p. m. Continuous northerly winds, with thick weather, lengthened passage, which was entirely unobstructed by ice. Inspector Smith reports mild winter, with advances from Upernavik favorable to easy navigation in Melville by Doctor Pavy and Henry Clay at Rittenbank. Well; party all well. Advise all concerned.

Leave Monday for Upernavik via Rittenbank.

GREELY,
Commanding.

To COPENHAGEN.

Official copy from the records of the Signal Office.

W. B. HAZEN,
Chief Signal Officer.

Nov. 9, 1883.

RITTENBANK, GREENLAND, *July 21st*, 1881.

To the CHIEF SIGNAL OFFICER, U. S. A.,
Washington, D. C.

SIR: I have the honor to report that the Lady Franklin Bay Expedition reached Rittenbank at 9.30 a. m., to-day. A Danish brig ready for sea permits this further report. At Godhavn Herr Krarup Smith, chief inspector of Northern Greenland, received me most kindly and promised all possible assistance. Unfortunately he was obliged to leave on a tour of inspection 12 hours after our arrival, having delayed his departure thus long on our account.

Through the kindness of his excellent wife I was, however, enabled to obtain a fair supply of dogs, dog-meat, dried fish, and seal-skins, which had been negotiated for through the energy of Dr. O. Pavy. Dr. Pavy was at Rittenbank on our arrival, but reached Godhavn the morning of July 20th. A contract at once was made with him to serve as act'g ass't surgeon of the expedition. We were prevented by fog from leaving Godhavn until 12.30 a. m., July 21st, and arrived here, 60 miles distant, as stated above, having been delayed a short time by thick weather. A good set of observations for time were obtained at Godhavn, p. m. of July 19th, a. m. of 20th, the only times on which the sun was to be seen during our stay.

Dr. Pavy has nine dogs, which makes, with the 12 bought, 21, and he has also three sledges and certain other trappings. He has also accumulated 3,500 lbs. of dried fish at this place. The arrangements made by Dr. Pavy at his own risk have been of marked benefit to the service, as a supply of dogs and food can rarely be obtained save by ordering in advance.

Mr. Henry Clay has been hired to accompany the expedition to L. F. B., at a nominal salary of $15.00 dollars per month and a ration, as a signal service assistant. Acting on the advice of Herr Inspector Smith, arrangements for certain clothing, the two Esquimaux hunters, and the balance of dogs have been deferred until we reach Upernavik, where I expect to find the inspector.

I hope to leave here to-morrow morning, and, proceeding through the Waigat Strait, reach Upernavik by July 23d. In addition to the mildness of the winter, I have to report that the spring has been unusually early. Everything now seems to favor a fortunate journey northward. Lieut. Lockwood has been sent with four men to-day to obtain some birds from a "loomery" several miles distant from here. All officers and men are in the best of health.

I am, very respectfully, your obedient servant,

A. W. GREELY,
1st Lieut., 5th Cavalry, Act. Signal Officer and
Assistant, Com'd'g L. F. B. Expedition.

Official copy from the records of the Signal Office.

W. B. HAZEN,
Chief Signal Officer.

Nov. 9, 1883.

UPERNAVIK, GREENLAND, *July* 26, 1881.
CHIEF SIGNAL OFFICER OF THE ARMY:

SIR: I have to report that I have this day forwarded to your office duplicate contracts made with Octave Pavy, M. D., July 20, 1881, at Godhavn, Gd., to serve as Actg. Asst. Surg. of this expedition, for reference to the Surgeon-General; also to the Adjutant-General, through you, a copy of oath administered to Dr. Pavy, on his entering on his duties.

I am, resp'y, yours,

A. W. GREELY,
1st Lt. 5 Cav. A. S. O. & Asst. Com'd'g L. F. B. Expedition.

Official copy from the records of the Signal Office.

W. B. HAZEN,
Chief Signal Officer.

Nov. 9, 1883.

UPERNAVIK, GD., *July* 29, 1881.
CHIEF SIGNAL OFFICER OF THE ARMY:

SIR: I have the honor to recommend that arrangements be made at St. John's, Nfd., *this year* for the following stores, to be ready and to be paid for next summer, when the relief steamer leaves:

Six tons dried seal meat (should be pressed in bales and kept *dry;* cost should be trifling, as it is used considerably for manure; has been sold fresh for 40c. a barrel): very necessary for dogs, and if not sent will cause much greater expenditure—probably ten times over; should be baled, covered with water-proof material. (75) seventy-five pairs seal-skin boots (with hair off, shaved or tanned), of *three largest sizes;* 50 prs. to be *unsoled with leather,* and 25 prs. to have *leather soles attached,* as is done for sealing use (should cost about $2.50 for plain boots and $5.00 for the soled boots); these boots should be best quality, and guaranteed to be water-tight. 150 pairs "Iceland stockings;" should cost about 40 to 50c. per pair; should be good quality to wear (but not the best); same as generally used among sealers. 5 "square flipper" seal-skins, *shaved;* or, if not to be had, 10 "old dog-harp" seal-skins (*the whole lot, either kind,* should cost about $30 to $35); needed for repair of boots, &c.; very important.

Proposals should be asked for the furnishing of these supplies of J. & W. Stewart, C. F. Bennett, Walter Grieve & Co., Browning Bros., St. John's, and Munn & Co., Harbor Grace. All things being equal, I would recommend J. & W. Stewart as very reliable. Care should be taken to insist on *good* articles.

Mr. Molloy, U. S. consul, would undoubtedly attend to the inspection and proposal. It is most important that these articles should be obtained at St. John's.

The clothing now had is barely sufficient for use during the coming twelvemonth, and a supply cannot be had in Greenland under less than a year, ordered in advance, and even then is uncertain. It is more than probable, too, that the cost would be really less in St. John's than here.

Action is necessary this autumn, as some of the articles are obtained in Labrador, and the seal meat must be caught in March.

I am, respectfully, yours,

A. W. GREELY,
1st Lieut. 5th Cavalry, A. S. O. and
Assistant Com'd'g L. F. B. Expd.

Official copy from the records of the Signal Office.

W. B. HAZEN,
Chief Signal Officer.

Nov. 9, 1883.

FORT CONGER, LADY FRANKLIN BAY,
Grinnell Land, August 15th, 1881.

To the CHIEF SIGNAL OFFICER OF THE ARMY:

SIR: I have the honor to make the following report regarding the progress of the International Polar Expedition, which I have the honor to command. Leaving St. John's, Nfdl., at noon, July 7th, the harbor of Godhavn, Greenland, was reached 9 p.m., July 16th. The voyage was made in the face of continuously adverse winds, experiencing two strong northerly gales and constant cloudy and foggy weather. The ship behaved admirably. The only ice seen south of Cape Farewell were a few icebergs off Funk Island, and about forty in 52° N., 53° 15' W. Pack-ice was fallen in with at 10.30 p.m., July 12th, in 61° 30' N., 53° 30' W., and was left behind at 3 a.m., July 13th. A second pack was encountered the same day at 2.30 p.m., in 62° 30' N., 53° 15' W., and passed through in an hour. Neither pack offered any obstructions to free passage or caused the slightest delay. They both consisted of ice-floes (varying from one to eight feet above the water), which, coming from the east coast of Greenland, had drifted with the southerly current from Cape Farewell into Davis Strait.

Not a dozen icebergs were seen in Greenland waters until Disco Bay was reached, when over a hundred were counted at one time. From Herr Krarup Smith, inspector of North Greenland, I learned that the past winter in Greenland (except a brief period of cold in March) had been one of marked and unusual mildness, and that the ice north of Upernavik had broken up very early. Delaying his vessel fifteen hours on the expedition's account, he left the next day for an official inspection of Proven and Upernavik, assuring me of all possible aid and assistance for himself and all other officials. On July 20th Dr. Octave Pavy joined the expedition as Acting Assistant Surgeon. At Godhavn twelve dogs, a large quantity of dog food, and some seal-skins were procured: A considerable quantity of *mattak* (skin of the white whale, a very valuable antiscorbutic), and a few articles of fur-clothing were obtained by barter, as they could not be bought for money. Hard-bread and tobacco were principally given in exchange. Valuable assistance was given in this matter by the wife of Inspector Smith and by Mr. Fleischer, chief trader and governor of Godhavn. The remains of the house, purchased in 1880, was taken on board, as well as 3,000 pounds of buffalo pemmican, placed at my disposal by H. W. Howgate, of Washington. Nine dogs, which were at Rittenbank, were also bought of O. Pavy. A good set of observations for time was made July 19-20, at the only hours the sun shone during our stay at Godhavn. Leaving Godhavn the morning of the 21st, the vessel reached Rittenbank the same forenoon. At that point were purchased a number of seal-skins, a large quantity of dog food, and other minor articles, which had been accumulated for the expedition through the energy of Dr. Pavy. The nine dogs before mentioned were taken on board. Mr. Henry Clay * there joined the expedition under the status of a Signal-Service employé. Being delayed by the fog, Lt. Lockwood was sent with a party to obtain birds form Awe Prins Island. He returned that evening with sixty-five guillemots (*Alca Awa or Alca Brünnichi*). It was said at Rittenbank that the spring had been the most forward one for years. Leaving Rittenbank 2.15 p.m., July 22d,

---

* Mr. Clay returned in the "Proteus" from Lady Franklin Bay.—RECORDER.

and running through the Waigat, the steamer was off Upernavik 9 p. m. July 23rd,
but owing to fog could not enter the harbor until the next morning. Two Esquimaux
whom I had understood would accompany the expedition were not available, and in consequence a trip to Proven, about 50 miles distant, was necessary to obtain others. Skin
clothing could not be obtained, except ten suits, which, having been made by order
of the Danish Government for the use of the International Polar Station of Upernavik
of 1882-'83, and were sold, through the kindness of Inspector Smith, to the expedition.
A severe storm setting in prevented Lt. Lockwood (whom Mr. Elborg, chief trader at
Upernavik had offered to accompany to Proven) from starting on the 24th. On the
morning of July 25th Lt. Lockwood left in the steam-launch "Lady Greely" (which had
been put into the water for the trip), taking a circuitous route inside the islands, rendered necessary by bad weather. Lt. Lockwood returned early on the 28th, bringing
for service with the expedition a native, Jans Edward, and a half-breed, Frederick
Thorley Christiansen, who were contracted with that day. Lt. Lockwood also procured about a dozen suits of skin clothing, which, though second-hand, are very serviceable. He had killed 120 guillemots during his voyage. The launch behaved admirably both as a sea-boat and under steam. Lt. Kislingbury, by my orders, made two
visits, July 24th and 25th, to the "loomery," near Sanderson's Hope, bringing back the
first day three hundred fine birds, and on the latter one hundred and fifteen, all guillemots (*Alca Awa*). Ten dogs (five of whom have since died of dog disease; must have
been sick when sold to me), were procured from Mr. Elborg. Additional dog food,
sledge fittings, dog harness, and seal-skins were also bought. It was through the
marked interest and kindly influence of Inspector Smith (whom I found at Upernavik)
that the expedition secured the services of the natives and obtained so fair a stock of
needed articles. The meteorological records of the past winter show it to have been
very mild, and the spring very early. Inspector Smith told me that in fourteen years
Upernavik has never been so green. Reports from Tessuissak were to the effect that
the ice, breaking up very early, was all gone. On the afternoon of July 29th the anchorage of Upernavik was left, and at 7 p. m., having run out the southern way, the
vessel was distant three miles from Upernavik, just off the island to the west. Running northward a few hours, the "middle passage" was taken, and at 7 a. m., July 31,
the engines were stopped, as the "dead reckoning" placed the vessel only six miles
south of Cape York, and dense fog prevented land from being seen. An hour later,
the fog lifting a few minutes, showed land about five miles distant. This experience
of the "middle passage" may be fairly said to have been without parallel or pre-
cedent. The run of the English expedition of 1875-'76, from Upernavik to 45 miles
south of Cape York, in seventy hours, is said to have been unprecedented. Our
passage by the same route, and to within five miles of Cape York, was made in thirty-
six hours, *half the time* taken by the expedition under Sir George Nares, to run a less
distance. Nothing in the shape of a pack was encountered in Baffin Bay, but in
about 75° 08' N., 63° 40' W. a pack was seen to the westward, whether open or compact was uncertain. A polar bear (*Ursus maritimus*) and a seal (*Phoca barbata*)
were killed, on small detached floes in the "middle passage". July 31st was lost
through foggy weather, obliging the vessel to "lay to." At 8.15 a. m., the fog lifting
disclosed Petowik Glacier, near to the north of which, in small patches of dirty red-
dish color, was seen the red snow among the "crimson cliffs" of Sir John Ross. Sighting the Cary Islands at 3.10 p. m. that day, two parties were landed on the southeast
island at 5.45 p. m. The party under Dr. Pavy obtained from the cairn on the summit
the record left by Mr. Allen Young in 1875 and 1876, which form enclosures "A" and
"B"; copies were left in the cairn, and an additional record, enclosure "C." With Lieut.
Lockwood, I found and examined the whale-boat and depot of provisions left by Sir
George Nares in 1875, which were in good and serviceable condition. A record in the
boat was taken away (enclosure "D"), but a copy of it and a new record (enclosure "C")
were left in its place. At 12.30 p. m., August 2nd, Littleton Island was reached. A personal and exhaustive search of seven hours was necessary to find the English mail, which,
in four boxes and three kegs, have been forwarded to you, in order that they may be
returned to England. There was a very small cairn near the mail, but with no record. A record, enclosure "H," was left by me. Lt. Lockwood with a party landed
about 6½ tons of coal as a depot of fuel for possible future use. It is in and around a
large cask, on low ground, on the southwest side of the island, facing Cape Alexander. Lieut. Kislingbury and Dr. Pavy, by my orders, visited Life-Boat Cove to communicate with the Etah Eskimos, and see the "Polaris" winter quarters. Several photographs of the surroundings were taken by Sergt. Rice, and a number of relics brought
off, which will be forwarded to you. The transit instrument was found about twenty
feet from the cairn. The Etah Eskimos have evidently quitted the place, as all traces
were old, a year certainly, and probably two or three years. In searching on Littleton Island for the Nares cairn about fifty small cairns (many evidently for game) were
found, in two of which records from S. S. "Erik," Capt. Walker, June 20, 1876, were
found, and form enclosures "E" and "F." A cairn carefully built, and with an aper-
ture at the base, probably that of Sir George Nares, was found open and empty. Lt.

Lockwood, who later was sent to go over the ground a third time, concluded with me that the open cairn was that of Sir George Nares. A record was made by Lt. Lockwood for deposit, but a message sent him when the English mail was found caused him to withdraw it, or he was erroneously informed that I had found the cairn sought for. It probably has been plundered, as a piece of a London newspaper, *The Standard*, was found by me in the snow on the west side of the island. It contains a notice of a lecture by Sir George Nares in 1875. It forms enclosure " G." Some repairs to the wheel of the ship caused several hours delay, but Littleton Island was left at 10.45 p. m. The weather being very fair and no ice visible, I did not dare to take time to examine the 240 rations at Cape Sabine, but directed the captain to run direct for Cape Hawks. On August 3rd Cape Sabine was passed at 1.50 a. m., and Cape Camperdown at 4.10 a. m. At 8.40 a. m. off Cape Hawks, and at 9.10 a. m. lay to about two miles north of it, between the mainland and Washington Irving Island. Sent two parties, under Lt. Lockwood and Dr. Pavy, to examine respectively the south and north end of Washington Irving Island. With Lt. Kislingbury, Mr. Clay, and a number of the men I proceeded to the main shore and examined the English depot of 1875. The jolly-boat was found in good condition, and being short of boats it was taken by me. I have named it the "Valorous," it having belonged to H. M. S. "Valorous," connected with the Nares expedition. There was a large quantity of bread (some mouldy), two kegs of pickles, two partly full of rum, two barrels of stearine, and a barrel preserved potatoes. A keg of *picalilli* (I having none in my stores), one of the kegs of rum were taken, and three cans potatoes, to test them and the method of cooking them. The remaining stores were placed by my party in a better condition to resist the weather. Several photographs of the surroundings were made by Sergt. Rice. Starting again at 11.10 a. m., and running out to the southward, Lt. Lockwood's and Dr. Pavy's parties were picked up at 11.40 a. m. Lt. Lockwood found, in a cairn on the summit, a record of Capt. Nares, deposited in 1875, and countersigned by him in 1876, which forms enclosure "T." A copy was left, together with a new record (enclosure"K"). Passed Cape Louis Napoleon 1.10 p. m., and Cape Frazer at 3 p. m. Washington Land was first sighted at 3.55 p. m., through openings in the fog, which commenced setting in. About 5 p. m. the 80th parallel was crossed. At 5.30 p. m. abreast of Cape Collinson, where 240 rations are cached, but which I dared not visit, fearing dense fog would set in and delay seriously our northward passage. At 10 p. m., after running slow through a dense fog, it was necessary to stop until the next day (Aug. 4th), when, the fog clearing at 11.15 a. m., Franklin Sound was sighted about eight miles N. E. (true). It was passed at 11.45 a. m. At 2 p. m. the ship stopped in the N. E. end of Carl Ritter Bay, where I had decided to place a small depot of provisions in case of a retreat southward in 1883. About *two hundred and twenty-five* bread and meat rations were landed by a party under myself, which Lt. Kislingbury and Dr. Pavy accompanied. The depot was made on the first bench from the sea, just north of a little creek in the extreme N. E. part of the bay. About 7.45 p. m., off Cape Lieber, a heavy pack against the land was passed by a detour to the eastward, and at 9 p. m., August 4th, the vessel was stopped for the *first time by ice* in the extreme S. E. part of Lady Franklin Bay, only eight miles from destination. The pack was a very heavy one, and, running from Cape Baird northeastward in a semicircle, reached the Greenland coast (where it touched the land) just south of Offley Island, near the mouth of Petermann's Fiord. The pack consisted of thick polar ice, ranging from 20 to 50 feet in thickness, cemented together by harbor ice from two to five feet thick. It was impossible to do aught but wait. The vessel was tied to the pack off Cape Baird, and awaited a gale. On August 5th I went ashore at Cape Lieber with Lt. Lockwood, Dr. Pavy and party, to examine the ice from the cliffs. Lt. Lockwood erected a cairn on the highest peak. No other cairn could be seen on it or from it, nor on other peaks visited by Dr. Pavy and myself. Occasional lanes of water could be seen through the rifts of the fog-cloud which covered Hall Basin, but the main pack was firm and unchanged. On August 6th, the pack moving slightly, obliged the vessel to change its mooring place from time to time. Aug. 7th the pack drove us out of Lady Franklin Bay, and during that day and the 8th we were gradually driven south. Probably twenty-five miles of ice in huge fields passed southward of us during those two days. Every opportunity was improved to steam around such fields to keep head against the southerly current. On the evening of Aug. 8th the steady north wind had forced the whole pack down towards us, while the fields previously driven southward, packed fast together, formed a huge compact barrier, stretching from Carl Ritter Bay across to Hans Island. But a mile or so of open water remained. A *nip* appeared most probable, and preparations were hastily made to unship screw and rudder. During the night matters improved somewhat, but during the 9th and 10th we were forced slowly southward to within about 5 miles of Hans Island, having lost about 45 miles of latitude. About noon of the 10th the long-desired southwest gale set in, acccompanied by snow, starting the pack northward. The snow cleared the next morning, but the gale fortunately continued. Open water was visible on the west coast as far northward as could be seen. At 7.30 a. m.

we ran rapidly northward, and about 1 p. m. again passed Cape Lieber, and at 2.40 p. m. had crossed Lady Franklin Bay. Either ice-foot, or pack-ice jammed against the shore, covered Watercourse Bay, but a narrow lane permitted the vessel to enter Discovery Harbor, just inside Dutch Island, where harbor ice about 18 inches thick was found covering the whole harbor as well as the western half of Lady Franklin Bay. The vessel forced her way about ¼ mile through ice of the character above named, and then stopped, pending my decision as to the locality of the station. While Lieut. Lockwood was sent to examine Watercourse Bay and the coal-seam, I visited alone the "Discovery" winter quarters, and found in a cairn two tin cases, one labeled "Records," and the other "General information." They form enclosures "L," "M," "N," "O," "P," to this report. Lieut. Lockwood, returning early morning August 13th, reported the place an excellent one for camp, the bay partly clear, but shallow. He thought it probable the vessel could come within about 200 yards of the shore. The bay, however, was of such shape that, while discharging, the vessel would be unprotected against ice, as it is exposed to all winds from N.E. to S.S.W. The coal was so located that it could be readily mined after ice forms, and could, if required, be hauled without difficulty to Watercourse Bay or to Discovery Harbor. I reluctantly decided to settle at Discovery winter quarters, owing to the uncertainty that would attend unloading at such a place. It was fortunate that I so decided, for. sending Dr. Pavy to ground overlooking Watercourse Bay, on Aug. 13th, he reported it full of pack-ice. On the 12th the vessel broke her way through two miles of heavy ice and anchored off the cairn, about 100 yards from shore, at about 3 p. m. At 3.30 p. m. the men were divided into two gangs, to work day and night, by four-hour reliefs, until the cargo was discharged. The general cargo was discharged in 60 hours—by 3.30 a. m. (to-day) August 14th. At this time coal is being landed, of which I have about 140 tons, enough to last two winters without mining any. Work on the house is progressing rapidly, though but three or four men can be spared at present for that work. The foundation has been finished, floor-stringers laid, and about one-eighth of the frame is now up. Fourteen musk oxen have been killed, and enough meat is on hand for issue three times a week for the coming seven months, besides ten days' rations of dried birds. The post has been named Fort Conger, in honor of Senator Conger, of Michigan. Anything of importance will be added as an appendix. Photographic views have been, and will be, taken once each day, from which you can best judge of the progress and condition of affairs. I feel it proper to here state that in my opinion a retreat from here southward to Cape Sabine, in case no vessel reaches us in 1882 or 1883, will be safe and practicable, although all but the most important records will necessarily have to be abandoned. Abstracts could and would be made of those left.

I am, respectfully, y'rs,

A. W. GREELY,

1 *Lt. 5th Cav., A. S. O. & Ass't Com'd'g L. F. B. Exp'd'n.*

Official copy from the records of the Signal Office.

W. B. HAZEN,
Chief Signal Officer.

1, 15, '84.

FORT CONGER, GRINNELL LAND,
August 17th, 1881.

CHIEF SIGNAL OFFICER OF THE ARMY:

SIR: I have the honor to recommend that in connection with the vessel to visit this station in 1882 there be sent some captain of the merchant service who has had experience as a whaler and ice-master. Five enlisted men of the Army are requested to replace men invalided or who are found to be unfit otherwise for the work. One of the number should be a Signal Service sergeant. Sergeant Emory Braine, 2d Cavalry, and Sergeant Martin Hamburg, Company E, 10th Infantry, are recommended most highly, and without they are physically or morally unfitted within the year, their detail is requested. The two remaining men should be such as have had some sea experience. All the men should be rigidly examined as to their physical condition. The ice-master should be expected to see that every effort is made to reach this point by the vessel sent. In case the vessel cannot reach this point, a very possible contingency, a depot (No. A) should be made at a permanent point on the east coast of Grinnell Land (west side of Smith Sound or Kennedy Channel), consisting of ninety-six cans chocolate and milk, ninety-six cans coffee and milk, one-half barrel of alcohol, forty-eight cans mutton, forty-eight beef, one keg rum, forty-eight cans sausage, forty-eight cans mulberry preserves, two barrels bread, one box butter, forty-eight cans condensed milk, one-half barrel onion pickles, forty-eight cans cranberry sauce, forty-eight cans soup, twenty-four cans tomatoes, one gross wax matches (to be in water-tight case), one eighth cord of wood, one wall-tent (complete), one axe and helve, one whale-boat. At Littleton Island, carefully cached on the western point, out of ordinary sight, with no cairn, should be placed an equal amount (depot B), but no boat. A notice as to the exact locality should be left in the top of the coal (preferably in a corked and sealed bottle), buried a foot deep, which was left on that island. A second notice should be in the edge of the coal furthest inland, and a third in the Nares cairn, now open, which is on summit southwest part of island.

The second boat should be left at Cape Prescott, or very near, in order that if boats are necessarily abandoned above that point one will be available to cross to Bache Island and go to the southward. These boats should be not exceeding forty feet and not less than twenty above high-water mark, and their positions should be marked by substantial scantling, well secured and braced, to the top of which a number of pieces of canvas should be well nailed, so that it may be plainly and easily seen. A second staff, with pieces of canvas, should be raised on a point which shows prominently to the northward, so a party can see it a long distance. Depots A and B should be made ready in Saint John's and be plainly marked and carefully secured.

The packages during the voyage should be easily accessible. Depot A should be landed at the farthest possible northern point. A few miles is important, and no southing should be permitted to obtain a prominent location. The letters and dispatches should all be carefully soldered up in a tin case, and then boxed (at Saint John's) and marked, or put in a well-strapped, water-tight keg, and should be left with depot A if such depot shall be at or north or in plain sight of Cape Hawks, and the newspapers and periodicals left at Littleton Island. If depot A is not so far north, the letters and all mail should be returned to the United States. After making depot B, at Littleton Island, the vessel should, if possible, leave a record of its proceedings at Cape Sabine. If the party does not reach here in 1882, there should be sent in 1883 a capable, energetic officer, with ten (10) men, eight of whom should have had practical sea experience, provided with three whale-boats and ample provisions for forty (40) persons for fifteen months. The list of all provisions taken by me this year would answer exceedingly well. In case the vessel was obliged to turn southward (she should not leave Smith Sound near Cape Sabine before September 15th) it should leave duplicates of depots A and B of 1882 at two different points, one of which should be between Cape Sabine and Bache Island, the other to be an intermediate depot between the two depots already established. Similar rules as to indicating locality should be insisted on. Thus the Grinnell Land coasts would be covered with seven depots of ten days' provisions in less than three hundred miles, not including the two months' supplies at Cape Hawks.

The party should then proceed to establish a winter station at "Polaris" winter quarters, Life-Boat Cove, where their main duty would be to keep their telescopes on Cape Sabine and the land to the northward. They should have lumber enough for house and observatory, fifty tons of coal, and complete meteorological and magnetic outfit. Being furnished with dogs, sledges, and a native driver, a party of at least six (6) men should proceed, when practicable, to Cape Sabine, whence a sledge party northward of two best fitted men should reach Cape Hawks, if not Cape Collinson. Such action, from advice, experience, and observation, seems to me all that can be done to insure our safety. No deviation from these instructions should be permitted. Latitude of action should not be given to a relief party who on a known coast are searching for men who know their plans and orders.

I am, respectfully, yours,

A. W. GREELY,
1st Lieut. 5th Cavalry, A. S. O. and Ass't, Commanding Expedition.

Official copy from the records of the Signal Office.

W. B. HAZEN,
Chief Signal Officer.

Nov. 9, '83.

FT. CONGER, L. F. BAY, GRINNELL LAND,
Aug. 17th, 1881.

CHIEF SIGNAL OFFICER OF THE ARMY:

SIR: I have the honor to request that the Danish Government may be moved to direct that the following-named articles be prepared and ready, if practicable, at Godhavn, for the use of this expedition in 1882, to be called for by the relief vessel of 1882:

Twenty-six (26) *temiaks*, large sizes.
Forty-six (46) seal-skin pants, large sizes.
Ten (10) sleeping-bags, lined with dog-skin, large enough for two men of large stature.
Five hundred pounds *mattak*—skin of white whale.
One hundred fifty (150) coils of thongs for traces and lines.
Ten (10) dogs (with 2 mo's' dog food, to last *en route*.)
Suitable seal-skins for twenty dog-harnesses.

The order for these should be made from Copenhagen by the first vessel, and no time should be lost in arranging therefor. The first Danish ship leaving in March—early—reaches Godhavn about the first of May. If all cannot be obtained, as much as practicable should be made ready.

I am, respectfully, yours,

A. W. GREELY,
1st Lt. 5 Cav., A. S. O. and Ass't, Com d'g Expedition.

Official copy from the records of the Signal Office.

————— —————,
Chief Signal Officer.

Nov. 9, 1883.

—————

FT. CONGER, GRINNELL LAND,
Aug. 17, 1881.

CHIEF SIGNAL OFFICER OF THE ARMY:

SIR: The captain of the vessel coming to this station in 1882 should be provided with the following charts, which can be obtained from the Navy Department: Nos. 235. 274, 276, 555, 787, 807, 2117, 2118, 2282, and 2382.

The following should be purchased: From 75° N. to 84° N., Admiralty chart, Apr. 20, 1875, corrected to July, '78 (later if can be had), sold by J. D. Potter, 31 Poultry and 11 King st., London.

I am, resp'y, y'rs,

A. W. GREELY,
1 Lt. 5 Cav., A. S. O., and Ass't Com'd'g Exp'd'n.

Official copy from the records of the Signal Office.

W. B. HAZEN,
Chief Signal Officer.

Nov. 9, 1883.

—————

FT. CONGER, L. F. BAY, GRINNELL LAND,
Aug. 17, 1881.

CHIEF SIGNAL OFFICER OF THE ARMY:

SIR: I have the honor to herewith transmit copy map of Robeson Channel and approaches, whereon is marked the course followed by the "Proteus" northward of the entrance to Smith Sound; also map of "Discovery" winter quarters. The house is located within fifty yards or so of the cairn, and runs N. and S. One hundred copies (lithographed) of these charts would be very useful, and I request they be furnished.

I am, resp'y, y'r,

A. W. GREELY,
1 Lt. 5 Cav., A. S. O. and Ass't.

(Five inclosures.)

Official copy from the records of the Signal Office.

W. B. HAZEN,
Chief Signal Officer.

Nov. 9, 1883.

—————

FT. CONGER, L. F. BAY,
Aug. 18, 1881.

CHIEF SIGNAL OFFICER OF THE ARMY:

SIR: I have the honor to report that the party remaining as the enlisted force at this place are all men well fitted for the work, and their relief, except on grounds of ill health or at personal request, is not recommended. Sgt. Gardner is not always accurate, but is willing, and time, with supervision, will correct that fault. Private Ryan indulged too freely in drink at St. John's, but on the trip and here proves a most excellent, reliable, and hard-working man.

I am, resp'y, y'rs,

A. W. GREELY,
1 Lt. 5 Cav., A. S. O. and Ass't, Com'd'g Exp'd'n.

Official copy from the records of the Signal Office.

W. B. HAZEN,
Chief Signal Officer.

Nov. 9, 1883.

FORT CONGER, GRINNELL LAND, LADY FRANKLIN BAY,
August 18th, 1881.

CHIEF SIGNAL OFFICER OF THE ARMY:

SIR: I have the honor to report that the weather continues fine and the health of the men good. I have ordered Corporal Starr to return to Washington, as he has developed a tendency to asthma, which unfits him in the opinion of the doctor for hard work in the field, because *possibly* he might be attacked. The house is entirely framed and partly boarded.

Everything perishable has been got under canvas.

I hope to send the party northward to Cape Henry in a week or so. In view of Corporal Starr's relief it would be well to send six men instead of five men.

The Captain hopes to sail to-night, I having promised to stop coaling at 6 p. m., when I shall have about 140 long tons coal, enough with proper margin for two years and more.

I am, respectfully, yours,

A. W. GREELY,
1st Lieut. 5th Cav., A. S. O. and Ass't, Com'd'g L. F. B. Expedition.

P. S.—24 additional musk oxen have been seen.

Official copy from the records of the Signal Office.

W. B. HAZEN,
Chief Signal Officer.

Nov. 9, 1883.

———

FT. CONGER, GRINNELL LAND,
August 18, 1881.

MY DEAR GENERAL:

*   *   *   *   *   *

I have kept all expenses down as low as I could. Am afraid may have trouble another year getting vessel. I would move early. Chester (Baird's man) recommends highly Capt. Buddington—who I know stands highly—as a suitable ice-master. He is an uncle of the "Polaris" Buddington, and an old whaler. Have, as I may say, no time for writing more, so many things demand my personal attention.

Ever faithfully yours,

A. W. GREELY,
1st Lt. 5 Cav., A. S. O., &c.

Gen. W. B. HAZEN,
Washington.

Official extract from the records of the Signal Office.

W. B. HAZEN,
Chief Signal Officer.

1, 15, '84.

———

[Telegram received, at 9, 12, 1881, 9.43 a. m., 8. N. Y., from St. John's, N. F., 12th.]

TO CHIEF SIGNAL OFFICER,
Wash'n, D. C.:

Entered Lady Franklin Bay one month from leaving St. John's. Obtained natives, skin clothing, and dogs at Godhavn, Rittenbank, Upernavik, and Proven.

Made most remarkable trip recorded from Upernavik, through "middle passage" to Cape York, in thirty-six hours. In six days and two hours from Upernavik, though delayed thirty-two hours by fog, entered Lady Franklin Bay, having meanwhile examined English depot, Cary Island; recovered entire English Arctic mail at Littleton Island; discovered transit instrument "Polaris" quarters, Life-Boat Cove; obtained record Washington Irving Island; overhauled English depot, Cape Hawks; and landed depot at Carl Ritter Bay. Vessel never met pack worthy of name nor stopped by ice until inside Cape Lieber, Lady Franklin Bay, eight miles from destination, where delayed one week, being forced back south of eightieth parallel. Entered Discovery Harbor, August eleventh, where station is located, Watercourse Bay being impracticable for landing. About hundred forty tons coal landed. Have killed here three full months' rations musk cattle. Weather fine. Building framed and being covered. Party all well.

GREELY,
Lt., Commanding.

LADY FRANKLIN BAY, *Aug.* 18*th*, 1881.

1.83 collect.

Official copy from the records of the Signal office.

W. B. HAZEN,
Chief Signal Officer.

Nov. 9, 1883.

————

The "Proteus" delayed by ice a few miles S. E. permits me to-day to report that one house is now covered, and it will be partly occupied to-morrow, Sunday. All well.

A. W. GREELY, *Lt.,&c.*

L. F. B., *Aug.* 20.

Official copy from the records of the Signal Office.

W. B. HAZEN,
Chief Signal Officer.

Nov. 9, 1883.

————

L. F. BAY, *Aug.* 25*th*, 1881.

All stores under cover. Freezing weather commenced. Observatory under way. House entirely done except inside work, which can be done at leisure. Start a small party north and one into interior in few days. Ice in L. F. Bay has unfortunately not gone out at all this year, and so steam-launch is kept here. No snow on ground. Party all well. "Proteus" delayed by ice at entrance to harbor for days, although channel open outside. Since Starr and Ryan are gone, seven men should come next year. Lowest temp., 22° on 20th.

A. W. GREELY.

Gen. W. B. HAZEN,
Chief Signal Officer, Washington, D. C., United States.

Official copy from the records of the Signal Office.

W. B. HAZEN,
Chief Signal Officer.

Nov. 9, 1883.

————

EXHIBIT N.

WASHINGTON, D. C., *January* 16*th*, 1883.

Captain G. W. DAVIS,
Recorder of Board:

SIR: As requested by the Board of which you are Recorder, I have the honor to submit the following regarding articles supplied to the Greely Relief Expedition of 1883, and which were designed for use in sledging expeditions.

SLEDGES.

Three sledges were furnished, two being seventeen feet in length, designed to carry heavy loads, and the other eight feet in length and proportionably lighter in all respects, but all being constructed upon the same plan, the design being to obtain the greatest amount of strength with the least possible weight of material.

These sledges were made alike at both ends, and consisted of double runners, made of the best hickory, one-fourth of an inch in thickness for the light sledge, and five-eighths of an inch in thickness for the heavier ones. The lower, or snow runners, were four inches in width, and the ice-runners were three inches wide. These were steamed and bent at the ends, which were brought together and secured in such manner as to give proper form to the sledge, whichever side might be uppermost. At intervals of two feet along the body of the sledge the runners were separated, and kept in position by posts twenty inches long, of suitable size, the ends of which rested in sockets of gun-metal securely riveted to the runners. The sockets were cast with a base three inches square, to rest on the runners, which gave them a broad bearing surface. Along the center line of the sledge the posts had slots, both on the inner and outer sides, formed by projecting shoulders, so constructed as not to weaken the wood. These slots were two inches wide, and three-eighths inch deep, and resting in them, running the entire length of the sledge, were placed the side-rails, upon which the beams rested. At either end these rails were separated by a piece of wood to which they were riveted, and which was made to fit against and join to the runners where their ends came together. The runners were shod with Norway iron one-tenth inch thick. To keep the upper and lower runners in position, and hold the ends of the posts firmly in the metal sockets, small rods of Norway iron were placed forward and aft of each post, passing between the side-rails, and through the runners and shoes, where they were countersunk and riveted.

The two sides of the sledge, being of course similar, were kept in position by cross-beams made of cask staves, or other suitable material, cut to the desired length. A slot large enough to admit the post was cut in each end of the cross-beam, so that the shoulder would rest on the inner side-rail, and the parts not cut away would pass on either side and beyond the post, where it would be secured by a lashing passed around the end of the cross-beam, the two side-rails, and the post.

It is a question whether diagonal lashings, extending from the metal socket at the ends of each post to similar points at the opposite ends of the adjacent posts, and passing between the side-rails, where they would cross, would not be better than the upright iron rods used. If of tarred stuff of suitable size, such lashings would have the requisite strength, would not be affected by moisture, and would not be gnawed by the dogs. They would give the necessary rigidity to the sides of the sledge, and in cases of breakage could be more readily cast off and replaced than could the iron rods.

It is believed that the lashings at the ends of the cross-beams, and the facility with which lashings could be passed from one of the upper runners to the other, above the load, when placed in position, would keep the sides upright, and resist any strain caused by the sledge sliding to one side or the other. To preserve the necessary rigidity, as between the two sides of the sledge whenever the resistance to one runner was greater than to the other, lashings extending diagonally from the posts on one side to those on the other would be sufficient, and being passed with a turn around the cross-beams would make a capital support for the load. It was expected that a traction-bar lashed underneath the side-rails, close to the nose of the sledge, would answer to haul by, and that if handles with a cross-bar for steering the sledge should be desirable, they could be similarly lashed at the rear end of the sledge.

The sledges for the Greely Relief Expedition of 1883 were made by Messrs. McDermott Brothers, of this city, and, including quite a number of spare parts, cost in the aggregate about one hundred and eighty dollars.

SLEDGING TENTS.

These were constructed of blue "denim," of the wedge or "A" pattern; were seven feet square at the base, and nine feet to the ridge. They were supported by two ice-chisels at each end, which were crossed and lashed about six inches from the ends of the handles, the ends projecting into ears or pockets on either side of the extreme ends of the ridge. Around these, when the poles were in position, a guy-rope was fastened and led down to a hummock of ice at convenient distance, or otherwise secured, and those at both front and rear of the tent being hauled taut, no ridge-pole was necessary.

At the base of the tent was sewed along its center a breadth of the cloth, one-half of which being brought up inside and fastened at the seams, formed convenient pockets, while the other half, resting on the snow or ice as a sod-cloth, was kept down and in position by snow or ice banked upon it, rendering the use of pins unnecessary.

The opening into the tent was through a hole three feet high and twenty-seven inches broad, the bottom of which was eighteen inches above the base of the tent. This was closed by a flap, something larger than the opening, stitched to the tent at the top, and fastened along the sides and bottom, where it overlapped by means of toggles.

When furnished with water-proof floor-cloths these tents were very complete, and would hold five men each. Being of dark color, they were more readily seen when pitched on the ice, and afforded protection to the eyes from the sun's rays. They were made for the Signal Service, at the Schuylkill Arsenal, Phila., under the direction of Captain Gill, M. S. K., at the cost (exclusive of transportation) of $14.82 each.

ALCOHOL STOVES FOR COOKING.

The principal feature of these was the placing around the boiler or vessel in which the boiling was done a metal jacket, made cylindrical in form, and of the size of the lamp. At the upper end it was brazed to the boiler, which it fitted at that end, and, owing to the increasing size of the boiler from the top downward, it formed an air space around the boiler where the heat from the lamp was confined and more perfectly utilized. Holes of suitable size near the top of the jacket afforded ventilation. The boiler held three gallons, and was furnished with a cover, and with a cock at the bottom extending through the jacket. It would contain when being transported the necessary mess-kit and utensils, and would melt snow and furnish tea or coffee for a party of five, besides cooking the pemmican with an expenditure of about one pint of alcohol.

Such stoves and boilers should be made of copper, but I am not able to give the cost.

SLEEPING-BAGS.

These were of sheepskin, bark-tanned, with the wool on. They should be single, one for each person, and without any lining. They were made with the wool inside, and sufficiently large to permit the occupant when dressed in fur clothing to turn easily. Their length permitted the legs to be fully extended. They were broader at the shoulders, narrowing towards the foot, and less towards the head. In general shape they were not unlike a coffin. Above the face was a circular opening about six inches in diameter, furnished with a flap to close when desired. From the bottom of this opening a slit was cut down to the middle of the bag, which was also supplied with a flap sewed fast at one edge and made to fasten at the other by means of small toggles. This, when open, permitted the occupant to sit up without getting out of the bag.

ICE CHISELS AND PADDLES.

These were made by using two-inch framing chisels from which the temper had been drawn, and the bevel made equal on the sides. Into the sockets of these were fastened securely handles of best ash, turned, one and one-half inches in diameter, and ten feet long.

Besides affording supports for the tents as already described, they served excellently as Alpen-stocks when clambering about ice-floes, and for detaching pieces of ice on which to cross narrow leads of water. Some of them were made with blades or paddles at the upper end, which were tipped with thin metal, and were useful when ferrying across a lead on a piece of ice. These implements were furnished from the Brooklyn Navy-Yard, and their cost is not known.

Boats, tents, sledges, and implements of all kinds should, when designed for Arctic work, be of dark color, to be more readily distinguishable when upon the ice.

I am, sir, very respectfully, your ob't servant,

W. H. CLAPP,
Captain 16th Infantry.

———

WASHINGTON, *Jan'y* 22, '84.

Captain G. W. DAVIS,
        Recorder Greely Relief Board.

SIR: Having been requested to prepare for the use of the Board a drawing of the sledges sent out with the Proteus Relief Expedition, I respectfully submit the accompanying, and request it may be made a part of my paper on the sledging outfit sent with that expedition.

I should add that the original design for this sledge was made by Chief Engineer Melville, of the Navy, while on board the "Jeannette," and his plan was modified by me to the extent of substituting bronze sockets for securing the posts to the runners, rather than framing them into the runners as he had proposed.

This change he highly approved—pronouncing the sledge as constructed all that could be desired. This opinion was concurred in by Lieut. Berry, also of the Navy, and by others of considerable Arctic experience.

I have the honor to be, your ob't servant,

W. H. CLAPP,
Cap't 16th Inf.

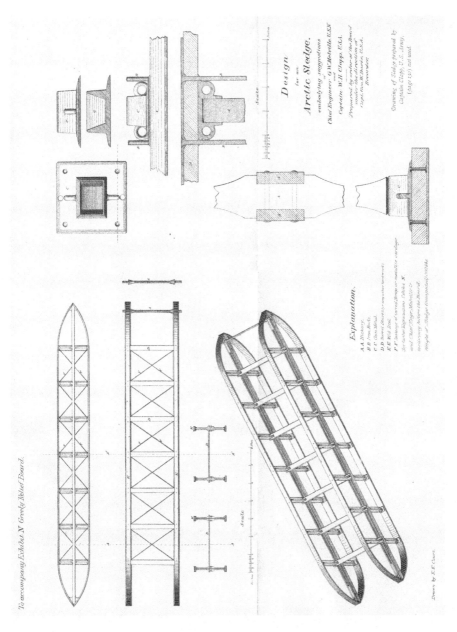

Design
for an
Arctic Sledge.
embodying suggestions
of
Chief Engineer G.W.Melville U.S.N.
and
Captain W.H. Clapp U.S.A.
Prepared by order of the Board
under the direction of
Capt. Geo.W. Davis, U.S.A.
President.

Drawing of Sledge prepared by
Captain Clapp, U.S. Army.
(Page iv) not used.

Explanation.

A A Hickory.
B B Iron Bolts.
C C Gun Metal.
D D Naval Wood (or any other hardwood)
E E Wild Zinc.
F F Lashings of twisted Rope or metallic wire
See further Explanation Tables N°
and Chief Engr Melville's
testimony before the Board.
Weight of Sledge (complete) 320 lbs.

Scale

Scale

Drawn by E.F. Carr.

The material originally positioned here is too large for reproduction in this reissue. A PDF can be downloaded from the web address given on page iv of this book, by clicking on 'Resources Available'.

EXHIBIT O.

BUREAU OF NAVIGATION, NAVY DEPARTMENT,
Washington, January 19, 1884.

SIR: By dirction of the Secretary of the Navy, I have the honor to forward herewith four letters relating to the subject under consideration by the Board of which you are president, referred to the Navy Department by Senator Miller, of California.

Very respectfully,

J. G. WALKER,
Chief of Bureau.

Brevet Major-General W. B. HAZEN, U. S. A.,
President Board of Officers to consider relief of Lt. Greely, &c., &c.

[Inclosure 1.]

U. S. REVENUE MARINE ST'M'R "RICHARD RUSH,"
San Francisco, Cal., Nov. 4th, 1883.

Hon. CHARLES J. FOLGER,
Secretary of the Treasury, Washington, D. C.

SIR: Referring to the unfortunate failure of the expedition sent to the relief of Lieut. Greely and party, resulting in the total destruction of one vessel and the return of the other without having accomplished anything, I most respectfully submit the following, and ask your favorable consideration. Lieut. Greely's instructions, as I understand them from the published accounts were, to be ready to break up his station at the opening of navigation of the present year 1883, and should no vessel come to his relief, to start south with his party and endeavor to reach Littleton Island not later than September, where the vessel sent to his relief was expected to remain, should it be found impracticable to reach Lady Franklin Bay. The latter place could not be reached this year, the ice being heavy and closely packed. This impassable condition of the ice would be known to Lieut. Greely, who would not fail to inform himself on the subject, and hasten his departure for Littleton Island, which place he probably reached without serious difficulty not many days after the departure of the "Yantic." On his arrival there, finding neither means of transportation nor shelter, food nor fuel on the island, he would naturally make an attempt to reach some of the Innuit settlements. As these settlements are small, and the inhabitants poor and unable to support a large party, it would be necessary to separate small parties going in different directions. Broken health by their long stay in the Arctic regions, wearied by the hardships already encountered in the toilsome journey from Lady Franklin Bay, disappointed and disheartened at not finding the succor they had a right to expect at Littleton Island, it is not improbable that some of the unfortunates might fail to reach an Innuit settlement. But when we refer to previous Arctic disasters and reflect upon the hardships men have endured from hunger and exposure in that most inhospitable region, and survived to reach the world with the knowledge gained, we have a right to hope that at least a part of them will survive the winter. When we reflect, further, that had aid been promptly rendered the loss of life or at least a portion of it might have been avoided in the case of both Franklin and De Long, we can readily see the necessity of prompt action if a like fate is to be averted in the present case. Had the Government sent several expeditions along the north coast of the continents of Asia and North America by land in the spring of 1881 instead of sending *one*, and that a vessel to go over the same ground which had already been traversed many times by a revenue steamer that was still keeping up an active search in all parts of the Arctic basin accessible to any vessel, De Long and his brave followers upon reaching the Lena Delta, after their most remarkable retreat over the frozen sea, might have found friends to greet them instead of death, through hunger and exposure.

Should all or a portion of the Greely party survive the winter, with the coming of spring they will look even more anxiously for assistance than when they strained their eyes in vain for signs of relief in the vicinity of Littleton Island. With the breaking up of the ice, assistance should be sent to them; not one vessel, but several. There are not only the chances to be considered of total failure through disaster in the case of a single vessel being sent, but also the chances of missing some of the members of the Greely party owing to the extent and exceedingly rough nature of the coast line to be searched. Considering the national character of the expedition under Greely, it seems to me proper that all branches of the public service should join in the search. I therefore respectfully ask to be allowed to take command of the steamer "Levi Woodbury," of the Revenue Marine Service, now stationed at Eastport, Maine, or such other suitable vessel as may be decided upon, when the proper time arrives, and join in the search. The cost will not be great, as no expensive repairs or alterations will be required; the vessel need only be in ordinary sea-going condition, and protected from chafe by a light sheathing of oak and an ice-breaker at the bows, as was the "Corwin.' Strengthening the vessel amounts to but little. If fairly caught between two large floes no vessel yet built could withstand the pressure. Safety lies in avoiding the nip. This our small, quick-moving revenue steamers are better capable of doing than any class of vessels afloat. The "Corwin" was saved from disaster by ice pressure on more than one occasion while under my command, when a slower working vessel could not have escaped total destruction. I respectfully ask your consideration of my proposition. Should you approve it, but not feel authorized under existing laws to detail a vessel for the duty, will you not refer it to Congress, with your indorsement? I should esteem it a great favor to be allowed to take part in the search, and in view of my two seasons' experience in Arctic ice navigation, believe I might be of some assistance in rescuing from certain death the remaining members of the unfortunate party.

I am, very respectfully, your ob't servant,

C. L. HOOPER,
Capt., U. S. R. M.

[Inclosure 2.]

U. S. REVENUE MARINE STMR. "RICHARD RUSH,"
San Francisco, Cal., December 16, 1883.

Hon. CHAS. J. FOLGER,
Secretary of the Treasury, Washington, D. C.

SIR: About the 4th of November I wrote you in relation to the Lady Franklin Bay Expedition, under command of Lieut. Greely, asking permission to join in the attempt at rescue which will be made with the opening of navigation in Greenland seas the coming spring. Not having received a reply to my communication, I take the liberty of again referring to the matter, which, in view of my anxiety, I trust you will excuse. If my proposition to join in the relief expedition in a revenue cutter should not meet with your approval, I respectfully ask permission to offer my services to General Hazen, U. S. A., Chief Signal Officer, who, I believe, contemplates dispatching a steam whaler on that duty as soon as spring opens. If possible to do so, I should very much prefer going in one of our own vessels, they being better suited to that kind of work than any other class of vessels not specially built for it. And, besides, a successful cruise would reflect credit upon the service, while an earnest attempt, although not crowned with success, would reflect no discredit upon us. This, however, is a secondary consideration, and if I cannot go in a revenue cutter, for the sake of joining in the work and making use of such poor ability as I possess as a sailor and navigator in trying to save the lives of the small party of our countrymen who are undoubtedly in great danger, I will gladly go in any way that I may. Trusting that my proposition may not meet with your disapprobation,

I am, very respectfully, your ob'd't servant,

C. L. HOOPER,
Captain, U. S. R. M.

[Inclosure 3.]

TREASURY DEPARTMENT, OFFICE OF THE SECRETARY,
Washington, D. C., Dec. 29, 1883.

Capt. C. L. HOOPER,
San Francisco, Cal.

DEAR SIR: I have received your two recent letters in reference to the Greely Expedition. Before I could reply definitely it was necessary first to determine whether there should be any expedition sent to the relief of Lieut. Greely. Since the receipt of your last letter I have talked with the Secretary of the Navy and the Secretary of War about the matter, and they are now discussing it. I do not believe it will be possible for a revenue cutter to go north without the authority of Congress. Whether you should be detailed to go in a naval vessel is another question, and I have some doubt whether you would care to go in a subordinate position or in any other way than in command of the vessel.

Yours, very respectfully,

CHAS. J. FOLGER,
Secretary.

[Inclosure 4.]

U. S. REVENUE MARINE STEAMER "RUSH,"
San Francisco, Jan. 4th, 1884.

Hon. JOHN F. MILLER,
Washington, D. C.

SIR: I respectfully ask your consideration of the inclosed copies of correspondence with the Hon. Secretary of the Treasury, in reference to relief for the Greely party. As you will see, the Hon. Secretary does not disapprove my plan of sending a revenue cutter to join in the relief, but believes the authority of Congress is necessary. This was done in the case of the "Corwin," when sent to search for the "Jeannette," and about six thousand dollars appropriated to defray the expense of putting the vessel in condition to battle with the ice.

If, after considering the matter, you do not disapprove it, may I ask that you will take such measures as you may think best, with a view to getting the desired authority for the Hon. Secretary to dispatch a vessel, and an appropriation of five or six thousand dollars to prepare her for ice work. I do not ask to go, to the exclusion of any one else, but that I may be one among the number.

Very respectfully, your ob't serv't,

C. L. HOOPER,
Capt., U. S. R. M.

JANUARY 16, 1884.

Respectfully referred to the honorable the Secretary of the Navy.

JNO. F. MILLER.

EXHIBIT P.

THE NEW YORK ASSOCIATED PRESS,
WASHINGTON BUREAU, 533 FIFTEENTH STREET,
Washington, D. C., Jan. 7, 1884.

DEAR SIR: I was called before the Greely Relief Board last week unexpectedly, having had no time for preparation or for the systematic arrangement of my ideas, and my suggestions, as they appear in the stenographer's notes, seem to me very fragmentary, unsatisfactory, and badly expressed.

If the Board will allow me to do so, I should like to read before it a letter with regard to sledging and Arctic management generally, which I wrote to Lieut. Greely in 1881, and which covers all or most of the points about which you questioned me. The original of the letter, after being twice taken north, now lies in the bottom of Smith Sound, but I have a copy which I should like to put at the service of the Board as a substitute for my extempore suggestions of Friday.

Very truly, yours,

GEORGE KENNAN.

Captain DAVIS.

WASH'N, *June 16,* 1882.

MY DEAR LIEUT. GREELY: I regretted very much that I did not have an opportunity to see you again before you left Wash'n for the North last summer, as I had a number of suggestions to make with regard to sledging devices, expedients, and equipments which I thought might be useful to you. I should have written you at Saint John's, but could not possibly get time to do so before you sailed. There seems to be a fair probability that Major Beebe, or some other officer of the service, will be able to communicate with you this summer, and I avail myself of the opportunity, first, to write you a friendly letter, such as I know, from my own Arctic experience, you will be very glad to get, and second, to make the suggestions which I desired and intended to make last summer. As I may be interrupted before I finish all that I have to say, I will begin with the suggestions and let the news take the chances of events.

My first suggestion relates to a shelter-tent for sledging parties. Before I had spent one winter in the field in Northeastern Siberia I was impressed with the necessity for some sort of shelter to protect myself from the tremendous storms which sweep across those Siberian steppes. Heavy wind, with dense snow-drift, was altogether the worst hardship we had to encounter, because it prevented us not only from traveling, but from enjoying any sort of comfort in camp. We could neither keep a fire nor cook, nor sit with our faces exposed, but were compelled to lie for 20, 40, or 60 hours at a time buried in a fur-bag, crawling out at intervals of 6 or 8 hours to get some-

11

thing to eat, compare notes, and curse the weather. We tried all sorts of tents, from the regulation Army tent to the Korak *polog*, but found them all inadequate. The great difficulty was that in a gale of wind, when we wanted shelter most, we couldn't get our tents up or make them stand. If we raised the frame first, it was almost impossible, even in half a gale, to stretch the canvas over it. If we tried to raise the frame and canvas together, the whole thing collapsed about our ears; and even if, on rare occasions, we succeeded in getting the tent up, the air inside was not much warmer than outside, and the tent generally blew over in the course of the night.

Now, since my return to America it has occurred to me that we might have escaped three-fourths of the suffering which we had to endure if we had exercised a little more ingenuity in the way of devising shelter. I have thought out a tent which seems to me free from most of the objectionable features referred to above, and which I think I could put up and make stand in any wind short of a gale which would blow the canvas all to pieces. The idea was suggested to me by the *polog*, or skin bedroom, of the Siberian Koraks, which affords more perfect shelter and comfort than any structure, except a house, which can be put up on an open steppe. Even that, however, has to be strengthened and protected by the large outer tent, and the latter is too heavy to carry and takes too much time to pitch.

My tent may be roughly described as follows: The frame-work, which is conical in form, consists of six, eight, or more light ashen poles, of such a length that when they are set up together in a cone the apex of the cone will be just within reach of a man's hand extended above his head. The ends of the poles at the apex of the cone are lashed together with a seal-skin thong, very much as the ribs of an umbrella are fastened together at the top; they are also fastened together (loosely) near the bottom by another thong, running around the base of the cone a foot or more from the ground and tied to each pole at such intervals as to govern the width to which the loose conical frame-work can be spread, just as the cloth of an umbrella governs the extent to which it can be opened; thus—

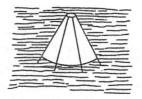

This frame-work, so tied together, can be shut up like an umbrella frame or opened out until the lower thong is tight. It will open so as to always cover a certain definite area, dependent upon the length of the lower thong. Every pole is armed at the bottom with a spiked ferule, to prevent slipping on ice or hard snow. This, with the exception of a few minor details, is all there is of the frame-work.

When in use this frame-work is to be anchored by ground tackle, laid out to windward and fastened to the apex of the cone by seal-skin thongs. The anchors consist of two pieces of inch-and-a-half planking, 30 inches long by 15 in width, with 10 or 15 large spikes driven through so as to project an inch and a half, or more, on the under side. Each anchor has a ring at one end, to which the line from the apex of the conical frame-work may be made fast. It is held down and made to *bite* by the weight of a loaded sledge, which is run up on it. Upon going into camp at night in a gale all you have to do is to take the frame-work from the sledge, spread it as you would open an umbrella and set it up on the snow, carry the anchors out to windward, run loaded sledges up on them, and attach them by lines to the apex of the frame-work, and the skeleton of the tent is fast beyond the possibility of overturn. The whole operation need not occupy two minutes, and I can hardly conceive of a storm which would interfere with it. The frame-work could be set up and anchored in the dark, by a man who was half frozen. The next thing is to get the canvas on it. Of course, it isn't possible to stretch a covering of canvas *over* a frame-work which has lines running out from its apex. It is therefore necessary to hang the tent up inside the frame, and this is the principal feature of the device.

The tent is cut to fit the inside of the conical frame-work, and has a tight bottom or floor continuous with the sides. In other words, the tent is virtually a conical bag with a flat circular bottom, and may be compared to the body of a conical oil-can, with a hook at its apex to hang it up by. When you have set up and anchored your frame-work, all that remains to do is to take the canvas bag which constitutes the tent in your arms and hang it up inside the apex of the frame-work by the hook in the corresponding apex of the tent. No wind can prevent you from doing this, and when it is done, no amount of wind can seriously interfere with the complete pitching of the tent. All that remains to do is to fasten the sides of the tent out to the poles by loop and toggle, or hook-and-eye fastenings. Loops or eyes may be permanently affixed to the poles at intervals of a foot or so with lines of corresponding hooks or toggles sewn up and down the sides of the tent opposite the poles. The bottom of the tent will of course rest on the ground, and, as the bottom or floor is all of one piece with the sides, no wind or snow can get in around the base of the cone. The only openings to the interior of this bag-like tent are a ventilating hole at its throat in the apex of the frame-work, and a slit for a door on the lee side of the base. Of course, when you get three or four men inside, the tent is further ballasted by their weight, since they lie on a bottom or floor which is sewn all around to the sides. My plan would be to warm this tent by a Florence kerosene stove. As the protection from wind would be perfect, it would burn without flickering or smoking, and would, I think, raise the temperature to such a degree—at least in a *fur* tent—as to prevent the deposition of moisture in the shape of frost on the sides. An alcohol stove, or any Arctic cooking apparatus would do, but I think a kerosene-oil stove would be found more effective and economical of fuel.

In a temperature of —40° out of doors I have seen the temperature of a Korak skin *polog* raised by a simple blubber and moss lamp to such a degree that it was perfectly comfortable to sit in it without furs. Of course a Florence oil-stove is five times as efficient as one of those miserable Korak lamps. A tent made of reindeer fur would be the best, and it would make up, or nearly make up, for its increased weight by enabling you to dispense with fur sleeping bags. I carried an unusually large fur tent to the mouth of the Anadyr and back with 30 days' dog food and 30 days' provisions for eleven men.

I have not fully covered all the details of this tent, because they must be worked out in practice according to circumstances. I don't see why the idea is not entirely practicable, and I am sure that such a tent could be set up and made to stand in almost any wind and upon any kind of a surface. The only question of serious difficulty which I can think of is the question of moisture. It is possible that the vapor from the men's breaths and from the cooking would so moisten the tent as to stiffen it with ice so that it could not be readily struck and packed up. This would not be as likely, however, to happen with a fur tent as with a tent of simple canvas. We never had the slightest trouble with moisture or frost in Korak *pologs*, even in temperatures of 50 below. The lamp kept the air warm enough to hold all the moisture in suspension inside the *polog*. It was only when the air made its escape and became chilled by contact with the outer air that frost formed, and even around such openings the quantity was not great and could be readily brushed off. Nares' and Payer's sledge parties seem to have been greatly troubled by the stiffening of their tents and clothing from the freezing of the moisture which they contained. We never experienced any such difficulty in Siberia, although we had temperatures as low as —68, and I think that in the case of the Nares and Payer sledge parties it must have been due, at least in part, to bad management. Men should so graduate the thickness of their clothing, in the first place, as to avoid getting into a profuse perspiration while at work, and then when they come into camp they shouldn't rush into a tent with their furs all full of snow and let it melt as they gradually get warm. That of course would load the air with moisture and dampen their clothing so that it would freeze stiff the next time they went out.

As I have before said, I don't think any serious inconvenience would be caused by moisture or frost in a *fur* tent made on the plan which I have suggested, provided men didn't rush into it with damp or snow-packed clothing on. Even in a light cotton duck tent made on that principle frost could hardly form more abundantly than it does in other tents, while the protection from weather, particularly wind, would be far more perfect. If these ideas strike you favorably, please give my tent a trial. Any sailor could make one in a few hours.

The next suggestions which I have to offer relate to clothing and sleeping-bags. From the fact that Kane, Markham, Koldeway, Payer, and Arctic explorers generally represent themselves as suffering intensely from cold in temperatures which we endured in Siberia with almost perfect comfort, I draw the conclusion that our clothing and equipment were much superior to theirs. Markham, for example, in his official report to Nares, describes night after night passed in misery in temperatures averaging about 35° below zero. Now, I have only to say that if a well man can't sleep out on the snow without any shelter whatever in a *calm* temperature of 35 below without suffering from cold, he is either insufficiently fed or improperly clothed. I am not particularly hardy, but I have slept out in that temperature just as comfortably as I ever slept at home in a bed, and even in a temperature of 50 below I have passed the night without suffering anything which could reasonably be called a severe hardship. I did not sleep much, and shivered away the night, but the suffering which I endured could not be compared for instance with that caused by even a moderate toothache. A complete Siberian equipment of furs, where one is not restricted by lack of transportation, consists of 3 pairs of fur stockings, 2 pairs of fur boots, one pair of *bootoolee* or over stockings, fur pantaloons (or leggings to cover the knees above the boots,) a fur hood, 3 prs. of mittens, a long squirrel-tail boa to wind around the neck and face, two *kookhlankas* or fur blouses, and a fur sleeping-bag. Some of these articles are luxuries rather than absolute necessities, but they are all needful if you wish to travel and camp out in comfort. I will take them up in order.

(1.) *Foot-covering.*—Foot-covering and sleeping-gear seem to me the most important part of a sledger's outfit. The freezing of the feet should be guarded against in every possible way, because it leads directly to total disability and death in the case of the individual, and because it compels the party to either abandon the disabled man or drag him on a sledge at the expense of slower progress and possible disaster resulting therefrom. Every naval Arctic expedition which has sailed from England since Parry, and almost every American expedition, has used blanket or duffle wrappings for foot-covering instead of fur stockings. All experience goes to show that this is a great mistake. In Siberia, where the temperature goes to 70 below, and where (in the vicinity of Verkhoyansk) the winter mean is more than 40 below, serious freezing of the feet is almost unknown. During my three years' stay there I did not see or hear of a single case, either among our own men or among the natives, while on the Nares expedition alone more than a dozen men had their feet seriously frost-bitten, four of them so seriously as to require amputation They didn't experience any lower temperatures than we did, and they didn't have in the field anything like the weather that a Siberian Cossack encounters in going from Verkhoyansk to Yakoutsk in January and February. And yet they lost their toes, while the Cossack goes through foot-whole, simply because they didn't know how to take care of their feet and a Cossack does.

I have tried all kinds of fur stockings, and in my judgment the best are those made of the heaviest and densest attainable fur of the adult reindeer. They should correspond in length with the boots, and should be made loose enough to give the freest possible play to the foot.

The boots should have a sole of seal-skin and uppers of seal-skin or fur from the leg of the reindeer. They should also fit very loosely—loosely enough not to pinch or draw over any part of the foot and should come up to the knee. A layer of dried grass or straw should be put into the boot for the fur stocking to rest on, and this, together with the stocking should be thoroughly *dried* at least once every day and oftener if necessary. As long as one's stockings are damp with perspiration the feet can be kept warm only by continuous exercise. The Siberian Cossacks are more particular about keeping their fur stockings dry than about any other single thing. I have seen them take off their boots and bare their feet to a piercing wind in the middle of the day in order to get on dry stockings, and they would no more think of going to bed at night without changing their stockings and thoroughly drying the moist ones than they would of trying to get to sleep with their eyes open. Every other duty may at times be slighted or neglected, but the changing and drying of stockings is never under any circumstances forgotten or omitted.

Where you have nothing but a lamp to dry your stockings by it becomes, of course, a difficult matter, and that is another reason why the tent which I have suggested (in connection with a kerosene-oil stove) seems to me almost a necessity. A Florence stove with two or three wicks and a drum heater would dry a large amount of fur clothing in a very short time, but you cannot use the stove unless you have a tent which will protect it perfectly from wind. This, ordinary tents will not do. If you should at any time find it impracticable for any reason to dry your fur stockings by artificial heat, change them all the same, and hang the moist ones up. They will part with some of their moisture by evaporation even when frozen. In such a case it would be well to keep one or two extra pairs of fur stockings to be worn only to sleep in, putting on the damp ones again in the morning to walk and work in. The sleeping stockings could thus be kept tolerably dry. I lay particular stress upon this subject of stockings, because in the course of three years of hard Arctic experience I learned its importance. Naval and Arctic Advisory Boards devote pages of instructions to matters which are not half as important to an Arctic expedition as this one subject of foot-covering. So far as I can discover from the records of recent Arctic expeditions the men's feet have been wretchedly cared for both by day and by night. Take for example Markham's report to Nares of his northern sledge journey from Cape Joseph Henry out over the ice. His men suffered from cold feet all the time in temperatures which a Siberian Cossack would laugh at. His second day's record says, "Passed a cold, wretched, and sleepless night, temperature inside the tent being minus 15°. Although our foot-gear was placed inside our sleeping-bags, nothing thawed; everything was frozen quite hard in the morning. The gauntlet mitts, (!) or hand-stockings, as they are called by the men, are admirable for the feet at night-time, but they do not suffice to keep them warm."

They *must* be admirable if, reinforced by a sleeping-bag, they won't keep the feet warm in a temperature of only —15°! The same day's record continues: "Halted at 4.45. John Radmore had all the toes of his left foot frost-bitten. Everything frozen perfectly hard. Our sleeping-bags resembled sheet-iron." The mean temperature for this day was —31°. Third day's record: "Slept a little less uncomfortably, though deprived of all feeling in our feet. Temperature inside the tent, minus 23°." Fourth day's record: "Another cold, sleepless night. Temperature inside the tent, —15°. A few slight frost-bites sustained; Daniel Harley rather severe in the big toe."

And so the report goes on, recording suffering, sleeplessness, and frost-bites in temperatures which we would have regarded in Siberia as fairly mild, and in which we never felt so much as serious inconvenience, still less suffering. Markham's men, as you see, used blanket foot-wrappings, and it is perfectly evident from every page of his report that they totally failed to answer the purpose for which they were intended. In fact their whole equipment was deplorably inadequate, although it weighed 714 pounds for 8 men, or about 90 pounds per man. A Siberian Cossack with half that weight of equipment will camp out in comfort in temperatures 20 degrees lower than that in which Markham says he passed "a cold, wretched, and sleepless night," and will sleep nine hours at a stretch without ever once having the sensation of cold feet. Personal hardiness, of course, counts for something, but dress is the main thing. I never should have gotten out of Siberia alive if I had passed "a cold, wretched, and sleepless night" every time the thermometer got down to —15°. Minus 35° was my lowest limit of *comfort*, but if there was no wind I didn't *seriously suffer* with cold feet at night until the thermometer went to the neighborhood of —50°. A man who is well fed, whose feet are covered with *dry* fur stockings and fur boots, and who has a sleeping-bag, ought not to suffer with cold feet at night in any temperature above —35°. I always carried with me a pair of *bootoolee* or thick reindeer-skin over-stockings, to put on over my boots at night when the cold was very severe, but I rarely had occasion to use them.

(2.) *Leg-covering.*—The Siberian Cossacks, as a rule, wear reindeer-skin trousers, but I found them cumbersome and used instead what the Russians call *nakalayniki*, which are a sort of knee-legging covering the leg from the top of the boot to the thigh. Mine were made of grey wolf-skin.

(3.) *Head-covering and face-protectors.*—The Siberan head-dress is a red fox-skin hood covering the head from the nape of the neck to the eyebrows, with a fringe of long, black bear-skin or of squirrel-tails around the face. The hood comes well forward over the cheeks so that when you stand sidewise to a wind it shelters the face from flying snow. The best face and nose protector I ever used was a sort of lady's *boa*, six or eight feet long, made of squirrel-tails strung together on a stout cord. This is wound around the neck and head until it comes up over the nose. You can breathe easily enough through the loose hairs, and yet they afford protection enough to the face to keep it from freezing even in a low temperature and a pretty high wind. As fast as the boa becomes covered with frost you turn it around or rewind it over the face so as to bring a dry part of it in front. It is so long that this can be done almost a dozen times before you use up all the dry portions of it. When you come into camp it can be dried throughout ready for use again on the next day.

(4.) *Body-covering.*—The principal article of the Siberian dress—and, all things considered, the most valuable and satisfactory Arctic garment I have ever seen—is the *kookhlanka*, or fur blouse, worn in winter by all the inhabitants of Northeastern Siberia, native and Russian. It is practically a long, double, fur shirt, without any opening front or back from the neck to the lower edge. It is made of two thicknesses of heavy reindeer-skin, with the tanned sides put together, so that the fur comes inside and out. It is cut like a very large, very loose, shirt, long enough to reach the calf of the leg, but, as I said before, without any openings, except the neck and arm holes. The body of it is purposely made ample enough to contain the bodies of about three men, so that when it is girt about the waist with a sash the fur lies over the body in plaits, or folds, so as to practically double its thickness. At the back of the neck-hole there is sewn on a very large hood of the same material, which is so capacious that when it is drawn up over the head and the other hood, its sides can be brought together in front of the face, to protect the latter in storms, and while asleep at night. The *kookhlanka* is always worn tied about the waist with a sash, and it is generally pulled up through the sash until the skirts come about to the knee. It then drops over the sash in a fold all around the waist. The reasons why I think this garment is far in advance of anything worn elsewhere in the north are as follows:

First. It has no opening to admit wind. If a coat buttons or fastens up in front more or less wind always gets in where the sides are brought together.

Second. It does not permit a circulation of cold air up and down the body inside of it. If a loose coat or blouse is worn without a sash, the air which has been warmed by the body is continually escaping at the throat, and cold air is blown in at the bottom to take its place, so that the heat of the body is carried away by a current of constantly changing air.

Third. The *kookhlanka* above the sash is virtually a capacious bag full of warm air which cannot escape, and which surrounds all the vital parts of the body and affords great additional protection. In ordinary winter weather, in fact in all weather except the severest, I carried a bottle of water inside the breast of my *kookhlanka* to ice sledge runners with, and carried it there without its freezing. The upper part of the *kookh-lanka*, above the sash contains three or four gallons of air which is warmed by the body, and remains there, affording almost as much protection as an equivalent thickness of fur and without any corresponding weight.

Fourth. The *kookhlanka* is adjustable as to length. If you are walking, running, driving a sledge, or doing anything which requires the free play of the legs the *kookhlanka* can be pulled up through the sash so that the skirts are above the middle of the thigh, and all the slack is about the waist. In sitting still or in lying down to sleep at night the skirts can be pulled down over the knees so as to nearly cover the entire leg.

Fifth. By a little *wriggle* the arms and hands can be drawn into the body of the garment through the sleeves as they always are at night, and thus completely protected. It is very convenient, too, in the day-time to be able to draw your hands into the body of the *kookhlanka* when they get very cold and warm them under your armpits. Many a time I have relieved aching fingers in that way when I couldn't get them warm in any other. In like manner, if the nose or cheeks begin to freeze, you can draw your head down through the neck-hole into this reservoir of warm air as a turtle draws his head into his shell, and thus get at least temporary relief. That, too, is often done at night, especially by men who happen to have no sleeping-bag. I could enumerate many other useful features of the *kookhlanka*, but the above must suffice. If you ever try one you wouldn't, I think, be satisfied to wear anything else. I always carried two *kookhlankas* with me—one of medium weight for the day-time, and one heavy one made long enough to touch the ground all around, to sleep in. I picked up a magnificent sleeping *kookhlanka* among the Chukches the second winter I spent in Siberia. It was fully five feet long and three feet wide, and was made of the finest and thickest reindeer-skin I have ever seen. In that *kookhlanka* and a good fur sleeping-bag I slept on the snow many nights without shelter, but in perfect comfort, in temperatures ranging from —20° to —35°.

In the course of three winters' experience I was never subjected to the slightest inconvenience by reason of the freezing and stiffening of my clothing or my sleeping-bag. It simply did not happen. Why, I do not know, unless because we took proper care of our furs. Markham's furs and sleeping-bags seem to have been frozen hard and stiff more than three-fourths of the time. Our immunity from trouble of this kind could hardly have been due to any difference in the general condition of the atmosphere. Our temperatures were lower than Markham's and our extreme variations as great and as rapid as his. We traveled frequently for weeks at a time in fall and winter along the coast of the Okhotsk Sea (which was generally more or less open) in dense fogs rising from the water, and still our furs did not stiffen with frost. A thin rime of frozen mist frequently formed over them, but it could be readily whipped or brushed off, and never caused us any inconvenience. I remember camping out one night on the coast of Penzhinsk Gulf in a dense fog, with a temperature of — 25°. I slept warm and comfortable. My sleeping-bag, upon getting up in the morning, was covered with rime, like hoar frost, but it was perfectly soft and pliable and remained so. I think that the reasons why Markham had so much trouble with the freezing of clothing and passed so many wretched sleepless nights were as follows:

1st. Neither the clothing nor the sleeping-bags of his men were adapted to the purposes for which they were intended. The men wore during the day either canvas jumpers or duffle blouses, and slept at night in duffle bags. Canvas and duffle are very inadequate substitutes for reindeer fur. Duffle blouses are warm enough to work in, but every man should have something like a fur *kookhlanka* to put on as soon as he stops working and to sleep in. Every man should furthermore have fur stockings instead of blanket wrappings, fur boots instead of canvas and carpet moccasins, and a reindeer-skin instead of a duffle sleeping-bag.

2d. The men should avoid as far as possible getting into a profuse perspiration in the day-time by reducing the clothing worn while working at the drag-ropes to the lowest limit consistent with safety. It is a good deal better to be cold than to get your clothing wet or moistened through and through with profuse perspiration. Markham's men worked until everything they had on was moist with sweat, and then rushed into a tent and ot into a duffle bag. For a time the tent was filled with moisture from the men's warm bodies and damp clothing, and then, after the cooking-lamp was put out, the temperature inside the tent fell, the men's damp clothing began to get cold on their bodies, the duffle sleeping-bags, which had, of course, absorbed moisture from the men's wet clothing, began to freeze and lose their heat-retaining properties, the sides of the tent began to stiffen with the moisture which they, too, had absorbed, and general misery was the inevitable result.

On one of Nares, sledge expeditions, which lasted 20 days, the tent and its appurtenances increased in weight by the absorption of moisture from 91 lbs. 7 oz. to 189 lbs. The sleeping bags increased in the same way from 8 lbs. 2 oz. each to 17 lbs., and everything else in the shape of clothing in the same proportion. (Official Reports of the Nares Expedition, page 88). Now, this is unquestionably bad management. The moisture which saturates tents and clothing in that way doesn't come out of the terrestrial atmosphere when the thermometer ranges continuously below zero; it comes from the bodies of men and the cooking of food, and penetrates the fabrics in the shape of uncondensed vapor. It is therefore subject to control.

The course of procedure of a party of Cossacks under such circumstances would be somewhat as follows:

Their personal outfit (for six men) would consist (exclusive of clothes worn) of—

1 very small tent (to be used simply for the protection of the lamp in cooking and *not* for shelter).

6 spare *kookhlankas* (to sleep in).

6 reindeer-skin sleeping-bags.

6 pairs of spare stockings (reindeer-skin) and 6 pairs of spare mittens.

If they expected to cross ice where they might meet with sludge or wet snow, they would perhaps take spare boots, not otherwise.

The outfit of the Nares sledging party upon starting out was as follows:

1 large tent.

1 coverlet.

1 spare coverlet.

1 lower robe.

1 canvas floor-cloth.

1 water-proof floor-cloth.

6 sleeping-bags (duffle).

6 knapsacks (with extra foot-wrappings, mittens, &c.).

6 pairs traveling boots.

This outfit weighed, in round numbers, 300 lbs.; the outfit of the party of Cossacks would not exceed 225 lbs.; a difference in favor of the latter of 75 lbs. At the end of 20 days the outfit of the Nares party had doubled in weight from the absorption of moisture, thus making 600 lbs. The outfit of the Cossacks would not increase in weight at all, with the exception of the small tent, which would perhaps be ten pounds heavier. The difference of weight in favor of the Cossacks would then be 365 lbs.; and the difference in the condition of the men of the respective parties, and in the amount of suffering they had endured, would be incalculable.

The management of the men of the Nares party was about as follows:

1st. They loaded their sledges with 235 lbs. to the man and had to resort to "double banking" and "standing pulls" in order to make an average of two miles a day with from three to five journeys back and forth over the same ground. They were consequently overworked.

2d. They always floundered through deep snow, sometimes almost up to their waists, instead of using snow-shoes. This was wholly unnecessary exertion.

3d. They would get into a profuse perspiration during the day and come into camp at night with their clothing all damp.

4th. Finding it cold standing around in their moist clothing while supper was being prepared, they would all get into the tent and into their duffle bags, and the warmth of their still perspiring bodies, together with the heat from the cooking apparatus and the steam from the hot water and food, would raise the temperature and fill the tent with vapor, thus partially saturating both tent and contents with moisture.

5th. During the night everything would freeze stiff, the men would suffer so from cold as to be unable to sleep, and in the morning they would crawl out of their frozen duffle bags unrefreshed and miserable to begin another day of the same experience.

The management of the Cossack would differ from this in every particular.

1st. He would use a sledge with runners 4½ inches wide at the base instead of 2½ inches. He would not put a pound more weight on the sledge than its complement of men could comfortably draw without "double banking," "standing pulls," or repeated journeys over the same ground. He would allow say, 150 lbs. to a man instead of the 235 lbs. allowed by the Nares people, but for their average of 2 miles a day he would make ten, and thus with a little more than half the food they carried, he would accomplish 3 or 4 times the distance made by them, and do it without over-exerting or breaking himself down. In all middle temperatures and in traveling over snow he would ice his runners as often as once in four hours. Nobody who has'nt tried it can appreciate the difference which this little expedient makes.

2d. In dealing with deep soft snow he would use snow-shoes, lengthening out his drag lines to prevent interference of one man with another, and would redistribute the weights on his sledges so as to have the lightest go first and the heaviest last. In *very* light, soft and deep snow he would break a road for the sledges by sending men ahead on snow-shoes to trample down and consolidate the snow. As a further precaution, if when he started out he had any reason to expect deep soft snow, he would multiply the number of his sledges and divide up the whole number of his men into smaller sledge parties. For example, instead of taking 4 eight-man sledges and loading each of them with 1,200 lbs., he would take 8 four-man sledges and load each of them with 600 lbs. He would thus distribute the total weight to be carried over twice the area of snow which would have to sustain its weight in the first case· There is no doubt, in my mind, that this is the correct principle. If it were given me as a task to transport 1,500 lbs. of dead weight with a force of ten men across 150 miles of steppe covered with soft fresh snow four feet deep, and to do it in the quickest possible time, I shouldn't think of putting the whole 1,500 lbs. on one sledge to be drawn by my entire force. To drag a 1,500-lb., sledge through four feet of soft snow is an almost hopeless task. It can, of course, be done, but at a very low rate of speed —say three or four miles a day—and at the expense of exhausting labor. I should put the 1,500 lbs. on the ten sledges, each to be drawn by one man, and graduate the weights from 50 lbs. for the first sledge to 200 lbs. for the last, and I should expect the whole caravan to move at the rate of from 10 to 15 miles a day, and without any floundering or exhausing labor. The snow-shoes of the first man would make a track in which a sledge with only 50 lbs. on it (I would even empty the first sledge entirely, if necessary) could be drawn without difficulty at a slow walk. For the 2d sledge the track would be a little better, for the 3d still better, and by the time the heavier sledges got along there would be quite a decent path. It is true I should be dragging about 300 lbs. of extra weight in the shape of nine extra sledges, but this slight disadvantage would be far more than counterbalanced by the wide distribution of my dead weight. A man carries extra weight when he puts on snow-shoes, but it pays.

3d. The Siberian Cossack would avoid as far as possible getting into a profuse perspiration. He would work coolly and steadily, and would graduate his clothing to the temperature and to the work which he had in hand, stripping down if necessary (as I have seen them do) to shirt, trousers, and light boots without stockings. He prefers always to shiver rather than to sweat while at work. His aim seems to be to keep as cool as possible while at work and as warm as possible while at rest. He will even sit on a sledge all day with cold feet rather than get into a perspiration by running to warm them—especially if he fears that he will not be able to find wood for a fire at night. One bitter cold day during my first winter in Siberia I spent half the afternoon running beside my sledge to warm my feet which were aching with cold. As a consequence I got into a profuse perspiration, and twenty minutes after getting back on my sledge I would be colder than ever, and would have to run again, keeping on all the time my heavy furs, and starting the perspiration anew by every run. Finally, one of my old Cossack drivers drove up beside me and said, "It's bad, Bahrin, to run so much. Why do you do it?" I replied that my feet were cold. "Do they stay warm after you run?" he asked. "No," I said, "and so I have to run again." "Toto" ("that's it") he replied gravely, "you have to keep running, and you get yourself all in a sweat running in heavy furs, and then when you sit still a few minutes you get cold again and your wet fur stockings freeze around your feet, and it is worse than if you hadn't run. When night comes you will try hard to keep warm because your underclothes will be wet." "But," I said, "what do you do when your feet ache?" He shrugged his shoulders, and then added, "If they ache, neecheevo (it is nothing). If they get so cold that they stop aching then I run until they ache again; but get into a sweat—no!" The result of this management is that when a Cossack goes into camp at night his clothing is fairly dry and his kookhlanka absolutely so. Before going to bed he hanges his fur stockings and dries the ones he has taken off if possible; puts on his spare kookhlanka over the other if it is very cold, spreads down his sleeping-bag in the lee of a sledge with a pillow if he has one, crawls into it, pulls the capacious hood of his sleeping kookhlanka over his head and face, draws his hands and arms out of the sleeves into the breast of his inner kookhlanka, and quietly goes to sleep in a temperature of −35°. Frost forms around his face in considerable quantities and in the morning he whips it off of his fur hood with a little stick. Otherwise his clothing and sleeping-bag are as dry, soft, and pliable as they were the night before, and they will continue so until the last day of his journey. I have seen this whole operation performed hundreds of nights, and I know it by heart. It is hardly necessary to point out the superiority of this equipment and this management to those of the Nares sledging parties.

I have omitted to say that in storms when the snow flies the Cossack does not allow the fur of his kookhlanka to become packed with the flying flakes, but puts on over it what is called a kamlay, which is a long, loose shirt of wash-leather, and wears it until he gets into his sleeping-bag at night.

The Siberian sleeping-bag is made of reindeer-skin, and those used by the Cossacks are generally short, coming up only to the waist, or at most to the armpits. The best one I ever had was of double California blanketing, lined with wolf-skins, and was about seven feet long, slit down the sides so as to make a flap which could be turned back, and then thrown up loosely over the head. This bag, however, was three times as heavy as those used by my Cossack drivers. The Cossacks after getting into their bags sometimes tied the mouths of them around their bodies loosely with their waist-sash to prevent the escape of any of the air which had been warmed by their bodies. With a long bag, however, I did not find this necessary. I think a good fur sleeping-bag is almost indispensable to comfort in the field. Reindeer-skin weighs more than duffle or blanketing, but it is far warmer, and all my experience goes to show that it is best to secure comfort at night, even at the expense of increased weights. As I said before, however, the equipment of a Cossack taken as a whole is not only warmer than that of one of Nares' sledgers but is considerably lighter. Markham's "coverlet," "spare coverlet," "lower robe," "canvas floor-cloth," and "waterproof floor-cloth" were, in my opinion, mere rubbish. If a man has two good *kookhlankas* and a sleeping-bag he needs no "upper robes," "lower robes," and "coverlets."

My letter seems to be getting to a preposterous length, and I must make my suggestions briefer.

With regard to sledges, I have nothing to say except that I would have the base or friction surface of the runner 4¼ inches wide instead of 2¼ inches, as it is in the regulation McClintock sledge. Such a runner goes far more easily over the deep soft snow which you will have to deal with than the cutting runner of a McClintock or Nares sledge. I am afraid you will not find your boat-sledge as useful or practicable as you anticipated. As I have not seen it, however, I may be entirely mistaken about it. I presume all of your sledges are, as they should be, lashed together with thongs and not pinned. A sledge ought not to be rigid in any part, and the most indestructible ones I have ever seen were almost as flexible and elastic as a long basket. The Siberian sledge is spanned just forward of the middle by an arch 2½ or 3 feet high, made out of a steamed and bent sapling, whose ends are firmly lashed on each side to the uprights of the runners. This arch serves as a convenient handle by which the sledge may be dragged from one side to the other, lifted or held back in descending hills. It seems to me to answer the purpose better than the "up-standers" of the Eskimo sledge. If I were you I should take pains to ice my sledge-runners for travel over snow. By rubbing them down with a cloth saturated with water you can put on one thin layer after another until the icing is ¼ to ⅜ of an inch in thickness. Care must then be taken to avoid bare places of ground, stones, and ice. Such an icing will last on snow half a day and will lighten wonderfully the labor of dragging the sledge. I should also, if I were in your place, make some experiments with a Hudson Bay sledge, with a view to ascertaining whether it is not better than any other in deep soft snow. It consists, as you doubtless know, of two or three long thin boards lashed together side by side by means of cross-pieces, and turned up at the forward end in this way:

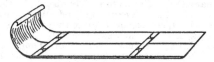

Its dimensions are, I believe, 7 to 9 feet in length by 2½ to 3 in width. I have always thought that this form of sledge, which is about the same thing as the Canadian *toboggan*, might be drawn over deep soft snow by men on snow-shoes much more easily than any other, because it would run on the surface, or sink in very little. It would be worth while to make some experiments with it in comparison with sledges of other kinds. It would also be worth while to make some careful and accurate experiments upon the amount, in weight, of food with which a sledge party can go the greatest distance. To illustrate what I mean, suppose 3 men start out with 3 sledges loaded with 18 lbs. of food each to see how far they can get from their base of supplies and back. Suppose that they eat daily 3 lbs. of food per man, and that with their light loads they can march at an average rate of speed for the whole time they are out of 25 miles a day. Their food will last them 6 days, in which time, at 25 miles a day, they can make 150 miles, or go to a distance of 75 miles from their base and back. Take that for one extreme of the problem—the extreme of limited food and high speed. Suppose, again, that three men start out with three sledges loaded with 300 lbs. of food each, to make a similar experiment. Suppose that no one of the three men can draw his own sledge single-handed, and that every sledge has to be advanced separately by the united strength of the whole party. Every man will then have to go five times over every mile of ground made good, and we will suppose that in that way the party is able to make an average for the whole journey of 3 miles per day. Their food at 3 pounds daily per man will last them 100 days, in which time they will make 300 miles, or reach a point 150 miles from their base and get back. Now, it is evident that neither of these parties has so managed as to secure the best results in the shape of distance. The first party has not gained enough in speed by taking light loads to make up for the shortness of the time it can stay in the field, and the last party has not gained enough in the number of days it can stay in the field to compensate for the slowness of its progress. Somewhere between these two extremes there is a proportion between speed and food-weight which would enable a party of 3 men to surpass either of the above records. Suppose, for example, that 3 men take 150 lbs. of food each, and are able, with that load, to make an average of 2 miles an hour, or 15 miles a day throughout their journey. They can stay in the field 50 days, in which time, at the average rate of 15 miles a day, they will make 750 miles, or reach a point 375 miles from their base and get back.

Of course these estimates are mere suppositions which make no pretentions to probability, but they illustrate what I want to bring out, viz, that somewhere between the maximum of speed with a minimum of food-weight on the one hand, and the minimum of speed with a maximum of food-weight on the other, there is a mean proportion of food-weight to speed which will secure the best results in point of distance. A man who carries no food at all can't go far, because he can't stay in the field. A man who loads himself down with food so that he can make only a mile a day can't go far, because, although he can remain indefinitely, in the field, he practically accomplishes nothing. What is the effective mean between these two extremes? Galton, in his "Art of Travel," says that the amount of weight which a man can carry with the best results is four-ninths of the amount which he can just stand up under. In other words, if he can just stagger under 270 lbs. his proper load is 120 lbs. This rule holds good, he says, no matter how muscular force is exerted in moving weight from place to place. By this rule, if, with the snow in a certain condition, a man can just move a sledge weighing 360 lbs., that is, drag it 20 feet with the exertion of all his strength, the proper weight for him to haul with the snow in that condition is 160 lbs. This agrees generally with my experience.

This whole question is one of great practical importance in Arctic sledging, and deserves investigation by careful experiment. Captain Nares says in his report that "the distance to which a sledge party can go depends upon the number of days they can stay in the field, and this in turn depends upon the amount of food they can carry." But this statement is incorrect, for the reason that it leaves out the most important factor of the problem, viz, *speed*. It would be better to say that the distance to which a sledge party can go depends upon the balancing of force, food-weight, and speed. There is a certain proportion between those factors which, if maintained, will give the highest possible result in distance. If any one of those factors is then increased or diminished at the expense of another, the distance made will fall short of the highest attainable distance. The salient features of the orthodox British sledging-school are few sledges, heavy food-weight, and low rate of speed. The Siberian sledging system is founded on many sledges, so as to widely distribute the total weight, light food-supply, and high speed. English explorers (and some Americans, as for instance Schwatka) load 10 dogs with 1,500 lbs., or more, so that the animals can just haul the load at a very slow walk, and are then satisfied with 10 miles a day (Schwatka's average). The Siberian Cossacks reduce the load for 10 dogs to 500 lbs., and make an average of 40 miles a day. There is no question as to which is the better of these two methods as far as distance is concerned. 1,500 lbs. of food will keep 10 dogs in the field 75 days, and in that time they will, by the first method, make 750 miles. 500 lbs. of food will keep the 10 Cossack dogs in the field 25 days, and in that time they will make 900 miles. I made 600 miles in 19 days during the short days of January, and 400 miles in 7 days in March and the first week of April. Of course such speed as this can only be made with light loads and good dogs, and under favorable conditions.

Wrangel averaged from 17 to 35 miles a day, even out on the Arctic Ocean among heavy hummocks and dealing with substantially the same obstacles as those which Markham, Aldrich, and Beaumont encountered. Seventeen miles a day was the lowest average he ever made, and that was when he went 175 miles from land out on the rough ice of the sea.

Before I stop I must describe the Siberian snow-shoe to you as I think you will find that very useful. It consits of a thin strip of board from 4 to 6 feet in length, by 8 inches in width, turned up at the forward end like a skate. It is covered all over the bottom with bristly skin from the fore-leg of the reindeer, so put on that the hairs all point backward. Sometimes seal-skin is used instead of reindeer-skin. The hair of whatever skin is used should be stiff and should lie down closely—that is, grow at an acute angle to the skin. The foot of the wearer is attached to the snow-shoe by a simple toggle so arranged as to let the heel rise from the shoe at every step, only the toe remaining fast. The snow-shoe is never lifted from the snow. The walker simply scuffles along in the snow sliding his snow-shoes ahead alternately, but not making the slightest effort to raise them up. The exertion is very light and the speed rapid, as the walker gets a spring from this long thin elastic board at every step and then slides more or less every step as if he were skating. The bristly hair on the bottom of the shoe lets it slip forward as if on soaped glass, but prevents the slightest slip backward and gives you a firm footing when you have occasion to pull. You can walk up a steep mountain side covered with crusted snow, and not slip back an inch.

I have known Tonguses around the Okhotsk Sea to make more than 100 versts (70 miles) a day on these snow-shoes, when the snow was crusted over enough to bear a man's weight, *with* snow-shoes, but not without.

Among the miscellaneous suggestions which occur to me are the following:

Try some experiments upon the cream-colored reindeer moss as food. If the stomach will digest and assimilate it, its use may save many lives in Arctic regions. Nordenskjold cooked some and ate it as an experiment, in Spitzbergen. He found it "bitter but nutritious," and thought it "could be eaten with relish by hungry men." The Siberian Koraks take it from the stomach of the reindeer after it has been partly digested and eat it in that shape. The questions to be settled are, will the human stomach bear the moss or the juice of it without pain, nausea, or any evidence of gastric disturbance; and, second, will it temporarily sustain life? The fatness of winter-killed reindeer shows that this moss is full of flesh and blood-making elements. But can the human stomach extract them from it? I should chop the moss up fine and try it raw, then boiled, and, finally, if the stomach wouldn't take it in either way, I should try soup made of it, or the water in which it had been thoroughly boiled. I don't suppose that this moss will *taste* good, but it is desirable to know whether it will sustain life, or help to sustain life, in the last extremity. If I had been in poor De Long's place I should have given it a trial before I died. It grows abundantly throughout the Arctic regions, and would be of great value in Arctic exploration if any way could be found to make the human body assimilate the food elements in it.

If you have occasion to make a sledge journey for the purpose of accomplishing *distance*, don't forget to consider the Cossack plan of dividing your total weight up into small loads, distributing it on a good many sledges, and then, as fast as the sledges are emptied, sending them back to your base, each with its complement of men. It's a waste of food to keep men with the party who are not absolutely needed to haul, and as the total weight is daily growing less, the hauling force may be from time to time correspondingly diminished. The sledges which are to be the first to go back should be put in the lead to break roads and do the brunt of the work, so as to save the strength of the men who are to keep on. The sledges which go back may then be sent out again to meet the party on its return with fresh supplies of food, or to make caches at points agreed on, which the returning party can pick up. There ought to be no danger in sending two men back with a light sledge. Wrangel did it when he was out 150 miles from land on the Arctic Ocean and 300 miles from his base. The men should be taught to find their way without the aid of officers. Don't overload your sledges with food. The ability to make *speed* is quite as important as the ability to stay a great many days in the field, and the *morale* of men who are making 15 miles a day is far better than that of men who are just struggling along at the rate of 3 or 4 miles a day. Men's minds and spirits should be considered as well as their bodies, and there is nothing so cheering as the consciousness of making good progress. "Double-banking" of sledges, and going back and forth over the same ground to advance sledges separately, is heart-breaking work.

In going over ice in the fall you will often meet with sludge under fresh-fallen snow in places where the ice has cracked and let water up through. The temperature of the air may be minus 25°, and yet this water will remain unfrozen because it is protected by the overlying blanket of snow. Such sludge is very dangerous to the feet, and they should be kept out of it by the use of snow-shoes.

JUNE 20.

I have just heard that your mail closes to-day, and I must bring this letter to an abrupt close. I intended to write you an account of the "Jeannette" disaster from my point of view, but shall have to omit it. You will get the principal facts from the newspapers.

And now, my dear Lieut. Greely, with my most cordial wishes and regard, I must bid you good-bye. You have been often in my thoughts during the past winter, and will be until you return, as I hope, in health and safety, crowned with honors. God bless you.

Faithfully, yours,

GEORGE KENNAN.

EXHIBIT Q.

Schedule of provisions supplied to U. S. S. "Rodgers," based upon a strength of 40 men for two years, with an allowance for the establishment of depots.

[See page 820, Report Secretary of the Navy, 1881.]

Articles.		Quantity.
Biscuit, in barrels	pounds	24,000
Salt beef, in barrels	do	4,000
Clear salt pork (fat), in barrels	do	16,000
Flour, in barrels, 150 barrels	do	23,400
Rice, in barrels	do	2,000
Dried apples, in boxes	do	2,000
Pickles, assorted, in kegs	do	3,000
Sugar, in barrels	do	10,000
Tea, in chests	do	2,000
Coffee, in tins	do	5,000
Butter, in tins	do	3,500
Dried vegetables, Alden or Smith process	do	3,000
Canned tomatoes	do	3,000
Beans	gallons	1,000
Molasses	do	260
Vinegar	do	500
Preserved beef	pounds	12,000
Pemmican, in tins	do	20,000
Canned soups	cans	1,000
Canned meats	pounds	12,000
Sauer-kraut (imported), in kegs	kegs	100
Split peas	pounds	2,000
Lard	do	5,000
Cheese, in tins	do	4,000
Hominy, in tins	do	2,000
Corn meal, in tins	do	2,000
Oat meal, in tins	do	2,000
Macaroni	do	1,000
Onions, dried (Alden's, or similar process)	do	1,000
Smoked tongues	do	500
Smoked hams	do	1,000
Condensed milk	do	1,500
Oysters, in tins	do	500
Chocolate	do	1,000
Dried herbs	do	24
Celery seed	do	20
Raisins	do	1,000
Gooseberries, dried } or other fruits, cherries, {	do	1,200
Rhubarb, dried ... } or currants, etc. {	do	1,200
Cranberries, in barrels	do	1,200
Baking-powder (Royal)		100
Mustard (Coleman's)		50
Black pepper		50
Red pepper		20
Spices, assorted		50
Salt, table		500
Seeds, mustard, cress, radish, cabbage, &c	pounds	50
Lime-juice, in kegs (small)	do	
Buckwheat flour	gallons	250
Dried prunes	pounds	100
Pepper sauce, pints	do	300
Tomato catsup	bottles	300
Tobacco, Navy	do	200
Tobacco, smoking	pounds	2,000
Sardines	do	100
Olive oil, quarts	½ boxes	1,000
Shaker corn (Smith's)	dozen	30
Pipes, brier-wood, with stems	pounds	1,200
S. W. soap	gross	1
Hops	pounds	1,000
Orange and lemon peel	do	10
Currie powder, ¼-pound bottles	do	45
Whisky	bottles	100
	barrel	1

WAR DEPARTMENT,
OFFICE COMMISSARY-GENERAL OF SUBSISTENCE,
Washington, D. C., Feb. 20, 1884.

Capt. GEO. W. DAVIS,
   U. S. Army, Recorder, Board of Officers, &c., Washington, D. C.

CAPTAIN: In compliance with the request of the Board of Officers, convened by Executive Order, dated Dec. 17, 1883, to consider an expedition to be sent for the relief of Lieutenant Greely and his party at Lady Franklin Bay, I have the honor to inclose herewith a list of subsistence stores transferred to Lieut. P. H. Ray, 8th Infantry, at San Francisco, Cal., July 12, 1881, for the use of Point Barrow Expedition; also a list of subsistence stores furnished Lieut. A. W. Greely, 5th Cavalry, in charge of the expedition to Lady Franklin Bay, May 18, 1881. The latter list also shows, as requested, the number of *rations* of each article, which is a component of the Army ration; also the total number of meat rations, bread rations, coffee rations, &c. As many of the articles furnished—extracts, canned fruits, spices, &c.—are not components of the ration, are simply furnished for sales (not issues), and no fixed quantity of them has ever been established as a ration, or as equivalent to the daily allowance of any article of the ration, it is impracticable to express them in rations. At most, their value as equivalents could only be approximately given; therefore, those articles are not grouped with the ration articles, but the quantity simply of each article is given.

Respectfully, your ob'd't servant,

R. MACFEELY,
Com. Gen'l Subs.

ENCLOSURE 1.

List of subsistence stores transferred to Lieut. P. H. Ray, 8th Inf., at San Francisco, Cal., July 12, 1881, for the use of Point Barrow Expedition.

Articles.	Quantities.	Articles.	Quantities.
Pork	1,600 lbs.	Onions, aldens	60 lbs.
Bacon	2,500 "	Oysters	96 cans.
Salt beef	2,000 "	Onions (cans)	48 "
Fish, pickled mackerel	30 "	Peaches	96 "
Corned beef (2-lb. cans)	744 cans.	Peaches, dried	100 lbs.
Hard bread	1,000 lbs.	Pears	48 cans.
Beans	400 "	Peas, green, French	200 "
Beans, baked (3-lb. cans)	192 cans.	Pepper, red (tins)	1 tin.
Rice	300 lbs.	Pepper, red (bottles)	32 bots.
Cheese, Y. A	58 "	Pickles, cucumber (gallons)	20 gallons.
Tea, black E. B	60 "	Pickles, olives (gallons)	10 "
Tea, Oolong	40 "	Pineapples	24 cans.
Tea, green Japan	100 "	Potatoes	1,050 lbs.
Sugar	1,100 "	Potatoes, Alden's	110 "
Vinegar	61 "	Preserves, damson	48 cans.
Candles, adamantine	320 "	Prunes	100 lbs.
Soap	300 "	Raisins, L. L	20¼ boxes.
Salt, fine	500 "	Salt, table	200 lbs.
Soap (salt-water)	27 "	Sardines	100¼ boxes.
Pepper, black	25 "	Sauce, cranberry	192 cans.
Yeast powder (¼-lb. tins)	128 "	Sauce, Worcestershire	24 bots.
Wicking	10 "	Soap, toilet, transp. glyc	111 cakes.
Allspice	6 "	" " " "	66 "
Apples, dried	520 "	" " " "	24 "
Bacon, breakfast	323 "	" " Yankee	24 "
Butter	432 "	Soap, toilet, B. Winds'r, large	96 cakes.
Chocolate, sweet	48 "	Soup, ass't'd	24 cans.
Cigars, ass't'd	2,000, No.	Starch, corn	60 lbs.
Cinnamon	6 lbs.	Sugar, cut loaf	800 "
Cloves	2 "	Sugar, gran	100 "
Coffee, Java	755 "	Sugar, powdered	30 "
Corn, green	408 cans.	Syrup	48 gallons.
Crackers, ass't'd	200 lbs.	Tapioca	50 lbs.
Flavoring, ex. lemon (2-oz. bots.)	48 bots.	Tobacco, chewing	200 "
" " vanilla (2-oz. bots.)	24 bots.	Tobacco, smoking, Durham	200 "
Flour, family	7,200 lbs.	Tomatoes (2½-lb. cans)	600 cans.
Ginger	12 "	Tongue	48 "
Ham, deviled	48 cans.	Wheat, cracked	100 lbs.
Ham, S. C	1,546 lbs.	Mustard	10 "
Hops	10 lbs.	Brushes, clothes	12, No.
Jelly, currant	96 cans.	" hair	6 "
Lard	480 lbs.	Brooms, whisk	24 "
Macaroni	50 lbs.	Can-openers	12 "
Mackerel, fresh (1-lb. cans)	48 cans.	Needles, ass't'd	200 papers.
" " (2-lb. cans)	24 "	" darning	50, No.
Matches, safety	720 boxes.	Needle-books	20 "
Milk, Eagle	432 cans.	Pins	24 papers.
Mushrooms	24 "	Thread, cotton, white and blk	180 spools.
Nutmegs	1 lb.	Thread, linen, white and black	216 "
Oatmeal	100 "	Cotton, darning	32 balls.
Oil, olive (gallons)	12¼ gallons.	Towels	72, No.

ENCLOSURE 2.

List of subsistence stores furnished Lieut. A. W. Greely, 5th Cav., Commanding Lady Franklin Bay Expedition, May 18, 1881.

8,400	pounds pork	11,200	rations.	
3,000	" bacon	4,000	"	
4 600	" salt beef	3,345⅓	"	
864	2-lb. cans beef, corned	2,304	"	
120	2 " " " roast	320	"	
242	pounds bacon, bkf	322⅔	"	
729	" ham, S. C	972	"	
				22,464⅙
144	1-lb. cans ext. of beef.			
24	2 " " " mutton.			
48	1 " " crab meat.			
24	2 " " clams.			
96	2 " " salmon.			
48	2 " " lobsters.			
96	2 " " oysters.			
48	" " shrimps.			
552	lbs. cheese.			
504	cans eggs, con'd.			
744	" soup.			
17,899	pounds hard bread	17,899	rations.	
980	" cornmeal	784	"	
6,450	" flour, fam	5,733⅓	"	
				24,416⅓
500	" macaroni.			
1,720	" oat meal.			
25	" tapioca.			
140	" cracked wheat.			
280	" farina.			
40	" corn starch.			
2,659	pounds beans	17,726⅔	rations.	
576	3-lb. cans beans, baked	3,840	"	
420	lbs. peas, split	2,800	"	
595	" rice	5,950	"	
1,120	" hominy	11,200	"	
				41,516⅔
960	2½-lb. cans onions.			
100	gals. onions.			
1,248	2½-lbs. cans potatoes.			
456	3 " " apples.			
60	1-gal. " apples.			
100	lbs. do., evap.			
96	cans asparagus.			
144	" green corn.			
144	3-lb. cans peaches.			
250	lbs. evap., do.			
48	2-lb. cans pears.			
96	" peas.			
48	2-lb. " pineapples.			
960	3-lb. " tomatoes.			
120	2 " " lima beans.			
48	3 " " quinces.			
244	lbs. prunes.			
1,008	cans gooseberries.			
1,900	pounds Rio coffee, ro	23,750	rations.	
196	" Java do.	2,205	"	
304	" tea	15,200	"	
				41,155
404	" chocolate.			
3,060	pounds sugar, bro	20,400	rations.	
1,060	" " gran.	7,066⅔	"	
108	gals. syrup	5,400	"	
192½	" molasses	9,625	"	
				42,491⅔

267	gals. vinegar	26,700	rations.	26,700
96	bots. pickles.			
250	gals. do.			
18¼	bbls. sauer-kraut.			
510	lbs. candles	34,000	rations.	34,000
240	lbs. soap	6,000	rations.	
200	" " salt water	5,000	"	
				11,000
288	cakes " toilet.			
1,568	lbs. salt	39,200	rations.	
190	" do. table	4,750	"	
				43,950
75	lbs. pepper, bl'k	30,000	rations.	30,000
10	" " Chili, col.			
12	bots. " Tobasco.			
108	lbs. yeast powder	2,700	"	2,700
100	" hops.			
5	lbs. allspice.			
3,024	" butter.			
5	" cinnamon.			
5	" cloves.			
24	bots. lemon ext.			
24	" vanilla.			
100	p'k'ts gelatine.			
10	lbs. ginger.			
48	cans jam.			
144	" jelly.			
78	lbs. lard.			
288	boxes matches.			
1,920	cans milk.			
198	lbs. mustard.			
5	" nutmeg.			
12	bots. olive oil.			
96	pipes.			
240	pipe-stems.			
144	cans preserves.			
96	jars do.			
140¼	lbs. raisins.			
1,008	cans cranb. sauce,			
24	" Wor. & Tobin's sauce.			
1.000	lbs. tobacco, plug.			
325	" " smoking.			
24	bots. celery extract.			
180	lbs. figs,			
192	cans gooseberries.			

SIGNAL OFFICE, WAR DEPARTMENT,
Washington City, Feb'y 23, 1884.

The PRESIDENT,
Board on Expedition for Relief of Lieutenant Greely, Washington, D. C.

SIR: In compliance with your request of 18th instant, for a list of such articles of food supplied to Lieutenant Greely and taken by him to Lady Franklin Bay, and also a list of food supplies furnished Lieutenant Ray while in command of Point Barrow, other than the articles of subsistence stores furnished these officers by the Commissary Department, I have the honor to inclose herewith the lists requested.

I am, very respectfully, your obedient servant,

W. B. HAZEN,
Brig. and Bvt. Maj. Gen'l, Chief Signal Officer, U. S. A.

Three enclosures.

[Enclosure 1.]

Food supplies furnished Lieutenant A. W. Greely.

24 cans (3 lbs.) tamarinds.
48 bot's (pints) horse radish.
24 cans (2 lbs.) orange marmalade.
50 lbs. pitted cherries.
96 cans (2 lbs.) blueberries.
48 " (2 lbs.) whortleberries.
24 " (2 lbs.) white ox-heart cherries.
48 " (3¼ lbs.) Cala. grapes.
48 "   "   pears.
72 " (3 lbs.) squash.
48 "   "   okra.
144 " (2 lbs.) carrots.
144 "   "   turnips.
144 "   "   beets.
120 "   "   sausage.
24 " (5 lbs.) peach butter.
24 "   "   quince   "

24 cans (5 lbs.) pear butter.
12 "   "   plum   "
24 " (3 lbs.) plum   "
24 " (¼ lbs.) currie powder.
6 jars Canton ginger.
12 pkgs. herbs, assorted.
12 bot's extracts "
6 kegs, 2 galls., olives.
8¼ bbls. cider.
128 lbs. Brazil nuts.
144 lbs. dates.
30 " cocoanut (Schepps.)
100 galls. lime-juice.
100 " N. E. rum.
125 " lime-juice.
3,667 pounds dried fish.
3,540 " pemmican.

The above is a correct list of stores furnished Lieutenant Greely for subsistence purposes by the Signal Office from the appropriation "Observation, Arctic Seas," &c., as shown by the records of that office.

LOUIS V. CAZIARC,
1st Lieutenant, 2d Artillery, Acting Signal Officer.

SIGNAL OFFICE, WAR DEPARTMENT,
Washington, D. C., Feb. 23, 1884.

[Enclosure 2.]

List of subsistence stores, Signal property, received by 1st Lieut. P. H. Ray, com'd'g Point Barrow Expedition, 1881–'82.

1,542 pounds ship bread, 40 gallons lime-juice, 20 pounds corn-meal, 270 pounds pemmican, 1 barrel whisky (45 galls.).
The above is a correct list of stores furnished Lieut. Ray for subsistence purposes by the Signal Office from the appropriation "Observation, Arctic Seas," &c., as shown by the records of that office.

LOUIS V. CAZIARC,
1st Lieut., 2d Artillery, A. S. O.

SIGNAL OFFICE, WAR DEPARTMENT,
Washington, D. C., Feb. 23, 1884.

[Enclosure 3.]

List of subsistence stores, Signal property, received by 1st Lieut. P. H. Ray, commanding Point Barrow Expedition, 1882–'83.

1,000 pounds canned corned beef, 300 pounds canned baked beans, 25 pounds canned sweet chocolate, 48 cans clams, 50 pounds buckwheat flour, 100 pounds Graham flour, 50 pounds pumpkin flour, 20 gallons cucumber pickles, 5 gallons pickled olives, 1,000 pounds potatoes, 475 pounds Alden's potatoes, 75 gallons maple syrup, 500 pounds corn-meal, 500 pounds hard bread.
The above is a correct list of stores furnished Lt. Ray for subsistence purposes by the Signal Office from the appropriation "Observation, Arctic Seas," &c., as shown by the records of that office.

LOUIS V. CAZIARC,
1st Lieut., 2d Artillery, A. S. O.

SIGNAL OFFICE, WAR DEPARTMENT,
Washington, D. C., Feb. 23, 1884.

EXHIBIT R.

Medical outfit of U. S. S. "Rodgers" for two years' service in Arctic regions, 1881.

[From Report of Secretary of the Navy, pp. 821 and 822.]

Articles.	Quantity.
MEDICINES.	
Acaciæ pulvis, 8-oz. bots ....lb.	½
Acidum aceticum, 8-oz. bots.........lb.	½
Acidum carbol. cryst., 2-oz. g. s. bots.lb.	½
Acidum carbolicum, imp., 1-lb. bots lb.	4
Acidum citricum, 8-oz. bots ....lb.	6
Acidum muriaticum, 4-oz. g. s. bots..oz.	4
Acidum nitricum, 4-oz. g. s. bots ....lb.	1
Acidum salicylicum, 2½ gr. pills ....no.	500
Acidum sulphuricum, 4-oz. g. s. bots.oz.	8
Acidum sulphur. aromat., 4-oz. g. s. bots............. ....lb.	½
Acidum tannicum, 1-oz. bots ....oz.	1
Acidum tartaricum, 8-oz. bots.......lb.	4
Aconiti radicis ext. fluid, 2-oz. bots..oz.	2
Æther, 8-oz. tins.......................lb.	6
Ætheris spiritus comp.,4-oz.g.s.bots.lb.	1
Ætheris spiritus nitros,8-oz.g. s.bots.lb	½
Alcohol, pint bots.....................pts.	4
Aloin, ½-gr. pills ....no.	500
Alumen, 8-oz. bots ....lb.	½
Ammoniæ aqua, 8-oz. g. s. bots.......lb.	2
Ammonii carbonas, 4-oz. bots........lb.	¼
Ammonii chloridum, 8-oz. bots ......lb.	1
Ammoniæ spirit. arom.,4-oz.g.s.bots.lb.	½
Antimonii et potass. tart., 1-oz. bots.oz.	1
Argenti nitras, 1-oz. bots ......oz.	4
Argenti nitras fusa. 1-oz. bots.......oz.	4
Atropiæ sulphas, 1-dr. g. s. bots .....dr.	2
Belladon. ext. alc., 1-oz. g. jars . .... oz.	1
Bismuth, subcarb., 2-oz. bots ....oz.	2
Buchu ext. fluid, 8-oz. bots ....lb.	1
Camphora, 4-oz. bots .. ..lb.	½
Cannabis indic. ext. alc., 1-oz. g. jars.oz.	1
Cantharidis (plasters) ....no.	20
Cantharidis tinct., 2-oz. bots ....oz.	2
Capsici ext. fluid, 4-oz. bots ....lb.	¼
Chloral hydras, 1-oz. g. s. bots.......oz.	4
Chloroformum purificat., 1-lb. g. s. bots ....lb.	2
Chloroformum impurum ....lb.	8
Cinchonæ ext. fluid. comp ,8-oz. bots.lb.	1
Colchici sem. ext. fluid, 4-oz. bots....oz.	4
Collodium, 1-oz. bots ....oz.	2
Colocynth ex. comp., 1-oz. g. jars ....oz.	2
Copaiba, 1-lb. bots.....................lb.	5
Creta præparata, 8-oz. bots...........lb.	1
Cupri sulphas, 2-oz. bots ....oz.	2
Digitalis tinctura, 2-oz. bots ... .oz.	2
Ergotæ ext. fluid, 4-oz. bots ....oz.	4
Ferri chlorodi tinctura,8-oz. g.s.bots.lb.	3
Ferri et potass. tart, 8-oz. bots.......lb.	3
Ferri subsulph. liq., 1-oz. g. s. bots...oz.	8
Ferri sulphas, 5-lb. box....... ......lb.	10
Filicis oleo-resina........................oz.	4
Gentianæ extractum, 1-oz. g. jars... oz.	4
Glycerina, 8-oz. bots....................lb.	6
Glycyrrhizæ ext., paper..............lb.	½
Glycyrrhizæ pulvis, 4-oz. bots.......oz.	4
Hydrarg. chlor. corros., 1-oz. bots . ..oz.	2
Hydrarg. chlor. mite., 2-oz. bots......lb.	¼
Hydrarg. iodid. viride, 1-oz. bots.....oz.	2
Hydrarg. nitrat. unguent, 2-oz. jars..lb.	8
Hydrarg. pilul., 3 gr. each............no	500
Hydrarg. unguent, 8-oz. jars.........lb.	2
Hyoscyami ext. alc., 1-oz. g. jars.....oz.	1
Iodinium, 1-oz. g. s. bots ....oz.	1
Iodoformum, 1-oz. bots ....oz.	1
Ipecacuanhæ pulvis, 4-oz. bots......lb.	¼
Ipecacuanhæ pulvis comp.,8-oz. bots.lb.	1
Jalapæ ext., 1-oz. g. jars ....oz.	1
Lavand. spirit comp., 1-lb. bots......lb.	1
Lini farina, 5-lb. tins ....lb	25
Linum, 5-lb. tins ....lb.	5
Magnesia, 4-oz. bots.....................lb.	¼
Magnesii sulph., 8-lb. tins ....lb.	16
MEDICINES—Continued.	
Menth. pip. ol., 1-oz. bots ....oz.	1
Morphiæ sulphas, 1-dr. bots .. ..oz.	1
Morrhuæ oleum, 1-pt. bots ....pts.	40
Myrrha, 2-oz. bots.......................oz.	2
Nucis vomicæ ext. alc., 1-oz. g. jars ..oz.	1
Olivæ oleum, 1-pt. bots............ pts.	20
Opii pulvis, 2-oz. bots ... .oz.	4
Opii tinctura, 1-lb. bots ....lb.	4
Opii tinctura camph., 1-lb. bots .....lb.	6
Pepsina, 1-oz. bottles..................oz.	2
Pilul. cathart. comp., 1-oz. bots......no.	500
Pilul. rhei comp ....no.	200
Plumbi acetas, 8-oz. bots ....lb.	½
Podophylli resina, ½-oz. bots .... oz.	½
Potass. arsenit. liq., 4-oz. bots ....oz.	4
Potass. acetas, 8-oz. bots..............lb.	½
Potass. bicarb., 8-oz. bots..............lb.	½
Potass. bichromas, 8-oz. bots., battery.lb.	3
Potass. bitart., 8-oz. bottles .... lb.	1
Potass. chloras, 8-oz. bots..............lb.	½
Potass. et sod. tart., 1-lb. bots..........lb.	4
Potass. nitras, 8-oz. bots...............lb.	¼
Potass. permanganes, 1-oz. bots .....oz.	2
Potassii bromidum, 8-oz. bots.........lb.	2
Potassii iodidum, 8-oz. bots...........lb.	2
Pruni virg. ext. fluid, 8-oz. bots ......lb.	½
Quiniæ sulphas ....oz.	4
Resinæ ceratum, 1-lb. tins ....lb.	2
Ricini oleum, 1-pt. bots...............pts.	20
Rhei ext. fluid, 4-oz. bots ....oz.	4
Rhei pulvis, 4-oz. bots...................oz.	4
Sapo.......................................lb.	5
Saponis linimentum, 1-lb. bots ......lb.	5
Scillæ syrupus, 1-lb. bots..............lb.	2
Senegæ ext. fluid, 8-oz. bots............lb.	½
Sennæ ext. fluid comp., 8-oz. bots....lb.	½
Sinapis pulvis, 2-lb. tins ....lb.	10
Sodii bicarbonas, 1-lb. bots ....lb.	4
Sodii boras, 8-oz. bots..................lb.	½
Sodæ chlor. liquor, 1-lb. g. s. bots.....lb.	5
Sulphur.... .. ..lb.	1
Terebinth. oleum, 1-pt. bots........pts.	2
Theobromæ oleum, 2 oz	8
Tiglii oleum, 1-oz. bots.................oz.	1
Valerianæ ext. fluid, 8-oz. bots........lb.	1
Vaseline....................................lb.	10
Zinci. carb. præcip., 1-oz. bots.......oz.	8
Zinci sulphas, 1-oz. bots...............oz	2
Zingiberis ext. fluid, 8-oz. bots.......lb.	2
Additional.	
Simonis oleum, pur ...., ...oz.	4
HOSPITAL STORES.	
Brandy, 1-pt. bots ....pts.	24
Corn-starch, 2 lb. tins..................lb.	10
Extract of beef, 2-oz. jars ....lb.	5
Nutmegs ....oz.	2
Sugar, white, 5-lb. cans................lb.	10
Tapioca, 2-lb. tins ....lb.	6
Tea, black, 8-oz. tins.....................lb.	1
Whisky, 1-pt. bots....................pts.	36
Wine, port, 1-pt. bots..................pts.	12
Wine, sherry, 1-pt. bots ....pts.	12
SURGICAL INSTRUMENTS.	
Aspirator ....no.	1
Bougies, gum...............................no.	12
Bougies, o. p.................................no.	6
Catheters, gum.............................no.	6
Catheters, o. p..............................no.	3
Catheters, silver...........................no.	3

Medical outfit of U. S. S. "Rodgers," &c.—Continued.

Articles.	Quantity.	Articles.	Quantity.
SURGICAL INSTRUMENTS—Continued.		DISPENSARY FURNITURE—Continued.	
Case, dental, No. 1 ....no.	1	Measures, glass, 1-ounce....no.	2
Case, expeditionary and boat....no.	1	Measures, glass, 1-drachm ....no.	1
Case, general operating, small....no.	1	Mortar and pestle, glass....no.	1
Case, pocket ....no.	1	Mortar and pestle, wedgewood....no.	1
Case, urinary....no.	1	Percolator....no.	2
Cupping-glasses....no.	12	Pill-boxes, paper ....doz	2
Galvanic battery ....no.	1	Pill-boxes, wood....doz.	2
Laryngoscope ....no.	1	Pill-tile....no.	1
Ophthalmoscope....no.	1	Psychrometer ....no.	1
Razor ....no.	1	Scales, apothecary's ....no.	1
Razor-strop....no.	1	Scale-case ....no.	1
Scarificator....no.	1	Scissors....pairs.	2
Speculum, anal ....no.	1	Sheepskins ....no.	1
Speculum, aural ....set.	1	Spatulas, 6-inch ....no.	1
Stethoscope, double....no.	1	Spatulas, 5-inch ....no.	1
Stomach-pump ....no.	1	Spatulas, 4-inch ....no.	2
Syringes, enema....no.	1	Spatulas, 3-inch ....no.	1
Syringes, hypodermic (sp. req.)....no.	1	Spirit lamp ....no.	1
Syringes, p. glass ....no.	6	Test-case....no.	1
Syringes, p. rubber ....no.	6	Test-tubes ....no.	12
Syringes, self-injecting ....no.	2	Tubing, glass ....lb.	¼
Thermometers, clinical....set.	1	Twine ....lb.	¼
Tourniquets, field ....no.	12	Vials. assorted ....doz.	4
Tourniquets, screw....no.	3	Weights, apothecary's ....set.	1
Urinometer....no.	1		
SURGICAL APPLIANCES.		HOSPITAL FURNITURE.	
Bandages, roller ....no.	12	Basin and pitcher, metal....no	1
Bandages, Esmarch's ....no.	1	Basin, tin, dressing ....no.	2
Bandages, suspensory ....no.	12	Bed-pan ....no.	1
Binder's boards ....no.	2	Brush, dust....no.	1
Buckskins ....no.	2	Bucket, tin ....no.	1
Cotton batting, 1-lb. packages ....lb.	2	Bucket, wood....no.	1
Flannel ....yds.	8	Candlesticks ....no.	2
Gypsum, calcined, 5-lb. tins....lb.	15	Close-stool, small ....no.	1
Ligature, silk....oz.	¼	Feeding-cups ....no.	2
Ligature, wire, 1-yd. rolls ....yds.	2	Knives and forks....no.	2
Lint, patent, about 40 yds ....lb.	4	Ladle ....no.	1
Muslin ....piece.	1	Lamp, hanging bulkhead....no.	2
Muslin, oiled, 1-yd. rolls....yds.	2	Lantern, hand....no.	2
Needles, thimble, and thread....set.	1	Mugs ....no.	2
Pencils, hair....no.	12	Pans ....no.	1
Pins ....lb.	¼	Sauce-pans ....no.	2
Plaster, adhesive, 5-yd. rolls....yds.	15	Shovels, dust....no.	1
Plaster, isinglass, 1-yd. rolls ....yds.	2	Spit-cups....no.	1
Silk, gray ....yds.	4	Spoons, table ....no.	2
Splints....set.	1	Spoons, tea ....no.	3
Sponge, bath....lb.	1	Tea-pot....no.	1
Sponge, surgical ....lb.	2	Tumblers ....no.	2
Tape....pieces.	2	Urinals, glass ....no.	1
Tape-line....no.	2	Wine-glasses ....no.	2
Trusses, single ....no.	6		
Trusses, double....no.	2	BEDDING.	
Wax, yellow....lb.	1	Pillow cases, gum....no.	3
DISPENSARY FURNITURE.		Sheets, gum ....no.	3
		Towels ....no.	12
Apparatus-stand ....no.	1	BOOKS.	
Apparatus, atmospheric....no.	1	Dispensatory....no.	1
Boat medicine-chest....no.	2	Park's Hygiene ....no.	1
Corks, bottle ....gross	¼	Formulary ....no	1
Corks, vial....gross.	¼	STATIONERY.	
Cork-extractor ....no.	1		
Corkscrew ....no.	1	Blank book, foolscap, 4-quire ....no.	2
Funnels, glass....no.	2	Blank book, foolscap, 2-quire ....no.	2
Funnels, gutta-percha....no.	1	Blank book, small quarto....no.	4
Gallicups....no.	6	Envelopes, official ....no.	25
Grater, nutmeg ....no.	1	Envelopes, small ....no.	50
Lamp, nursery ....no.	2	Erasure, knife....no	1
Litmus paper, red....bot.	1	India rubber ....pieces.	1
Litmus paper, blue....bot.	1	Ink, black ....bot.	2
Measures, tin, pint....no.	1	Ink, red ....bot.	1
Measures, tin, ½-pint....no.	1	Inkstands ....no.	1
Measures, glass, 8-ounce....no.	4	Lead-pencils ....no.	6
Measures, glass, 4-ounce....no.	1		
Measures, glass, 2-ounce....no.	1		

Medical outfit of U. S. S. "Rodgers," &c.—Continued.

Articles.	Quantity.	Articles.	Quantity.
STATIONERY—Continued.		STATIONERY—Continued.	
Medical journals ....no.	2	Paper, wrapping, blue ....qrs.	2
Mucilage ....bot.	2	Paper, wrapping, white ....qrs	2
Paper, blotting ....qrs	1	Penholders..........................no.	12
Paper, envelope.....................qrs.	2	Penknives.......................... no.	1
Paper, filtering....................qrs.	1	Pens, steel ....box.	1
Paper, foolscap ....qrs.	10	Portfolios ....no.	1
Paper, official ... .qrs.	5	Quills ....no	24
Paper, letter.......................qrs.	10	Rulers ....no.	1
Paper, ruled, note ....qrs.	5		

WAR DEPARTMENT,
SURGEON-GENERAL'S OFFICE,
Washington, D. C., February 7, 1884.

Captain GEO. W. DAVIS,
    14th U. S. Infantry, Washington, D. C.

SIR: I am instructed by the Surgeon-General to transmit to you, as requested in your letter of the 2d instant, a copy of the invoice of hospital supplies issued to Acting Assistant Surgeon Geo. S. Oldmixon, in July, 1881, for the use of the detachment commanded by Lieutenant P. H. Ray, 8th U. S. Infantry, stationed in 1881-'2 and '3 at Point Barrow, Alaska; also a copy of the invoice of hospital supplies issued to Lieutenant A. W. Greely, 5th U. S. Cavalry, in May, 1881, for the use of the detachment commanded by him, and known as the "Lady Franklin Bay Expedition."

I have to inform you also that the medical officer (Dr. Oldmixon) who accompanied the expedition to Point Barrow has not made to this office any report on the health and sanitary condition of the men composing the detachment.

Very respectfully, your obedient servant,

                D. L. HUNTINGTON,
                  Surgeon, U. S. Army.

Two inclosures.

[Enclosure 1.]

Invoice of medicines, hospital stores, bedding, &c., contained in 17 packages, issued to Act'g Asst. Surg. Geo. S. Oldmixon, U. S. Army, for Point Barrow, Alaska, expedition, by Capt. H. Johnson, Medical Storekeeper, U. S. A., at San Francisco, Cal., July 9, 1881.

Articles.	Quantity.	Articles.	Quantity.
I.—REGULAR LIST.		MEDICINES—Continued.	
MEDICINES.		Cerate, blistering, in 8-oz. tins......oz.	8
		Cerate, resin, in 1-lb. tins...........lb.	1
Acid, carbolic, for disinfection, in 1-lb.		Chloral, hydrate of, in 1-oz. g. s. bottles..... ....oz.	6
bottles, 95 per cent ....lb.	4	Chloroform, purified, in 8-oz. g.s. bottles...........................oz.	32
Acid, carbolic, pure, crystallized, in 4-oz. s. bottles ....oz.	8	Colchicum seed, fluid extract of, in 4-oz. bottles	4
Acid, citric, in 8-oz. bottles ....oz.	96	Colocynth, compound extract of, powdered, in 8-oz. bottles ....oz.	8
Acid, muriatic, in 8-oz. g. s. bottles...oz.	8	Copper, sulphate of, in 2-oz. bottles.oz.	4
Acid, nitric, in 4-oz. g. s. bottles.....oz.	8	Croton oil, in 1-oz. g. s. bottles ......oz.	1
Acid, sulphuric, in 4-oz. g. s. bottles.oz.	8	Ergot, fluid extract of, in 4-oz. g. s. bottles.............................oz.	4
Acid, tannic, in 1-oz. bottles.........oz.	3	Ether, compound spirits of (Hoffman's anodyne), in 8-oz. g. s. bot .....oz.	8
Alcohol, in 32-oz. bottles...........bott.	24	Ether, stronger, for anæsthesia, in 1-lb. tins ....oz.	8
Ammonia, carbonate of, in 8o-z. bottles. ....oz.	16	Ether, spirit of nitrous (sweet spirits of nitre), in 8-oz. g. s. bot . ...oz.	16
Ammonia, solution of, in 8-oz. g. s. bottles. ....oz.	16	Flaxseed meal, in tins ....lb.	24
Arsenite of potassa, solution of (Fowler's solution), in 4-oz. bot ....oz.	4	Ginger, fluid extract of, in 8-oz. bottles.................................oz.	
Bismuth, subnitrate of, in 2-oz bottles..... ....oz.	4		
Borax, powdered, in 8-oz. bottles ...oz.	8		
Camphor, in 8-oz. bottles ... .oz.	24		
Castor oil, in 32-oz. bottles........bott.	4		

Invoice of medicines, hospital stores, bedding, &c.—Continued.

Articles.	Quantity.
MEDICINES—Continued.	
Glycerine, pure, in 8-oz. bottles.....oz.	16
Iodine, in 1-oz. g. s. bottles....... oz.	3
Iron, solution of the subsulphate of, in 1-oz. bottles ....oz	4
Iron, tincture of the chloride of, in 8-oz. g. s. bottles.................oz.	16
Jalap, powdered, in 4-oz. bottles .....oz.	4
Lead, acetate of, in 8-oz. bottles.....oz.	8
Liquorice root, powdered, in 8-oz. bottles.............................oz.	16
Magnesia, sulphate of, in 8-lb. tins..lb.	8
Mercurial ointment, in 1-lb. pots ...lb.	1
Mercury, corrosive chloride of (corrosive sublimate), in 1-oz. bot.......oz.	1
Mercury, mild chloride of (calomel), in 2-oz. bottles.....................oz.	2
Mercury, ointment of nitrate of (citrine ointment), in 4-oz. pots. . oz.	4
Mercury, pill of (blue mass), in 8-oz. pots..............................oz.	8
Morphia, sulphate of, in ½-oz. bottles.oz.	1
Mustard seed, black, ground, in 6-lb. tins...............................lb.	6
Olive oil, in 1-pint bottles ....bott.	12
Opium, camphorated tincture of, in 8-oz. bottles ....oz.	16
Opium, compound powder of (Dover's powder), in 8-oz. bottles .....oz.	8
Opium, powdered, in 8-oz. bottles ...oz	8
Opium, tincture of (laudanum), in 8-oz. bottles ....oz.	16
Pepper, cayenne, ground, in 8-oz. bottles ....oz.	8
Peppermint, spirit of, in 4-oz. bottles oz.	16
Pills, camphor (grains two), and opium (grain one), in bottles . no.	100
Pills, compound cathartic, in bottles no.	100
Podophyllum, resin of, in 1-oz. bottles.oz	1
Potassa, acetate of, in 8-oz. bottles..oz	8
Potassa, bicarbonate of, in 8-oz. bottles.. . .... oz	16
Potassa, bitartrate of, powdered (cream of tartar), in 8-oz. bot ....oz.	80
Potassa, chlorate of, powdered, in 8-oz. bottles ....oz.	24
Potassa, nitrate of, powdered, in 8-oz. bottles.. ....oz.	82
Potassa, permanganate of, in 1-oz. bottles.. .... oz.	2
Potassium, bromide of, in 4-oz. bottles...............................oz.	16
Potassium, iodide of, in 8-oz. bottles.oz.	16
Quinia, sulphate of, in 1-oz. bottles, or compressed in tins...............oz.	10
Rhubarb, powdered, in 4-oz. bottles.oz.	4
Rochelle salt, powdered, in 8-oz. bottles. ... .oz.	16
Santonin, in 1-oz. bottles . ...oz.	1
Seneka, fluid extract of, in 8-oz. bottles.................................oz.	8
Silver, nitrate of, in crystals, in 1-oz. g. s. bottles ....oz.	2
Silver, nitrate of, fused, in 1-oz. g. s. bottles.............................oz.	2
Soap, castile, in paper ....lb.	16
Soda, bicarbonate of, in 8-oz. bottles.oz.	16
Soda, chlorinated solution of, in 1-lb. g. s. bottles . .... lb.	2
Squill, sirup of, in 1-lb. bottles......lb.	5
Strychnia, in ⅛ oz. bottles...........oz.	⅛
Sulphur, washed, in 8-oz. bottles ...oz.	16
Turpentine, oil of, in 32-oz. bottles.bott.	4
Wax, white, in paper.................oz.	6
Zinc, sulphate of, in 1-oz. bottles....oz.	4
Myrrh, in 4-oz. bottles ....oz	8
HOSPITAL STORES.	
Arrow-root, in tins ....lb.	5
Barley, in tins ....lb.	5
HOSPITAL STORES—Continued.	
Beef, extract of, Liebig's, in porcelain jars ....lb.	8
Brandy, in 32-oz. bottles...........bott.	24
Candles, paraffine.....................lb.	8
Farina, in tins ....lb.	8
Milk, concentrated, in 1-lb. tins......lb.	16
Nutmegs, in 2-oz. bottles ....oz.	2
Pepper, black, ground, in 4-oz. bottles.oz.	8
Sugar, white, crushed, in boxes or tins...... ....lb.	24
Tea, black, in tins or original chests.lb	10
Whisky, in 32-oz. bottles ....bott.	12
II.—ARTICLES EXPENDABLE.	
INSTRUMENTS.	
Probangs.............................no.	6
Syringes, penis, glass................no.	12
Syringes, penis, rubber ....no.	6
Trusses, single ....no.	4
DRESSINGS.	
Bandages ....doz.	16
Bandages, suspensory ....no.	2
Binder's boards, 2½ by 12 inches.pieces .	6
Binder's boards, 4 by 17 inches ..pieces.	6
Cotton bats ....no.	2
Cotton wadding ....sheets.	4
Flannel, red, all wool ....yds.	3
Gutta-percha cloth ....yds.	3
Lint, patent........................... lb.	5
Lint, picked...... ....lb.	2
Muslin, unbleached, unsized, 1 yard wide ....yds.	5
Needles, cotton, thimble, in case....no	1
Oiled muslin, in 2-yard pieces......yds.	6
Oiled silk, in 2-yard pieces.........yds.	5
Plaster of paris, in 5-lb. tins ....lb.	10
Pencils, hair (assorted sizes) in vials.no.	12
Pins ....papers.	6
Plaster, adhesive, 5 yards in a can.yds.	10
Plaster, isinglass, 1 yard in a case..yds.	2
Silk, gray, for shades ....yds.	2
Silk, ligature..........................oz.	2
Splints.............................sets.	1
Splints, Smith's anterior...............no.	1
Splints, material for making, felt.pieces.	2
Sponge, fine, small pieces .. ..oz.	10
Tape, cotton, or twilled stay binding ....pieces.	2
Thread, linen, unbleached............oz.	1
Tow ....lb.	5
Towels ....doz.	1
Twine, ½ coarse ....oz.	8
STATIONERY.	
Blank books, cap, half bound, 4 quires, no..	8
Elastic bands, assorted, gross ....no.	1
Envelopes, printed, official 50, letter 50 ....no.	100
India rubber.......................pieces.	1
Ink, 2-oz. bottles ....no.	1
Ink, carmine, in 1 oz. bottles.........no.	1
Paper, blotting ....qrs.	2
Paper, writing: cap, 1 quire; letter, 2 quires; note, 1 quire.............qrs.	20
Pencils, lead.............................no.	12
Penholders ....no.	12
MISCELLANEOUS.	
Corks, velvet, best, assorted ....doz.	8
Lamp-wicks, pieces............. doz.	4
Pill boxes, ½ paper, ½ turned wood .doz.	3½
Sheepskins, dressed, for plasters....no	1

Invoice of medicines, hospital stores, &c.—Continued.

Articles.	Quantity.	Articles.	Quantity.
MISCELLANEOUS—Continued.		MISCELLANEOUS.	
Vials: six, 6-oz.; six, 4-oz.; six, 2-oz.; six, 1-oz ....doz.	4	Basins, tin, small, for dressers ......no.	2
		Basins, wash, hand..................no	2
III.—ARTICLES NOT EXPENDABLE.		Bed pans, delf, shovel shaped (metal for field)........................no.	1
INSTRUMENTS.		Buckets, leather.....................no.	2
Field case ....no.	1	Feeding cups .... no.	2
Pocket case ....no.	1	Funnels, tin, pint...................no.	2
Scissors, large and small............no.	2	Lanterns, glass......................no.	2
Speculum for the rectum............no	1	Measures, graduated, glass, 4-oz ....no	4
Spongeholders, for the throat.......no.	2	Measures, graduated, glass, minim..no.	3
Stethoscope ....no.	1	Measures, tin, gallon to pint, sets.. no	1
Stomach pump and tube, in case....no.	1	Medicine measuring glasses, large..no.	4
Syringes, hard rubber, 8-ounce .... no	2	Medicine panniers, furnished by the list, sets .... no.	1
Syringes, hypodermic ....no.	2	Mortars and pestles, wedgewood, 3½ to 8 inches ....no.	1
Syringes, rubber, self-injecting .....no.	2	Pill tiles, 5 to 10 inches .. ..no.	1
Tongue depressors, hinged ....no.	1	Scales and weights, prescription, one set of apothecaries' weights......no	1
Tourniquets, field ....no.	2	Spatulas, 3-inch and 6-inch ....no.	2
Urinometers........................no.	1	Spirit lamps (brass for field) ....no.	4
		Test tubes ....no.	12
BOOKS.		Urinals, glass ....no.	4
Anatomy, Gray's ....copy.	1		
Bumstead on Venereal...........copy.	1	ADDITIONAL ARTICLES.	
Chemistry, Fowne's ....copy.	1		
Diagnosis, Da Costa's ....copy.	1	Acid, salicylic...... .... oz.	40
Dispensatory ....copy.	1	Cosmoline, cerate.................. lbs.	4
Eye, Stellwag on ....copy.	1	Iodoform .... oz.	1
Meteorology, Loomis'.............copy.	1	Iron, persulphate of, powder ....oz.	4
Midwifery, Cazeaux's.............copy.	1	Pepsin...........................oz.	2
Physics, Ganot's ....copy.	1	Pills, morphia, sulph., ½-gr ....no.	300
Skin, Diseases of, Tilbury Fox...copy.	1	" quinia, bisulph., 2 " ......no.	500
Surgery, Gross'...................copy.	1	" " sulph., 2 " ....no	500
Therapeutics, Stillé's ....copy.	1	Plaster, mustard ....yds.	3
Morning report book ....no.	1	Vaseline, plain.....................lbs.	3
Order and letter book ....no.	1	Lint, marine.......................lbs.	10
Record of deaths ....no.	1	Sponge, chloroform ....no.	1
Register of patients, small, flexible covers...........................no.	2	Tubes, drainage ....yds.	3
		Tooth extracting case, O. P....... no.	1
BEDDING.		Tourniquet, Esmarch's.. ....no.	1
Bed sacks ....no.	10	Color Blindness, Jeffries on ....cop.	1
Blankets, gray, for the field ....no.	20	History, med., of post..............cop.	1
Blanket cases, canvas ....no.	2	Hygiene, Hammond...............cop.	1
Gutta-percha bed covers ....no.	4	Jurisprudence, Stillé & Wharton, 1 vol .... cop.	1
Pillows, hair ....no.	12	Jurisprudence, Stillé & Wharton, 2d vol. (2 pts.).......... cop.	1
Pillow-cases, white.................no	2	Practice of Med., Watson..........cop.	1
Sheets.............................no.	12	Lamps, side ....no.	1
		" stand......................no	1
FURNITURE.		Mattresses, elastic felt .... no.	4
Chairs, rocking.....................no.	1		
Clocks, wooden, small...............no.	1		
Tubs, bath, large...................no	1		

I certify that the preceding invoice is correct.
Station: Medical Purveying Depot, San Francisco, Cal.
Date: July 9, 1881.

H. JOHNSON,
Capt. and Medical Storekeeper, U. S. A.

A true copy.
S. G. O., P. D., Feb. 5, 1884.

J. H. BAXTER,
Chief Med. Purveyor, U. S. A.

[Enclosure 2.]

Invoice of medicines, hospital stores, bedding, &c., contained in 13 packages, issued to 1st Lt. A. W. Greely, U. S. Army, commanding Lady Franklin Bay Expedition, by Capt. F. O'Donnoghue, Medicine Storekeeper, U. S. A., at New York, May 23, 1881.

Articles.	Quantity.	Articles.	Quantity.
I.—REGULAR LIST.		MEDICINES—Continued.	
MEDICINES.		Opium, powdered, in 8 oz. bottles...oz.	8
		Opium, tincture of (laudanum), in 8 oz. bottles..........................oz.	16
Acid, carbolic, pure, crystallized, in 4 oz. g. s. bottles.....................oz.	12	Pepper, cayenne, ground, in 8 oz. bottles.............................oz.	8
Acid, citric, in 8 oz. bottles.........oz.	200	Peppermint, spirit of, in 4 oz. bottles.oz.	16
Acid, sulphuric, aromatic, in 8 oz. g. s. bottles ....oz.	16	Pills, camphor (grains two) and opium (grain one), in bottles.... .. ....no.	200
Acid, tannic, in 1 oz. bottles........oz	4	Pills, compound cathartic, in bottles.no.	200
Alcohol, in 32 oz. bottles...........bott.	24	Pills, opium, in bottles.............no.	200
Ammonia, aromatic spirits of, in 4 oz. g. s. bottles....................oz.	12	Podophyllum, resin of, in 1 oz. bottles................................oz.	1
Ammonia, carbonate of, in 8 oz. bottles.................................oz.	32	Potassa, bicarbonate of, in 8 oz. bottles................................oz.	16
Ammonia, solution of, in 8 oz. g. s. bottles...... ....oz.	16	Potassa, bitartrate of, powdered (cream of tartar), in 8 oz. bot ....oz.	160
Antimony and potassa tartrate of (tartar emetic), in 1 oz. bot ....oz.	2	Potassa, chlorate of, powdered, in 8 oz. bottles ....oz.	16
Arsenite of potassa, solution of (Fowler's solution), in 4 oz. bot ....oz.	4	Potassa, nitrate of, powdered, in 8 oz. bottles ....oz.	64
Belladonna, alcoholic extract of, in 1 oz. w. m. bottles..............oz.	2	Potassa, permanganate of, in 1 oz. bottles.............................oz.	4
Bismuth, subnitrate of, in 2 oz. bottles.................................oz.	16	Potassium, bromide of, in 4 oz. bottles ....oz.	12
Camphor, in 8 oz. bottles ....oz.	24	Potassium, iodide of, in 8 oz. bottles .oz.	24
Castor oil, in 32 oz. bottles.........bott.	4	Quinia, sulphate of, in 1 oz. bottles, or compressed in tins................oz.	10
Cerate, blistering, in 8 oz. tins......oz.	8	Rochelle salt, powdered, in 8 oz. bottles.................................oz.	16
Cerate, resin, in 1 lb. tins...........lb.	1	Seneka, fluid extract of, in 8 oz. bottles.................................oz	8
Chloral, hydrate of, in 1 oz. g. s. bottles................................oz.	32	Silver, nitrate of, in crystals, in 1 oz. g. s. bottles.........................oz.	4
Chloroform, purified, in 8 oz. g. s. bottles.................................oz.	64	Silver, nitrate of, fused, in 1 oz. g. s. bottles...............................oz.	2
Colchicum seed, fluid extract of, in 4 oz. bottles ....oz.	8	Soap, castile, in paper .... lb.	8¼
Colocynth, compound extract of, powdered, in 8 oz. bottles ......oz.	8	Soda, bicarbonate, in 8 oz. bottles .oz.	16
Copper, sulphate of, in 2 oz. bottles oz.	4	Soda, chlorinated solution of, in 1 lb. g. s. bottles.............. ......lb.	4
Croton oil, in 1 oz. g. s. bottles ......oz.	1	Squill, syrup of, in 1 lb. bottles......lb.	5
Ergot, fluid extract of, in 4 oz. bottles.... ....oz.	4	Sulphur, washed, in 8 oz. bottles...oz.	16
Ether, compound spirits of (Hoffman's Anodyne), in 8 oz. g. s. bot...... oz.	8	Turpentine, oil of, in 32 oz. bottles.bott.	3
Ether, stronger, for anæsthesia, in 1 lb. tins .. ..oz.	32	Wax, white, in paper.............oz.	6
Ether, spirit of nitrous (sweet spirits of nitre), in 8 oz. g. s. bot ......oz.	24	Zinc, sulphate of, in 1 oz. bottles....oz.	4
Flaxseed meal, in tins ....lb.	16		
Ginger, fluid extract of, in 8 oz. bottles.................................oz.	8	**II.—SUPPLEMENTARY LIST.**	
Glycerine, pure, in 8 oz. bottles ... oz.	32		
Gum arabic, powdered, in 8 oz. bottles ....oz.	16	MEDICINES.	
Iodine, in 1 oz. g. s. bottles........oz.	4	Aconite root, fluid extract of, in 8 oz. bottles ....oz.	16
Iron, solution of the sulphate of, in 1 oz. bottles ....oz.	4	Calabar bean, extract of, in ½ oz. bottles ....oz.	¼
Iron, tincture of the chloride of, in 8 oz. g. s. bottles................oz	16	Ipecacuanha, fluid extract of, in 8 oz bottles ....oz.	8
Lead, acetate of, in 8 oz. bottles ....oz.	8	Soda, sulphite of, exsiccated, in 4-oz. bottles ....oz.	8
Liquorice, extract of, in paper ..oz.	32		
Liquorice root, powdered, in 8 oz. bottles..... ....oz.	8	HOSPITAL STORES.	
Magnesia, sulphate of, in 8 lb. tins..lb.	8		
Mercurial ointment, in 1 lb. pots.....lb.	2	Brandy, in 32-oz. bottles ....bott.	12
Mercury, corrosive chloride of (corrosive sublimate), in 1 oz. bot .. oz.	1	Candles, sperm or composition, half-length, in boxes ....lb.	4
Mercury, mild chloride of (calomel), in 2 oz. bottles ....oz.	2	Farina, in tins ....lb	4
		Milk, concentrated, in 1-lb. tins.....lb.	16
Mercury, pill of (blue mass), in 8 oz. pots ....oz.	8	Nutmegs, in 2-oz. bottles...........oz.	2
Mercury, red oxide of, in 1 oz. bottles oz.	1	Pepper, black, ground, in 4-oz. bottles, oz	8
Morphia, sulphate of, in ¼ oz. bottles.oz.	6	Sugar, white, crushed, in boxes or tins, lb....................................	12
Opium, camphorated tincture of, in 8 oz. bottles...... ....oz.	24	Tea, black, in tins or original chests.lb.	20
Opium, compound powder of (dover's powder), in 8 oz. bottles...........oz.	8	Whisky, in 32-oz. bottles..........bott.	24

Invoice of medicines, hospital stores, bedding, &c.—Continued.

Articles.	Quantity.	Articles.	Quantity.
III.—ARTICLES EXPENDABLE.		**INSTRUMENTS—Continued.**	
INSTRUMENTS.		Speculum for the rectum...........no.	1
		Spongeholders for the throat.......no.	4
Probangs ....no.	6	Spray apparatus ....no.	1
Syringes, penis, glass ....no.	24	Stethoscope ....no.	1
Syringes, penis, rubber ....no.	12	Stomach pump and tube, in case....no.	1
Trusses, single.....................no.	4	Syringes, hard-rubber, 8-ounce......no.	1
		Syringes, hypodermic ....no.	2
DRESSINGS.		Syringes, rubber, self-injecting ....no.	3
		Tooth-extracting case, Army pattern,	
Bandages ....doz	32	....................................no.	1
Bandages, suspensory...............no.	4	Thermometer, clinical...............no.	1
Binders' boards, 2¼ by 12 inches.pieces.	12	Tongue depressors, hinged ....no.	1
Binders' boards, 4 by 17 inches..pieces.	12	Tourniquets, field ....no.	4
Cotton bats ....no.	2	Tourniquets, screw, with pad........no.	2
Cotton wadding ....sheets.	4		
Flannel, red, all wool ....yds.	6	**BOOKS.**	
Gutta-percha cloth.................yds.	3		
Lint, patent ....lb.	4	Anatomy, Gray's ....copy.	1
Lint, picked ....lb.	2	Dispensatory ....copy.	1
Muslin, unbleached, unsized, 1 yard		Hygiene, Parke's ....copy.	1
wide...............................yds.	10	Practice of Medicine, Flint's.....copy.	1
Needles, cotton, thimble, in case...no.	1	Surgery, Erichsen's ....copy.	1
Oakum, fine, picked ....lb.	5	Surgery, Guthrie's Commentaries.copy.	1
Oiled muslin, in 2-yard pieces .....yds.	4	Therapeutics, Waring's....... .. copy.	1
Oiled silk, in 2-yard pieces .... .. yds.	5	Therapeutics, Mechanical, Wales'.copy.	1
Pencils, hair (assorted sizes) in vials,		Register of Patients, small, flexible	
....................................no	12	covers.............................no.	2
Pins ....papers.	3		
Plaster, adhesive, 5 yards in a can.yds.	10	**BEDDING.**	
Plaster, isinglass, 1 yard in a case..yds.	10		
Silk, gray, for shades ....yds.	1	Bed sacks ....no.	20
Silk, ligature ....oz.	1	Blankets, gray......................no.	40
Splints ....sets.	2	Blanket cases, canvas...............no.	4
Splints, Smith's anterior .... no.	2	Gutta-percha bed covers ....no.	8
Splints, material for making, felt.pieces.	2	Pillows, hair ....no.	5
Sponge, fine, small pieces .... oz.	10	Pillow-cases, white, "linen".......no.	40
Tape, cotton, or twilled stay binding,		Pillow ticks ....no.	20
pieces	3		
Thread, linen, unbleached .. ..oz.	1	**MISCELLANEOUS.**	
Tow ....lb.	10		
Towels............ ....doz.	2	Basins, tin, small, for dressers......no.	2
Twine, ½ coarse....................oz.	8	Basins, wash hand ....no	4
		Feeding cups........................no.	2
MISCELLANEOUS.		Funnels, tin, pint...................no.	3
		Graters, nutmeg and large ....no.	1
Corks, velvet, best, assorted...... doz.	16	Measures, graduated, glass, 4 oz .. no.	3
Pill-boxes, ⅔ paper, ⅓ turned wood.doz.	8	Measures, graduated, glass, minim .no.	3
Sheepskins, dressed, for plasters ...no.	1	Medicine measuring glasses, large .no.	3
Vials—six, 6-oz.; six, 4-oz.; six, 2-oz.;		Pill tiles, 5 to 10 inches ....no.	2
six, 1-oz ....doz.	4	Spatulas, 3-inch and 6-inch ....no.	2
		Spirit lamps (brass, for field). ......no.	2
IV.—ARTICLES NOT EXPENDABLE.			
		ADDITIONAL ARTICLES.	
INSTRUMENTS.			
		Beef extract, Starr's...............lbs.	16
Cupping-tins, assorted sizes........no.	12	Balance,.in case.............. ......no.	1
Field-case ....no.	1	Vaseline, plain ....lbs.	6
Lancet, thumb ....no.	4	Mustard plaster...... ....yds.	6
Pocket-case ....no.	1	Acid, salicylic.......................oz.	160
Scarificators.......................no.	2	Esmarch's tourniquet ....no.	1
Scissors, large and small ....no.	2	Cosmoline cerate ....lb.	2

I certify that the preceding invoice is correct.

F. O'DONNOGHUE,
Captain and M. S. K., U. S. A.

MEDICAL PURVEYING DEPOT, U. S. A.,
NEW YORK CITY, *May 23d*, 1881.

A true copy.

J. H. BAXTER,
Chief Medical Purveyor, U. S. A.

EXHIBIT S.

WASHINGTON, *January* 28, 1884.

MY DEAR SIR: Concerning the stores left at Cape Hawks, I am very positive that there was some meat there.

I brought off one can myself, and others of the party brought off one or two more. We found the meat in good condition. There was about eight casks in all, 120 gal. casks, hooped with iron.

When Lt. Greely was going off in the boat, I heard him say that there would be enough of everything for him and his party for two months, in case he had to retreat that way.

When we arrived at Discovery Harbor we found 23 barrels of pork and beef in good condition, which I have not seen mentioned in any report.

Respectfully yours,

Capt. GEO. W. DAVIS.   J. W. NORMAN.

EXHIBIT T.

[Wm. Macnaughtan's Sons, Commission Merchants, 3 Howard st., east of Broadway.]

NEW YORK, 29*th Jan.*, 1884.

GENT'N: We learn that reindeer can be secured, raw, in Canada East, at $2.00 per skin, subject to change.

We inclose our correspondence with the Hudson's Bay Co., as it will prove of value to you.

Please return theirs to us. Anything this correspondence suggests to you we will be pleased to answer. Why would not buffalo robe overcoats prove indispensable in your equipment? They are made cheaply with great skill, and are easily obtainable.

Resp.,

WM. MACNAUGHTAN'S SONS.

Capt. GEO. H. DAVIS,
  Board of Officers, Relief Expedition, Washington, D. C.

[Enclosure 1.]

[Wm. Macnaughtan's Sons, Commission Merchants, 3 Howard st., east of Broadway.]

NEW YORK, 11*th Jan.*, 1884.

DEAR SIR: Will you have the kindness to give us full information on the following:

Do the men at your posts wear reindeer clothing, and is there a difference between reindeer and caribou? How are they dressed, the usual way, or in oil, and do they injure by water? How do the skins average in cutting, and do you use the light or heavy haired?

Please favor us with an early answer. This with anything further will be much appreciated.

Yours, very resp'y,

WM. MACNAUGHTAN'S SONS.

S. K. PARSON, Esq.,
  Hudson's Bay House, Montreal, Canada.

[Enclosure 2.]

HUDSON'S BAY HOUSE,
  Montreal, 14 Jan., 1884.

DEAR SIRS: In reply to yours of the 11th inst.: The men at some of our posts wear reindeer clothing, and, as far as I ever knew, there is no difference between reindeer and caribou. The felt side is dressed like moccasin leather, not smoked, and the hair is left on the other. They are not dressed in oil, and they get hard if they become wet.

I don't know what you mean by "how do the skins average in cutting." The light and heavy haired are both used, according to the part of the clothing required for.

In conclusion, I might add that all the deerskin clothing ever used at our posts is made by the Esquimaux themselves, and traded from them, and that our men rarely, if ever, wear it, except when traveling along the coast; and further, that any such clothing made by white men without proper patterns would, I consider, be utterly useless.

Faithfully yours,

S. K. PARSON.

Messrs. WM. MACNAUGHTAN'S SONS,
  3 *Howard Street, New York.*

[Enclosure 3.]

|Wm. Macnaughtan's Sons, Commission Merchants, 3 Howard st., east of Broadway.|

NEW YORK, 21*st Jan.,* 1884.

DEAR SIR: Your favor of the 14th is at hand. Please accept our thanks.

In asking "how the skins average in cutting," we meant how many skins are generally required to make an entire suit, and what does the suit consist of. Every dozen suits would consume about how many skins? You speak of their being tanned same as moccasins; is that the same as the dressed skin that we express to you to-day, or do you re-dress and re-tan such leather, and how?

Yours, very resp'y,

WM. MACNAUGHTAN'S SONS.

S. K. PARSON, Esq.,
  Hudson's Bay House, Montreal, Canada.

[Enclosure 4.]

HUDSON'S BAY HOUSE,
  Montreal, 25 Jan., 1884.

DEAR SIRS: Your parcel containing a dressed skin has just been delivered to me. I cannot tell you much about number of skins required to make suits, for, as I before mentioned, our people buy them ready-made from the Esquimaux. I should say from memory that there are about nine skins in each suit; the inner shirt or coat being made of 4 small skins out of the backs only; the outside coat and trousers would take about 5 large skins. As a rule it is only the young skins killed in August which are of use for clothing. If I had a skin of the kind, I would be glad to send it to you. The one you send is, in my opinion, quite useless for clothing, and is far too soft and spongy for almost every purpose.

I feel sure that any attempt to make clothing with the skins you are able to procure would prove a failure.

Faithfully yours,

S. K. PARSON.

Messrs. WM. MACNAUGHTAN'S SONS,
  3 *Howard St., New York.*

EXHIBIT U.

Extracts from official reports and other publications, descriptive of the depots of provisions, boats, &c., existing in Baffin Bay, Smith Sound, Kennedy and Robeson Channels.

Compiled by order of the Board by Captain GEO. W. DAVIS, *Recorder.*

CAPE YORK.

*   *   * "The dingy was a very light shallow cedar boat for use in perfectly smooth water and a very light cargo. *   *   * When I left the shelter of the land at Cape York, she was left above high-water mark above that point." (Garlington to Chief Signal Officer, Oct. 20th, 1883. Sig. Service Notes No. X., Washington, D. C., 1883.)

CARY ISLAND DEPOT.

"A depot of 3,600 rations were landed [July 27th, 1875] on the S. E. spit of the S. E. island, and a record deposited in a conspicuous cairn on the summit." (Nares' Report, page 4.)

July 31st, 1881. "Sighting the Cary Islands at 3.10 p. m. that day, two parties were landed on the S. E. island. * * * With Lieut. Lockwood, I found and examined the whale-boat and depot of provisions left by Sir Geo. Nares in 1875, which were in good and serviceable condition." (Greely to Chief Signal Officer, Aug. 15, 1881, Exhibit M, p. 142.)

* * * "Copy of record found in cairn on top of S. E., Cary Island, by U. S. S. 'Yantic,' Aug. 5, 1883."

Aug. 1st, 1876.—"I have this day inspected the 'A' depot left on this island by H. M. ships 'Alert' and 'Discovery,' and found everything apparently undisturbed and in good condition. * * * There were, in all, 31 casks and 12 cases, besides the tins of preserved meats, which were not counted." [Signed by Lt. Arbuthnot, R. N., Arctic yacht 'Pandora.'] (Capt. Wildes' report to Sec't'y of the Navy, Sept. 17, 1883.)

* * * "I found everything there [S. E., Cary Island, July 21st, 1883] undisturbed. From a careful examination of two bbls. of bread and three cans of meat, I estimated that sixty per cent. of the provisions are in good condition, while perhaps seventy-five per cent. could be eaten in an emergency. The boat was also in good condition. * * * The * * * depot is on the S. E., Cary Island, consisting of at least eighteen hundred rations and a whale-boat." (Garlington to Chief Signal Officer, Oct. 2, 1883. Sig. Service Notes No. X, Washington, D. C., 1883.)

CAPE ISABELLA.

July 29th.—"As the weather was so thick that no one on the ships, except those employed in establishing the cairn and small depot of provisions, could see its position [Cape Isabella], and there being, therefore, no reason for delaying the 'Discovery,' Capt. Stephenson proceeded. The cairn was built on the summit of the outer easternmost spur of the cape, at an elevation of about 700 feet above the water." (Nares' Report, p. 4.)

* * * "A cairn was erected on the outer spur of Cape Isabella, 700 feet above the water-line; a cask for letters and a few cases of preserved meat being hidden away on a lower point, about 300 feet high, magnetic west of the cairn." (Nares' Narrati~ vol. 1, p. 57.)

"At a less high elevation, in a secure niche amongst the rocks, were deposited an empty cask and about one hundred and fifty pounds of preserved meat." (Markham's Frozen Sea, p. 54.)

"Lieutenant Becker, however, on looking * * * behind some rocks about 20 yards off [Aug. 6, 1876] * * * discovered four wooden cases which lay in a crevice. * * * These I at once examined and found under them a cask which he suggested might contain the letters from the expedition [Nares']. But as the cases were marked 'New Zealand preserved meat,' and as I did not think it likely that the letters would be deposited in such an obscure place without some record being left at the cairn to say they were there, I concluded it to be a depot of provisions." (Report Lt. Arbuthnot, Sept. 25, 1876, to Capt. Allen Young, commd'g "Pandora," Nares' Report, p. 476.)

"A cask of letters, &c., has been placed with the depot of provisions." (Extract from record dated Aug. 6, 1876, left by Lieut. Arbuthnot of the "Pandora" on Cape Isabella, Nares' Rep., p. 478.) "On landing [Sept. 9th, 1876] a small mail of letters and newspapers which had been left by the 'Pandora' was found at the depot." (Nares' Report, p. 37.)

Sept. 4th.—"As a last resort the remaining whale boat was placed on Cape Isabella and its location marked by a tripod showing well to the northward." (Beebe's Report to Chief Signal Officer, Sept. 28th, 1882. Sig. Service Notes No. V, Washington, D. C., 1883.)

LITTLETON ISLAND.

Aug. 2nd.—"Lieutenant Lockwood with party landed about 6½ tons of coal as a depot of fuel for possible future use. It is in and around a large cask on low ground on the southwest side of the island facing Cape Alexander." (Greely to Chief Signal Officer, dated Aug. 15, 1881, p. 142. Exhibit M.)

Aug. 3d, 1882.— * * * "The stores were landed in a cove in the north end of the island, so well concealed as to be invisible from any point a few yards distant and covered with a 'paulin securely anchored down with rocks, and copies of a record with minute directions for finding the stores placed as directed in Lieut. Greely's letter of last year—two in the the coal on the southern end of the island and one in Nares'

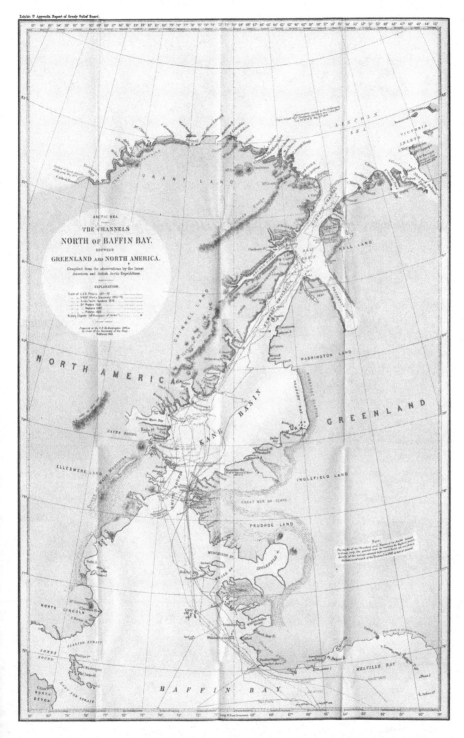

The material originally positioned here is too large for reproduction in this reissue. A PDF can be downloaded from the web address given on page iv of this book, by clicking on 'Resources Available'.

cairn on the summit of the S. W. part of the island." (Beebe to Chief Signal Officer, Sept. 28, 1882. Sig. Service Notes No. V, Washington, D. C., 1883.)

[The articles composing this cache were those indicated in Lt. Greely's letter to Chief Signal Officer, Aug. 17th, 1881. See Exhibit M, p. 141.—RECORDER.]

CAPE SABINE.

July 29th.—"A depot of 240 rations was established on the southernmost of the islets [at Payer Harbor] in a convenient position for traveling parties—a cairn being built on the summit of the highest and outer one, and a notice of our movements deposited here." (Nares' Report, p. 5.)

Aug. 18*th,* 1882.— * * * "On a long, low island near to and due west (true) from Brevoort Island was found a small depot of provision left by the ' Discovery' * * *. The depot consisted of one barrel of canned beef; two tins—forty pounds each—bacon; one barrel—one hundred pounds—dog biscuit; two barrels—one hundred and twenty rations each—biscuit, all in good condition; two hundred and forty rations—consisting of chocolate and sugar, tea and sugar, potatoes, wicks, tobacco, salt, stearine, onion-powder, and matches, all in fairly good condition. Three small casks that had contained rum and high wines were separated from the other packages, broken, and their contents evaporated or leaked out * * *. The cache was re-built, and made as secure as possible, marked by two oars found with the depot placed upright in the rocks, and a record of the 'Neptune' placed in the cache. A description of this depot and its position was afterwards left with the depot established on Cape Sabine." (Beebe to Chief Signal Officer, Sept. 28, 1882. Sig. Service Notes No. V, Washington, D. C., 1883.)

* * * "On the morning of the 31st [August] succeeded in effecting a landing and establishing a cache upon Cape Sabine, the northernmost land that had been attainable by us. The stores and whale-boat were placed in a sheltered spot, well secured and covered by a tarpaulin. A tripod made of scantling with an oar attached, to which pieces of canvas were well nailed, were placed upon a prominent point, showing well from the northward and securely anchored with rocks, and in a cairn beneath was placed a record giving the bearing of the cache." (Beebe to Chief Signal Officer, Sept. 28, 1882. Sig. Service Notes No. V, Washington, D. C., 1883.)

[The articles composing this cache were those indicated in Lieut. Greely's letter to to Chief Signal Officer under date of August 17, 1881. See Exhibit M, p. 141.—RECORDER.]

July 24th, 1883.—"Lt. Colwell succeeded in making land, and in caching the provisions about three miles west of Cape Sabine. They were secured as well as circumstances permitted, and covered with a tent-fly. This cache consisted of hard bread, tea, bacon, canned goods, tobacco, and sleeping-bags, estimated at five hundred rations. This cache was not disturbed again. * * * * * A large quantity of clothing, consisting of buffalo overcoats, fur caps and gloves, Arctic overshoes, uniform clothing, and underclothing, &c., was cached on Cape Sabine. Two sidereal chronometers were placed in the cache." (Garlington to Chief Signal Officer, Oct. 2, 1883. Sig. Service Notes No. X, Washington, D. C., 1883.)

* * * "I proceeded to gather together all the stores I could spare and reclaim from the bags of the crew of the 'Proteus' and make a cache of them on the rocks in Payer Harbor under Cape Sabine. The cache made there contained clothing—blouses, trousers, flannel shirts; socks, stockings, mitts, buffalo overcoats. fur caps, flannel drawers, undershirts, woolen and rubber blankets; all wrapped in rubber blankets, covered with a tent-fly and weighted down with rocks. The supply of clothing is sufficient for twenty-five men for six months. Near this cache is a new top-sail and two boats [bolts] of new canvass left by Captain Pike; a sufficient supply to furnish shelter for a large number of men.

"In a cove about three miles west of Cape Sabine a cache of provisions was made. This cache contained fifteen sleeping-bags, six hundred pounds of hard bread (three barrels and two painted canvas bags), an unknown quantity of bacon, about seven hundred pounds of canned meats, vegetables, and fruits, a box of tea (forty pounds), a box of gunpowder, a can of matches, a tin pot, and a quantity of clothing. all secured as well as possible in a crevice of the rocks, covered with two tent-flies, and the whole weighted down with stones. In a conspicuous cairn on the top of Brevoort Island, built by the Nares expedition, I deposited a notice of the loss of the 'Proteus,' a definite description of the locality of the caches of clothing and the provisions. .* * * The record of the late Mr. W. M. Beebe is in the same cairn. I did not disturb the cache left by the expedition of Mr. Beebe of last year further than to see if the stores were in good order and the boat serviceable. The depot of the English expedition on the small island south of Payer Harbor was not disturbed." (Garlington to Chief Signal Officer Oct. 20, 1883. Sig. Service Notes No. X, Washington, D. C., 1883.)

"A depot was landed from the floe at a point about three miles from the point of Cape Sabine, as you turn into Buchanan Strait. There were five hundred rations of bread, sleeping-bags, tea, and a lot of canned goods; no time to classify. This cache is about thirty feet from the water line, and twelve feet above it on the west side of a little cove under a steep cliff. Rapidly-closing ice prevented its being marked by a flag-staff or otherwise; have not been able to land there since. A cache of two hundred and fifty rations in same vicinity, left by the expedition of 1881, visited by me and found in good condition, except boat broken by bears. There is a cache of clothing on point of Cape Sabine opposite Brevoort Island, in the 'jamb' of the rock, and covered with rubber blankets. The English depot on the small island near Brevoort Island in damaged condition, not visited by me. There is a cache of two hundred and fifty rations on the northern point of Littleton Island and a boat at Cape Isabella." (Extract from Garlington's record left at Cape Sabine, July 24, 1883. Sig. Service Notes No. X, Washington D. C., 1883.) .

"Five hundred pounds of hard bread, sleeping-bags, and assorted subsistence stores were landed from the floe about three miles from Cape Sabine around point towards Bache Island. There is also a cache made last year along same shore. The depot was secured as well as possible. * * * A quantity of clothing was left on extreme point of Cape Sabine, and one barrel of beef, all poorly secured." (Extract from Garlington's record left at Littleton Island July 26, 1883. Sig. Service Notes No. X, Washington, D. C., 1883.)

"I estimated the number of rations put by Lieut. Colwell on that first boat as 500 rations; he thinks there were 650 rations." (Garlington's response to a question by the Board, January 2nd, 1884, page 42.)

"Q. I think you left some provisions at Cape Sabine. At what altitude above high water were those provisions placed, as you remember?—A. About ten or fifteen feet, and behind a corner of rocks which would protect them from the ice banking up.

"Q. You feel that they are perfectly secure from any danger from ice?—A. Yes; the only trouble would be from water running down the side of the cliff and getting under them, or a snow-slide might cover them up. When we left there was no snow nor any water coming into the hollow where I placed them.

"Q. Were they in a position where they might be destroyed by a slide of snow from above, or pushed out on the ice?—A. The cliff was almost perpendicular where I placed them, in a little crevice, and the chances are that a slide of snow would not come down in that crevice, but would go over it or pass around to one side. They are about thirty feet distant from the edge of the water." (Extract from testimony of Lieut. Colwell before the Board, January 4, 1884, p, 69.)

CAPE HAWKS.

Aug. 12th, 1875.—"A large depot of 3,600 rations of provisions was landed on the southern side of Cape Schott, and a notice of our progress deposited in a cairn on the summit of Washington Irving Island." (Nares' Report, p. 5.)

Sept. 1st, 1876.—"On the 1st of September we crossed Dobbin Bay, and succeeded in securing the ships to an iceberg, aground only a quarter of a mile from the depot of provisions left by us the previous spring a few miles north of Cape Hawks. * * By working in the cracks opened by the ebb tide some of the provisions were embarked; but there is still a boat and a large quantity of biscuit left on shore there." (Nares' Report, p. 34.)

Sept. 1st, 1876.—* * * "And as some of our provisions were getting low, on passing the large depot established in Dobbin Bay, on our way up, the previous year, we landed and brought off all the tea, sugar, and chocolate, and such other articles as we were likely to require." (Markham's "Frozen Sea," p. 398.)

* * * "But a boat and some biscuit still remain. If visited during the summer these will be found on the northern shore of a small bay a mile and a half distant from Cape Hawks, and about a quarter of a mile from the east point of the bay. During the winter, when covered by snow, it would be very difficult for a stranger to find the locality, unless, indeed, the pole marking it remains up." (Nares' Narrative, vol. II., p. 160.)

Aug. 3d, 1881.—"With Lt. Kislingbury, Mr. Clay, and a number of the men, I proceeded to the main shore and examined the English depot of 1875. The jolly boat was found in good condition, and being short of boats it was taken by me. * * * There was a large quantity of bread (some mouldy), two kegs of pickles, two partly full of rum, two barrels stearine, and a barrel of preserved potatoes. A keg of *pica-lilli* (I having none in my stores), one of the kegs of rum were taken, and three cans potatoes to test them and the method of cooking them. The remaining stores were placed by my party in a better condition to resist the weather." (Greely to Chief Signal Officer, Aug. 15, 1881, Exhibit M, p. 143.)

[Lieut. Greely in his letter to Chief Signal Officer, dated Aug. 17, 1881 (see Exhibit M, p. 145), refers to the Cape Hawks depot as containing "two months' supplies."—RECORDER.]

"Concerning the stores left at Cape Hawks, I am very positive that there was some meat there. I brought off one can myself and others of the party brought off one or two more. We found the meat in good condition. There was about eight casks in all—120 gallon casks hooped with iron. When Lt. Greely was going off in the boat I heard him say that there would be enough of everything for him and his party for two months in case he had to retreat that way." (J. W. Norman to Recorder of Board, Jan'y 28, 1884; Exhibit S, p. 176.)

CAPE COLLINSON.

Aug. 20th, 1875.—"A depot of provisions was landed at Cape Collinson for our future travelers bound to the southward along the coast." (Nares' Report, p. 10.)

"A small depot of 240 rations was landed on Cape Collinson, about 100 yards inshore and 30 feet above the water line. These provisions have not since been disturbed. During the winter they will be deeply buried in snow, and probably the mark piled over them will have broken down." (Nares' Narrative, vol. I, p. 102.)

Aug. 3d, 1881.—"Abreast of Cape Collinson, where 240 rations are cached, but which I dared not visit fearing denser fog." (Greely to Chief Signal Officer, Aug. 15, 1881, Exhibited M, p. 143.)

CARL RITTER BAY.

Aug. 4th, 1881.—"At 2 p. m. the ship stopped in the N. E. end of Carl Ritter Bay, where I had decided to place a small depot of provisions in case of a retreat southward in 1883. About 225 bread and meat rations were landed by a party under myself which Lt. Kislingbury and Doctor Pavy accompanied. The depot was made on the first bench from the sea, just north of a little creek in the extreme N. E. part of the bay." (Greely to Chief Signal Officer, Aug. 15, 1881, Exhibit M, p. 143.)

CAPE MORTON.

Aug. 23d, 1875.—"The 'Discovery' then landed a depot of 240 rations at Cape Morton for use of any traveling party exploring Petermann Fiord." (Nares' Report, p. 10.)

"On 2nd June [1876] I [Lieut. Fulford, H. M. ship 'Discovery'] visited the depot at Cape Morton, and found it to be in good condition; one bag of dog biscuit had been moved about ten yards from the depot, but no tracks were to be seen." (Nares' Report, p. 433.)

POLARIS BAY.

[A large depot of provisions, tools, and other supplies was abandoned by the "Polaris" at Thank-God Harbor, on the 12th of August, 1872."—RECORDER.]

"It has been reported by Sir George Nares, the commander of the expedition [1875–'6], that, in regard to the provisions deposited at Polaris Bay by the United States Polar Expedition, the whole of the provisions were used by the sledge parties from H. M. ships, 'Alert' and 'Discovery,' and that the depot no longer exists." (Sir Edward Thornton to Secretary of State, April 26th, 1877; see Exhibit H, p. 121.)

"Tuesday, 8th August. * * * I wish we could take the 20-ft. ice-boat, but she is too heavy. * * * Closed the house; secured everything and started at 10 p. m. in the 15-ft. ice-boat." (Lieut. Beaumont's journal, p. 392, Nares' Report.)

CAPE SUMNER—NEWMAN BAY.

"Two crews left their boats; one a whale-boat, twenty-four feet long, and the other the 'Heggleman' canvas boat, on Cape Sumner [about 1½ miles east of Cape Sumner, near mouth of small ravine] at the southern entrance of Newman Bay, in lat. 81° 51' N. * * * No list was made of the articles secured with the boats" [a fewcases of preserved meat and a little bread; about 500 cartridges, one shot-gun, two rifles, one box-chronometer, two sextants]. (R. W. B. Bryan to Navy Department Jan'y 9, 1875, p. 667, Narrative North Polar Expedition U. S. ship "Polaris.")

"The whale-boat is 26 feet long, 5 feet beam, and 3¼ feet deep, double planked, one plank stove on bluff of starboard bow, about 7 inches; easily repairable and otherwise in a servicable condition." (Stevenson to Nares, May 22, 1876, Nares' Report, p. 57.)

"The whale-boat lay bottom upwards on a flat piece of land about 100 yards from the beach, lashed down to heavy stones and frozen in by mud, while the canvas boat was with difficulty discovered buried in snow and lying about 80 yards from the whale boat and 200 from the tent. The whale-boat was stove in on the starboard bow, for which defect the materials necessary for repair were at hand, and was in other respects a good, serviceable boat." (Doctor Coppinger to Capt. Nares, Sept. 12, 1876, Nares' Report, p. 422.)

"Finding beneath her six 14-foot oars marked 'canvas boat,' we take and secure them alongside the whale-boat, so that the latter, at all events, may be thoroughly serviceable when wanted." (Nares' Report, p. 428.)

DISCOVERY HARBOR.

"When we arrived at Discovery Harbor we found 23 barrels of pork and beef in good condition, which I have not seen mentioned in any report." (J. W. Norman to Recorder, Jan'y 28, 1884, Exhibit S, p. 176.)

LINCOLN BAY.

Aug. 30th, 1875.—* * * "the opportunity was taken to land a depot of provisions for travellers, consisting of 1,000 rations. The depot was placed about thirty feet above the sea, on a hillside fronting the first dip in the coast hills from the extreme point of the bay. The cairn, which can be seen from the ice a mile from land, was built a few yards inshore of where these provisions were deposited. This depot was not subsequently disturbed by us, and no doubt still remains intact." (Nares' Narrative, Vol. I, p. 122.) [*Vide* Markham's "Frozen Sea," p. 135.—RECORDER.]

[NOTE.—In 1875 a depot of 2,000 rations was landed by Capt. Nares, from the "Alert," at Floe-Berg Beach, but all these stores were subsequently embarked. (*Vide* "Markham's Frozen Sea," p. 383.) Other minor depots were established, by sledging parties from the "Alert," at Pt. Richardson, View Point, near Cape Joseph Henry, and at Cape Chalon. But it cannot be learned from the report of Nares, nor from his "Narrative," or Markham's "Frozen Sea," that any of these stores now remain.—RECORDER.]

EXHIBIT V.

Room, Board of Officers considering relief expedition to Lieut. Greely and party at Lady Franklin Bay.]

WASHINGTON, D. C., *January* 5, 1884.

SIR: The Board of Officers created by Executive Order dated December 17, 1883, now considering a plan of relief of the Lady Franklin Bay Expedition, are desirous of securing from persons having personal knowledge of the navigation of the waters leading to Lady Franklin Bay an expression of opinion regarding the organization and conduct of the relieving force. Very extensive knowledge of the region in question and the adjacent waters was acquired by the officers serving with the English expedition of 1875-'6, commanded by Captain Sir Geo. S. Nares; and the Board to which, by order of the President, has been intrusted the preparation of a plan of rescue, would be glad to have the benefit of suggestions relative to the subject under consideration from Captain Sir Geo. S. Nares, Captain H. F. Stephenson, Captain Albert H. Markham, all of the Royal Navy; and to this end, on behalf of the Board, I have the honor to request that the proper steps be taken to acquaint the gentlemen referred to of the desire which has been expressed of profiting by the suggestions of these officers.

As the Board desires to complete its labors at an early day, it would be highly desirable that the request for the information referred to be communicated by cable.

Very respectfully, your obedient servant,

W. B. HAZEN,
Brig. and Bvt. Maj. Gen'l, Chief Signal Officer, U. S. A.,
President of the Board.

The Hon. SECRETARY OF THE NAVY.

Same to the Hon. Secretary of War.

NAVY DEPARTMENT,
BUREAU OF NAVIGATION AND OFFICE OF DETAIL,
Washington, 16 *February,* 1884.

SIR: By direction of the Secretary of the Navy, I have the honor to transmit herewith a copy of a letter from Captain Sir George Nares, R. N., to our minister at London, together with a copy of a letter transmitting to the latter suggestions from that officer, Captain Markham, R. N., and Major Feilden, H. B. M. A., addressed to the President of the Greely Relief Board.

Very respectfully, your obed't serv't,

J. G. WALKER,
Chief of Bureau.

Bvt. Major-General WM. B. HAZEN, U. S. A.,
Pres'd't of Board of Officers considering the relief of Lieut. Greely and party.

[Enclosure 1.]

LONDON, 10th *January*, 1884.

YOUR EXCELLENCY: I hasten to reply to your note of yesterday, inviting me on behalf of the Government of the United States to make such suggestions as may occur to me for the conduct of the party to be sent out for the relief of the Lady Franklin Bay Expedition under Lieutenant Greely, U. S. A.

Any suggestions regarding the conduct of an Arctic relief party must necessarily depend on the nature of the expedition itself. I, therefore, as a preliminary note, send you the following remarks.

An Arctic relief expedition should be self-supporting—it should consist of two vessels—one to act as a depôt for the retreat of the search party in case of accident to their vessel, to be stationed at the most advanced position that can be reached from the South with certainty each summer—the other vessel should be pushed forward to the station to be relieved.

If the depôt ship is not to be communicated with the following summer she should be prepared to pass two winters at her station. If she is to be communicated with (which entails sending out a third vessel early in the following season), stores and provisions for one year will be sufficient.

The advance vessel should in any case be prepared to pass two winters—otherwise (supposing her to be provisioned only for one) the commander's orders must allow for his abandoning his vessel for the safety of his own crew the first spring, at the very period when, if the relief had not been effected previously, he should be engaged in searching for those he was sent out to succour.

The present season is, I am afraid, already too far advanced for the purchase of ordinary ice vessels at a reasonable price, for the owners of those vessels have by this time made their arrangements for the coming fishing season—there is, therefore, no option except to purchase whaling vessels at an enhanced price to allow for a prospective voyage—to build new vessels—or to obtain the services of the two vessels named below.

It happens that H. M. S. "Alert," which is doubled and strengthened for ice navigation, has recently returned from foreign service, and I have little doubt but that the Admiralty would willingly dispose of her. Although perhaps not well adapted for ordinary naval service, she would form an admirable Arctic depôt vessel, and would not require much expenditure to fit her for Arctic service.

As an advance vessel it would be worth while to inspect the yacht "Pandora," late H. M. S. "Newport"—I understand that she is for sale; but whether she has sufficient accommodation and stowage room to carry two years' provisions for her own crew and one year's for the men composing Lieutenant Greely's party is uncertain; the fact, however, can be readily obtained.

On hearing from you further particulars regarding the nature of the relief expedition, whether it is to be composed of two wintering vessels, as I advise, or only one— I will send you suggestions for the conduct of the party.

I am, &c.,

G. S. NARES.

His Excellency J. R. LOWELL.

[Enclosure 2.]

LONDON, 1st *February*, 1884.

SIR: In preparing the accompanying report, as requested by you, embodying suggestions for the conduct of the expedition to be sent out for the relief of the Lady Franklin Bay Expedition by the United States Government, I have deemed it advisable to obtain the views of Major H. W. Feilden, H. M. Army, who served under my command in the British Expedition of 1875–'76, to Smith Sound and Grinnell Land, as naturalist on board H. M. S. "Alert," and whose acquaintance with the natural resources of the district is perhaps more extended than that of any other person.

I have also conferred with Captain Albert H. Markham, R. N., whom you invited to report on the same subject, and, thinking that it will be more valuable than sending in separate reports, I have, with the concurrence of that officer, embodied our joint views in the accompanying statement.

I have the honor to be, &c.,

G. S. NARES,
Captain, R. N.

His Excellency JAMES RUSSELL LOWELL.

LONDON, 1st *February*, 1884.

To the President of the Board for the relief of the Lady Franklin Bay Greely Expedition, Washington :

SIR : In response to the invitation transmitted to us by His Excellency the Minister of the United States in London, we have the honor to submit for consideration the following suggestions which may prove useful in drawing up the instructions for the guidance of those entrusted with the conduct of the expedition about to be despatched for the relief of Lieutenant Greely and his party.

To ensure success, the expedition must, in our opinion, be thoroughly and efficiently equipped, competently commanded, and, above all, be under the direct auspices and supervision of the Government.

We would strongly deprecate the despatch of an expedition that was to combine any other object, such as whaling, with that of the primary undertaking.

In the first place, we are very strongly of opinion that the main relief party should consist of two ships ; one of these should be engaged in advance, in the actual search, proceeding, if necessary, as far north as Discovery Bay; whilst the other should be used as a depôt ship, placed in such a convenient position that, in case of accident to the advance ship, there would be no necessity for her crew to retreat to the Danish settlements in Greenland.

In such an eventuality the officers and men of the ship destroyed would merely have to fall back upon their consort, from which sledging expeditions would be despatched in quest of Lieutenant Greely and his party.

Both these ships should be fully equipped for ice-navigation ; should, of course, be steamers, but possess sail power as an auxiliary.

They should be provisioned for at least two years, and should be provided with complete sledging equipments, which should certainly include pemmican and other provisions generally used by sledging parties.

Too much care cannot be taken in the selection of provisions of a suitable nature, but the experiences derived, in connection with this matter, from recent American Arctic expeditions can leave little to be desired. It appears to us that the possibility of adding frozen meat to the general stock of provisions should not be overlooked.

We think there is a great probability that Lieutenant Greely's party has already left Discovery Bay. Adopting this view, one of the ships should, we think, be despatched as early as the 1st of May, 1884, certainly not later, with orders to proceed to Godhaven, in Greenland, and to push on as early as possible to Upernavik, so as to meet Lieutenant Greely should he have succeeded in finding his way south to any of the Danish settlements.

If he has not done so, it is quite possible that he may have passed the winter somewhere between Cape York and Life-Boat Cove. It is therefore very desirable that this region should be searched early in the season.

There are two ways of carrying out this duty : either by sending a special Government vessel independent of the main relief expedition, or by inviting the co-operation of the whaling vessels. The latter should in any case be requested to keep a good lookout for the party journeying south in boats. However, should one of the whaling vessels meet them the captain would, by returning with them to the south, necessarily have to give up his chance of making a successful fishing voyage. It is, therefore, worthy of consideration whether the vessel that communicates with the Greenland settlements early in the season should not be ordered to proceed to the northward through Melville Bay, with the whaling vessels, at the first breaking up of the ice. If Lieutenant Greely's party is not fallen in with near Cape York, it would then be the duty of the commander of the vessel to diligently search the Cary Islands and the coast line to the northward, prior to the arrival of the main relief party ; every endeavor being made to communicate with the Eskimos of those regions, who will be sure to have tidings of the absent party, should they have been in the vicinity.

The two main relief vessels should time their arrival at Upernavik about the first week of July, and in the event of no tidings of Lieutenant Greely's safety being forthcoming at the Danish settlements they should proceed to the northward in company.

Failing, intelligence of the party having been obtained on the Greenland coast north of Cape York, including Littleton Island, Cape Isabella should be visited, and the cairn on the summit of that headland examined.

Supposing that no tidings or traces of the missing party are forthcoming at the entrance to Smith Sound, it will then devolve on the commanding officer of the relief expedition to organize further plans for prosecuting his search through Kennedy Channel, even, if necessary, to Discovery Bay.

In such an event it appears to us essential to consider the course of action that would probably have been pursued by Lieutenant Greely up to the present date.

What Lieutenant Greely's views were in August, 1881, may be gathered in some measure from his letter to the Chief Signal Officer, U. S. A., dated Fort Conger, August 17, 1881,* which was brought back to the United States by the S. S. "Neptune" ["Proteus"], after her successful voyage with the members of the international expedition to Discovery Bay in the autumn of 1881.

Lieutenant Greely, in that communication, appears to have fully recognized the contingency that the relief ship of 1882 might not be able to reach Discovery Bay; but it does not quite appear that he realized the possibility of the ship not making good her passage to some point on the east coast of Grinnell Land (west side of Kennedy Channel), where at some prominent point he recommended a depôt† should be landed.

He further requested that a similar depôt to No. A might be placed on Littleton Island, and a boat at Cape Prescott, to enable his party to retreat across the waterway between that point and Bache Island, and thence to Cape Sabine.

He evidently contemplated that under every circumstance "Depôt No. A" would be placed in the autumn of 1882 at least as far north on the shores of Grinnell Land as Cape Hawks.

His views as to the relief to be afforded in 1883 are thus expressed in the above quoted communication:

"If the party does not reach here (Discovery Bay) in 1882, there should be sent, in 1883, a capable, energetic officer, with ten (10) men, eight of whom should have had practical sea experience, provided with three whale-boats, and ample provisions for forty (40) persons for fifteen months. In case the vessel was obliged to turn southward (she should not leave Smith Sound near Cape Sabine, before September 15th), it should leave duplicates of depôts A and B, of 1882, at two different points, one of which should be between Cape Sabine and Bache Island, the other to be an intermediate depôt, between two depôts already established. Similar rules as to indicating locality should be insisted on. Thus, the Grinnell Land coast would be covered with seven depôts of ten days' provisions, in less than three hundred miles, not including the two months' supplies at Cape Hawks.

"The party should then proceed to establish a winter station at Polaris Winter Quarters, Life-Boat Cove, where their main duty would be to keep their telescopes on Cape Sabine and the land to the northward.

"Being furnished with dogs, sledges, and a native driver, a party of at least six men should proceed, when practicable, to Cape Sabine, whence a sledge party northward, of the two best fitted men, should reach Cape Hawks, if not Cape Collinson."

It is clear, therefore, that whenever Lieutenant Greely decided to retreat from Discovery Bay his plans would be based on the supposition that Depôt No. A of 1882 had been placed at or to the northward of Cape Hawks; that a large supply of stores would have been cached at or near Cape Sabine, and that a relief party would winter at Life-Boat Cove in the winter of 1883–'84 even if the relief ship had turned south in the autumn of 1883.

The results of the relief expeditions of 1882 and 1883 may be briefly summarized as follows:

On the 10th August, 1882, the steamer "Neptune," with a relief party and stores on board, reached her most northern point in Smith Sound, latitude 79° 20', being twelve miles from Cape Hawks and seventeen from Cape Prescott, but was there stopped by the ice. The record‡ of the voyage shows that from the above date to the 28th of August, 1882, repeated but unsuccessful attempts were made to reach Cape Hawks. On the morning of the 31st August a landing was effected on Cape Sabine, western side of Smith Sound, and there stores and a whale-boat were placed (presumably Depôt A), but no distinct mention is made as to the amount of provisions left. On the 3d September, 1882, Mr. W. M. Beebe succeeded in landing stores on Littleton Island (presumably Depôt B), and the "Neptune" then turned homeward.

In 1883 the steamer "Proteus," carrying Lieutenant Garlington, U. S. A., relief party and stores, rounded Cape Alexander at the eastern entrance of Smith Sound on the 22nd July, and entered Pandora Harbour; that same afternoon Smith Sound was crossed to the western side and a landing made at Payer Harbour, in the vicinity of Cape Sabine. Lieutenant Garlington satisfied himself that the *stores* left there from the "Proteus" ["Neptune"] in 1882 were in good order, though the whale-boat had been slightly damaged by bears. At 8 p. m., on the evening of the 22nd July, the "Proteus" was again underway and attempted to force a passage to Cape Hawks; she was, however, caught in the ice-pack, crushed, and sunk early on the morning of the 23rd July, 1883, between Cape Sabine and Cape Albert.

Lieutenant Garlington, assisted by Lieutenant Colwell, U. S. N., succeeded in saving some stores from the "Proteus," out of which some 500 rations were cached by those officers about three miles west of Cape Sabine.

The relief party and crew of the "Proteus" then crossed the sound to Littleton Island, which they reached on the 25th July. From there they started southward in

---

* Sig. Ser. Notes, No. X, pp. 22, 23, Washington, 1883.
† For contents of this depôt (A) *vide* Sig. Ser. Notes, No. X, p. 22, Washington, 1883.
‡ Sig. Ser. Notes, No. V, Washington, 1883.

13

their boats for the Danish settlements in Greenland, reaching Upernavik on the 24th August, 1883, after a most fortunate boat-voyage, entailing, however, great exposure and suffering on the party.

There has been, therefore, no depôt of provisions, stores, or boat established anywhere north of Cape Sabine since Lieutenant Greely's party arrived at Discovery Bay in 1881; so, whilst retreating along the east coast of Grinnell Land to Smith Sound, their only means of subsistence, until reaching Cape Sabine, would be the supplies brought away with them from Fort Conger, the animals procurable on the journey, and the depôts left behind by the British Expedition of 1875-'76.

When, in the autumn of 1882, the party at Discovery Bay realized that relief had failed to reach them that year, Lieutenant Greely would at once husband his remaining stock of provisions. Discovery Bay being a peculiarly favorable position for procuring musk oxen, he in all probability, eked out his subsistence with a considerable supply of meat. Consequently, if he decided to start southward from that station in July, 1883, as we think he would, and run the risk of passing the relief ship on her way north, it may reasonably be hoped that the party had with them a large supply of food, dependent of course on the capacity of the boats at their disposal.

The first difficulty would be to cross Lady Franklin Sound, 10 miles wide, but, with provisions advanced in the spring of 1883, this part of the journey would probably be accomplished before the first week of August. By that time Kennedy Channel would be comparatively free of ice, and few troubles need be expected while proceeding south along the shore of Judge Daly Promontory. In latitude 80° 5′ N. the British expedition left a cache of 240 rations, sufficient to last Lieutenant Greely's party for at least ten days; with this supply, in addition to his own resources, he would be the better able to face the forty miles of the route before reaching Cape Hawks in latitude 79° 30′ N., where, although he would not find the expected Depôt A, he would find a boat and a supply of biscuit left there by the British expedition. The party would then be sixty miles from Cape Sabine, where they knew that a cache of 240 rations had been left by the British Expedition, and where, in addition, we now know he would find the stores left by the "Proteus" ["Neptune"] in 1882, besides a whaleboat, also the 500 rations left by Lieutenant Garlington and Lieutenant Colwell, three miles west of Cape Sabine, in 1883.

Reaching this position would probably be the most difficult part of the journey, but once at Cape Sabine, and strengthened by this supply of provisions, and supplemented with an additional whale-boat, it would be an extraordinary misadventure if an opportunity did not offer in the fall of 1883 for the party to cross over Smith Sound and reach the neighborhood of Littleton Island. No doubt extreme disappointment would be felt when the absence of a relief party and want of a winter station at Life-Boat Cove ("Polaris" winter quarters) was discovered; but as, in all probability, Lieutenant Garlington's record announcing the loss of the "Proteus" would have been found at Cape Sabine, the disappointment would have been in a great measure anticipated. Once arrived at Littleton Island, with the help of the depôt left there in 1882 by the "Proteus" ["Neptune"], and with assistance from the Eskimos of Etah, there is no reason why the winter of 1883-'84 should not be passed in safety.

If, on the other hand, Lieutenant Greely and his party, owing to contingencies, such as sickness, may have determined, rather than risk the hazard of a boat-journey in 1883, to chance the arrival of a relieving ship at Discovery Bay in the fall of 1883, and have remained there, the position of the party, though precarious, is not, we think, by any means hopeless.

With the addition of supplies of musk oxen, birds, hares, and perhaps a few seals, we may hope that they will not be absolutely without supplies before August, 1884.

The relief of Lieutenant Greely's party differs in one vital respect from the Franklin search expeditions. In that case expedition after expedition was pushed into an unknown area; the uncertainty of where Franklin had been lost intensifying a hundred-fold the difficulties of the quest.

Now there is a definite objective to strike for, and the difficulties to be overcome are those arising from the forces of nature in the Polar world, but in a comparatively well-known area.

We will now suppose that the search of the relief expedition of 1884, between Cape York and Littleton Island and Cape Isabella, has proved fruitless; in this event the commander of the expedition would naturally attempt to reach Cape Sabine, and there will probably be no very great difficulty in his making good a landing at that point.

If Lieutenant Greely's party is not found there, then only two conclusions can be arrived at: Either they are still at Discovery Bay, or else the party has met with misfortune in its attempt to retreat southward.

In this case the depôt ship should move into Payer Harbour; the other ship should take advantage of any favorable movement in the ice, and, keeping to the land water, *always carefully avoiding the main pack*, proceed northwards. Patience and skill would, there is little doubt, be rewarded in the end, and it may reasonably be hoped that an opportunity of gaining Discovery Bay will offer itself during the navigable season of 1884.

The east side of the entrance to Smith Sound, after being carefully examined for traces of the missing party, should be shunned, particularly during strong southwest and west winds, for those are the winds that give favorable opportunities of reaching Grinnell Land and proceeding northwards, along the eastern coast.

As a precaution, in case of an accident to the advance ship and her crew having to retreat by land, depôts and a boat should be placed at or near Cape Prescott, and some other points further north, as proposed by Lieutenant Greely.

It may be suggested, if not already provided for, that great advantage would accrue from heliography; a pair of instruments, therefore, on both ships, and a trained operator in each vessel, might be of the greatest service.

We now arrive at our final consideration: Supposing the advance ship is unable during the navigable season of 1884 to reach Discovery Bay, or to find Lieutenant Greely's party along the coast of Grinnell Land, its fate must be ascertained.

The depôt ship should find winter quarters, not later than the 1st September, in the safest and most convenient station near Payer Harbour, on the west side of Smith Sound; this would enable her sledge parties to start early in the spring of 1885, along the east shore of Grinnell Land, and, with those from the advance ship, complete the search of the whole coast line. Payer Harbour itself has the disadvantage of being somewhat too exposed a station for winter quarters, but the leader of the expedition may be safely intrusted to decide that point. Port Foulke, or Pandora Harbour, offer more eligible wintering stations than Payer Harbour or any other known place in its vicinity on the west side of Smith Sound, but wintering on the Greenland side of the sound would involve uncertainty in the despatch of the sledge parties along the shores of Grinnell Land in the spring of 1885, for it must be borne in mind that the ice in Kennedy Channel is not to be relied on remaining unbroken during the winter months, and is certain to break up early in the spring.

No dependence should be placed on detached boat relief expeditions, except in the extreme case of the advance vessel becoming disabled early in navigable season of 1884, for no boat party can, in addition to the provisions necessary for their own support, convey sufficient supplies to relieve a large distressed party of men, and return with them to their station.

Too much reliance should not be placed by such parties on the natural resources of the shores of Grinnell Land. But although the British Expedition of 1875–'76 did not actually meet with any musk oxen, reindeer, or bears, between Port Foulke and Discovery Bay, traces of them were seen, and with good fortune a retreating boat party might come across some of these animals, walrus, or a few seals. After leaving the warmer waters of Baffin Bay, the great breeding haunts of sea-fowl are left behind. Port Foulke is the most northern summer haunt of the little auk, where it breeds in countless numbers, and contributes largely to the summer food of the Eskimos of Etah. Neither does Brünnich's guillemot, the well-known Arctic loom, extend its breeding range beyond the entrance of Smith Sound. Along the shores of Grinnell Land a few black guillemots nest, but not gregariously. At certain localities, such as the more protected bays, a few eider ducks will be found, whilst on the fresh-water lakes a considerable number of brent geese rear their young. None of these birds are to be obtained without an expenditure of time beyond the capacity of travelling parties, with whom delay means consumption of the stores they are carrying with them. The bird life of that region will not afford to sledge or boat parties more than an occasional addition to their rations, and cannot be reckoned on as a certain means of subsistence, such as the loomeries and aukeries of Baffin Bay afford during the breeding season of those birds.

In conclusion, we think it would be advisable to obtain the good-will and assistance of the Cape York district Eskimos by the timely and judicious distribution of presents, and the leader of the relief expedition should receive directions to this effect. Finally, we are desirous of expressing our heartfelt sympathy with the United States regarding the object of the contemplated expedition, and our readiness to afford, at any time, any information or assistance, that it may be in our power to render.

We have the honor to be, sir, your obedient servants,

G. S. NARES,
Captain, R. N.
A. H. MARKHAM,
Captain, H. M. S. "Vernon."
H. W. FEILDEN,
Major, H. B. M. Army.

EXHIBIT W.

U. S. CONSULATE, SAINT JOHN'S, N. F., *Feb'y 2nd*, 1884.

Gen'l W. B. HAZEN,
Chief Signal Officer U. S. A., Washington, D. C.

SIR: I herewith beg to enclose original agreement received from Mr. Syme for hire S. S. "Proteus." I have concluded the purchase of the "*Bear*" and hope to get her off for New York next Saturday. She will have to coal and take in about 200 tons stone ballast in the after hold. I should recommend the hiring of some of her present crew, as they are all sealers and sailors. The chief engineer, Mr. Stynes, holds a first-class certificate, and has been used to the seal fishery as engineer for a number of years.

He was employed by me as engineer of the "Gulnare," Lieut. Doane, on an Arctic trip. If you can use your influence to get him employment I shall consider it a personal favor. Any stores required, such as boots, clothing, dogs, meat, &c., had better be engaged here as soon as possible.

I am, sir, your ob't servant,

THOS. N. MOLLOY.

[Extract.]

U. S. CONSULATE, SAINT JOHN'S, N. F., *Feb'y 2, '84.*

Gen'l W. B. HAZEN, U. S. A.,
Washington, D. C.

* * * * * * *

DEAR SIR: Anything required by the expedition, such as boots, had better be engaged this month, other articles later in the season. If you can induce the commander of the expedition to take his choice of men from the present crew, I think it would be to the advantage of the expedition, as they are all experienced sailors and sealers. The engineer, Styne, is a first-class officer, and has a great desire to proceed. He was chief engineer of the "Gulnare," under Lieut. Doane, U. S. A., on an Arctic trip.

* * * * * * *

Yours, very respectfully,

THOS. N. MOLLOY.

Abstract miscellaneous correspondence.

No.	Date.	From whom received.	Subject.
1	Dec. 21, 1883	Secretary of the Navy........	Transmits communication from Commander H. C. Taylor, U. S. Navy, requesting that Lieut. N. R. Usher, U. S. Navy, be heard before Board.
2	Dec. 19, 1883	Commander H. C. Taylor, U. S. Navy.	Recommends Lieut. N. R. Usher, U. S. Navy, as a suitable person to proceed upon a relief expedition.
3	Dec. 19, 1883	Lieut. George T. T. Patterson, 14th Infantry, U. S. Army.	Requests his name be submitted for duty with proposed expedition.
4	Dec. 27, 1883	General W. B. Hazen, Chief Signal Officer.	Incloses communications from the files of his office of persons suggesting plans of, and volunteering to accompany an expedition for relief of Lieutenant Greely and party.
5	Sept. 11, 1883	Secretary of State	Transmits, through War Department, a communication dated Uxbridge, Ontario, Canada, Aug. 28, 1883, with inclosures, from R. Commander John P. Cheyne, British Royal Navy, relative to relief of Lieutenant Greely by means of balloons.
6	Sept. 14, 1883	George E. Tyson..............	Through War Department, offering his services for relief of Greely party.
7	Sept. 15, 1883	J. E. Marcussen..............	Volunteers to accompany expedition.
8	Sept. 16, 1883	J. H. Stevens	Presents a plan for the rescue of Lieutenant Greely by means of sleds.
9	Sept. 16, 1883	Lieut. J. E. Macklin, 11th U. S. Infantry.	Desires to be one of a Greely relief party.
10	Sept. 17, 1883	Lieut. W. P. Evans, 19th U. S. Infantry.	Offers his services in connection with proposed expedition for relief of Greely.
11	Sept. 17, 1883	George W. Melville, Chief Engineer, U. S. N.	Submits through Navy Department a method for relief of Greely party.
12	Sept. 18, 1883	Gustav F. Seivern............	Calls attention to a boat invented by him for use in Arctic regions.
13	Sept. 18, 1883	C. O. Duthok................	Recommends use of balloons in searching for Greely.
14	Sept. 18, 1883	Joseph Keefer................	Requests employment on relief expedition.
15	Sept. 24, 1883	J. B. Brainard................	Requests employment on relief expedition.
16	Oct. 9, 1883	James Craig	Requests, through Navy Department, an appointment for his son as geologist on proposed expedition.

APPENDIX. 189

Abstract miscellaneous correspondence—Continued.

No.	Date.	From whom received.	Subject.
17	Nov. 6, 1883	Lieut. P. H. Ray, 8th U. S. Infantry.	Tenders his services to command expedition, provided same is sent out under auspices of Chief Signal Officer.
18	Dec. 7, 1883	Lieut. W. C. De Hart, U. S. R. M.	Offers his services as commander of expedition.
19	Dec. 12, 1883	L. E. Ralston	Volunteers to accompany expedition.
20	Dec. 13, 1883	Major H. W. Feilden, H. B. M. Army.	Submits his views relative to relieving Greely party.
21	Dec. 15, 1883	Lieut. W. C. Brown, 1st U. S. Cavalry.	Requests to be detailed on relief expedition.
22	Dec. 21, 1883	H. H. McGrew	Offers services to accompany Greely relief.
23	Dec. 21, 1874	Dr. A. P. Mason	Offers to accompany expedition as surgeon.
24	Dec. 20, 1883	Adjutant-General, U. S. A.	Furnishes copy of telegram to Lieutenant Schwatka, U. S. A.. requesting him to prepare a paper as to organization and conduct of party for relief of Lady Franklin Bay people, together with copy of Lieutenant Schwatka's reply.
25	Dec. 21, 1883	......do	Transmits copy of telegram from Lieutenant Schwatka stating that his recommendation for Greely's relief would be sent by mail.
26	Dec. 23, 1883	General N. A. Miles, U. S. A	Recommends Lieutenant Schwatka to command Greely relief expedition.
27	Dec. 28, 1883	Cyrus Smith	Desires the adoption of his fuel-saving device for steam-boilers or heating-stoves by the proposed expedition.
28	Jan. 5, 1884	F. B. J. Rust	Expresses willingness to appear before Board and give experience acquired as member of scientific corps of Dutch Arctic Expedition, 1882–'3.
29	Jan. 7, 1884	Dr. I. C. Rosse	Declines to appear before Board.
30	Dec. 31, 1883	Sergt. C. Madsen, 5th Cav'y	Tenders his services to accompany expedition.
31	Dec. 31, 1883	Dr. F. E. Coulter	Requests, through War Department, appointment as physician to expedition.
32	Jan. 8, 1884	S. K. Parson, agent for Hudson's Bay Co., Montreal, Canada.	States inability of his company to furnish within 60 days sufficient reindeer-skins to make 100 suits of clothing.
33	Jan. 10, 1884	Wm. Macnaughtan's Sons	Submit estimate for buckskin clothing.
34	Jan. 10, 1884	Chief Clerk War Department.	States War Department is unable to print proceedings of Board on account of reduced state of appropriation.
35	Jan. 11, 1884	Wm. Macnaughtan's Sons	Will report in a short time whether they can supply reindeer-skins.
36	Jan. 7, 1884	R. Laidlaw, E. Heimbacher, and E. S. Eveleigh.	Desire appointment as photographers to relief expedition.
37	Jan. 14, 1884	F. B. J. Rust	Submits brief outline of his Arctic experience.
38	Dec. 31, 1883	L. Y. Coggins, for Otis Young.	Submits plan for constructing ships for Arctic service.
39	Jan. 15, 1884	Secretary of War	Transmits copies of letters from the State Department, dated the 11th and 12th instant, inclosing copies of dispatches from United States Minister to England respecting steps to be taken for Greely's relief.
40	Jan. 15, 1884	J. W. Norman	Requests employment with relief party.
41	Jan. 9, 1884	E. M. Philibaum	Volunteers services for expedition.
42	Jan. 18, 1884	Secretary of War	Transmits copies of letters, dated the 16th and 17th instant, from Department of State, inclosing copies of telegrams, dated the 10th, 16th, and 17th instant, from U. S. consul at Saint John's, Newfoundland, respecting the purchase of a vessel to be used for relief of Lady Franklin Bay expedition.
43	Jan. 21, 1884	Navy Department	Calls attention to letters from L. Y. Coggins for Otis Young, Frank Reynolds, and Robert Laidlaw & Co., previously forwarded without letters of transmittal.
44	Jan. 10, 1884	H. M. Sutherland	Volunteers to accompany expedition.
45	Jan. 11, 1884	W. Gibson, vice-consul, Glasgow, Scotland.	Transmits through Lieut. J. A. Tobin, U. S. N., a memorandum from Lewis T. Merrow & Son, ship brokers, Glasgow, Scotland, respecting the sale of a steamer to the U. S. Government for the relief expedition.
46	Jan. 22, 1884	Secretary of War	Transmits copy of letter, dated 19th instant, from State Department, inclosing copy of telegram from U. S. Minister at London, England, relative to purchase of vessel for Arctic navigation.
47	Jan. 23, 1884	Wm. Macnaughtan's Sons	State they shortly expect to have information from Hudson's Bay Co. relative to reindeer-skins.
48	Jan. 25, 1884	H. Clay	Transmits, through Hon. A. S. Willis, a plan for relief of Greely.
49	Jan. 26, 1884	Dr. Thomas H. Carroll	Requests appointment as surgeon.
50	Jan. 29, 1884	Navy Department	Submits copy of letter from Messrs. Delamater & Co., of New York, relative to building a steamer for Greely expedition.
51	Jan. 29, 1884	Hudson's Bay Company	State they are unable to furnish in 60 days sufficient reindeer-skins for 100 suits of clothing.

INDEX.

Printed in the United States
By Bookmasters